SPEAK TO THE EARTH

Creation Studies In Geoscience

Edited by
GEORGE F. HOWE

**Presbyterian and Reformed Publishing Company
1975
Creation Research Society Books
1989**

Copyright © 1975
Presbyterian and Reformed Publishing Co.

Second printing, October 1989
Creation Research Society Books

ISBN 0-940384-07-8

Library of Congress Catalogue Card No. 75-15446
Printed in the United States of America

ACKNOWLEDGEMENTS

The editor is deeply grateful for the consistent help of two individuals in the area of refereeing manuscripts and tending to managerial details—John N. Moore and Walter E. Lammerts. Other scientists who gave unstintingly of their time in analyzing geological papers were: Harold Armstrong, Thomas G. Barnes, Clifford Burdick, Stuart Nevins, Bernard Northrup, Emmett L. Williams and many others. The editor is indebted to these people and their efforts have improved the quality of these papers. Various publishers have graciously allowed republication of pictures or whole papers which have appeared in other books or journals and credit references are listed in each case.

TABLE OF CONTENTS

ACKNOWLEDGMENTS AND INTRODUCTION
GEORGE F. HOWE

PALEONTOLOGY AND ORIGINS
1. THE SISQUOC DIATOMITE FOSSIL BEDS 1
   BERNARD E. NORTHRUP. 1969. 6(3):129-131. December.
2. IS THE CAPITAN LIMESTONE A FOSSIL REEF? 16
   STUART E. NEVINS. 1972. 8(4):231-248. March.
3. RESEARCH ON THE JOGGINS PETRIFIED TREES 60
   HAROLD G. COFFIN. 1969. 6(1):35-44, 70. June.
4. A NOTE ON THE UNSATISFACTORY NATURE OF THE HORSE SERIES OF FOSSILS AS EVIDENCE FOR EVOLUTION 86
   FRANK W. COUSINS. 1971. 8(2):99-108. September.
5. FOSSIL MAN: ANCESTOR OR DESCENDANT OF ADAM? 104
   R. DANIEL SHAW. 1970. 6(4):172-181. March.
6. DISCOVERY OF HUMAN SKELETONS IN CRETACEOUS FORMATION 127
   CLIFFORD L. BURDICK. 1973. 10(2):109-110. September.
7. HUMAN FOOTPRINTS IN ROCKS 131
   WILBERT H. RUSCH, SR. 1971. 7(4):201-213. March.

RESEARCH IN CATASTROPHISM
8. PALEOECOLOGY AND THE FLOOD 161
   HAROLD W. CLARK. 1971. 8(1):19-23. June.
9. THE CYCLICAL BLACK SHALES 172
   WALTER G. PETERS. 1971. 7(4):193-200. March.
10. FIELD EVIDENCE OF RAPID SEDIMENTATION... 190
    WALTER G. PETERS. 1973. 10(2):89-96. September.

11. THE MESA BASALT OF THE NORTHWESTERN UNITED STATES 211
    STUART E. NEVINS. 1971. 7(4):222-226. March.

12. POST-FLOOD STRATA OF THE JOHN DAY COUNTRY, NORTHEASTERN OREGON 221
    STUART E. NEVINS. 1974. 10(4):191-204. March.

13. FRANCISCAN ROCKS—A REVIEW 253
    BERNARD E. NORTHRUP. 1970. 6(4):161-171. March.

14. THE CREATIONIST AND CONTINENTAL GLACIATION 279
    WILLIAM A. SPRINGSTEAD. 1973. 10(1):47-53. June.

15. THE ARK OF NOAH 294
    HENRY M. MORRIS. 1971. 8(2):142-144. September.

GEOLOGICAL EVIDENCE FOR A RECENT CREATION

16. DECAY OF THE EARTH'S MAGNETIC MOMENT AND THE GEOCHRONOLOGICAL IMPLICATIONS 300
    THOMAS G. BARNES. 1971. 8(1):24-29. June.

17. ON THE RECENT ORIGIN OF THE PACIFIC SOUTHWEST DESERTS 314
    WALTER E. LAMMERTS. 1971. 8(1):50-54. June.

18. A BAT IN A STALAGMITE 324
    ROBERT HARRIS. 1971. 8(2):144. September.

19. COMETS AND A YOUNG SOLAR SYSTEM 327
    HAROLD ARMSTRONG. 1971. 8(3):192-193. December.

20. TIME, LIFE AND HISTORY IN THE LIGHT OF 15,000 RADIOCARBON DATES 331
    ROBERT L. WHITELAW. 1970. 7(1):56-71, 83. June.

21. A CRITICAL EXAMINATION OF RADIOACTIVE DATING OF ROCKS 365
    SIDNEY P. CLEMENTSON. 1970. 7(3):137-141. December.

22. THE EMPIRE MOUNTAINS—A THRUST FAULT? 376
    CLIFFORD L. BURDICK AND HAROLD SLUSHER. 1969. 6(1):49-54. June.

23. THE GLARUS OVERTHRUST 388
    WALTER E. LAMMERTS. 1972. 8(4): 251-255. March.

ASTRONOMY AND ORIGINS

24. SOME ASTROMICAL EVIDENCES FOR A
    YOUTHFUL SOLAR SYSTEM 401
    HAROLD S. SLUSHER. 1971. 8(1):55-57. June.

25. CRITIQUE OF STELLAR EVOLUTION 409
    GEORGE MULFINGER. 1970. 7(1):7-24. June.

THERMODYNAMICS AND CREATIONISM

26. THERMODYNAMICS: A TOOL FOR CREATIONISTS 447
    EMMETT L. WILLIAMS. 1973. 10(1):38-44. June.

INTRODUCTION

While trying to impress the greatness of God upon his friends, Job suggested that they should "Speak to the earth . . ." and that it would teach them (Job 12:8). This same wise advice can be given to scientists who perform geological research—let the earth "speak" for itself concerning origins. It has been said that the best research is that in which the experimenter poses questions to nature and then receives answers back in the form of experimental data which he interprets. It is in this sense that geologists must "speak to the earth" and let it yield information upon which origins theories may be erected. All origins theories involve *a priori* commitments which lie outside the domain of experimental science. And yet any useful theory of origins must also fit favorably with all valid observations from field and laboratory.

The twenty-six papers which follow are geoscience manuscripts published in the Creation Research Society Quarterly from June 1969 to March 1974 (note bibliographic information of this nature given in the index and at the onset of each article). These papers were selected for reprinting in book form because of their experimental or observational character. A symposium of this sort demonstrates that creationist geologists do perform experiments and that creationist theories are a suitable basis for creative scientific research. Likewise this volume should serve as a stimulus fostering more original geological studies and the present editor of the Quarterly, Dr. Donald B. DeYoung welcomes such papers. Correspondence should be directed to him at Grace College, 200 Seminary Drive, Winona Lake, IN 46590.

A certain amount of selection was required in preparing the list of papers for reprinting and this is lamentable because there are other valuable papers in earth science for which there was not room in this book. Readers should realize that many back volumes of the Creation Research Society Quarterly can be purchased at a nominal cost and such correspondence should be directed to the membership secretary, Dr. Glen W. Wolfrom, P.O. Box 14016, Terre Haute, IN 47803.

For more than 125 years geology has been considered to be the handmaiden of general evolutionism (macroevolutionism) to the extent that some people deem the two fields inseparable. However, these authors show that in five general areas of their field creationism holds forth a viable alternative to evolutionism. It is, of course, for the reader to decide if the creationist option is better and more credible in terms of correlating scientific data than the evolution view. The only scientific way to decide such a question is to "Speak to the earth . . ." and listen very carefully to the data that come in response.

GEORGE F. HOWE
The Master's College
P.O. Box 878
Newhall, CA 91322

I

THE SISQUOC DIATOMITE FOSSIL BEDS

BERNARD E. NORTHRUP*

Introduction

One of the evidences commonly used in the classroom to imply necessity of extended geological chronology is the remarkable accumulation of diatomaceous earth in the Lompoc area of Santa Barbara County, California. Recently the author investigated these very extensive deposits to make a critical examination of the field evidences, suspicious that uniformitarian dramatization, oversimplification and distortion may have misrepresented the facts.

The student is usually told that these extensive beds, built up of the skeltons of microscopic, silica-collecting algae of the sea, are the normal result of the long, still, silent rain of death that is constantly taking place in the oceans today.[1] For this remarkable deposit (which extends from 200 feet below sea level[2] to more than 1,500 feet above sea level in places) to have attained this thickness, historical geologists estimate an accumulation period of from 33,000 to 1,500,000 years. This is estimated to have been between two and five million years ago.[3]

These estimates are based upon argument from the present rate of deposition, without any consideration of indications that this deposit is not at all an accumulation at present rates. It is simply a calculation based upon ocean basin deposition, which is variously estimated to be taking place at a rate from 1/500 of an inch per year to as much as ½ inch per year. On this basis, 66 foot samples from the Atlantic Ocean floor have been estimated to represent as

---

*Bernard E. Northrup is professor of Old Testament at the Baptist Bible School of Theology, Clarks Summit, Pennsylvania. He holds the Th.D. degree.

much as 1,500,000 years.[4]

The deposition estimate for the Miocene Sisquoc formation, as these diatom deposits are called, is undoubtedly also based upon assumptions concerning fairly stable ocean temperatures and currents. Neither does it appear to take into consideration such factors as the diatom's recently observed reproductive spurts, reproducing by division among ice crystals in frigid sea water at $-1.75°$ Centigrade.[5]

While the number of diatoms in the great oceans may reach as high as 100,000 per quart, this is dwarfed into insignificance by the noteworthy discovery of a phenomenal 6,330,000 diatoms found in a liter of sea water in the Kiev Canal in Russia.[6] This multiplication in cold waters is one reason for the abundance of whales in the Arctic, since the diatom and the chain of life supported by it provides much food for the great creatures.[7] (Editor's Note: Obviously, if during the ice age following the flood reproduction of diatoms were at the rate of those in the Kiev Canal, then the mentioned estimate of 1,500,000 years would be reduced drastically.)

It would be impossible, of course, for one to field-check abundance of diatoms in sea water of the Miocene epoch during which the bulk of the Lompoc deposits were supposedly made. Neither is it possible to estimate water temperatures during those deposits nor at the time the diatoms lived. These must be differentiated, for the diatom ooze was undoubtedly built up long before the event which brought this onshore deposit into being. Probably a good paleontologist could evaluate the types of diatoms found, and together with the evidences presented by the fossilized herring mackerel, perch, whales, and even sea birds contained therein, form a reasonable estimate of water temperatures during both growth and redeposit.

A field trip demonstrated that evidence was entirely and indisputably out of harmony with the normal classroom presentation, so much so that it reminded one of the story of Plato's cave. According to the sage, an observer was fixed with his back to the mouth of a cave, knowing only those truths about the world outside which he could deduce from the shadows on the inner walls of the cave.[8]

THE SISQUOC DIATOMITE FOSSIL BEDS 3

I am convinced that reality in geological time has been grossly misrepresented on the walls of the contemporary science classroom by the deceptive shadows of evolutionary uniformitarian time values.[9] At Lompoc this distortion is remarkably evident. The fossils that were trapped in the abrupt deposition which left this unique graveyard tell a story violently contradictory to the classroom interpretation. Every fossil found supports a denial that it had been buried at a geological "snail's pace."

Diatomaceous Beds Described

These deposits at Lompoc contain some of the world's most

Figure 1. Enlargement of remarkable arrangement by J. Rinnbeck of 266 diatoms, scales and spicules (pin head sized). (Courtesy of Karl Dern.)

Figure 2. Photomicrograph of a collection of diatoms. (Courtesy of Horace Nelson.)

beautiful examples of fossilization. The researcher finds it easy to forget that entire mountains under his feet, glistening white, dull grey, very soft pink or occasionally nearly jet black in veins, are entirely composed of fossils. Because of their microscopic size, these little cell wall skeletons of purest glass, massed together in inestimable quantities, simply appear to be a delicate chalk-like clay. Yet this diatomaceous earth is of a gently compacted mass that is often in the form of almost absolutely pure opal fossils.

The delicate individual size of diatoms is shown by photomicrographs of a diatom arrangement in Figure 1 (which also includes some scales of sea urchin and sponge spicules). This remarkable arrangement by Rinnbeck includes 266 separate items, although it is actually the size of a pinhead. It was among a series of microscope exhibits displayed at the Philadelphia centennial years ago. The original microscope slide is in the possession of Karl Dern, a retired employee of Johns Manville, who now lives in San Mateo, California (see also Figure 2).

Strangely, in the pure beds of silica, both in Johns Manville's deep quarry and on Dicalite's high Brush Ridge, there are obsidian-like streaks of dark brown to black bands of thoroughly cemented opal (see map, Figure 3). Though rarely of soft gemstone quality, they display concoidial fractures when shattered. No meaningful explanation has been found for this veining phenomenon.

It is easy to speculate that these thoroughly hard veins resulted from subsurface percolation of mineral saturated waters. That later crustal movement has compressed and heated these, perhaps by means of escaping subterranean gases, has been proposed. The veins, however, seem to follow no particular pattern. Sometimes they are many inches thick, yet diminish to disappear when traced across the face of a cut.

At times they are so common that they render the quality of the product so poor that it has to be stored on a temporary dump awaiting such a time that processing would become profitable.[10] These hard bands, of course, were useless for the filtration, adhesive, bulkage, abrasion and other products which are the ultimate destiny commercially for these diatom skeletons. So also are the fish fossils when too many of them are embedded in the diatomite.[11]

Materials from the three quarries which I have visited are marketed in an astounding number of forms from floor sweepings to filters to fine silver polishes. A vast proportion of this remarkable industry stems from the purchase of a five cent sack of common table salt on September 27, 1922 by a laboratory employee of the Celite Company (purchased in 1928 by Johns Manville Company). I have a dated copy of my friend's handwritten laboratory report on the experiment which first transformed diatomite (silica) into sodium silicate, or "Hy-Flow," as it is called in the industry today because of its new filter flow characteristics. This transformed the industry.

But it was not in the economic history or its values that I was interested particularly. Contained within these marine contoured rolling hills of diatomite are beautifully preserved biological forms so perfect that individual scales, bones, fins, even veins, upon occasion, may be studied. This is possible by the fineness of the particles of diatomite in which they were buried. Perhaps the very

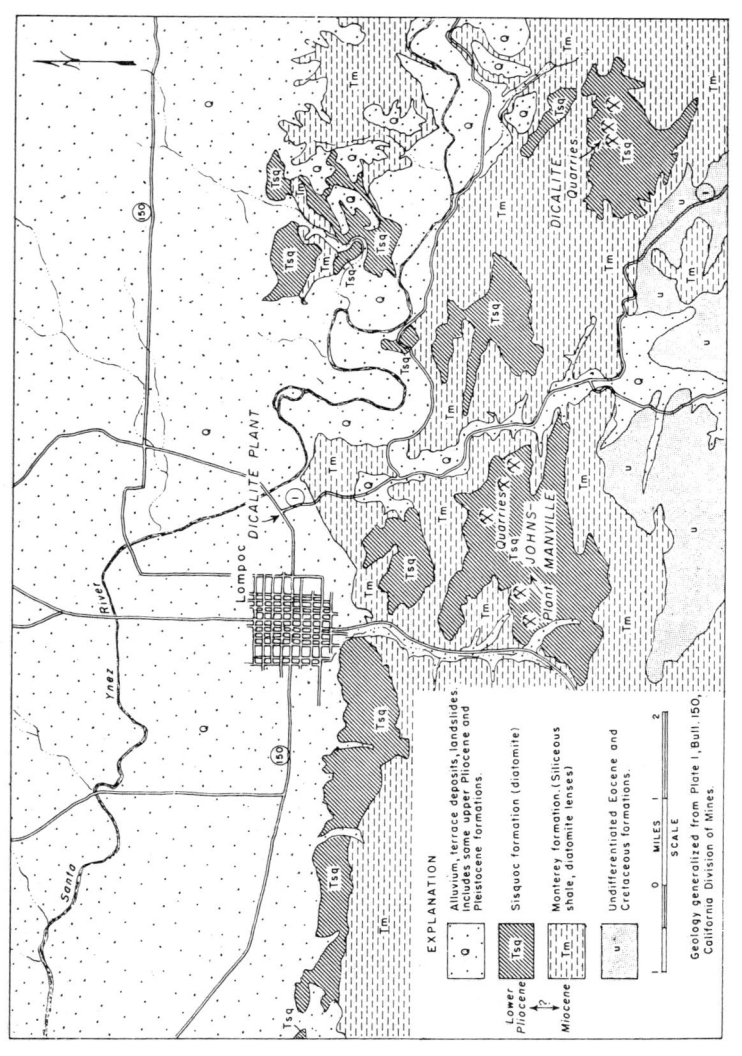

Figure 3. Geologic map of Lompoc area, Santa Barbara County, showing distribution of diatomite-bearing Sisquoc formation. From "Mineral Commodities of California" by O. P. Jenkns. Bulletin 176. California Division of Mines, December, 1957. Used by permission.

nature of the diatomaceous material contributed to the preservation of the soft parts and controlled decay.

These fish fossils are not mere carbonaceous impressions. In a number of specimens which the author opened, intestinal materials were still preserved as fine red dust which lay loosely in the body cavity. Often the delicate form of an eye was completely observable.

Frequently every scale was in place, and the only distortion visible was that of dislocation in the spinal cord and the pressing of the delicate rib bones and the lower fins out of alignment as the body was compressed to a few thousandths of an inch in thickness. In one case, a slight fault had displaced the head of a herring in two planes by one half of an inch. The distortion otherwise leaves the physical form well preserved in every way.

As a rule these fish were found lying in the bedding plane of the diatomite, which fractures easily along this plane. This made recovery of the fish fossils a fairly simple matter, except for the fact that diatomite is somewhat to exceedingly brittle, particularly after weather exposure. As a result, many of the blocks on which I worked were beginning to crumble on the surface, and did not fracture as well as those in other areas.

Mr. Bob Hendy, the geologist at the Johns Manville's "Celite" quarries, kindly escorted me in a four wheel company vehicle throughout their extensive quarries. He remarked that fossil fish finds have become rather uncommon, and that the company now somewhat regretted giving their very large collection of fish and bird fossils to Stanford University. A display at the gate and in an administration building is rather small, but it does include a fossilized bird and some ear bones of whales, along with herring. A superb example of mackerel is on display in the Lompoc Chamber of Commerce offices.

Normal Deposition Questioned

It is deposition of fossils in the normal bedding plane of the diatomite that first suggested that these fishes and birds had simply fallen to the bottom after death, to be slowly covered by the slow "rain" or "snow" of diatom structures from the waters above. There are several factors, however, that make this simple uniformitarian explanation impossible.

First, the perfect condition of the bodies of the fossilized fish repudiates slow deposition (Figure 4). Frequently the fish were

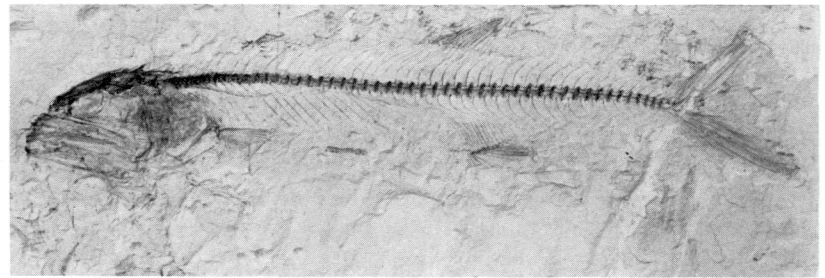

Figure 4. Xyne Grex **fossil. (Courtesy of Karl Dern.)**

recovered with every scale in place. The supposed gradual deposition of millions of carcasses, untouched by other bottom feeding fishes, and their painfully slow burial by the postulated 1/1500 to ½ inch per year deposition rate simply is not possible. The body structures of these fossils were preserved without any indication of deterioration and putrefaction. This proposed gravecloth of silica could scarcely cover a needle. How could it preserve the body of a fish an inch or more thick? Or how could a whale carcass be buried?

Secondly, there are fossils found which show that the rate of deposition was extremely rapid. Some are clearly deposited by a violent action which has torn scales and even removed fins from the body. In other fossils the scales lie in the diatomite layers around, *below* and in layers *above* the body. This requires exceedingly rapid burial! The typical fish, whether still alive or not at the time of deposit, was tumbled into position while surrounded by moving diatom ooze above and below. Its scales were torn loose by violent movement; they were deposited almost simultaneously with the fish.

Furthermore, there were places where fossils were found partially matted against each other. This made it impossible to recover either fossil whole, and they were unwisely discarded in many cases, for their specimen value was not recognized immediately. One workman, who spent some time with me in the office of Mr. Don Goodhue,[12] told me that he has found layers high on a ridge where thousands of fish fossils were heavily matted together in a layer more than a foot thick. These were so well preserved that they actually retained a distinct odor of fish when a fragment was broken off to expose unoxidized surfaces.

As a rockhound he was particularly interested in whalebone which is found occasionally. At least two specimens are known, one of which has been removed to the Santa Barbara museum. Presence of these large marine vertebrates is also significant evidence against slow burial. Long before uniform deposition could have buried them, their bones would have been scattered and then dissolved.

Very large quantities of whalebone have been found about 100 miles to the north, behind the first coast range, near Paso Robles, in the elevated valley followed by highway 101. One vertebra which I have noted from alluvium deposits there is more than 12 inches in circumference, and is quite well petrified. The bone structure is clear, and one pad is still observable on the end. A rancher friend there has a large horse trough filled with ribs and vertebra. Many other specimens have been carried away.

A Mechanism Proposed

It would appear that a violent upheaval had transformed the long Salinas Valley from an ideal breeding and calving ground for whales into a trap for such giant mammals. They now make their annual visits to remote Scammon's Lagoon in Baha California.[13]

When that uplift occurred in geological history I do not know, but I have observed that wave terraces and deltas are beautifully preserved along many sections of this unusual valley. Thus one may assume that they are Pleistocene, realizing that Pleistocene strata in the catastrophist's view are within historical times. An uplift that was sudden enough to trap whales in the Paso Robles area may have been involved in the Pleistocene uplift that left temporary beaches above Lompoc and lowered the sea level as much as 1,300 feet below very evident beach terraces in the area above Los Angeles.[14]

It is possible that a catastrophic intrusion of massive Arctic currents was an important factor in transporting the diatom ooze to Lompoc. If, as the author believes, the Miocene and the Pleistocene epochs are nearly contemporary steps in an extremely brief and violent crustal movement and upheaval in early historical times, then it may be that the diatom beds are, indeed, remains of arctic life forms swept down the coast by a moving coast line.

If one assumes that the so called "Cenozoic era" was actually a short catastrophic period, then it is possible also that a chain of events in rapid sequence swept Miocene diatoms ashore, trapped offshore life in "milk of Silica" (diatom ooze), and then soon killed the Paso Robles whales thereafter. The catastrophic nature of this uplift may be indicated by presence of fossilized sand dollars of remarkably modern form in water wells hundreds of feet deep in beds of sand.

Entombment of multitudes of shallow water fish with larger marine animals at Lompoc is in itself fascinating. That fossilized ear bones of whales are found in the same beds is significant evidence of catastrophism—that is, mixing of creatures such as shallow water fish (still alive) with remains of whales which had died previously. These whale ear bones would come from bottom deposits. They are portions of dismembered and decayed skeletons which are most resistive to dissolving processes which destroy bone in ocean depths. One may propose that these had been carried into place with the diatom ooze from the continental shelf at least. Their presence in beds containing undecayed, almost undistorted fossils of soft bodied fishes and birds which could never sink to deep water deposits without being torn apart and dissolved is most significant evidence for catastrophe. This combination of the two extremes could only speak of abrupt, violent burial.

A further indication of extreme violence is the fact that among the *Xyne Grex* specimens there are many indications that these fish were trapped in terror while they were yet alive. These herring, now apparently extinct, exhibit their terror by their mouths, often wide open as if grasping for their last breath in suffocation. Their fins lie widely spread and their backs are fiercely arched at the gill case and the body is twisted as if in agony. Indeed, this position of the head, thrown back as if the neck were broken, is characteristic of the Brush Ridge specimens and is found in many of them. Sizes of specimens at this site varied from an inch long minnow of unknown species to small "sunperch" and herring of a size comparable to those living today.

It is obvious form a careful examination that these fish were suddenly and violently trapped. They apparently suffocated in a strange, misplaced medium which unexpectedly overcame them, engulfing them in a solution that was at least as dense as milk of magnesia. Very possibly this was diatom ooze, disturbed from a large ocean basin, which had been literally scooped from its resting place—possibly from the continental shelf, possibly in some now forgotten arctic basin. If what the geologist calls Cenozoic was, as I believe, characterized by rapid continental movement to the west, it is likely that basin-scouring tsunsami waves would form and sweep on to the rising coast.

If the Cenozoic era was a fearsomely rapid and abrupt series of events, as postulated presently, then the Mesozoic "era" was already in the throes of the oncoming final ice age, the Pleistocene epoch. This may account for the vast deposits of diatoms, which thrive in arctic seas. Perhaps a comet or meteor struck the earth after the flood causing the land mass to divide. Collision fallout from this event may have changed the albedo of the earth and the "ice age" may have followed soon after, scouring the newly lifted Alps, Rockies, and, of interest here, the Coast Range.

But in accounting for the remarkable quantities of diatoms, one should not forget that there is evidence that polar regions of an ancient continent were possibly still covered by a vast ice sheet left previously ("Paleozoic era") by the Noahic flood. Absence of Paleozoic deposits in the Canadian Shield might be used to support this contention. Such an icy condition after the flood would contribute ideal conditions for the phenomenally abundant multiplications of the diatoms in the seas of the world. In any case, it seems clear that there were vast quantities of diatom ooze available at the time of this catastrophic deposit. Ocean pockets of ooze were suddenly redeposited near or on shore as the result of violent crustal movement. No uniformitarian explanation can account for all factors involved at the moment of death and burial of fossil fish.

(It should be noted that George M. Price presented similar data regarding the diatomaceous beds, and he too regarded them as evidence for catastrophism.[15])

Perhaps the most remarkable feature contradicting uniformitarian deposition is occurrence of many fossil skeletons that simply do not follow the bedding plane in the diatomite. The bedding plane evidently represents a temporary surface. Not all fish lie flat, as would be expected if they were slowly and uniformly covered. Of course a fish which has deposited slowly, standing on end, would decay long before it could possibly be covered by the diatom "snow." Such a fossil, commonly found at Brush Ridge, had to be covered instantly.

Repeatedly I was disappointed in my search for "perfect" specimens which would exhibit the entire fish laterally on the bedding plane. Rather I found instead that only part of the fish lay in the bedding plane which had split open so easily. In my eagerness to find a nice display piece, I discarded numerous fossils which crossed bedding planes, as would be expected according to my contention that these had been catastrophically deposited. "They have their heads and tails a million years apart," commented a puzzled plant workman, who helpfully spent some time with me when I was first orienting myself to the area and the situation. He, like myself, was unable to reconcile field fact with classroom theory.

Conclusions

In the light of all these factors it is presently concluded that the diatom deposits were formed by material forced on shore by westward movement of the continental shelf with accompanying compressions and faults which elevated these ranges which traverse Point Arguello. They were deposited conceivably in unconsolidated ooze form on the Pacific Ocean bottom after the Noahic flood.

Their delicate bodies may have been among final sediments which precipitated out of the quieting flood waters. Or, as I have suggested, their affinity for cold waters may have brought a tremendous spurt of reproduction after the flood when combined factors of icy waters and silica filled waters made this possible.

It is true that the diatom has not been identified in deposits older than the Jurassic period of the Mesozoic era, but this is simply the old argument from silence. If these are extremely abrupt periods, as proposed, following close after the creative week, there is no problem. The disturbance of the diatoms into solution (out of ocean basin deposit) and their transport through the fish-filled waters of the continental shelf I attribute to an abrupt movement of the continent following the very extensive separation of the continents.

This event, which I identify with Genesis 10:25, would involve abrupt overriding of the East Pacific Rise by the continental shelf. This would literally scoop up these deposits and hurl them into the coastal waters. Their compression and uplift would be completed in the final stages of the Pleistocene Epoch about 2000 B.C. (Editor's note: Some will interpret Genesis 10:25 [as Matthew Henry does] to refer to a division of nations politically [in keeping with Genesis 10:32 even though a different verb for "division" is used] rather than to a physical partitioning of an early continent into several fragmentary continents. Furthermore, some creationist workers envision only one great earth catastrophe since creation—the Noachian deluge.

This view of the formation of the Lompoc diatomite deposits finds agreement in an isolated comment on deposits of microflora ooze found in Von Engeln and Caster:

> The peculiar significance of the deep sea deposits is that they do not appear, except under very special circumstances as constituents of this thick series of sedimentary marine strata that constitute the bedrock over most of the land areas of the earth. They are never lifted to make continental tracts. Where found, *extreme local diastrophism is responsible.*[17]

It is presently postulated that this compression series which affected Point Arguello in this way was at the same time completing the entire coastal range, trapping vast basins behind San Francisco's Golden Gate Ridge and the small range now cut by Carquinez Straits which drains the Great Central Valley of California.

Presence of fossil sand dunes high above the San Francisco Bay in the new Sierra Monte development south of the city is one of many evidences used to support this. These recent channels now drain the entire basin from Redding to the Grapevine south of Bakersfield. The shoreline of this enormous lake is plainly visible along the new Freeway 5 miles south of Tracy, where delta fans are evident below erosion valleys high above the valley floor.

It is significant that diatomite of low grade may be found scattered from King City far north of Lompoc to well south of Los Angeles, as well as in the Great Valley west of Bakersfield.[18] Here the presence of many fossil shark's teeth in "Sharkstooth Hill" bears mute testimony to the dramatic changes in the western continental shelf in those tumultuous times. Today a large folded range stands between Bakersfield and the coast.

It is the author's opinion that California is a fertile area for a Christian geologist studying the weaknesses of uniformitarian theory. The diatom itself bears mute testimony to this weakness. Furthermore, the Christian biologist should find the reproductive traits of the diatom significant. The fact that over 25,000 varieties of the diatom have been classified, and that fossil and modern forms are identical, though supposedly separated by millions of years and countless reproductive divisions,[19] should provide a check on the postulates of biological change. The stability of these 25,000 created varieties of this microscopic plant which flourishes invisibly to the human eye is an exquisite testimony to their infinite Creator.

REFERENCES

1. An example copied from the Lompoc Chamber of Commerce map follows: ". . . Diatomaceous earth—a soft powdery substance created from the fossilized remains of microscopic plants which grow beneath the water and built up layer after layer of 'sea snow' for thousands of years."
2. Bob Hendry, geologist at the Lompoc Johns Manville plant, in private discussion, August, 1968.

3. "After 50,000 centuries research puts the diatom to work." A booklet published in 1941, from the series, "Research at Johns Manville," pp. 7-8.

4. Von Engeln and Caster. 1952. Geology. McGraw and Hill, New York. "It will be appreciated that, although formanifera, Pteropods, Radiolarian and diatom remains fairly rain down through the oceanic deeps, their accumulation over the ocean floor in the sense of thickness of deposit, is at an extremely low rate because of microscopic size of the organisms and because some of the remains dissolve as they sink" (p. 324).

5. Meguro, Ito, and Fukushima, 1966. "Diatoms and the ecological conditions of their growth in sea ice in the arctic ocean." *Science,* 152:1089-1090.

6. Ferdinand C. Lane, 1947. The mysterious sea. Doubleday and Co., New York, p. 87.

7. *Ibid.*

8. The Dialogues of Plato, The republic. Book 7, Great Books of the Western World, Encyclopedia Britannica, Chicago. Vol. 7:388-389.

9. Bernard E. Northrup, 1968. Harmonizing geology with Genesis. The author has available a four page chart and the explanative sheets displaying his conclusions concerning precise relationships of Historical Geology and Biblical accounts of creation and catastrophes ($1.00).

10. According to Bob Hendry, geologist at Lompoc Johns Manville plant.

11. Superintendent Don Goodhue and interested employees of Grefco's Dicalite plant during an extended conversation, August, 1968.

12. *Ibid.*

13. Earl Stanley Gardiner, 1960. Hunting the desert whale. Morrow, New York.

14. Raymond C. Moore, 1958. Historical geology. 2nd edition. McGraw Hill and Co., New York, pp. 474-477.

15. George M. Price, 1923. The new geology. Pacific Press Publishing Association, Mountain View Calif., pp. 200-201.

16. William H. Matthews, 1968. Fossils. Barnes and Noble, p. 1990.

17. Von Engeln and Caster, *op. cit.*

18. Moore, *op. cit.*

19. Reference #3 above.

II

IS THE CAPITAN LIMESTONE A FOSSIL REEF?[†]

Stuart E. Nevins*

Introduction

One has only to refer to the index of any recent historical geology text to find a number of examples of so-called fossil organic "reefs." These "reef" deposits, which are found in various portions of the geological column, have been recognized by many observers to be very difficult to reconcile with Biblical chronology.

The great thickness of calcium carbonate found in a single ancient "reef" appears to represent thousands of years of accumulation of coralline and algal organisms one on top of another if cemented at roughly the same rate as modern organic reefs. How then can the Noachian Flood be considered important in rapidly depositing certain portions of the geological record if strata implying very slow rates of accumulation are common? Doesn't the occurrence of so many fossil "reefs" require that many thousands of years be added to the relatively short duration of earth history implied in the book of Genesis?

That the so-called "reefs" of the fossil record provide difficulty for biblical chronology was recognized by John C. Whitcomb and Henry M. Morris in *The Genesis Flood*.[1] They suggest that many of these fossil "reefs" are not *in situ,* organically-bound frameworks, but fossiliferous debris which has been transported in the waters of

---

[†]Research for this paper was supported by the Research Fund of the Creation Research Society. Contributions for the support of such research projects may be mailed to Richard Korthals, 7227 Thomas St., River Forest, Illinois 60305, and may be designated for the Research Fund.

*Stuart E. Nevins holds an M.S. degree in geology and is assistant professor of geology at the Christian Heritage College, El Cajon, California.

the universal Noachian Flood. Many structures which may appear to be *in situ,* they propose, are products of resedimentation.

Harold W. Clark[2] in his book *Fossils, Flood and Fire* considers that Permian "reefs" were growing before the Flood and, therefore, suggests that these structures are organically constructed in quiet water over a period of time longer than the year of the Flood. Clark argues that the rate of growth of Paleozoic "reefs" need not be as slow as the rate for modern reefs. He is not obligated to the long period of time advocated by uniformitarian geologists.

The problem of fossil "reefs" was also brought to many people's attention in an article by J. R. van de Fliert[3] written as a critique of *The Genesis Flood.* Van de Fliert advocates that strict adherence to the Biblical chronology is untenable because of the very long period of time necessary to form a single fossil "reef." He mentions several "barrier reefs" in the stratigraphic record as particular problems and insists that modern historical geologists are correct in estimating the age of many of the earth's sedimentary deposits in the order of hundreds of millions of years.

The problem of fossil "reefs" is therefore a crucial issue to Bible-believing Christians.

In response to a research challenge from several members of the Creation Research Society, an investigation was conducted into one of the so-called "barrier reefs" of the fossil record. This is the world famous "Permian Reef Complex" of the Guadalupe Mountains of southeastern New Mexico and western Texas (more commonly referred to by geologists as "Capitan Reef"). The purpose of the present research paper is to evaluate critically the stratigraphic, lithologic, and ecologic criteria which have led many modern geologists to consider the Capitan Limestone and associated sediments as an example of a fossil "barrier reef."

Terminology

To avoid confusion many terms must be defined. They are used widely by modern geologists. These definitions are found in the Appendix.

Definition of "Reef"

Before beginning an analysis of the data relevant to "Capitan Reef" it is necessary that agreement be obtained on the definition of the term "reef." Geologists of the past have used different criteria to define "reef," the term has been misapplied to many fossil deposits which have been understood to be deposits of tumbled debris, sheet-like strata, or of other non-reefal origin.

The layman usually pictures a reef as a massive structure composed of solid, organically-bound, *in situ* organisms on or near the shore of the ocean. He may recognize that a reef has a particular topographic expression (it rises above the surrounding depositional surface), has an internal structure which is largely unbedded or obscurely bedded, and is chemically composed mainly of calcium carbonate ($CaCO_3$). To those in the nautical profession, the term "reef" has very precise meaning denoting an organic structure which intercepts waves and is a hazard to navigation.

Present-day reefs have been grouped into three main classes: *fringing reefs*—linear reefs which occur at the shoreline; *barrier reefs*—linear or curved reef strips which follow the shoreline yet are separated from it by a lagoon usually many tens of feet deep; and *atolls*—circular reef strips which surround empty lagoons.

In the study of ancient "reefs" the historical geologist would be severely handicapped by definitions as specific as those just stated. When examining a stratum which is suspected to contain a "reef" deposit, it is often very difficult to determine whether the organisms were bound together at the time they lived. This is often due to recrystallization of the carbonate after deposition which obscures many of the features of the deposit. There is always extreme difficulty in estimating the depth of water and the position of the shoreline at the time the organisms lived mainly because these are rarely apparent in the stratigraphic outcrop.

The geometry of the suspected "reef" deposit is sometimes changed by erosion subsequent to the period of deposition. Also, the stratigraphic outcrop contains no isochronous datum lines which can tell the geologist what the characteristic topographic expression of the deposit was at a particular moment in time. For many reasons the historical geologist has been content with using a very vague definition of ancient "reefs."

W. C. Krumbein and L. L. Sloss in their text, *Stratigraphy and Sedimentation,* begin their discussion of fossil "reefs" with the following admission concerning that misuse of the term:

> Recognition of the oil-trapping potentials of mound-like carbonate masses and the relationship of some of these to modern organic reefs has led to the rather indiscriminate application of the term "reef" to almost any permeable carbonate mass that exhibits a degree of upward convexity. The development of a definition that would cover ancient organic reefs, but which would exclude unrelated masses of similar geometry, is hampered by a number of factors.[4]

The inappropriate use by geologists of the term "reef" which reflects a very poor definition is also emphasized by J. Keith Rigby:

> The term "reef" has been applied loosely to several structures by different workers. Locally, it has been used for merely a faunal association, even though the organisms are present as loose, discrete fragments and the rocks in which they occur are evenly bedded in moderately thin layers. The term also has been applied to carbonate lenses in noncarbonate sequences, even though these lenses are of bedded, unbound detritus, oolites, or crinoid columnals. It also has been applied to sheetlike deposits of *in situ* corals or algal crusts or other reef-associated organisms even though the deposit is widespread, thin, and with no demonstrable topographic expression. Massive tumbled blocks also have been considered to be reefs, particularly if the blocks are abundantly fossiliferous and occur in distinctly more thinly bedded rocks. The term "reef" also has been applied to large carbonate structures which may be truly of reef origin at their margins, but which are composed mainly of bedded, clastic debris.[5]

Thus, we see that part of the misconceptions associated with the "reef" problem comes from the vague definition of the term "reef." Since the term has been widely misapplied, we have abundant reason here to question the authenticity of the "reef" interpretation of many geologists. If we were to ask for a more strict definition of the term "reef," it is evident that many (and probably most) of these ancient deposits would not qualify for consideration as "reefs."

Probably the greatest difficulty in identifying so-called ancient "reefs" is that the modern examples generally have little resemblance to those of the past. Krumbein and Sloss recognize that modern and ancient "reefs" are products of different environments. They write:

> . . . much of our knowledge of modern reefs is derived from the study of oceanic realms in which reefs are found on seamounts or islands that rise from abyssal depths. The data have but little applicability to the majority of ancient reef masses available for investigation, since the latter are products of relatively shallow epicontinental seas, commonly associated with restricted euxinic or evaporitic environments that are not duplicated among modern settings. Finally, the dolomitization and recrystallization of carbonate rocks serve to obscure many of the details of structure, texture, and paleontology, that would aid in relating ancient reefs to their modern counterparts.[6]

W. H. Easton in his popular text, *Invertebrate Paleontology*, has suggested that the reason for dissimilarity between modern and ancient "reefs" is also due to differences in the type of organisms forming each. Modern reef-forming organisms (mainly scleractinian corals and coralline algae) were not responsible for building Paleozoic "reefs."

Furthermore, most of the ancient "reef" organisms are extinct today and their ecologic affinities are to some degree unknown. Easton recommends that the ancient deposits should *not* be referred to as "reefs." Specifically,

> Recent coral reefs are not typical of coral growths in the past. Intergrown build-ups as large as the Great Barrier Reef east of Australia are unknown in the fossil record. Moreover, many tropical "coral reefs" of today actually consist of more than 50 per cent (some as high as 80 per cent) of calcareous red algae such as *Lithothamnium* and *Halimeda*. It is also true that ancient reefs commonly (or even mostly) consisted of less coralline material than other material. For instance, many Paleozoic reefs were composed largely of tabulate corals and stromatoporoids, or even of crinoids or brachiopods. For this reason it has

seemed desirable for a word to be coined which has neither the connotation of corals nor of rocks and shoals such as mariners have in mind when they speak of reefs. The term *bioherm* has achieved wide acceptance by geologists for build-ups of any kind of organic skeletal material. In addition, the companion term, *biostrome,* refers to stratified deposits of fossils or fossil debris which do not stand in any appreciable relief above the general surface of deposition.[7]

Since the modern and ancient deposits differ, there are very few features of modern reefs which can be used to identify ancient "reefs." Thus the "reef complex" problem becomes very apparent because we do not know exactly what characteristics to expect in ancient "reefs."

In the previous discussion some of the problems relating to identification of fossil "reefs" have been presented. Yet, many geologists feel that ancient "reefs" exist in the stratigraphic record. How is this identification made? The recognition is based mainly on three logical schemes which come from different subfields of geology. These subfields are 1) stratigraphy, 2) lithology, and 3) paleoecology.

1) *Stratigraphy,* a discipline of geology which deals with the position and geometry of stratified rocks, is claimed by many geologists to prove the existence of "reefs" in the fossil record. These geologists say the presence of a reef should modify the sedimentation of an area to such an extent that three typical depositional environments (the "reef core," the "backreef," and the "forereef") should exist and be readily apparent from study of the strata.

Since a reef cannot exist without modifying surrounding sedimentation, the environments and strata associated with the alleged "reef" proper are termed a "reef complex." Very characteristic facies relationships should exist in an ancient "reef" and any synchronous depositional surface should change laterally in a seaward direction from "backreef" to "reef core" to "forereef." Furthermore, a study of the position of each environment of the so-called "reef complex" should show that the "reef core" rose topographically above the surrounding depositional surface.

2) *Lithology,* the megascopic and microscopic study of the com-

position and structure of rocks, is also alleged to be very useful in identifying different environments of an alleged fossil "reef complex." The "reef core," which represents the actual "reef" proper accumulated in the zone of breaking waves, is made of organically-bound sediments and precipitated calcium carbonate from *in situ* organisms. This unbedded framework must be wave-resistant and lack large bodies of mud, silt, or sand which could be easily eroded by waves. Cavities within the "reef core," however, could be filled with fine sediment which has been "baffled" down into the framework.

The "forereef" is on the seaward side of the "reef" and is located in deeper water. Here bedded deposits dipping at some angle away from the massive "reef core" form from fossil fragments and chunks of "core" which have been torn loose by waves and rolled downslope.

The "backreef" is thought to represent a broad and shallow lagoonal environment behind the "reef core" where there is little turbulence caused by waves. Here fine grained materials such as mudstone or siltstone, or chemical precipitates such as calcium carbonate or calcium sulfate are deposited.

3) *Paleoecology,* the study of the relationship between ancient organisms and their environment, is considered by many geologists to distinguish the various parts of the "reef complex." Thus, the "reef core" should be characterized mainly by rugged life forms which could bind themselves and other sediments. Thin-shelled or free-floating forms would be at a disadvantage. The "backreef" should logically contain fragile organisms and forms which could tolerate higher salinity. Due to the depth below the photic zone, the majority of the "forereef" environment should lack *in situ* growths of algae. Many of the organisms of the "forereef" could be expected to be out of place due to transportation from the "reef core."

Having discussed the problems and techniques used to recognize fossil "reefs," an attempt can now be made to formulate a definition of the term "reef" which will be both restrictive and useful to the geologist. J. Keith Rigby defines "reef" as follows:

> Reefs are considered as largely unbedded or obscurely bedded, massive structures which are composed of solid, organically

bound, *in situ* organisms, and which were at least potentially wave-resistant structures that rose topographically above the surrounding depositional surface.[8]

Another excellent definition was made by William G. Hart who suggests that a "reef" is:

. . . a wave-resistant organic build-up composed of frame-builders, cementing organisms, and detrital fill which modifies the surrounding sedimentation.[9]

Combining the better features of both Rigby's and Hart's definitions, we attempt a definition which clearly encompasses the stratigraphic, lithologic and ecologic criteria which have been useful in identifying so-called fossil "reefs." It is suggested that a "reef" is a largely unbedded, wave resistant structure composed of *in situ*, organically-bound, frame-building organisms, cementing organisms, and sediment filling which modifies the surrounding sedimentation. This definition can be used to assess the "reefishness" of many of the so-called "reefs" of the fossil record. It will be employed when examining "Capitan Reef" which is one of the most widely claimed examples of an ancient "barrier reef."

General Description of Capitan Limestone

While the Capitan Limestone is present in several areas in southeastern New Mexico and western Texas, one of the best exposures occurs in the Guadalupe Mountains southwest of Carlsbad, New Mexico. The very light gray limestone which is about 2,000 feet thick outcrops in a narrow strip up to five miles wide and about 47 miles long (see Figure 1).

This limestone tends to form the southeast escarpment of the northeast-southwest trending Gaudalupe Mountains. Carlsbad Caverns and Guadalupe Mountains National Parks are located in the Guadalupe Mountains and the exceptional scenery and enormous caverns are due to the distinctive Capitan Limestone.

The Permian Capitan Limestone has been considered for the past 40 years by many geologists to be a classic example of a fossil "barrier reef." Probably more has been written on the Capitan than any other ancient "reef" in North America. K. H. Crandall[10] was the first to publish data in 1929 advancing the "barrier reef" explanation.

Since then numerous authors have supported Crandall's idea. The "reef" interpretation has been solidly "enthroned" in the literature and in geologists' minds by popular guidebooks and textbooks.

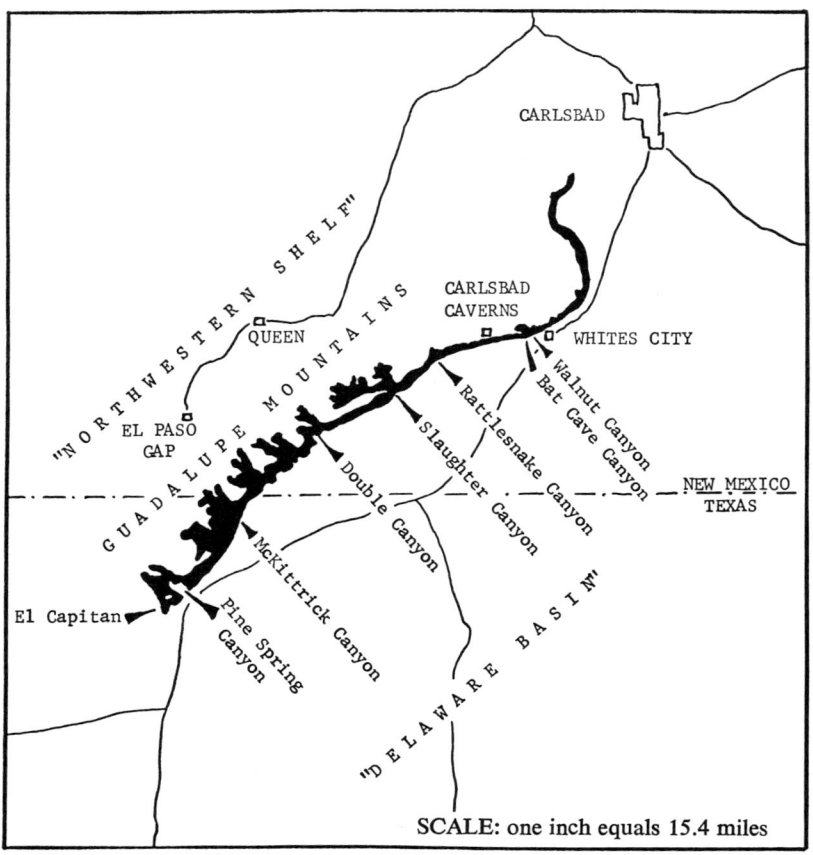

Figure 1. Location map of Guadalupe Mountains in southeastern New Mexico and western Texas. The zone of outcroppings of Capitan Limestone is blackened.

IS THE CAPITAN LIMESTONE A FOSSIL REEF? 25

Only a few notable articles[11, 12, 13] have taken exception to the popular view.

According to advocates of the popular interpretation, one of the best exposures of Capitan Limestone illustrating the appropriateness of the "reef" view is in the Guadalupe Mountains. By far the greatest amount of data on the Capitan comes from this area.

In order to test the "reef" interpretation for the Capitan Limestone of the Guadalupe Mountains, extensive literature search and field investigation was conducted. Since the Capitan is most readily studied in the field where it is cut by canyons on the southeast side of the Guadalupe Mountains, seven canyons were studied in the field research. These are Walnut Canyon, Bat Cave Canyon, Rattlesnake Canyon, Slaughter Canyon, Double Canyon, McKittrick Canyon, and Pine Spring Canyon (see Figure 1). The present research concentrated on the stratigraphy, lithology, and to some extent the paleoecology of the Capitan Limestone.

Stratigraphy

Strata of the Permian System[14] and of the Guadalupian Stage of the Middle Permian are well exposed in southeastern New Mexico and western Texas. For a number of years many geologists have attempted to interpret the environment of deposition of these strata.

To the southeast of the Guadalupe Mountains the Bell Canyon and Cherry Canyon formations (predominantly strata of fine grained quartzose sandstone with some beds of limestone) are present over wide areas. Because of the regular bedding of the fine material in widespread strata and the lack of fossils, the Bell Canyon and Cherry Canyon formations are interpreted to be deposited in a marine basin (called the "Delaware Basin") which was about one to two thousand feet deep.

To the northwest of the Guadalupe Mountains strata of dolomite, sandstone, and evaporite of the Tansill, Yates, Seven Rivers, Queen, and Grayburg formations are present. These are presumed to have been deposited at the same time as the Bell Canyon and much of the Cherry Canyon formations. These strata of dolomite, sandstone, and evaporite to the northwest of the Guadalupe Mountains are considered by many geologists to have been deposited in a shallow sea or broad lagoon (called the "Northwestern Shelf") because of the chemical characteristics of the rocks and persence of rare shallow marine fossils.

Thus, many geologists envision the existence of an oceanic basin (the "Delaware Basin") to the southeast of the Guadalupe Mountains, and a shallow sea or broad lagoon (the "Northwestern Shelf") to the northwest during the Guadalupian Stage of the Permian. The Guadalupe Mountains, then, are of particular interest because they are generally considered to have been an area of transition between the shallow sea and the deep ocean.

The alleged transition zone is represented by a distinctive type of limestone and dolomite known as the Goat Seep Limestone (dolomitized limestone with rare fossils) and the Capitan Limestone (limestone and dolomitized limestone with common shallow marine fossils). The Capitan Limestone and Goat Seep Limestone, which are thought to represent a "barrier reef," inter-tongue laterally to the northwest with the Tansill, Yates, Seven Rivers, Queen, and Grayburg formations. To the southeast the Goat Seep Limestone and Capitan Limestone intertongue laterally with the Bell Canyon and Cherry Canyon sandstones and limestones. The interpreted environments and facies relationship between formations are shown in Figure 2.

Many geologists who hold to the above interpretation have also

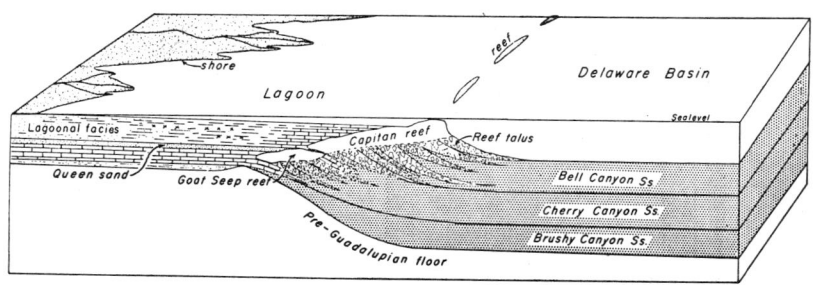

Figure 2. Block diagram showing different ecologic and depositional environments alleged to be associated with "Capitan Reef." (After Carl O. Dunbar and Karl M. Waage.[15])

speculated on how the strata and depositional environments developed over millions of years. A common explanation given to students is that at the beginning of the Guadalupian Stage a shallow sea covered much of the area. To the northwest was a land area which continually supplied sediments to the sea. At or near the shore of this sea, "Goat Seep Reef" began to grow and trap sediments on its shoreward side. This started a differentiation between "shallow sea" and "deep-sea basin."

Because of nutrient-rich waters upwelling from the stagnant basin to the highly saline shallow sea, "reef" growth was ideal and a linear "barrier reef" ("Capitan Reef") developed. Waves tore chunks of "reef core" loose and these rolled down the steep slope on the basinward side of the "reef" to form vast "talus" deposits.

Supposedly, while sea level rose gradually over millions of years, "Capitan Reef" could not grow upward at a fast rate but grew basinward over the talus deposits. A broad and shallow lagoon existed behind the "barrier reef" which trapped sediments coming from the land. Basin sediments may have come from the land through narrow breaks in the "reef." "Reef" construction was concluded when sea level began to lower.

After the Guadalupian Stage was deposited, the sea occupied "Delaware Basin" and was very shallow. As the sea dried up it left vast amounts of evaporites (anhydrite, gypsum, salt, etc.) comprising the Castile Formation which exists to the southeast of the Guadalupe Mountains. The southeast escarpment of the Guadalupe Mountains is the shelf-basin margin caused by the Permian "reef complex."

Figure 3 shows two different stratigraphic interpretations through the Guadalupe Mountains. The top illustration displays the conventional diagram advocated by geologists who hold the "barrier reef" view. Notice that the Capitan Formation is divided into two units—a "reef core" unit above a "reef talus" unit.

The "reef core" unit is thought to represent the organically-bound build-up which formed a wave-resistant "reef." The "reef talus" unit is considered to represent the "forereef" deposits which accumulated on the seaward side of the "reef core." Thus, P. B.

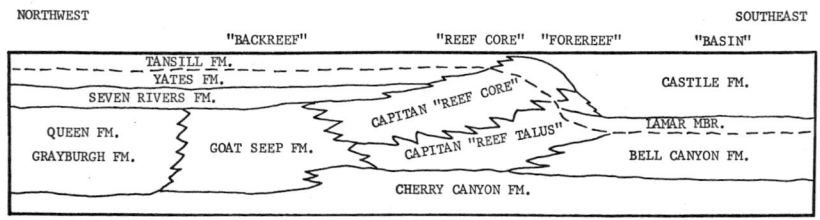

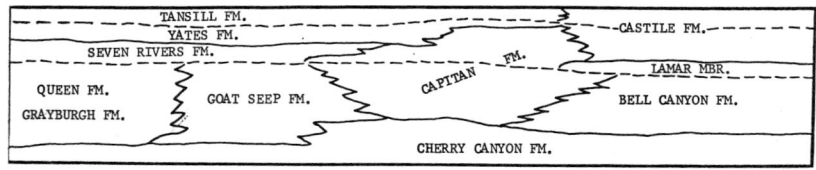

Figure 3. Two generalized cross-sectional diagrams through the Guadalupe Mountains showing different stratigraphic interpretations before any flexure or erosion of strata. Top, diagram suggested by advocates of the "barrier reef" view modified from P. T. Hayes and R. L. Koogle[16]). Bottom, diagram proposed from our research. Dashed lines are interpreted to be synchronous depositional surfaces. Vertical thickness of strata is variable but approximately 3,000 feet; horizontal width of diagrams is about nine miles (note the use of extreme vertical exaggeration).

King[17] and P. T. Hayes and R. L. Koogle[18] of the U. S. Geological Survey differentiated the two units in their geological mapping. They map the boundary between the two units of the Capitan Limestone at a prominent topographic break.

Figure 4 shows the mouth of Slaughter Canyon and the supposed lithologic boundary between the unbedded (massive) "reef core" and the bedded and steeply dipping rocks of the "reef talus" unit.

Our field work does not support the above division of the Capitan. Lithologic data presented later in the paper will be used to show the absence of lithologic change at the topographic break. Furthermore, we will show that the alleged "reef core" lacks large masses of frame-building organisms and, therefore, is a poor example of the wave-resistant portion of the proposed "reef complex."

Also, it will be suggested that there is absence of demonstrable "reef-derived" talus in what is interpreted to be the "forereef" por-

IS THE CAPITAN LIMESTONE A FOSSIL REEF? 29

tion of the Capitan. The distinction of a massive reef core" unit from a bedded and steeply dipping "reef talus" unit is therefore *imaginary*.

In our interpretation of the stratigraphy (see Figure 3, bottom diagram) we have avoided making the division. The Capitan Formation is shown as a single unit. It is noteworthy that C. W. Achauer,[19, 20] a petroleum geologist, refuses to make the distinction between "reef core" and "reef talus" for similar reasons.

Advocates of the "barrier reef" interpretation also imagine characteristic facies relationships to exist. Thus, "back reef," "reef core," "forereef," and "basin" sedimentation are considered to be coeval. In Figure 3 (top diagram) the dashed line is used to indicate a

Figure 4. Capitan Limestone at the mouth of Slaughter Canyon. The massive cliff-making limestone alleged to be "reef core" is above beds thought to be "reef talus" which dip steeply toward the camera. At the extreme left are "back-reef" beds of the Yates and Tansill formations. Vertical exposure is about 1,000 feet.

synchronous depositional surface. The base of the Tansill Formation is correlated in time with the Lamar Limestone Member (calcilutite) of the "basin" deposited Bell Canyon Formation.

According to W. W. Tyrell[21] the Tansill-Lamar correlation is based on the presence of common species of fusalinids (small planktonic animals the size and shape of a grain of wheat) in both units. This time correlation surface is considered to pass through both the alleged "reef core" and "forereef talus" of the Capitan.

C. W. Achauer,[22] however, disputes this paleontological correlation with statigraphic evidence. His field work seems to indicate that the Lamar Limestone Member passes into the upper part of the Capitan Limestone but does not pass into the Tansill Formation.

Figure 5. "Backreef," "reef core," and "forereef talus" in McKittrick Canyon, The massive cliff-making "reef core" (calcisiltite) is above so-called "reef talus" (sponge-algal limestone). "Backreef" beds of Yates and Tansill overlie the "reef core."

Figure 6. Laminated gypsum of the Castile Formation.

Achauer correlates the Lamar Member through the upper Capitan with the Seven Rivers Formation. Harold S. Cave,[23] a geologist who is also critical of the "barrier reef" view, correlates the Lamar Member with the Grayburg Formation.

Our field work also does not substantiate the Tansill-Lamar correlation. In the stratigraphic diagram presented in Figure 3 (bottom diagram) we correlate the Lamar through the upper Capitan with the Seven Rivers or Queen formations. Figure 5 shows alleged "back-reef," "reef core," and "forereef" beds in McKittrick Canyon. The "talus" of the "forereef" Capitan in the foreground is stratigraphically above beds which correlate in time with the Lamar Member, yet, these foreground beds appear to merge into the massive "reef core" Capitan and not into the Tansill Formation above the Capitan. The Tansill seems to consistently cap the "reef core" Capitan (except where removed by erosion). To suggest the Lamar-Tansill correlation here seems inappropriate.

The Tansill Formation in a southeast direction must be correlated in time with the Castile Formation because of the presence of intertongueing between Capitan and Castile as noted by C. L. Jones[24] and H. S. Cave.[25] Yet, advocates of the "barrier reef" view commonly place the deposition of the evaporites of the Castile Formation gypsum, anhydrite, salt, and limestone (see Figure 6) after the entire Gaudalupian Stage. Thus they deny Capitan-Castile intertongueing to any large extent. The evidence which suggests simultaneous evaporite-carbonate deposition is difficult for the "reef" view. Could ocean waters which had reached a high enough concentration to precipitate calcium sulfate have been conducive to reef growth?

Advocates of the "barrier reef" interpretation also suppose that considerable topography existed at the junction of the "Northwestern Shelf" and "Delaware Basin." The dashed line in Figure 3 (top diagram) is thought to represent a synchronous depositional surface. Notice that the surface rises about one thousand feet as it passes through the Capitan Limestone.

The need for this topography is seen in Figure 7. Here beds of "Delaware Basin" rocks are seen approaching the alleged "reef" to

Figure 7. Strata of sandstones of Brushy Canyon, Cherry Canyon, and Bell Canyon formations below the prominent peak (El Capitan), the upper portion of which is Capitan Limestone.

the northwest. In the right foreground of Figure 7 are standstones of the Brushy Canyon Formation, and in the center left are sandstones of the Cherry Canyon Formation. The peak at the right is El Capitan, the upper portion of which is Capitan Limestone.

While the Brushy Canyon and Cherry Canyon formation pass under the Capitan Limestone, the Bell Canyon Formation, which lies above the Cherry Canyon and below the Capitan, intertongues with the Capitan. There seems to be a rise in altitude of synchronous beds through the Capitan. Upholders of the "reef" view who endorse the Tansill-Lamar correlation must imagine Bell Canyon strata correlating in time with strata which overlie the Capitan—hence a change in altitude of synchronous beds of about one thousand feet.

Since our field work does not suggest the Tansill-Lamar correlation, but that the deposition of the Lamar Member of the Bell Canyon Formation is contemporaneous with the upper Capitan, we see considerably less change in altitude of synchronous beds. Yet, even our interpretation must allow for some change in altitude. How is this accounted for?

Those who hold the "barrier reef" view maintain that the change in altitude is due largely to the depositional slope which existed during Guadalupian time between the supposed "shelf" and the "basin." They tend to deny evidence of large tectonics (deformations by folding). But, if the southeast side of the Gaudalupe Mountains where the Capitan outcrops is a zone of flexure of strata, the change in altitude of synchronous strata need not be caused by original deposition along a junction between "shelf" and "basin." Harold S. Cave says:

> Since publication of the paper entitled, "Permian Stratigraphy of Southeastern New Mexico and Adjacent Parts of Western Texas," by K. H. Crandall, . . . it seems to have been a generally accepted fact by many geologists that the generally southeast dips shown in the Capitan limestone outcrops in the general Carlsbad Cavern area are the result of foresetting in reef building. It is herein suggested that the dips in question are, in large part at least, comparable with other formational dips coming off the southeast and east flanks of the Gaudalupe Mountains. Hence said dips could well be perfectly normal inclinations resulting from the post-Cretaceous orogeny that built the mountains.[26]

Our field work showed evidences of tectonics (orogeny). Probably the most obvious evidence of flexure through the Capitan comes from the steep angle of dip of the alleged Capitan "reef talus." In some places these beds dip at angles of 45° away from the supposed "reef core." (Commonly encountered dips are usually about 20°.)

Due to the buoyancy of rocks and sand in water it is nearly impossible to accumulate materials at such steep angles. Tectonics seems at least in part necessary to imagine formation of this slope. Achauer[27] observes that some rock fragments in the Capitan "reef talus" can be fit together along fracture planes, and such is evidence of tectonics.

IS THE CAPITAN LIMESTONE A FOSSIL REEF?

Evidence is available to suggest uplift of the Capitan "reef core" and/or downwarping near the base of the "reef talus." Thus, in Figure 8, beds of Yates and Tansill formations can be seen dipping at 8° toward the northwest away from the "reef core." When Tansill beds are present on top of Capitan "reef core," they usually dip toward the "basin" (southeast) at 5° or more. Bell Canyon beds are also warped upward as they approach the Capitan "reef talus."

Since our field work indicates that at least a major part of the structural features associated with the Capitan Formation are post-depositional, we have avoided including these on our stratigraphic diagram (Figure 3, bottom diagram). Thus, our time lines pass through the Capitan horizontally (or nearly so) with little distortion.

In the previous discussion several stratigraphic objections have been presented to the classical "barrier reef" interpretation of the Capitan Limestone. Those who maintain that the Capitan Limestone and associated strata represent a fossil "reef complex" with simultaneous deposition of "backreef," "reef core," and "forereef" do so on very scanty evidence.

Lithology

One of the best ways to disprove the young age of the earth's sedimentary deposits implied by biblical chronology would be to find evidence of long history within the stratigraphic record. Such an evidence would be a large organically bound framework composing the "reef core" of a fossil "barrier reef." It would take thousands of years to cement a framework of algal and coralline organisms one on top of another if deposited at roughly the same rate as modern reef core.

If several fossil "reef cores" could be found at various levels in the stratigraphic succession, evidence for slow accumulation over long periods of time would be well documented. Lithology should either substantiate or refute the presence of these alleged "reef cores" in the ancient sedimentary deposits.

When geologists first suggested the "barrier reef" interpretation for the Capitan Limestone 40 years ago, they were primarily impressed by the stratigraphy. Since the Capitan had massive limestone

Figure 8. Beds of Yates and Tansill formations in Rattlesnake Canyon dipping at 8° toward the northwest away from the "reef core."

above steeply dipping beds of brecciated material, the proposal was that it represented a "reef" on the junction between "shelf" and "basin" environments. Little consideration was given to the lithology of the Capitan at that time. The lack of large organically-bound frameworks was known, but it was reasoned that recrystallization had destroyed them, or that future field investigations would find some.

Today there is wide agreement among geologists that the alleged Capitan "reef core" lacks large organically-bound frameworks. One of the first geologists to clearly note the absence of "reef core" was Donald L. Baars:

> In cross-section the Capitan complex . . . is composed of steeply dipping "fore-reef" beds of skeletal sands and gravels that in-

terfinger basinward with clastics of the relatively deep Delaware Basin. The skeletal particles deposited on the basinward slope grade abruptly to a massive limestone facies in a shelfward direction. *This so-called "reef core" is, upon close inspection, massive but composed of calcilutites (lithified lime muds) which would not now be considered "framebuilt" or particularly wave resistant in the unlithified state.*

This facies is narrow, and in some places is lacking. Core sediments (or, in some cases, the fore-slope skeletal sands) grade abruptly shelfward to beds of definite intertidal character, demonstrating very shallow water to mud-flat environments. *Diligent search has shown that reefoid structures are rare indeed, and are not responsible for the shelf construction but occur only as superficial small structures.*[28] (Emphases added.)

Probably the most qualified person to speak concerning Capitan "reef core" is C. W. Achauer who has examined hundreds of slabbed and etched samples and hundreds of thin sections under the microscope. He agrees with Baars concerning the lack of framework, but correctly observes that the "reef core" is not mostly clay-size materials as Baars suggests, but predominantly silt- and sand-size debris, as follows:

> Most of the Capitan lacks reef cores or large masses of colonial frame-building organisms. . . . Primarily the Capitan consists of silt- and sand-size skeletal debris derived from many kinds of organisms that thrived along the edge of the Northwest shelf.[29]

Examination of the so-called "reef talus" should also provide clues about the supposed binding of the "reef core." Achauer says, "The Capitan lacks stratified deposits of bioclastic debris which can be shown to have been derived from reef cores."[30] And R. J. Dunham says:

> Use of this criterion [examination of the binding of the "reef talus"] on the surface Capitan reef and on the subsurface Scurry reef indicates that the binding was wholly or largely inorganic, which accords with other evidence. . . . The Capitan reef and the Scurry reef thus are examples of a large class of stratigraphic reefs that are not ecologic reefs, not "really reefs." Organisms provided their skeletal debris, their bulk; but organisms did not provide their rigid framework (except perhaps locally, and incidentally).[31]

Based on our field work, we can conclude that the Capitan Limestone lacks an organically-bound framework. The Capitan is composed largely of calcarenite and calcisiltite. Fossils, except where noted in the discussion on paleoecology, are usually fragments and are not cemented in an organic framework.

The massive so-called "reef core" limestone tends to be very hard and poorly stratified due to some recrystallization of calcite. The lower portion of the Capitan has been partially dolomitized. Calcirudite "fossil hash" is sometimes found in both the "reef core" and "reef talus."

Figure 9 shows what may be called typical Capitan "reef core"

Figure 9. Cut and polished slab of typical Capitan "reef core" rock from McKittrick Canyon. It is calcisiltite which was not wave-resistant. Structure is blurred due to recrystallization. An encrusting bryozoan is present in the upper left (2X actual size).

from McKittrick Canyon. The sample comes from the lower part of the massive cliff in the center of Figure 5. The limestone (calcisiltite) is composed mainly of silt-size particles of broken skeletal calcite and calcite of nonorganic origin. There is no wave-resistant framework present! A small encrusting bryozoan cemented in the silt matrix is present in the upper left.

There is some evidence of recrystallation of the calcite (a characteristic of "reef core" limestone) which tends to obliterate fossils and make the rock extremely hard. Some geologists have actually maintained that recrystallization has destroyed the framework which is postulated to have existed, but this view seems rather extreme be-

Figure 10. Cut, polished, and etched slab of Capitan Limestone from Pine Spring Canyon containing pisoliths (large concentrically laminated spheres) and ooliths (small gray spheres) (1.5X actual size).

cause of the presence of unrecrystallized fossils.

Many of the most perfect fossil specimens presented later come from the "reef core" and these are also cemented in calcisiltite or calcarenite matrix. Arguing for destruction of the organic framework by recrystallization therefore seems pointless.

Figure 10 shows Capitan from Pine Spring Canyon near the boundary between Capitan and Tansill formations. The limestone is composed predominantly of pisoliths (the larger concentrically layered spheres) and ooliths (the smaller, gray, pellet-like spheres). The origin of the two is still uncertain. Some geologists speculate that both objects formed from sticky particles which have rolled collecting clay- and silt-size particles. Other geologists postulate

Figure 11. Cut, polished, and etched slab of Capitan "reef talus" (calcisiltite) from McKittrick Canyon. Many different fossils are evident due to the absence of recrystallization (1.5X actual size).

that the pisoliths formed from weathering and recrystallization around nucleii. One thing seems certain, they are not evidence for an organic framework.

A sample of what may be considered somewhat representative of Capitan "reef talus" is seen in Figure 11. It was collected in McKittrick Canyon near the foreground in Figure 5. The term "reef talus" is certainly misleading because this sample shows no evidence of having originated from the destruction of "reef core." It is very much like what has been called "reef core" as it is composed of calcisiltite matrix with abundant broken fossils.

The only notable lithologic difference between this sample and the "reef core" sample of Figure 9 is the presence of recrystallization in the latter. A cross-section of a whole, thin-shelled brachiopod is seen in the lower right of Figure 11. To the left of center is an encrusting bryozoan. No organic binding is evident.

It is most evident that "Capitan Reef" is very different from modern reefs when careful lithologic examination is conducted. Since "Capitan Reef" does not contain large masses of demonstrated "reef core," and "reef talus" which can be shown to be derived from destruction of "reef core," there is ample justification in denying its alleged reefal origin.

"Capitan Reef" in the Guadalupe Mountains did not build large organically-bound, wave-resistant, colonial frameworks and therefore did not *require* thousands of years of *in situ* growth. The presence of calcisiltite, calcarenite, and calcirudite in the alleged "reef core" suggests that the broken fragments were transported and deposited. *In situ* material is very rare if it exists. The rate of deposition need not be anything comparable to modern reefs.

Paleoecology

Many factors hinder proper ecologic interpretation of "Capitan Reef." The fact that most Paleozoic "reef-building" organisms are extinct restricts our knowledge of any biological affinities of these organisms. Recrystallization and dolomitization also tend to obscure some fossils and their matrix. The presence of exotic organisms

42 SPEAK TO THE EARTH

transported from different environments to a single portion of the "reef" also presents problems.

What is known about the ecology of Capitan organisms does not lend exclusive support to the "barrier reef" interpretation. Concerning the ecology of Capitan organisms, P. B. King says:

> From a study of the calcitic limestone, it is clear that lime-secreting organisms contributed to the formation of the rock. Brachiopods, various molluscs, and some other groups are very abundant in certain beds. These organisms, however, do not show any special adaptation to a reef environment. There is not, for example, a noteworthy abundance of thick-shelled forms that would

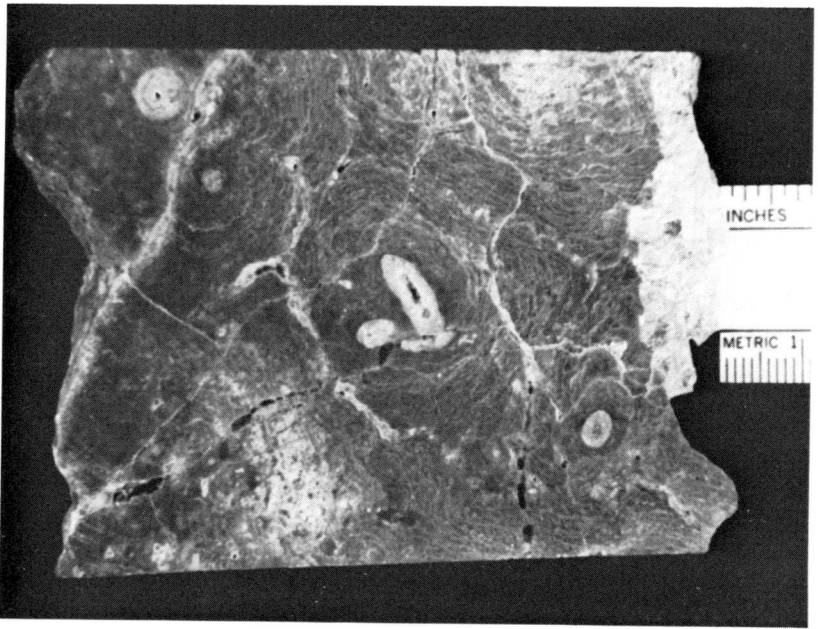

Figure 12. Cut and polished slab of spherical, concentrically laminated algae from Capitan "reef talus" of Slaughter Canyon. Nuclei are commonly a broken piece of bryozoan or other fossil fragment. Rolling of the spheres is evident and there is little evidence of organic framework or wave-resistant characteristics.

thrive in strong currents and pounding waves of the exposed parts of a reef and would, therefore, contribute a considerable amount of limestone to the deposit; instead, the assemblage seems to be a normal neritic fauna, such as would grow in any region of clear, shallow water.[32]

The possibility that organisms found in the Capitan were capable of withstanding the turbulence of a wave environment is denied by Achauer. Of the alleged "reef-building" Capitan organisms he says:

> . . . the most prominent forms are calcareous sponges and bryozoans. These organisms may have been capable of forming, and actually may have formed, sediment baffles in the Capitan; however, they did not build a wave-resistant structure in the Capitan, nor probably did they have the ecologic potential to do so.[33]

According to advocates of the popular "reef" view, algae were responsible for the major part of sediment trapping and binding, and, hence, are thought to be the major "reef-forming" organisms. Our field work and subsequent laboratory analysis of rock samples gave special attention to algae.

Figure 12 shows the commonest type of algae observed. These are small, spherical, cabbage-like (although of smaller size) colonies which tend to be crowded together. They seem to be composed mainly of filamentous green and blue-green algae which formed crude laminations around a bryozoan or other fossil fragment.

The majority of the structure, however, is not algae but frequently lime mud which was trapped between algal laminations. Promoters of the "barrier reef" interpretation feature this type of rock as a prime example of "reef core." Samples very similar to Figure 12 are on display at the exhibits at Carlsbad Caverns National Park labeled as "reef core" rock.

What is interesting about these algal structures is that they are most common in the so-called "reef talus" with sponges as stratified beds between layers of calcisiltite (such as Figure 11), calcarenite, and calcirudite. The "reef talus" beds in the foreground of Figures 4 and 5 are composed largely of this type of algal structure.

That this type of algae composes an *in situ* "reef core" within the "reef talus" deposits is most unlikely because of its position in the alleged "reef complex." Algae can grow only in shallow water where sunlight is available and should not live hundreds of feet below the alleged wave intercepting portion of the "reef." Since these algae are filamentous and build structures by trapping mud between calcareous laminations, there is little evidence of rigid framework or wave-resistant characteristics.

Some geologists may argue that these colonies of algae are not *in situ* "reef cores" when found in the "reef talus," but are transported from the wave-intercepting "core" of the deposit where they are truly *in situ*. Careful mapping by Achauer of this algal and sponge deposit shows that it is characteristic of the "forereef" posi-

Figure 13. Photomicrograph of Capitan "reef core" algal sphere (right) in a nonorganically bound matrix of silt-size particles (left). Algal structures have dominant orientation of calcite crystals that is not found in the matrix (35X actual size).

tion and is sometimes in the "reef core" area. Both the "reef core" and the "reef talus" of Figure 4 in Slaughter Canyon, according to Achauer,[34] are composed of this association.

This algae and sponge relation is found with the Lamar Limestone in McKittrick Canyon which has been considered a deep water deposit and proceeds up the sloping beds of "reef talus" to near the massive "reef core" in Figure 5. The "reef core" in Figure 5 is not characterized by algae or sponges but by calcarenite and calcisiltite.

Such data are most perplexing. Achauer[35] correctly observes that the algae and sponge association common to the alleged "forereef" is the most "reef-like" structure in the entire Capitan complex. The most "talus-like" part of the Capitan in McKittrick Canyon seems to be the alleged "reef core!"

There is good evidence that even these "reef-like" algal structures are of transported origin. The characteristic roundness of these structures with enclosed fossil fragment nucleii suggests that they have been rolled. Also, microscopic examination (see Figure 13) shows that colonies are usually in a matrix of nonorganically-bound calcisiltite.

Evidences of what may be a sediment trapping organic framework are seen in Figure 14. This rock is from the Capitan "reef core" just below the Tansill Formation in Slaughter Canyon. What appears to be "stromatolitic algae" occur as a mat in growth position over nonorganically-bound calcarenite bearing abundant dasyclad algae.

According to John M. Cys,[36] some stromatolitic structures in the Capitan have been shown to be of inorganic origin. Several features of Figure 14, to the contrary, indicate algal origin.

If these are *in situ* algae, then the Noachian Flood evidently was not responsible for depositing them. However, it is possible that resedimentation (transport, deposition, and burial) has occurred with the mat of algae being redeposited in appearance of growth position.

If many more mats could be found in the appearance of growth position, then *in situ* growth would seem necessary. At the present time it seems appropriate to reserve judgment about the *in situ* character of these algae.

The dasyclad algae, a green algae forming a nonorganically-bound structure in the bottom of Figure 14 and in Figure 15, are distinctive forms common in the Capitan. While alive, their thalli were composed of a central fleshy stem with branches arranged in whorls. Calcite was secreted as a cylinder enveloping the central stem and the bases of the branches. After fossilization the only remaining parts are the hollow lime cylinders with pores in the walls where branches penetrated.

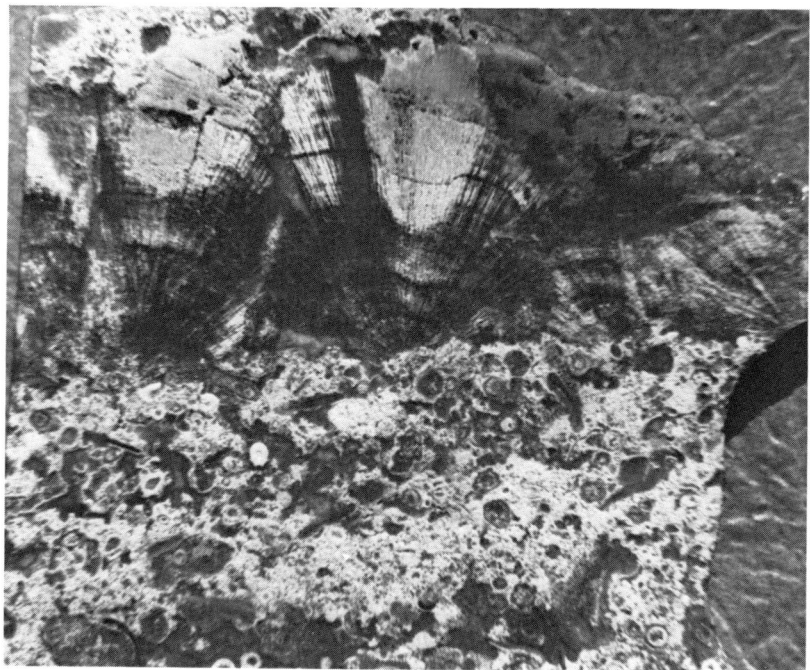

Figure 14. Cut, polished, and etched slab of Capitan "reef core" showing "stromatolitic algae" structure apparently in growth position over nonorganically-bound calcarenite with abundant dasyclad algae (1.5X actual size).

IS THE CAPITAN LIMESTONE A FOSSIL REEF? 47

The presence of dasyclad algae in the "reef core" and "forereef" as well as in the "backreef" seems to present problems for the "reef" view. How could algae of such delicate structure have survived in a wave environment?

Another type of algae found in the Capitan belongs to the extinct family of lime-secreting red algae called Solenoporaceae. This family very closely resembles the modern calcareous red algae of the family Corallinaceae which commonly form 50 to 80 percent of reefs at the present.

What is amazing in our study of the algae of the Capitan is the unimportance of Solenoporaceae as a "reef-builder." It was not

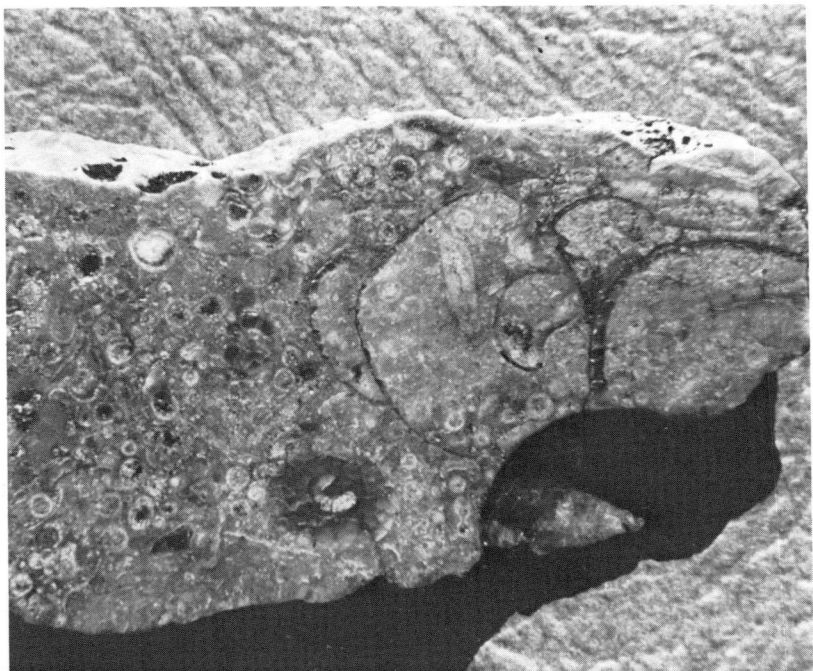

Figure 15. Cut, polished, and etched slab of Capitan Limestone from Walnut Canyon which is very closely associated with "backreef" beds. Dasyclad algae (left) and cross-sections of brachiopods (right) are in a nonorganically-bound matrix (2X actual size).

found as a frame-builder or as a sediment-binder but simply as an encrusting form often around fenestrate bryozoans. Thus, one of the organisms which should have been well adapted to a wave environment, building strong organic structures and binding sediments, is relatively insignificant in the so-called "Capitan Reef."

Calcareous sponges are found in the "reef core" and "forereef" areas. They have the ecologic potential to build frameworks and bind sediments to form a "reef." But the sponges are usually small, the largest being up to two or three centimeters in diameter and not more than ten or twenty centimeters long (Figure 16 shows a cross-section of a sponge).

The sponges are not found in colonial frameworks, but are usually

Figure 16. Naturally weathered rock surface showing cross-section of a sponge from Capitan "reef talus" in McKittrick Canyon. Matrix is nonorganically-bound calcarenite (actual size).

separate from each other embedded in a nonorganically-bound matrix of calcarenite. They therefore do not seem to have formed wave-resistant frameworks in the Capitan. Attempts to determine if these sponges are in growth position *(in situ)* seem to be somewhat subjective although Achauer[37] thinks that some are in position of growth.

As noted earlier, sponges are associated with transported algal spheres in deposits which are somewhat typical of the "forereef" or "reef talus" environment. The "reef core" as stated earlier is dominantly calcisiltite or calcarenite with a characteristic lack of what are considered to be wave-resistant, frame-building sponges or algae.

Two general types of bryozoans are very common in the Capitan. First there are small encrusting forms which are usually found as

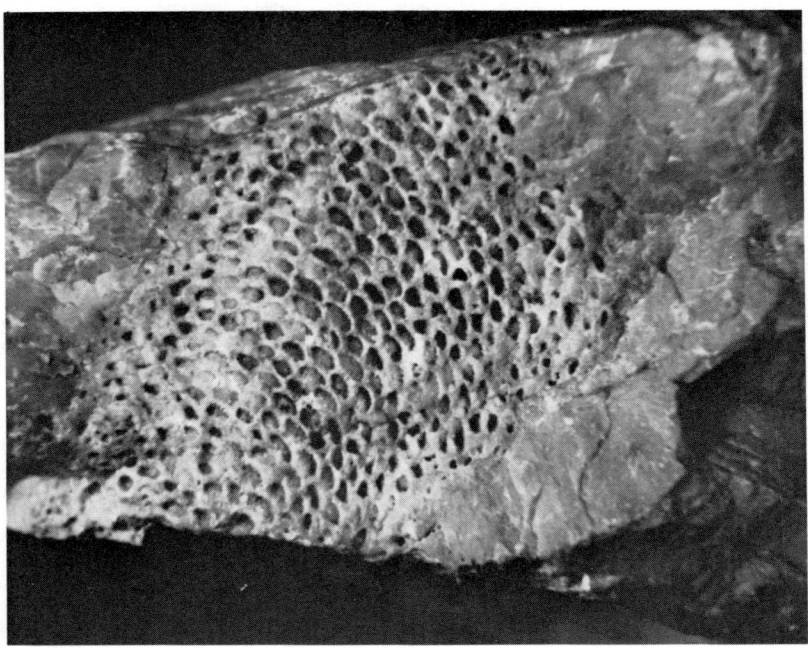

Figure 17. Fenestrate bryozoan from Capitan "reef core." This fragile creature could not have survived in a wave environment. Matrix is calcisiltite (actual size).

fragments. These are found embedded in calcisiltite or calcarenite "reef core" rock (see Figure 9), or in the central part of concentrically laminated algal spheres (see Figure 12), or in supposed "reef talus" beds (see Figure 13). Encrusting bryozoans were evidently shallow marine creatures, but they show little ability to build wave-resistant frameworks and could not bind sediments.

The second variety are the fenestrate bryozoans (see Figure 17). They are large fans having a lacy net-like frame which has great delicacy and beauty. When alive, the fans stood erect attached to the substrate by a flimsy base. Fenestrate bryozoans, which are *common* to the Capitan "reef core," most certainly could not withstand a wave environment and they could not bind sediment. They

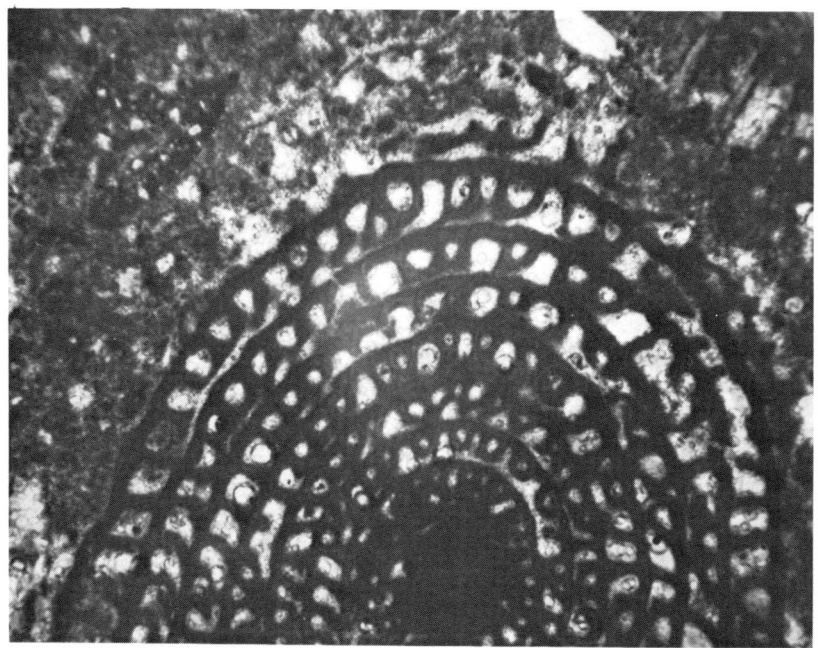

Figure 18. Photomicrograph of fusalinid in silty matrix from Capitan "reef core." The sample is from Carlsbad Caverns National Park elevator shaft #2 at a depth of 499 feet below the surface (35 X actual size).

IS THE CAPITAN LIMESTONE A FOSSIL REEF? 51

are mute testimony of the inadequacy of the "reef" interpretation.

Fusalinids are also common to the Capitan (see Figure 18). They are the size and shape of a grain of wheat and form by coiling around a central axis. These are planktonic animals which show no special adaptation to a "reef" environment. When observed in the "reef core," fusalinids are usually cemented by calcarenite or calcisiltite, and their tests often show preferred orientation, an evidence of current action during deposition.

Brachiopods are very frequently encountered in "backreef," "reef core," and "forereef" deposits. Many of the skeletal fragments making up the limestone are pieces of broken brachiopods. Whole brachiopods are fairly common (see Figure 19) and just a few species com-

Figure 19. Brachiopods (Spurmularia guadalupensis) in Capitan calcerenite from Carlsbad Caverns elevator shaft #2 (½ X actual size).

prise the majority of those observed. These brachiopods were sessile, bottom dwelling creatures which could not bind themselves to the substrate and show no special adaptation to a wave environment.

Other fossil forms found in the Capitan Limestone include crinoids (animals with a floating "head" having numerous radiating arms and long jointed stem which attached to sea floor—not frame-builders and not able to thrive in surf environments), cephalopods (chambered, coiled mollusks which could swim—not a "reef-builder"), pelecypods (thin shelled clams which are not especially adapted to surf zones), and trilobites (arthropods characterized by a body having three parts or lobes—probably not a surf animal). *Corals, creatures which could be considered ideally adapted to a reef environment, are very rare in "Capitan Reef."*

From the above discussion it appears that the fossil flora and fauna of "Capitan Reef" represent a shallow water assemblage which was not especially adapted to a wave or strong current environment. "Reef-forming" organisms which could bind sediments and build frameworks are either altogether absent or largely inconspicuous.

Other Alleged Fossil "Reefs"

Are the stratigraphic, lithologic, and ecologic characteristics of "Capitan Reef," as described above, also found in other alleged Late Paleozoic "reefs"—or is the Capitan somewhat unique?

The lack of frame-builders is noted in "Goat Seep Reef" by P. B. King:

> Like the other limestones along the margin of the Delaware Basin the Goat Seep limestone is quite generally dolomitized, with the result that many of the details of its original structure are now lost. Not many reef-building organisms have been collected from it. No corals have been found, but Dr. Girty reports the presence of sponges. It is not possible, therefore, to determine whether the Goat Seep reef was built by organisms or by inorganic growth.[38]

Oil companies have been intensely interested in Pennsylvanian and Permian rocks in the subsurface in northern Texas. Here the

IS THE CAPITAN LIMESTONE A FOSSIL REEF? 53

so-called "Horseshoe atoll" (also known as "Scurry Reef") has been penetrated numerous times by drill bit. Concerning this limestone deposit P. T. Stafford says:

> Because of certain characteristics of the Horseshoe atoll, applicability of the terms "reef" or "atoll" to this carbonate mass may be questioned. The relationships of the different lithologic types in the Horseshoe atoll are unlike those of any reef described in the literature. Rock composed of a growth lattice of organisms was not observed; only detrital limestone has been noted. In areas that would commonly be considered reef core, calcirudite is found. Furthermore, the slopes on the flanks of the Horseshoe atoll are generally low compared to those of the so-called Capitan reef of western Texas and New Mexico or the Quaternary reefs in the Pacific.[39]

Donald L. Baars comments on some alleged "reefs" of the Pennsylvanian System of New Mexico, and that a demonstrated "reef core" is absent:

> Banks composed of carbonate sediments are present in rocks of Upper Pennsylvanian (Virgil) age in both the Sacramento and San Andreas Mountains of south-central New Mexico. . . . The bioherms are made up of skeletal debris and carbonate muds, with the chief constituent being codiacean algae. . . . Although some geologists have argued for a reefal origin of these buildups, there is no evidence of a rigid framework or wave-resistant characteristics.[40]

Mississippian bioherms in New Mexico were studied by Lloyd C. Pray. He begins his paper with the following statement:

> Abrupt mound and ridge-shaped carbonate masses of Mississippian (Osagian) age that are up to 350 feet thick crop out in southern New Mexico where they were first reported and described in considerable detail by Laudon and Bowsher (1941). These structures and apparently similar ones in the subsurface of north-central Texas have commonly been referred to as "crinoidal bioherms." Although the New Mexico occurrences have been known and examined by many geologists, including the writer, since 1941, their genesis has remained obscure, particularly the nature of the core facies. *The most enigmatic aspect has been the identity of the frame-builders, if indeed frame-builders were ever present.*[41] (Emphasis added.)

Thus, it seems that many highly fossiliferous limestones of the Late Paleozoic are in no sense organic frame-built reefs. Since general characteristics can be associated among fossiliferous limestones of the Late Paleozoic, it would seem logical to seek a common mode of origin.

Capitan Limestone: What Is It?

The above comments on the Capitan Limestone have shown the inadequacy of the "barrier reef" interpretation. So far remarks on what the Capitan *is* have been very brief. In a word the Capitan is here considered to be a *biostrome*—a highly fossiliferous stratified deposit which shows little topographic relief and is surrounded mostly by nonfossiliferous strata.

To the southeast of the Guadalupe Mountains the Capitan intertongues with gypsum, limestone, and sandstone, while to the northwest it intertongues with dolomite, siltstone, sandstone, and limestone. The lower dolomitized unit of the Capitan appears to be very continuous to the northwest where it passes laterally into the dolomitized Goat Seep Limestone and then into the Queen and Grayburg formations. Thus, the Capitan is not a narrow facies from 3 to 5 miles wide but a position of a widespread layer of limestone. The formation names seem to confuse the true geometry of the deposits.

When was the Capitan Limestone deposited relative to the Noachian Flood? Did it accumulate before, during, or after? In our opinion some of the most obvious evidences of the universal Noachian Flood occur in Late Precambrian and Early and Middle Paleozoic strata. Here are found vast blanket-like marine sediments covering entire continents with a lack of subaerial deposits such as widespread lava flows. When volcanics are found in the Late Precambrian and Early and Middle Paleozoic strata, they show many evidences of submarine extrusion.

In a previous paper[42] it was shown that most of the Cenozoic strata (which were deposited after both the Paleozoic and Mesozoic strata) could not have been deposited during the Flood and they were interpreted to be post-Flood. This conclusion was based on

IS THE CAPITAN LIMESTONE A FOSSIL REEF?

the observation that Cenozoic lava flows in the northwestern United States are commonly subaerial.

The Mesozoic strata also seem to be post-Flood as subaerial lava flows are well documented. Thus, in the Meridian Formation (Triassic) of central Connecticut, basalt strata with manifold evidences of subaerial flow are up to 500 feet thick and are continuous laterally over distances up to 30 miles. Sedimentary strata between and above the Meridian flows contain abundant dinosaur footprints.[43]

Also, enormous Triassic or Jurassic lava flows of the Parana Basin of Brazil probably covered at least 375,000 square miles to a depth of up to 2,000 feet.[44] Similar flows to those in Brazil deposited about the same time are found in South Africa.

It is our opinion at the present time that the Late Paleozoic strata are associated with the final stages of the Noachian Flood. Thus, the Capitan Limestone, which is among the youngest of the Late Paleozoic strata, could be either deposited during the last part of the Flood or shortly thereafter. If fossils such as Figure 14 can be well documented as *in situ* occurring on several horizons, then the Capitan would have to belong to our post-Flood era.

Since the Capitan is composed largely of loose, unbound sediments and fossils, much of the material could have been transported by flood waves. Studies on the texture of the Bell Canyon and Cherry Canyon sandstones show that the grain size *increases* toward the southeast (toward the Gulf of Mexico) and this indicates the source direction of the sand.[45]

It is possible that much of the Capitan sediment was washed into its present location by tidal waves from seismic disturbances or meteorite impact immediately after the Noachian Flood. The data certainly do not *require* many thousands of years for the Capitan to accumulate and, therefore, seem to present little problem for Biblical chronology. Instead, the lack of large organically-bound structures, which would grow during thousands of years, suggests that deposition was very rapid.

Acknowledgments

I wish to thank the Creation Research Society Research Fund

chairman for amply funding field investigations during the summer of 1971 in southeastern New Mexico and western Texas. The permission of Carlsbad Caverns and Guadalupe Mountains National Parks to collect hand specimens of limestone was essential to completion of the project. I am grateful for the cooperation of Carlsbad Caverns National Park and Humble Oil Company for graciously allowing me to examine well cores and rock thin sections of Capitan Limestone.

Appendix: Terminology

General terms:

Reef: a largely unbedded, wave-resistant structure composed of *in situ*, organically-bound, frame-building organisms, cementing organisms, and sediment filling which modifies the surrounding sedimentation.

Reef Complex: the suite of environments and resulting sediments associated with a reef.[46]

Terms relating to stratigraphy:

Stratigraphy: a discipline of geology which deals with the position and geometry of stratified rocks.

Reef Core: the wave-resistant, *in situ*, organically-bound portion of a reef complex.

Forereef: the sediments on the seaward side of the reef core which are composed largely of transported debris (also known as "reef talus").

Backreef: the sediments on the shoreward side of the reef core often deposited in a lagoon.

Biostrome: a nonorganically-bound fossiliferous limestone which has no appreciable topographic relief but tends to be a widespread layer.

Bioherm: a nonorganically-bound fossiliferous limestone which rose topographically above the surrounding depositional surface.

Formation: a mappable rock unit.

Member: a subdivision of a formation.

Facies: refers to lateral variance in rock type within a stratigraphic interval.

Cenozoic Strata: the most recently deposited strata noted for fossil mammals.

Mesozoic Strata: strata deposited immediately before Cenozoic strata and are known for dinosaur fossils.

Paleozoic Strata: strata deposited immediately before Mesozoic strata and have abundant marine organisms.

Precambrian Strata: the oldest strata which have few fossils.

Tectonics: deformational processes in the earth's crust.

Terms relating to lithology:

Lithology: a discipline of geology which deals with the megascopic and microscopic composition and structure of rocks.

Limestone: a sedimentary rock composed chiefly of calcium carbonate—$CaCO_3$.
Dolomite: a sedimentary rock composed chiefly of calcium-magnesium carbonate—$CaMg(CO_3)_2$.
Calcite: a mineral composed of calcium carbonate.
Calcilutite: limestone composed chiefly of clay-size particles.
Calcisiltite: limestone composed of chiefly silt-size particles.
Calcarenite: limestone composed of chiefly sand-size particles.
Calcirudite: limestone composed chiefly of particles larger than sand-size.
Dolomitized: refers to limestone which has been partially changed to dolomite through the addition of magnesium ions.
Recrystallized: refers to limestone in which the original crystal structure of calcite has been modified.
Calcareous: containing calcium carbonate.
Anhydrite: mineral composed of calcium sulfate—$CaSO_4$.
Gypsum: mineral composed of calcium sulfate and water—$CaSO_4 \cdot 2H_2O$.
Evaporite: rock composed of anhydrite, gypsum, or salt.
Pisolith: a sphere of concentrically laminated limestone or dolomite generally larger than 2 mm.
Ooliths: a sphere of limestone or dolomite usually smaller than 2 mm.

Terms relating to paleoecology:

Paleoecology: the study of the relationship between ancient organisms and their environment.
Stromatolitic algae: algae which build structures which have more or less planar lamination.
Dasycladaceae (Dasyclad): family of fragile green algae which construct calcareous tubes.
Solenoporaceae: extinct family of calcareous red algae having the ability to construct organically-bound frameworks.
Corallinaceae: modern family of calcareous red algae which build modern reefs.
Scleractinida: order of modern corals which build modern reefs.
Bryozoan: member of phylum of colonial animals which build calcareous structures.
Fusalinid: extinct animal about the size and shape of a grain of wheat.
Brachiopod: member of phylum of marine shelled animals with two unequal shells or valves.
Crinoids: marine animals with a floating "head" having numerous radiating arms and long jointed stem which attaches to the sea floor.

REFERENCES

1. John C. Whitcomb, Jr., and Henry M. Morris, 1961. The Genesis flood. The Presbyterian and Reformed Publishing Co., Philadelphia. pp. 408-409.
2. Harold W. Clark, 1968. Fossils, flood and fire. Outdoor Pictures, Escondido, Calif., pp. 82, 106.
3. J. R. van de Fliert, 1969. Fundamentalism and the fundamentals of geology. *Journal of the American Scientific Affiliation* 21, 3:79-80.

4. W. C. Krumbein and L. L. Sloss, 1963. Stratigraphy and sedimentation (second edition). W. H. Freeman & Co., San Francisco. p. 573.

5. J. Keith Rigby, 1969. Reefs and reef environments, *American Association of Petroleum Geologists Bulletin*, 53:738.

6. Krumbein and Sloss, *op. cit.*, p. 575.

7. W. H. Easton, 1960. Invertebrate paleontology. Harper & Row, Inc., New York, pp. 202-203.

8. Rigby, *loc. cit.*

9. William G. Hart, 1969. Microfacies analysis of the Permian reef complex (Guadalupian), Carlsbad Caverns, New Mexico. Unpublished Master's thesis, Texas Technological College, San Antonio, Texas.

10. K. H. Crandall, 1929. Permian stratigraphy of southeastern New Mexico and adjacent parts of western Texas, *American Association of Petroleum Geologists Bulletin*, 13:927-944.

11. Harold S. Cave, 1954. The Capitan—Castile—Delaware Mountain problem. Guidebook of southeastern New Mexico (Fifth Field Conference), New Mexico Geological Society. pp. 117-124.

12. Donald L. Baars, 1964. Modern carbonate sediments as a guide to old limestones, *World Oil*, 158:95-100.

13. C. W. Achauer, 1969. Origin of Capitan Formation, Gaudalupe Mountains, New Mexico and Texas, *American Association of Petroleum Geologists Bulletin*, 53:2314-2323.

14. The "Permian System" in southeastern New Mexico and western Texas is an objective, well defined stratigraphic interval and should not be confused with the "Permian Period" which is thought by many geologists to have been a vast interval of time (45 million years) which elapsed over 200 million years ago.

15. Carl O. Dunbar and Karl M. Waage, 1969. Historical geology. John Wiley & Sons, Inc., New York, p. 295.

16. P. T. Hayes and R. L. Koogle, 1958. Geology of the Carlsbad Caverns West Quadrangle, New Mexico—Texas. Map published by U.S. Geological Survey.

17. P. B. King, 1948. Geology of the southern Gaudalupe Mountains, Texas. U. S. Geological Survey Prof. Paper 215. 183 pp.

18. Hayes and Koogle, *loc. cit.*

19. Achauer, *op. cit.*, pp. 2314-2315.

20. C. W. Achauer, 1971. Discussion: origin of Capitan Formation, Gaudalupe Mountains, New Mexico and Texas, *American Association of Petroleum Geologists Bulletin*, 55:313-315.

21. W. W. Tyrell, 1964. Petrology and stratigraphy of near-reef Tansill-Lamar strata, Guadalupe Mountains, Texas and New Mexico. Roswell Geological Society Guidebook. pp. 66-75.

22. Achauer, 1971, *op. cit.*, p. 215.

23. Cave, *op. cit.*, p. 122.

24. C. L. Jones, 1954. The occurrence and distribution of potassium minerals in southeastern New Mexico. Guidebook of southeastern New Mexico. New Mexico Geological Society. pp. 107-112.

25. Cave, *op. cit.,* p. 121.
26. *Ibid.,* p. 119.
27. Achauer, 1969, *op. cit.,* p. 2321.
28. Baars, *op. cit.,* p. 99.
29. Achauer, 1969, *op. cit.*
30. *Ibid.*
31. R. J. Dunham, 1970. Stratigraphic reefs versus ecologic reefs, *American Association of Petroleum Geologists Bulletin,* 54:1931-1932.
32. King, *op. cit.,* p. 86.
33. Achauer, 1969, *op. cit.*
34. Achauer, 1971, *op. cit.,* pp. 313-314.
35. Achauer, 1969, *op. cit.,* p. 2320.
36. John M. Cys, 1971. Origin of Capitan Formation, Gaudalupe Mountains, New Mexico and Texas: discussion, *American Association of Petroleum Geologists Bulletin,* 55:312.
37. Achauer, 1969, *op. cit.,* p. 2321.
38. King, *op. cit.,* p. 52.
39. P. T. Stafford, 1959. Geology of part of the Horseshoe atoll in Scurry and Kent counties, Texas. U. S. Geological Survey Prof. Paper 315-A, p. 12.
40. Baars, *op. cit.,* p. 100.
41. Lloyd C. Pray, 1958. Fenestrate bryozoan core facies, Mississippian bioherms southwestern United States, *Journal of Sedimentary Petrology,* 28:261.
42. Stuart E. Nevius, 1971. The Mesa basalt of the northwestern United States, *Creation Research Society Quarterly,* 7 (4):222-226.
43. P. D. Krynie, 1950. Petrology, stratigraphy and origin of the Triassic sedimentary rocks of Connecticut, *Connecticut Geological and Natural History Survey Bulletin 73.* 247 pp.
44. C. L. Baker, 1923. The lava field of the Parana Basin, South America, *Journal of Geology,* 31:66-79.
45. Advocates of the "barrier reef" view need to have the sand coming from the northwest and must be able to explain how it escaped being trapped in the "backreef." Where in any modern environment are limestones and sand from the shore and evaporites being deposited behind a barrier reef while sand from the shore is being deposited in widespread strata in deep water beyond the reef?
46. The term "reef complex" may also have meaning to the psychologist when describing a geologist's tendency to indiscriminately call *any* highly fossiliferous and unbedded limestone deposit a "reef." A geologist encumbered with such a bias may be said to possess a "reef complex."

III

RESEARCH ON THE CLASSIC JOGGINS PETRIFIED TREES

HAROLD G. COFFIN*

Introduction

Along the upper end of the Bay of Fundy, and on the outer east coast of Nova Scotia, a classic phenomenon of great interest is seen. Upright petrified stumps embedded in the cliffs have been exposed by marine erosion. It is a singular experience to walk along the beaches and see trees up to five meters tall and one meter in diameter standing out from the cliffs in what appear to be their original positions of growth (Figure 1).

Coal is mined along the Bay of Fundy and in other Upper Carboniferous deposits of Nova Scotia. Petrified trees arise from the upper surfaces of some of the coal seams or are distributed in the strata between seams.

Charles Lyell visited[1] the cliffs near Joggins in 1842. A young Canadian scientist, William Dawson, accompanied him during a later visit, and went on to make a comprehensive study[2] of the Carboniferous of Nova Scotia. They followed the stratigraphy worked out by William E. Logan,[3] the first director of the Geological Survey of Canada. Richard Brown[4] recorded some of the unique features of the coal measures of the Sydney, Nova Scotia, area and helped settle the controversy concerning the relationship between some of the common fossils associated with coal, namely the *Stigmaria* roots and *Lepidodendron* trees.

---

*Harold G. Coffin, Ph.D., is Research Professor at the Geo-Science Research Institute affiliated with Andrews University, Berrien Springs, Michigan 49104.

Figure 1. A beautiful petrified tree (Sigillaria) **originating in shale and extending up into sandstone. Joggins, Nova Scotia.**

Trees most commonly involved are the lycopod genera *Sigillaria, Lepidodendron,* and the coniferous *Cordaites;* the first two are often upright whereas the latter one is not (Figure 2). The roots of the upright lycopods have been shown to change in morphology to become unquestioned and typical *Stigmaria* roots.[5] I also found one example near Sydney Mines that clearly demonstrated this relationship between the stigmariae and the lycopod trees.

The trunks of the two giant club-moss genera apparently were hollow or had soft pulp centers because all the vertical stumps were filled with sediments and only the outer wood or bark remained as a thin film of coal (Figure 3). Horizontal trees of this type were almost always flattened.

Cordaites, a coniferous tree somewhat resembling the Paraná Pine of the Southern Hemisphere, was not hollow. It had long spatulate

Figure 2. Two Cordaites petrified logs in prostrate position. None were found upright. Joggins.

or lanceolate leaves with parallel striations on the surface which caused early taxonomists to misplace it among the Monocotyledons.

Two Possible Viewpoints

In the early days of geological investigation and observation, keen students of the earth such as Nicolaus Steno and John Woodward largely accepted the Genesis Flood as a reality and interpreted the structure of the earth's surface and the organic evidences found within as the result of this event. When coal was definitely established to be plant debris, the mode of its emplacement in the sediments was generally assumed to be the result of drift on the waters of the Noachian Deluge.

A new view was voiced in the writings of Hutton and Playfair, and crystallized under Lyell. Under these and other opponents of

Figure 3. Erect lycopod stumps were hollow and filled with sediments when buried. Joggins. Note that the sandstone bed passing along the top is not found inside the tree.

catastrophism, the autochthonous* concept of coal formation became dominant and has remained dominant except for some weakening of the view under the impact of Henry Fayol's clear and forceful presentations for drifting which he produced near the end of the nineteenth century.[6]

Among the factors which served as strong arguments for *in situ* accumulations of plant remains were the reports and studies[7] of erect trees and spreading roots and rootlets (*Stigmaria* and appendages)

---

*The term "autochthonous" refers to coal formation from indigenous plant remains which grew in the place where coal is found (i.e., *in situ*). The term "allochthonous," refers to coal formation from plant remains which have been transported by some force from place of original growth to present location.

Figure 4. Stigmaria with radiating appendages. This Stigmaria was traceable a few feet to the right where it joined an erect tree. Point Aconi, Cape Breton Island, Nova Scotia.

apparently found in place in the ancient soils. Despite serious anomalies connected with the uniformitarian interpretation of the vertical trees the spreading roots and rootlets, and the surrounding sediments, the trees and stigmariae, probably more than any other factors, cemented the thinking for autochthonous coal formation (Figure 4). This view of coal origin necessitates abundance of time for geological processes to function at uniform rates. Thus this belief was a major contributor to the establishment of the geologic time scale. Few other formations appeared to have as many and as convincing evidences of *in situ* conditions as did the Carboniferous.

Dawson considered each level of trees to represent a ground surface or soil level. Taking also the *Stigmaria* root zones and the coal seams to be soil levels, he recorded 85 such horizons and felt

Figure 5. This petrified stump is filled with coarse sandstone but surrounded by shale except at the top. Hammer at base gives scale. Point Aconi, Cape Breton Island.

this to be the minimum number of soil levels revealed along several miles of sea cliffs in the Joggins region.[8]

The growth of forests and the establishment of soils for at least 85 levels, required the rhythmic rise and fall of the land for the burial of each level. Incomplete cyclothems are continuous through more than 14,000 vertical feet in the Joggins area.[9] The difficult requirement for the land surface in the same locality to be suitable for the exacting conditions of bog formation following many of the emergencies from the sea was considered justified by the evidence.

Ten Evidences for Allochthonous Origin

Although the autochthonous origin of the coal, trees, and *Stigmaria* roots at Joggins has been assumed since Dawson's research, substantiation of this view appears difficult. Evidences in favor of an allochthonous origin and rapid sedimentation are enumerated below:

1. The coniferous *Cordaites,* although mingled with erect lycopod trees, has not been found erect (Figure 2). If the trees are in growth position the solid, more durable trees, rather than the hollow fragile ones, would be expected to remain standing in the midst of invading seas and depositing conditions.[10]

2. Just under 70% of the hollow vertical tree trunks contain sediment unlike or having different bedding than the surrounding matrix. Often the type of sediment lying just above the broken-off stump top also fills its hollow cavity. A few examples had internal sediments unrelatable to any overlying or surrounding strata (Figure 5). It could be postulated that the original matrix was completely removed and replaced by another, or the stumps were moved to a new location after infilling, but neither of these possibilities is compatable with the *in situ* theory.

3. A distinctive soil level is usually missing (Figures 1, 3, 5, 6, 20). Only a small number of the vertical trees arise from coal. The majority originate in shale or sandstone which exhibit no change in texture or organic context. Several trees in the same stratum may arise from different levels—none of which qualify as ancient soil zones.

Petrified stumps arising from a coal surface almost never send roots into the coal, but spread their roots onto or just above the coal. A modern peat bog exposed in cross-section near Sydney Mines by eroding seas has had at least two living forests growing on its surface in post-Pleistocene times. These forests were killed and the stumps buried by accumulating peat. The tops of the stumps of the most recent forest protrude above the present peat bog surface.

Such a situation seems not to have been attained in the coal seams and petrified trees. Stumps of trees that grew in or on peat, now coalified, should be easy to recognize if the trunks extended into the sediments above the coal.

4. The presence of overlapping erect trees seems to preclude the

amount of time needed for their normal growth in their present positions (Figure 6). The major portion of the lower trunk would have protruded above ground during the entire life of the upper tree if both are in growth position. The hollow interiors of both were filled when sandy mud buried them. The trees are three meters apart and the nearly horizontal bedding, easily traceable between them, negates the suggestion that they were simultaneously on an even surface.

5. A variety of organic remains are found in the sediments within the stumps, including forms unexpected for trees *in situ*. Leaves, needles, fruits, twigs, and branches would fall into hollow upright stumps; but the presence of sections of *Stigmaria* roots and *Calamites* stems is less understandable without recourse to an allochthonous theory of origin (Figure 7). Three examples of *Stigmaria* and one of *Calamites* inside hollow stumps were found by the author in the North Sydney area, and Brown[11] makes reference to one.

Bones of several species of amphibians or reptiles have been found

Figure 6. Overlapping erect trees only a few feet apart, Glace Bay, Cape Breton Island.

Figure 7. Stigmaria with radiating appendages positioned in the sediments inside an erect tree. Sydney mines. Cape Breton Island.

68   SPEAK TO THE EARTH

inside the vertical stumps.[12] The carcass or bones of an amphibian or reptile within a hollow stump before erosional removal of the stump, would travel with the stump and be buried in sediments when the stump was buried. Swimming animals might seek out floating rafts of trees and plant debris during a flood. Animal tracks, also seen in the Joggins sediments, fail to provide useful insights because they could be produced under a variety of situations and conditions[13] (Figure 8).

6. Remarkably beautiful preservations of delicate organic structures are found. Foliage which accumulates on a modern ground surface seldom remains intact for more than one or two seasons. Just below the surface, vegetable matter has lost much of its original form and identity by decay. Especially problematic would be such fragile structures well preserved below the roots of vertical trees in

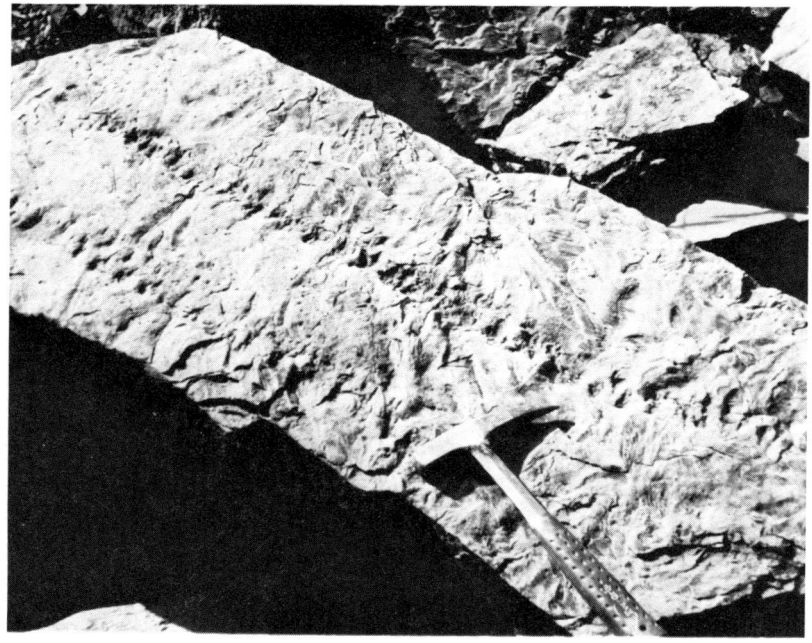

Figure 8. Tracks on sandstone. Joggins.

growth positions. The trees mentioned under item 4 above, exhibited this feature well.

7. Diagonal petrified trees, tipped forty-five or more degrees, are occasionally seen in the cliffs (Figure 9). The roots are at right angles to the stumps and not parallel to the bedding. Such trees speak of rapid burial or transport *in toto* along with the sediments.[14]

8. A marine tubeworm *Spirorbis* (Figure 10) is frequently attached in abundance to vegetable matter in the coal and to the prostrate and erect trees, both inside and outside the hollow stems. The postulated limnic habitat for Carboniferous *Spirorbis* is highly questionable and goes against almost every facet of evidence available.[15] The presence of this annelid almost forces the conclusion that the trees were exposed to deep marine intrusions or floated in saline water.

Figure 9. Diagonal tree in sandstone near Alder Point, Cape Breton Island.

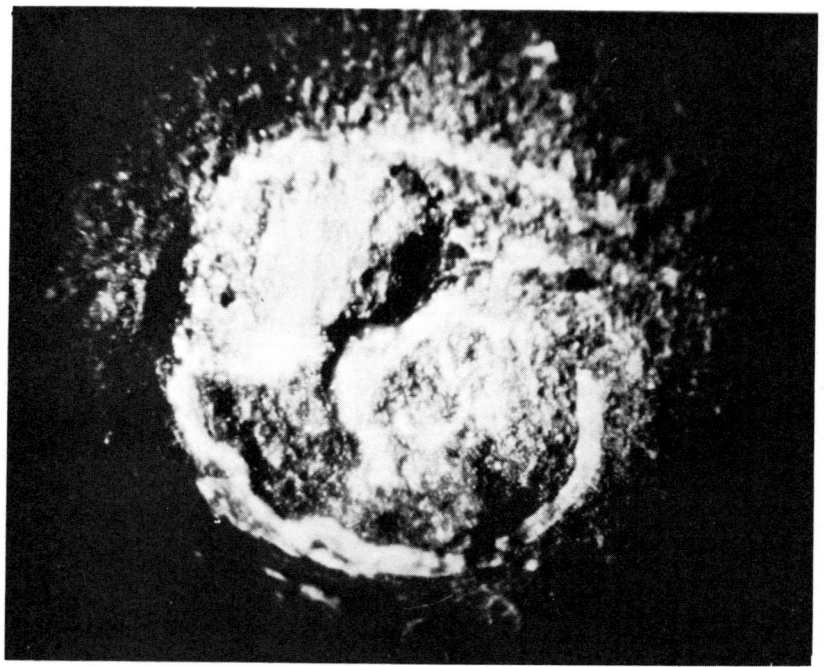

Figure 10. Cross section through the small tubeworm, Spirorbis, in organic sediments at Joggins.

9. Sediments often bank up against the vertical stumps and have a saucer-like bedding within the hollow interiors (Figure 11). This settling of sediments along with well-preserved fossils suggests rapidity of depositing processes.

10. The vertical lycopod stumps often penetrate two or more strata, one of which rarely may be a coal seam. Polystrate trees, 11.5 meters or more tall,[16] would necessitate rapid fallout of sediments at least that deep in that location to prevent decay of the upper parts of the stumps.

Most of the sandstones are cross-bedded, contain ball and pillow structures, show local unconformities, cut and fill phenomena, or are ripple marked; all features of rapid water flow or movement current.

Shales, on the other hand, do not show clearly current and flow evidences. The fine nature of the sediments of which shale is composed probably would not settle out except in water that was relatively quiet or deep enough to allow materials to sink below surface agitation.

In addition to these two sediment types and the gradations between them, there are occasional strata of conglomerate especially in the lower part of the Carboniferous. These are composed of pebbles and flat cakes of shale that appear to have been ripped up from a partly dried but unindurated shale bed on which the conglomerates were laid.

The cyclothems of Nova Scotia are mostly incomplete. Throughout much of the over 14,000 feet of Carboniferous strata, sandstone and shale alternate and the thickness of the individual beds varies greatly (Figure 13). Although plant remains are scattered through most of this depth, coal as such is missing from much of the sequence.

I know of no count of the total number of cyclothems in this

Figure 11. Longitudinal section through standing tree in shale. Shale on left inside tree; shale on right banked up against outside of tree. Sydney Mines.

Figure 12. Minor unconformities in bedding near Joggins.

Carboniferous deposit but the number must be in the hundreds. Hundreds of emergences and submergences of the land is an unreasonable explanation. An explanation of the unsolved problem of the formation of cyclothems bears directly, of course, on the issue of the autochthonous versus allochthonous deposition of plants and coal.

Upright Fossil Trees Interpreted

If the *in situ* position of these stumps is questioned, their upright orientation in the strata calls for some explanation. Trees and logs floating in an upright position are not rare under certain conditions. Saturated timbers that have gotten away from log booms and have drifted for some time in the waters of Puget Sound in the Northwest, often float upright with their tops barely visible at the surface of the water. Loggers from British Columbia and Alaska say trees

RESEARCH ON THE CLASSIC JOGGINS PETRIFIED TREES 73

or stumps ripped out of the ground by ocean storms or logging operations frequently float upright. I have noticed and photographed recent stumps sitting upright along the beach or among piles of driftwood along the Bay of Fundy where they were left by high tides or storms.

Francis[17] reports, ". . . it is natural for short stems attached to heavy roots or trees to float upright, with the roots downwards, when transported by deep water, particularly if the roots enclose a ball of clay or gravel."

Ager[18] makes the following comment:

> E. D. McKee (personal communication, 1963), has told of palm trees being swept from a Pacific atoll during hurricanes and coming to rest in considerable depths of water in an upright position because of their heavy, stone-laden roots, so that even trees in position of life may not be completely beyond question.

While sailing along the coast of New Guinea the Challenger Ex-

Figure 13. Cliffs near Joggins showing rhythmic sedimentation.

pedition ran into long lines of driftwood brought down perhaps by flooding rivers. The following appears in the report:

> Much of the wood was floating suspended vertically in the water, and most curiously, logs and short branch pieces thus floating often occurred in separate groups apart from the horizontally floating timbers. The sunken ends of the wood were not weighted by any attached masses of soil or other load of any kind; possibly the water penetrated certain kinds of wood more easily in one direction with regard to its growth than the other, hence one end becomes water-logged before the other.[19]

Travelers from the Amazon region of South America report frequent observance of trees floating upright down the river, especially following high water and floods.

Upright trees have been uncritically taken as *a priori* evidence of unchanged growth position but much caution is advised against such automatic assumptions. Stevenson,[20] in his monograph on the

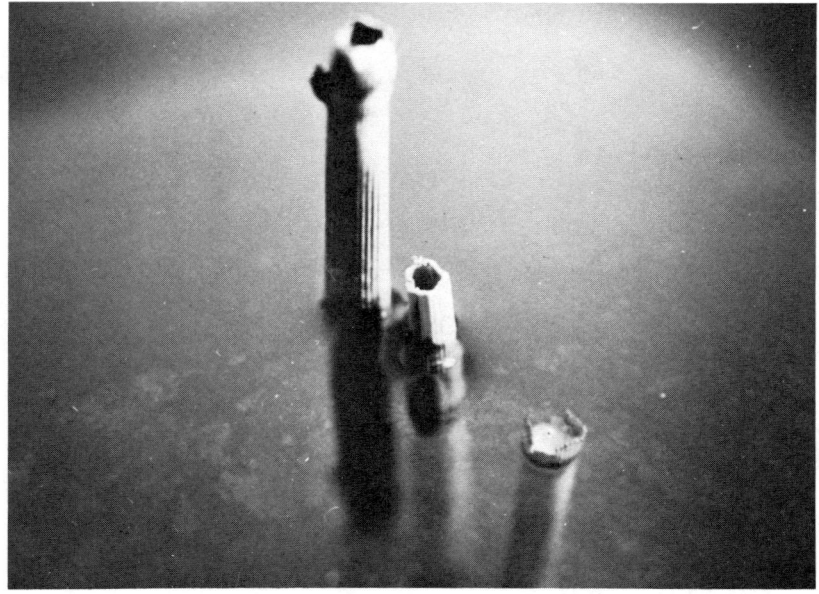

Figure 14. Cluster of Equisetum **floating upright.**

Figure 15. Individual stems of Equisetum suspended from the surface or standing upright on the bottom. To facilitate obtaining a sharp focus, the stems were moved to near the front of the tank, but they are not leaning against the glass or each other.

formation of coal beds, decides that upright trees are not important in settling the problem of autochthonous or allochthonous origins of coal.

Results of Flotation Experiments

Flotation experiments have been undertaken by the author with *Equisetum* in an attempt to clarify the vertical position of *Calamites* stems. Some findings: (a) Clusters of horsetail stems attached to the same roots float upright because of the heavy rootstock and associated soil (Figure 14). (b) Individual stems floated horizontally for some days until they became saturated and swung into an upright position suspended from the surface of the water. (c) As saturation increased, they sank and rested on the bottom of the tank in a vertical position (Figure 15). (d) Eventually a few days later they fell over to lie prone. Contemporaneous sedimentation would have incorporated many of them upright in the sediments.

The *Calamites* stems in Nova Scotia strata are generally single. They are probably not in growth position but have been buried by

76 SPEAK TO THE EARTH

the clastic deposits in a way similar to that suggested by the flotation experiments.

Henry Fayol[21] undertook flotation experiments for several years in an artificial pond. This comprehensive research gave percentages for the vertical and horizontal floating of living trees similar to those for prone and erect petrified trees in the coal measures of Central France. His results with *Equisetum* were the same as those of this investigator.

Seven Points of Interpretation

The problem of the *Stigmaria* and associated appendages has long puzzled paleobotanists. There are aspects dissimilar to anything seen today that make it impossible for researchers to be unanimous in their conclusions on the stigmariae. However, few question the *in situ* position of the structures even though the true nature' of

Figure 16. Appendages extending up and down from a Stigmaria. This Stigmaria has been flattened as is true for many. Sydney Mines.

their function is not known. Rootlet-bearing stigmariae have been traced several feet toward *Lepidodendron* or *Sigillarian* trees where they become the flaring roots of the trees. Thus the stigmariae and their rootlets assume a position like roots to a tree.

Present thinking on *Stigmaria* is aptly summarized by Arnold,[22]

> The true morphology of stigmariae and its relation to the stem, remains, even after more than a century of research, one of the great unsolved problems of paleobotany. . . . Modern research has thrown little additional light on the *Stigmaria* problem and the remains are generally ignored by presentday paleobotanists.

The following points concern interpretation of the stigmariae as true roots *in situ*. If the stigmariae are not assumed to be in growth position, the dead end of the present state of knowledge is bypassed by a new approach that holds promise of a solution to the problem.

1. Appendages extend from *Stigmaria* in parallel orientation (Fig-

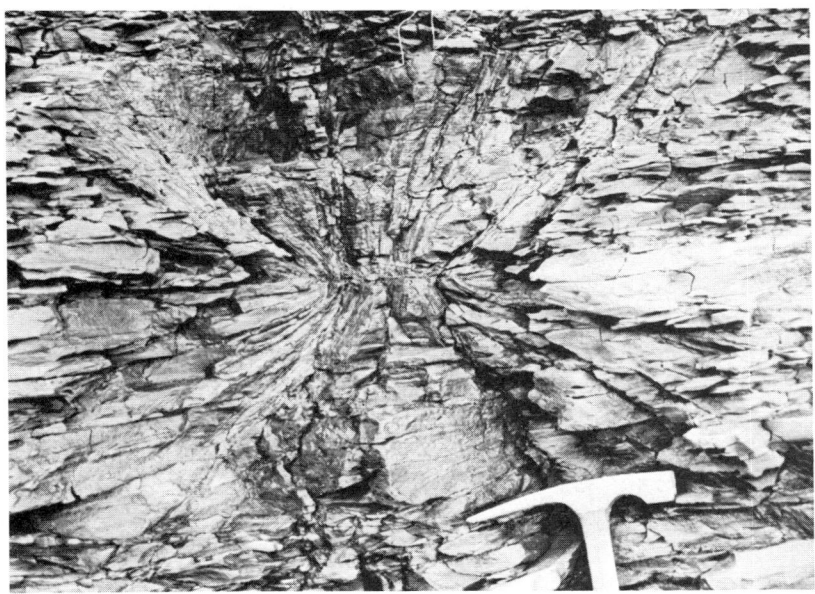

Figure 17. Cross section through Stigmaria **showing radiating appendages. Sydney Mines.**

ure 16). These "rootlets" follow each other around bends and corners in a manner untypical of normal rootlets which pursue an independent course through the soil. Occasionally all of the appendages may be confined to the same horizontal plane on which the *Stigmaria* rests.

2. Appendages usually radiate from the *Stigmaria* in all directions into the rock; consequently, many of them have an upward orientation which would be termed negative geotropism if they are in position of growth (Figure 17). Yet a nearly universal characteristic of normal rootlets is positive geotropism.

Furthermore, if these are true roots that grew where now located, some of the appendages were positively geotropic, some were negatively geotropic, and some were not sensitive to gravity; but no noticeable difference in morphology is apparent. "Rootlets" which

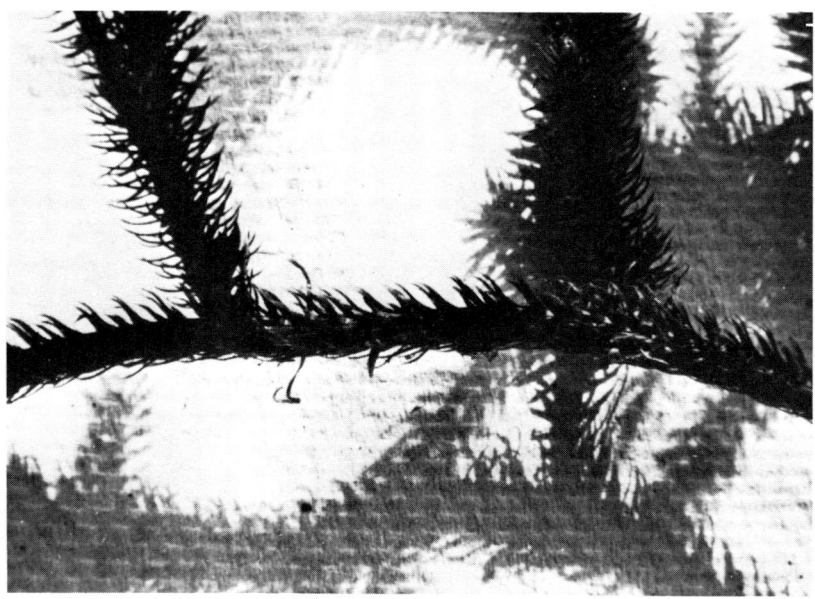

Figure 18. Creeping stem and upright shoots of Lycopodium. Note that the scale-like leaves are spirally arranged around the stem and the lower ones do not extend as broadly from the stem as do the upper ones.

extend upward are usually longer and less bent than those penetrating downward. This feature has significance when comparison is made with the living *Lycopodium* (see item 4 below).

3. Stigmariae do not have the dendritic branching and resulting taper in diameter of roots. Long sections often have the same diameters at the two ends as illustrated by one somewhat flattened, 20 meter length found by this investigator near Sydney Mines with diameter measurements of 6.5 cm by 10 cm at both ends.

4. Stigmariae have remarkable resemblances to the creeping stems or rhizones of the modern clubmoss *Lycopodium*. In both, appendages which are poorly equipped with vascular tissues are attached in spiral arrangement. Both have little or no taper and

Figure 19. A section of Stigmaria with radiating appendages. These appendages are poorly developed compared to others but note that those extending upward are clearly visible; whereas, those extending downward are rare or absent. Spirally arranged pits or points of attachment of the appendages are visible. Sydney Mines.

have large fibrous vascular cylinders. The lower scale-like leaves around the creeping stems of *Lycopodium* are shorter and assume a more accute angle of attachment; whereas, the upper ones are longer and extend nearly perpendicularly from the stems.

As mentioned above, this feature is also true for stigmariae and "rootlets" (Figures 18 and 19). Thus it is probable that the "rootlets" of *Stigmaria* are not "rootlets" at all but slender leaf-like appendages. Several paleobotanists have been impressed with the possibility that stigmariae are giant rhizomes or creeping stems.[23]

An evidence for *in situ* burial that requires more detailed consideration is the report of plant parts such as roots growing into or penetrating the tissues of trees, before carbonization. Among the examples cited in the literature are: (a) *Stigmaria* "rootlets" penetrating from one level down into the trees of a lower level,[24] (b) *Stigmaria* protruding through the wall of a stump,[25] and (c) *Stigmaria* "rootlets" growing into the tissue of *Stigmaria*.[26]

My study of the stigmariae indicates that "rootlets" and plant fragments are often found in the sand or shale inside the stigmariae even though these structures are seldom more than 10 cm. in diameter. These phenomena may be interpreted as intrusions by growth from outside, but the scattered and fragmentary nature of the plant structures and the presence of bedding, obviously water laid, inside the stigmariae leave this interpretation open to question.

In no case was I able to find any actual penetration of the carbonaceous wall of the *Stigmaria* by "rootlets" or other plant structures that might have grown into it. The possibility of stigmariae and "rootlets" being rhizomes or creeping stems casts some shadow on the ability of *Stigmaria* "rootlets" to grow into other *Stigmaria* in a manner one would expect of true rootlets.

Even if growth penetration is a correct observation, it is not overly relevant because whether the coal and plant specimens are autochthonous or allochthonous, penetration by growing plant parts could be a reality. In the latter case, the growth into partly decayed or soft tissues by a rootlet or underground stem would have taken place before the forest was rafted to the position of burial.

5. Quantitative measurements of orientation of sixty-nine stig-

mariae in locations near Sydney Mines and Joggins indicate a strong parallel orientation. Measurements were taken in shale and sandstone directly above and below coal seams. These stems, often visible for several feet, have the typical radiating appendages assumed to indicate *in situ* plants.

Orientation measurements of stigmariae in coal have been taken and with similar results.[27] Thus stigmariae below, in, and above coal seams have similar patterns of positioning. Yet the parallel orientation, which agrees with current direction as determined by cross-bedding and ripple marks, strongly speaks against their being in position of growth. Parallel orientation for roots of living trees growing unrestricted in sand or soil would certainly be unexpected.

6. Stigmariae are found in limestone, crude coal composed mostly of mussel shells, and other odd sediments which would not be considered suitable soils for the growth of roots.

7. Isolated sections of *Stigmaria* unattached to upright lycopods and with radiating appendages are found. Most notable of these are the ones found inside erect stumps (Figure 7). It would appear that the appendages were stiff and their radiating position little affected when the sections were dropped or moved about in soft sediments.

Excellent Natural Object Lesson

One short section of cliff near Sydney Mines constitutes a good case history which includes several of the points brought out above. A large, upright petrified tree (probably *Sigillaria*) originated in the same bed where compass measurements established the parallel orientation of stigmariae with each other and with the dominant current (Figure 20). Thus, if the stigmariae were not in growth position, it is doubtful that the tree would be.

The erect tree passed through a bed of shale 1.5 meters thick which contained abundant quantities of exquisitely preserved fern leaves—good evidence of rapid sedimentation. The upper one meter of the tree was filled with sediments approaching that of crude coal. No one-meter bed of coal existed outside the tree, but there was, however, directly above the broken top a 7-cm. seam of this dark gray deposit.

82   SPEAK TO THE EARTH

Apparently the last meter of the hollow tree was filled with this material when it was washed out over the surface. In this case it is obvious that the thin organic layer lying directly over the tree cannot be a growth level but was a water-laid deposit.

The Nova Scotia Carboniferous sediments are rather typical of the Paleozoic coal measures of North America and Europe. Thus the objections to *in situ* theory for the coal deposits of Nova Scotia apply in some degree to the Carboniferous in general. However, before broad generalizations beyond Nova Scotia are made, research must be undertaken in other areas.

Tentative Model of Deposition

A completely satisfactory hypothesis of the depositing conditions involved in the laying down of the vegetable and organic debris that has become coal and the positioning of the erect trees and

Figure 20. A lycopod tree with unusual features best ascribed to an allochthonous burial (see text): Point Aconi.

the parallel *Stigmaria* sections cannot be presented without much more research, but a brief and tentative model is as follows:

Plants were torn up by erosion and transgressing seas. As the stumps floated in the water they became saturated and slowly swung into an upright position. Clusters of horsetails washed out into the sea and floated vertically until they became saturated and sank. Individual stems tipped upright after a period of soaking. While plant flotsam was drifting, tubeworms and mussels fastened themselves to the floating mass, and fishes swam among the debris.

Eventually the stumps and *Calamites* sank down into the muds at the bottom or were stranded on a mud flat when the tide retreated. Continuing fallout of sediments from the water above or tidal movements and wave action caused sediments to accumulate around and in the stumps. This occurred repeatedly in a sinking basin, thus producing many superimposed strata containing erect stumps and other plant remains.

Following deposition, the whole area was warped, causing a tilting of up to twenty degrees in some parts of the basin. Later still, glaciers scoured the tilted surface and left erratic boulders, glacial till, eskers, and other evidences. With the rising of the ocean when continental glaciers melted, the Bay of Fundy and the Atlantic Ocean cut back the cliffs and exposed the interesting fossils and coal seams of Nova Scotia.

REFERENCES

1. Charles Lyell, 1843. On the upright fossil trees found at different levels in the coal strata of Cumberland, Nova Scotia, *Proceedings of the Geological Society of London,* 4:176-178.

2. J. W. Dawson, 1854. On the coal-measures of the South Joggins, Nova Scotia, *Quarterly Journal of the Geological Society of London,* 10:1-41; 1859. On the lower coal-measures as developed in British America, *Quarterly Journal of the Geological Society of London,* 15:62-76; 1866. On the conditions of the deposition of coal more especially as illustrated by the coal-formation of Nova Scotia and New Brunswick. *Quarterly Journal of the Geological Society of London,* 22:95-169; 1891. Acadian geology. Fourth Edition. Macmillan and Co., London, 833 p.; 1894. Note on the genus *Naiadites,* as occurring in the coal formations of Nova Scotia, *Quarterly Journal of the Geological Society of London,* 50:435-442.

3. W. E. Logan, 1845. Section of the Nova Scotia coal measures as developed at the Joggins . . ., *Canadian Geological Survey Progress Report,*

1843:92-159 and 1908. *Nova Scotia Institute of Science Proceedings and Transactions,* 11:419-499.

4. Richard Brown, 1846. On a group of erect fossil trees in the Sydney coal-field of Cape Breton. *Quarterly Journal of the Geological Society of London,* 2:393-396; 1848. Description of an upright *Lepedodendron* with *Stigmaria* roots, in the roof of the Sydney main coal, in the island of Cape Breton, *Quarterly Journal of the Geological Society of London,* 4:46-50; 1850. Section of the lower coal-measures of the Sydney coalfield, in the island of Cape Breton. *Quarterly Journal of the Geological Society of London,* 6:115-133.

5. E. W. Binney, 1846. Description of the Dukinfield *Sigillaria, Quarterly Journal of the Geological Society of London,* 2:393. Also Richard Brown. 1848. Description of an upright *Lepidodendron* with *Stigmaria* roots, in the roof of the Sydney main coal, in the island of Cape Breton. *Quarterly Journal of the Geological Society of London,* 4:46.

6. John J. Stevenson (see Reference 20) notes what he considers to be a resurgence of the concept of the allochthonous origin of coal around the turn of the last century. However, from a perspective of 55 years beyond his writings it can be said that the autochthonous theory is still held by the large majority.

7. W. E. Logan, 1842. On the character of the beds of clay immediately below the coal-seams of S. Wales, *Proceedings of the Geological Society of London,* 3:275-277. This interesting note by Logan was one of the first to point out the abundance of stigmariae and appendages in the underclays below coal seams and he proposed that this clay was the soil on which the coal producing plants originated and the stigmariae and appendages represented roots still *in situ.* See also J. W. Dawson. 1866. On the conditions of the deposition of coal . . ., *Quarterly Journal of the Geological Society of London,* 22:95-169.

8. Dawson, *op. cit.,* pp. 2-10.

9. Logan, *op. cit.* (see Reference No. 3 above), 1845, pp. 92-159; and 1908. 11:419-499.

10. In the Joggins cliffs, the majority of the *Cordaites* logs are somewhat lower in the Pennsylvanian section than the erect lycopods but, near McCarren Brook, both appear in the strata but again the conifers are all prone, whereas some of the lycopods are erect.

11. Richard Brown, 1850. Section of the lower coal-measures of the Sydney coalfield, in the island of Cape Breton, *Quarterly Journal of the Geological Society of London,* 6:127.

12. Charles Lyell and J. W. Dawson, 1953. On the remains of a reptile . . . from the interior of a fossil tree . . ., *Quarterly Journal of the Geological Society of London,* 9:58-63. J. W. Dawson, 1863. Notice of a new species of *Dendrerpeton,* and of the dermal coverings of certain Carboniferous reptiles, *Quarterly Journal of the Geological Society of London,* 19:469-473; 1892. Notice of the discovery of additional remains of land animals in the coal-measures of the South Joggins, *Quarterly Journal of the Geological Society of London,* 18:5-7. Margaret C. Steen, 1934. The amphibian fauna from

the South Joggins, N. S., *Zoological Society of London, Proceedings,* Pt. 3, pp. 465-504. R. M. Sternberg, 1941. Carboniferous dipnoans from Nova Scotia, *American Journal of Science,* 239:836-838. See also *Papers of National Museum of Canada,* 1963, No. 22, pp. 1-13; *Proceedings of Linnean Society of London,* 1966, 177:63-97; *Science,* 1967, 158:56-59.

13. C. M. Sternberg, 1933. Carboniferous tracks from Nova Scotia. *Geological Society of America Bulletin,* 44:951-964, plates 35-37. He makes this remark on some unusual tracks discussed and illustrated in the paper. "Superficially they resemble the track of some of the wading birds, but of course there is little probability of their having been made by birds."

14. For further examples of diagonal trees see 1966. Prolegomena to a study of cataclysmal sedimentation, *Creation Research Society Annual,* 3:16-37.

15. H. G. Coffin, 1968. A paleoecological misinterpretation, *Creation Research Society Quarterly,* 5:85.

16. F. M. Broadhurst, 1964. Some aspects of the paleoecology of non-marine faunas and rates of sedimentation in the Lancashire coal measures, *American Journal of Science,* 262:865.

17. Wilfrid Francis, 1961. Coal, its formation and composition. Edward Arnold (Publishers) Ltd., London, p. 28.

18. Derek V. Ager, 1963. Principles of paleoecology. McGraw-Hill Book Co., Inc., New York, p. 85.

19. Challenger Expedition, 1885. Report on the scientific results of voyage of the H.M.S. "Challenger" during the years 1873-76 under the command of Captain Nares and Captain Thompson. Narrative Vol. 1. H. M. Stationery Office, London. See also Fauth, Ph. 1913. Horbigers glacial-kosmogenic. Eine neue entwickelungs-geschichte des weltalls und des sonnensystems. Kaiserslautern, Kayser, p. 443.

20. John J. Stevenson, 1911-1913. Formation of coal beds, *Proceedings of American Philosophical Society.* Vols. 50-52.

21. Henry Fayol, 1886. Études sur le terrain bouiller de Commentry. Livre premier; lithologie et stratigraphie, *Bull. de la Soc. de l'industrie minérale,* 2e série, 15$^{3-4}$, Saint-Étienne. 543 pp.

22. Chester A. Arnold, 1947. An introduction to paleobotany. McGraw-Hill Book Co., Inc., New York, pp. 123-124.

23. C. Grand' Eury, 1890. Géologie et paléontologie du bassin houiller du Gard. Étienne. H. Graf zu Solms-Laubach, 1894. Ueber *Stigmariopsis* Grand' Eury. Palaent. Abh. (Dames and Kayser) N.F. Bd. 2, Jena. A. C. Seward. 1898-1919. Fossil plants. Hafner Pub. Co., Inc., New York. Reprint 1963. Vol. II.

24. Dawson, *op. cit.,* p. 29.

25. *Ibid.,* p. 230.

26. A. C. Seward, 1898-1919. Fossil plants. Hafner Pub. Co., Inc., New York. Reprints 1963. Vol. II, p. 245.

27. W. F. M. Kimpe and A. A. Thiadens, 1951. On the occurrence of coal raft above and rhizome inclusions in seam Finefrau B, South Limbourg, Holland. Third International Congress of Sedimentology. Groningen-Wageningen, Proceedings, pp. 167-173.

IV

A NOTE ON THE UNSATISFACTORY NATURE OF THE HORSE SERIES OF FOSSILS AS EVIDENCE FOR EVOLUTION*

FRANK W. COUSINS**

Introduction

Construction of family trees to show possible connecting links between various species and larger groups of the animal kingdom is widely used in the presentation of the case for evolution. It is a particularly subtle form of presentation, since it is often assumed by the reader that the drawing itself is evidence for the connecting links which the drawing forcefully suggests (see Figure 1).

Two recent cases† come readily to mind in which, with absolutely *no evidence* to support their case, bodies of learned men have spent prodigious labor simply to show that a paleo-biological tree may be drawn for their chosen group of animals. This of itself is not objectionable, but the unwary are easily ensnared intellectually by the erudition of the case to believing that such was *in fact* the way the development of that group of animals proceeded *in nature*—indeed the case is inevitably concluded in that manner by the authors of the scheme.

---

*Editor's Note: This article is based on a chapter in the book entitled, *Symposium on Creation*, III, and is reprinted here by the kind permission of the editor, Mr. Donald W. Patten, and the publisher, Baker Book House, Grand Rapids, Michigan.

**Frank W. Cousins is a consulting engineer, a chartered electrical engineer, and a fellow of the Royal Astronomical Society.

†"Genesis of the Hymenoptera and the Phases of Their Evolution," S. I. Malyshev, London, 1969, (63/—). "The Cnidaria and Their Evolution." Symposia of the Zoological Society, London, No. 16. Edited by W. J. Rees. London, 1966. (1051—).

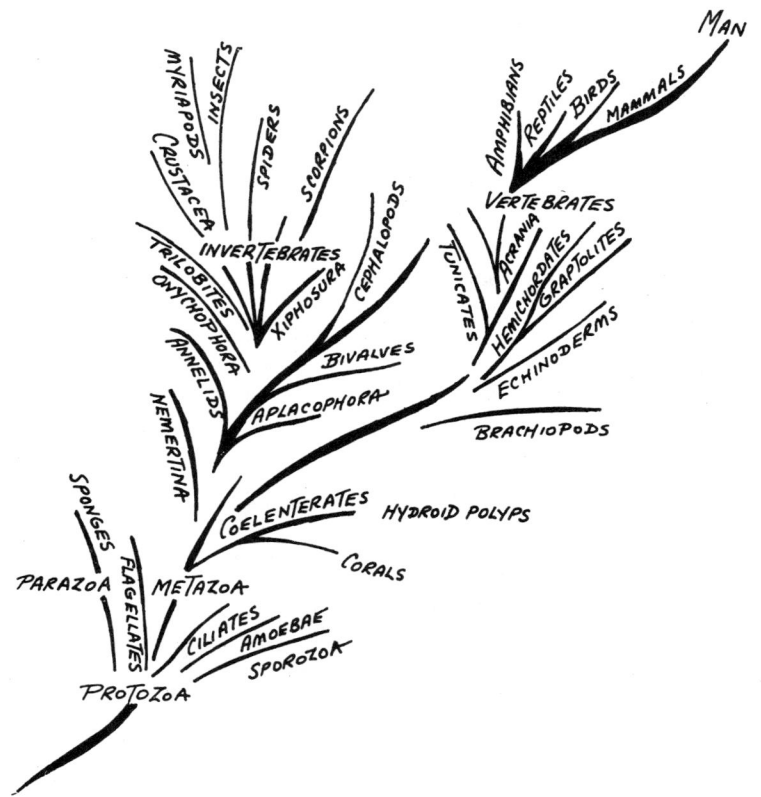

Figure 1. From "Fossil Man, a Reappraisal of the Evidence," by F. W. Cousins, 1961, published by The Evolution Protest Movement, Havant, Hampshire, England.

ANIMAL PHYLOGENY
after de Beer

This phylogenetic tree is typical of the way evolutionists present their case. It is redrawn by the author from deBeer's *Atlas of Evolution*, Nelson, 1964, p. 155. In presenting it deBeer says: "Animals evolved from Protophyta by loss of chlorophyll and acquisition of holozoic nutrition. From Protozoa, Parazoa produced sponges, and Metazoa gave rise to two main groups leading to the highest invertebrates and to vertebrates respectively." There is no evidence of such an evolutionary chain. There is no evidence at the outset of the chain that a single protozoan has changed into a single metazoan.[6] The author found no difficulty in drawing this phylogenetic tree, but the lines, the slope of the lines, the thickness of the lines, the graceful upward curve of

If one now turns to, allegedly, the most powerful evidence in support of the case for evolution (i.e., transformation across the species), one will often be invited to consider the case for the alleged evolution of the horse. That this is indeed so, I quote from a recent paper by Professor F. H. T. Rhodes:[1]

> ... at a lower taxonomic level, between genera, for example, we also have a substantial number of transitional sequences. One of the best of all is the sequence of horses linking the whippet-sized, primitive, Eocene form Hyracotherium with the living horse. This was one of the first fossil sequences ever described. It was first described by Kovalevsky in 1874, and it was later amplified by Marsh, and interpreted by Huxley. The beautiful gradational sequence which these fossils show is now so well described (e.g., Simpson,[††] 1951) that we need only summarise its major features. These involved the increase in body size, the increase in size and change in the shape of the skull, changes in the teeth, involving the premolarisation of the molars, and the deepening of the teeth from low crowned to high crowned, together with the infilling of the depressions in the upper surfaces with cement. With these were associated changes in the limbs, with the gradual reduction in the number of toes, and in the whole change in construction of the limbs associated with the change in posture from pad-footed to spring-footed. Now this series is incontrovertible. It provides clear evidence of the transition of one genus to another over a period of something like seventy million years.
>
> Secondly, at all taxonomic levels, there are now, in a limited number of cases, examples of continuity. Let us first of all take high taxonomic levels. Here we have, especially in the vertebrates, remarkable transitional forms between various classes. Between the crossopterygian fish and the amphibia, we have the ichthyostegids, part fish, part amphibia, known from the Upper Devonian or Lower Mississippian of Greenland. The early Upper Devonian Elpistostege is intermediate between ichthyostegids and osteolepids (Westoll, 1938, 1943, 1958). Between birds and reptiles, we have the renowned Archaeopteryx.

---

the lines, should not be mistaken for evidence of actual genealogical links (from V. H. Heywood and J. McNeill, Phenetic and Phylogenetic Classification. Nature, vol. 203, No. 4951, pp. 1220-1224, Sept. 19, 1964).

††Simpson, G. G., (1951), Horses, Oxford University Press, New York.

and from Dr. G. A. Kerkut's book,[2]

> It would not be fitting in discussing the implications of Evolution to leave the evolution of the horse out of the discussion. The evolution of the horse provides one of the keystones in the teaching of evolutionary doctrine, though the actual story depends to a large extent upon who is telling it and when the story is being told.

I will now proceed to show that the evolutionists' view concerning the horse as valid evidence for transformation is open to serious doubt. I hope to show further that the general presentation of their arguments cannot carry the conviction which is universally granted to it by those unskilled in biology, who, not unnaturally, accept that biologists view the evidence with dispassion, as far as that is even possible, in the presentation of the controversial case which they espouse.

I turn to the powerful arguments mounted by the late Professor H. Nilsson in his *Synthetische Artbildung*.[3] Unfortunately, this encyclopaedic work is expensive and rare; further, it is written in the German language and thereby not openly accessible to readers who are not German scholars. I am much indebted therefore to my friend, Mr. C. H. Greenstreet, for having made, at my request, a translation of the relevant portion of *Synthethische Artbildung,* on the horse, which it is my pleasure to present for the first time in English. I am also indebted to the kindness of the publishers of *Synthetische Artbildung,* Messrs. C. W. K. Gleerup of Öresundsvägen, Lund (Sweden), for permission to publish this translation and thereby give these important ideas to a wider audience. The pictures, footnotes, the introduction, conclusion, and the extensive bibliography presented here are my contribution to this study, and they form no part of the original pieces by Professor Nilsson.

The Horse

How innumerable are the family trees that only hold together because "connecting lines on paper" form the intermediate bridges! Without these, the construction of a family tree would be almost impossible. For it is particularly the connecting corners that in reality are almost always lacking. One can easily satisfy oneself of this everywhere in the relevant literature.

Here someone interrupts: "But no! even if all the other family trees are demolished, *one* nevertheless remains, paleobiologically sound, continuously and consequentially constructed, established through the whole Cenozoic,* the family tree of the horse."**

It is true that people have spoken of the evolutionary "parade horse," proudly calling attention on the one hand to the completeness of a long transformational series, while on the other hand contemptuously emphasizing the nature of the series as a rather detached piece of bravura.

The enthusiasts are many. One can still see in the latest reviews of evolution, which are no longer written by natural philosophers or pure morphologists, how the family tree of the horse is compared to a true *experimentum crucis*. It is set out thus in the book *The Cause of Evolution* by the geneticist and biostatistician J. B. S. Haldane[4] (and in the recent *Atlas of Evolution* by the pre-eminent Darwinian, Sir Gavin deBeer,[5] see Figure 2).

We must at all events look somewhat more closely to see how deeply the credibility of their evolutionary series is anchored, despite the fact that the biostatistician readily accepts it. For it is certainly clear that neither the number of the forms nor the possibility of arranging them in a series is proof on its own.

It is very instructive to remind oneself how the oldest, Eocene fossils of this series were first interpreted. Davies[6] gives a good survey of this. He is so far from entertaining anti-evolutionary thoughts that he wrote his book rather as a polemic against the real English critic with respect to the theory of evolution, Dewar.[7]

Owen[8], the discoverer of the first eozoic† fossil in the London

---

*Cenozoic—the age of the mammals, said to extend from about 60 million years to the present.
 **The idea of evolution in the horse began with Kowalewskii working with European and Asian forms; see Kowalewskii, V. D. (1842), "Sur l'Amchiterium aurelianeuse et sur l'histoire paleontologique des Chevaux," Mem. Acad. Imp. Sci. St. Pet. 7, vol. 20.
 †Eozoic—a term suggested for the Pre-Cambrian system, but little used. It means the "dawn of life."

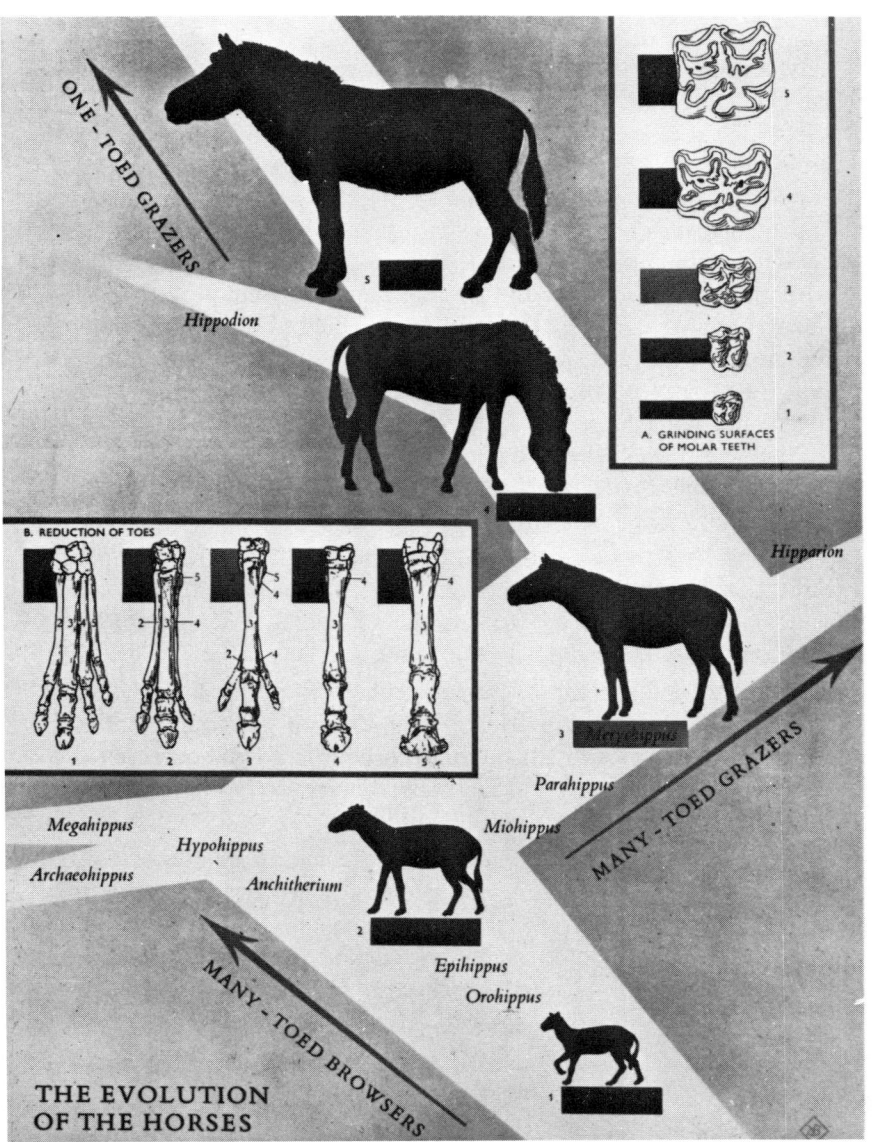

Figure 2. The evolution of the horse according to deBeer, Atlas of Evolution, 1964.

clay, explained the skull fragment as a new ungulate genus, which he named *Hyracotherium*. The name refers to the Genus *Hyrax*, the "Klippschliefer" or "Daman"††, which is today native to the mountains of Africa and Western Asia. Owen did not want to assert that *Hyracotherium* resembles the "Klippschliefer" more than any other genus of pachyderm, only that the size of the animal appeared to come closest to that genus. Its binary name was *Hyracotherium leporinum:* by the specific name he wanted to call attention to certain features of the skull that seemed to him to resemble the rodents. When later he was able to describe an almost complete skull and parts of the limbs, he did not dare to identify the two forms, but named the new form *Pholophus vuliapeps,* that is to say a type with a fox's head but multiple back teeth as in the hoofed animals. This form has been included by the later paleontologists in the genus *Hyracotherium.*

As will be at once seen from this state of affairs, Owen found an indication of correspondence of characteristics of *Hyracotherium* with several orders, including that of the ungulates. But he made no mention of a relationship with the equids.

When, toward the end of the nineteenth century, still further finds of *Hyracotherium*-like fossils had been made, it was found that these approached other forms, including the tapirs and rhinoceroses. The Eozoic hoofed animals of the perissodactyl* type were therefore collected into one family, Lophiodontidae.**

Very early on, however, already in the middle of the seventieth year of the previous century, the roots of a family tree of the present day horse were produced from this material. The finds of the American paleontologist Marsh and others were schematically exhibited for a lecture given by Thomas H. Huxley in New York,

---

††Daman—from the Arabic name *Daman israil,* sheep or lamb of Israel (it has no resemblance to a sheep). The Syrian rock-badger or "cony" of Scripture (*Hyrax syriacus*) is the name also extended to the species found at the Cape, *Hyrax capensis* (the Saphan of the Scriptures).

*Perissodactyla Odd-Toed Ungulates—an order of mammals containing horses, tapirs, and rhinoceros.

**Lophiodon—a fossil mammal of the Eocene Period related to the tapirs.

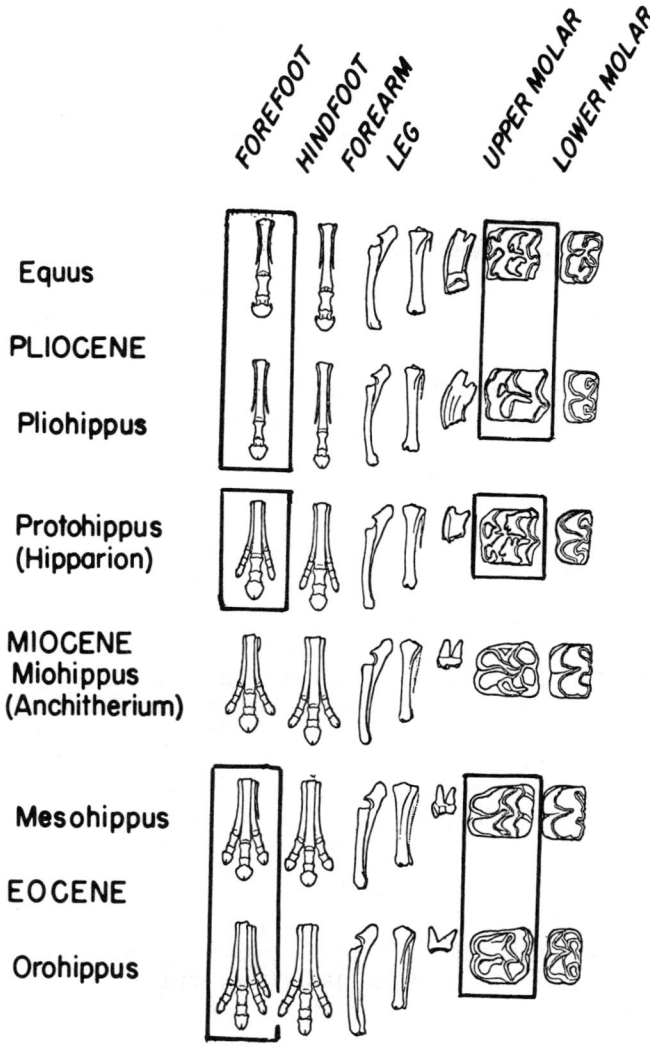

Figure 3. Alleged genealogy of the horse (after Marsh, Polydactyl horses, American Journal of Science, 1879, p. 505). The parts in the black boxes are the parts used by deBeer to make his case in 1964. See Figure 2.

where there were seen in increasing order and in series the front and back feet, the forearms, the rear leg bone, the tooth types, and the surfaces of the back teeth. (The author has reproduced the picture in Figure 3.) From this work the ancestry of the horse was at once *complete*. It was published by Marsh in 1879 and then found quick entry into many publications and text books; indeed it is still seen today, in full or in part, almost unchanged.

Since then, more than 70 years have passed and a quantity of further finds have been made. The continuity of the series has in certain cases become more intimate. Osborn, the outstanding expert on fossil horses, which have so greatly increased in number, thus also gained so strong an impression of the gradual transitions that he regarded the whole process of "becoming horse" as a displacement of the proportions of characteristics, as a pure case of transformism in the Darwinian sense. After discussion of the horse series he summarized his opinion in the following characteristic statement (Osborn,[9] p. 268):

> The above examples illustrate the general fact that *change of proportion* make up the larger part of mammalian evolution and adaptation. The gain and loss of parts, which is so conspicuous a phenomenon in heredity as studied from the Mendelian standpoint, is a comparatively rare phenomenon. The changes of proportion are brought about through the greater or less velocity of single characters and of groups of characters; for example, the transformation of the four-toed horse of the base of the lower Eocene into the three-toed embryo of the modern horse is brought about by the acceleration of the central digit and the retardation of the side digits. This process is so gradual that it required 1,000,000 years to accomplish the reduction of the fifth digit, which left the originally tetradactyl horse in the tridactyl stage; and it has required 2,000,000 years more to complete the retardation of the second and fourth digits, which are still retained in the chromatin and develop side by side with the third digit for many months during the early intra-uterine life of the horse.

According to Osborn the little toe also required 1,000,000 years to be continuously reduced away. He reckoned, however, with only 3,000,000 years for the whole Cenozoic Period. Now this period

HORSE SERIES OF FOSSILS UNSATISFACTORY EVIDENCE 95

is estimated to be at least 30,000,000 years.* The reduction of a given toe thus required 10,000,000.** The thought is not a little ingenuous.†

If one asks oneself: Is the continuity then really so marked as the series of *Hippi* (the names too are continuous) set up as long ago as 1879 indicate?

We ask the best European expert on fossil horses, Abel,[10] who is also familiar with the American finds. In his *Palaeobiology and Family History* which is thus 50 years more recent than Marsh's treatise, the horse problem is dealt with from the modern point of view, so that the work can be said to be representative of the present position of the relevant research.

In Figure 4 I have represented the family tree of the equids, after page 288 of Abel, in a comprehensive scheme, to which are added the geological stages and formations for both Europe and North America. As one sees, a hypothetical family tree is also made very prominent here. Many forms have been added, but they branch off from the main stem and disappear. Here too everything seems to proceed in unbroken and undisturbed temporal series. A parade horse in truth steps forward, perfect, out of the darkness.

However, when one carefully studies Abel's portrayal of the genesis of the horse, one is not a little surprised at several comments.

Attention is still drawn, as before, to the complete continuity of the family tree of *Equus,* so that one at once gets the impression that the development has proceeded quite undisturbed. In this case

---

*It has increased twofold from c. 1930. It is now 60,000,000 years, not 30,000,000. The argument of Nilsson is thereby greatly reinforced.

**This figure would now be 20,000,000 years.

†Editor's Note: It is obvious to the reader that Nilsson placed some faith in the supposed vast ages of the uniformitarian geologic column, as did Douglas Dewar and certain other creationists of a previous generation. Creation Research Society stands unalterably opposed to the long-ages hypothesis and in favor of a relatively recent creation (although not necessarily 4004 B.C.). Yet it is of interest, as author Frank Cousins points out, that the evidence favoring the creation of horses is so clear that it cannot be denied whatever one holds about the so-called "science" of stratigraphy or the supposed vast epochs of geologic time.

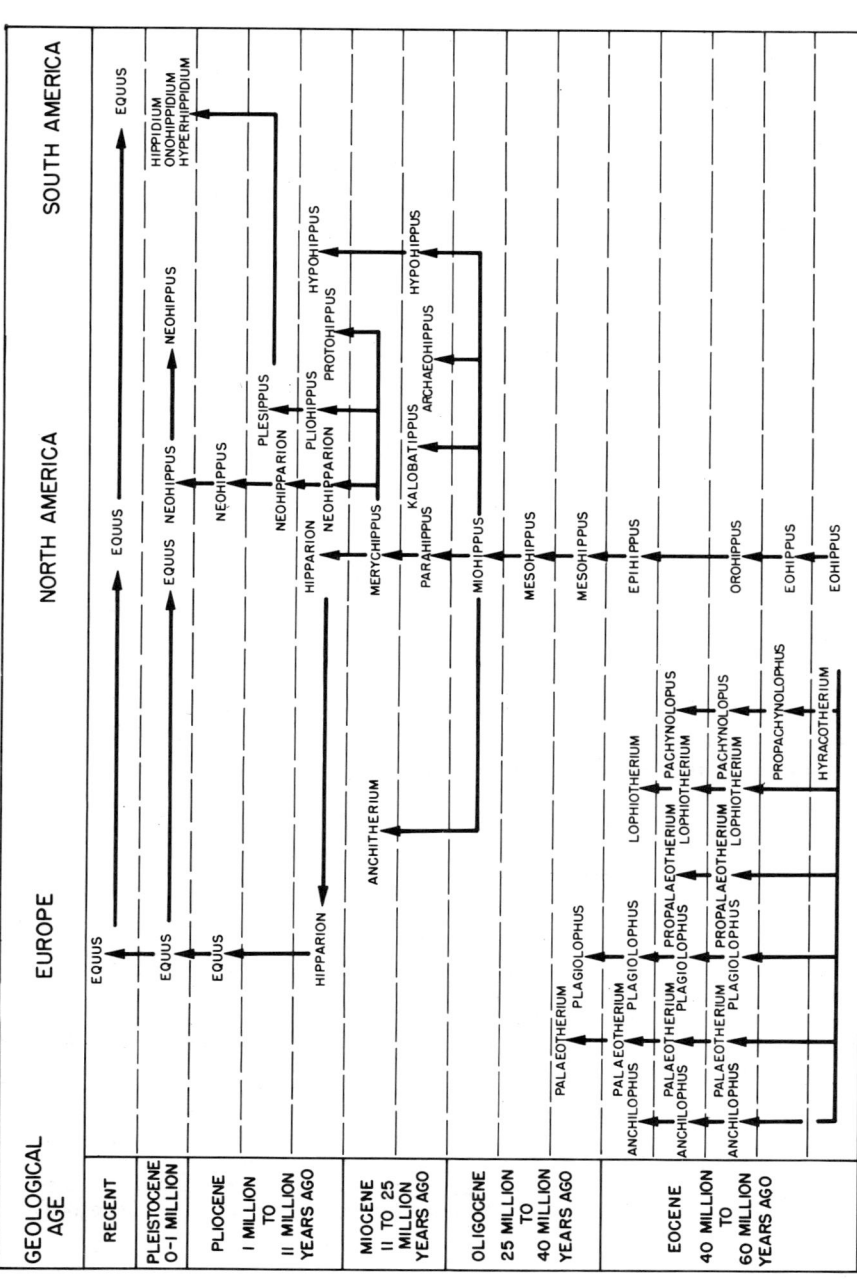

Figure 4. The family history of horses, after O. Abel (slightly simplified).

one does not expect discontinuities, either biological or geological. However, Abel speaks of "Old horses" and "New horses." The latter further form two clearly independent groups: that of small and more primitive new horses and that of the large equus-like. The last group begins with *Merychippus*. And the appearance of this genus is depicted as follows:

> However, the horse series itself shows very clearly that the phylogenetic development of a tightly-closed stem took place in quiet, uniform, one can say always uniform forms, and that then, in the series mentioned here, which it is true does not include all genera of the North-American horse, an era of much faster transformation set in that appeared almost stormy. This era is characterized by the origin of the *Merychippus* type.[10]

And in another place he asserted,

> that at the same time as in North America there occurred the formation from *Merychippus* of numerous new stems occurred in almost explosive form (Middle and upper miocene), there also took place in the case of the whales the origin of the two families of the physeritides and the ziphuds.[10]

A "stormy," "explosive" transformation of the horse tree, we can thus also say an emicative process, thus took place during the latter half of the Miocene. This applies both with regard to the degree of change in character and the production of new forms. "I have the impression," Abel[10] also said, "that the biggest jump shown by the horse, apart from the gap between *Mesohippus* and *Epihippus,* lies in the formation of the *Mercychippus.*"

The last statement also refers to a new break in the skeleton of the tree. I have just mentioned that Abel distinguished between old and new horses. *Epihippus* is the last of the old horses, while *Mesohippus* is the first of the new horses. Between these we have a very considerable jump. For the first were small animals, only as big as foxes, with four-toed forefeet; only with the latter did the large, three-toed type first occur.

Abel's attempt to reconstruct the biology and environment of these obviously very peculiar and very little horse-like "old horses" is of very great interest. This brings us back to Owen's *Hyraco-*

therium. This European genus is named *Eohippus* in North America. For their being synonymous Davies put forward the following argument, which is certainly worth reading:

> I here assume the generic identity of the *Hyracotherium* with *Eohippus,* as seems the inevitable conclusion from Forster Cooper's recent revision of the English fossils (1932). Technically, this means that the name *Eohippus* must be abandoned in favour of the prior name *Hyracotherium;* but in writing for the general reader I feel justified in using the highly appropriate name *Eohippus* (drawn horse) instead of the misleading *Hyracotherium.*[11]

Davies is thus inclined to suspend the priority rule of nomenclature, at least for the layman so as not to shake their evolutionary convictions by a misleading name for the proposed starting forms of the family tree.

Perhaps, however, the basis of Davies' rejection of the name *Hyracotherium* is not only the avoidance of a false etymological meaning. Indeed the first supposed ancestors are, as mentioned above, very little horselike both morphologically and in habitat. This was just as little the case with regard to their manner of life and whole ecological situation, as Abel, with the support of several investigators, imagined these to be. He depicted *Hyracotherium* and its environment very vigorously in the following manner:

> The oldest horses were not steppe-dwellers, but were small animals, which in looks and in their whole outward appearance must have presented the picture much more of a Chilean (Puduhirsch) deer or a Javanese deer (*Kantschils tragulus*) than that of a dwarf recent horse. Matthew has drawn attention to the fact that these oldest horses were thicket-dwellers, which rescued themselves in the case of urgent danger not by speedy flight but by a jump into the protective thickets, and which mainly lived on soft leaves and succulent vegetables, and this view is thoroughly to be endorsed. Prolonged running on hard steppes and browsing on the hard grassy plants of the steppes would not have been possible for these little old horses.[12]

Why have these eocene animals become true horses, since they remind one so little both morphologically and biologically of horses?

HORSE SERIES OF FOSSILS UNSATISFACTORY EVIDENCE 99

Are there today no animals that both look and live like these? Yes. It seems to me quite odd that no one has thought of the genus of animals from which the current name of Owens, *Hyracotherium*, was formed, namely *Hyrax*. It already shows in its incomplete material hyracoid traits, but no equine ones. And the former have become progressively more striking as the type has been made more complete through new finds.

Hyrax is a quite remarkable animal in the present-day fauna, which fits into no order since it imitates many orders. Mostly it is placed in the genus of hoofed animals, but it has also been placed amongst the insectivores and the rats; indeed, people have also sought to find traits of the elephants, marsupials and edentates.* The truth is that we find here just as peculiar a recent combination form as the South American hoatzin was among the now living birds. Owen has already found *exactly the same* with regard to *Hyracotherium*.

Hyrax, like *Hyracotherium*, is a small animal, about the size of a rabbit or fox. Like these, *Hyrax* has four toes on the forelimbs and three on the hind limbs, a quite striking similarity. The back teeth of the two genera exhibit many similarities and resemble those of the rhinoceri more than those of the horse. It must be added that *Hyrax* is a very shy animal that usually lives on mountain ledges and in thickets of the highlands, and when it chances to come out of the edges of the woodlands into grassy plains it takes fright extraordinarily easily and quickly disappears back into the thickets. Its way of life and name thus remind one as exactly as possible of those postulated for *Hyracotherium*.

Thus *Hyracotherium* does not resemble the present day horse in any respect, but on the other hand is quite *amazingly similar* to the present day damans. One can also express this state of affairs by saying that *Eocene "horses" are still living today*. Naturally these cannot be regarded as horses, for this would mean that evolution is standing quite still. Since the rest fit into none of the *recent* orders, one speaks of them, to save ridicule, as little as possible.

---

*Edentata—an order of mammalia characterized by the absence of front teeth (the ant eater, armadillo, sloth, etc.).

They would in fact only fit into the Eocene order *Lophiodontidae,* but this would be too absurd.

Hyracotherium is an Eocene genus. Beside it several closely connected European genera are placed and, as is seen from Figure 4, the genera *Propachynolophus* and *Pachynolophus* follow in the middle and upper Eocene, while *Hyracotherium* disappears in the lower Eocene. Thus a beautiful transgressive development appears to take place here. A revision of the European old horses by Forster Cooper[13] has, however, shown that those genera cannot be distinguished. Thus *Hyracotherium* lived during the whole Eocene and the development stood still. The names alone appear to have developed.

One still meets with the opinion that the horses became successively bigger. This is of course correct insofar as *Equus* is bigger than *Hyracotherium,* just as the horse of the present-day fauna is bigger than the daman, and between the two extremes there are in both cases several intermediate forms of ungulates. Now people were so firmly convinced of the increase in the size of horses in the geological strata that in some cases the ages of the strata have even been determined by the size-type of the horse-remains found therein.* As Cooper pointed out, there is no strong parallelism in this respect. *Eohippus* which appeared in the lowest Eocene, is the largest form of the Eocene horses. All middle and upper-Eocene forms are smaller. Only in the Oligocene did there come, with *Mesohippus,* a sudden significant increase in size. Here there appeared a type of horse that was also changed in many respects: a type of small new horse, which is about as big as a sheep.

With this there comes to light the first lacuna in the hypothetical family tree of our horse. In these animals of genera *Mesohippus* and *Parahippus,* both the front and hind feet are three-toed, and they differ from the old horses in many other characteristics, into which we cannot go here. Their way of life was also new. Thus Abel[14] thought that they were steppe-animals which inhabited floodplains formed during the Oligocene. A type both morphologically

---

*This is a good example of the circular reasoning of the "science" of stratigraphy.

and biologically new occurred with the Oligocene and lived until the Lower Miocene. Then this too disappeared.

Thereafter the real horse, the new horse, first appeared. The breaking of a hypothetical evolution series can hardly be more definite than with the appearance of this type. One-toedness dominated, although quite clear rudiments of two side-toes may occur. But an important deviant type occurred with respect to the teeth and the nature of the dentition. The teeth of the horse are very high, prismatic, not rooted, (enamel-folded) and richly covered in cement. In this respect they are structures unique in the whole fauna. Animals with teeth first occur in the upper Miocene. These "hypsodental ungulates" appear all at once, without intermediate stages. They are even naturally variable, just like other groups, since they at once appeared in full bloom. With *Merychippus* and *Hipparion* there is a rich group of Equus-like forms which are all separated from the former "brachydontal" groups by a gaping evolutionary gap. These former groups have died out, totally eliminated from the search. Here one cannot speak of evolution. The complete extinction of an ungulate fauna and the sudden appearance of another—and this at once richly differentiated, which I have described above as an emicative occurrence—is rather a creative fact.

The family tree of the horse is beautiful and continuous only in the textbooks. In the reality provided by the results of research it is put together from three parts, of which only the last can be described as including horses. The forms of the first part are just as much little horses as the present-day damans are horses. *The construction of the whole Cenozoic family tree of the horse is therefore a very artificial one, since it is put together from nonequivalent parts, and cannot therefore be a continuous transformation series.* Its evolutionary value is therefore made totally untenable through the new research.

Conclusion

Since Nilsson's work on the horse, reported here, there is no new evidence known to me which leads me to wish to change the conclusions he reached. His work was closed before 1954, but

Dr. G. A. Kerkut of the Department of Physiology and Biochemistry at the University of Southhampton, writing in 1960, and reprinting his researches in 1965 (see reference 2) appeals forcefully for biologists to put their house in order regarding the basic information on the horse and the fossils *per se.*

He points out that the basic information on the known fossils has not been given since 1926 and 1930 and that it is difficult to find out how many specimens of a given genus are available for study. There are, he thinks, probably 100 mounted skeletons of fossil horses in the world. There are no mounted skeletons of *Eohippus, Archaeohippus, Megahippus, Stylohipparion, Nannippus, Calippus, Onohippidium* or *Parahippus* and none in the USA of *Anchitherium* or *Hipparion.*

He then draws attention to the genera of the horse family. Kowalewski in 1874 knew of three; Lull in 1917 described 15, Simpson listed 26 in 1945, and Kerbut wonders how valid these genera really are. The Eocene is now dated at 60 million years and no one yet knows how to place the alleged 26 genera in relation to themselves within this vast time period which is open to severe criticisms on the dating methods used.

We still have a few of the Przewalski horse extant. The Prague Zoo keep the records of this animal believed to be the horse pictured in the Lascaux Caves (15,000 years ago?). A herd of eight was sighted in Mongolia in 1966. Dr. R. M. Stecher in a paper in 1968 in *Acta Zoologica et Pathologica* gives results of vertebrate counts from the spines of 61 skeletons of the Przewalski horse and he compares these with similar counts from four other horses—the domestic horse, donkey *(E. asinus),* mule *(E. caballus* and *E. asinus)* and hemione *(E. hemionus).* He also attempts to relate these figures to the number of pairs of chromosomes in a cell of each horse.

Przewalski horses have the longest thoracic segment in the spine, the next to the longest lumbar segment, the shortest sacral segment, and the next to the smallest number of lateral joints in the lumbar spine. It has also the highest chromosome count—66 pairs against 64 of the domestic horse, 63 of the mule, 62 of the donkey, and 54 in the hemione.

Dr. Stecher then makes the *completely invalid* assumption that this suggests evolution within the horse since the horse spine has changed and these changes are correlated with the chromosome count. It suggests, to my mind, nothing of the kind; it shows conclusively that the spines and chromosome counts are different in different animals and absolutely no evolutionary argument can legitimately be imported into his researches. He should know that we classify everything by constitutional differences and a study of the morphology of the horse cannot be used to decide on the reasons for the constitutional differences.

Horse evolution is still a matter of conjecture and not based on clear and unassailable evidence. The horse family is unique and separate and the evidence can, without any weighting, be fitted to the case for special creation.

REFERENCES

1. F. H. T. Rhodes, 1966. The course of evolution, *Proceedings of the Geologists' Association,* vol. 77, Part 1.
2. G. A. Kerkut, 1960. Implications of evolution. Pergamon Press, London, p. 144.
3. H. Nilsson, 1954. Synthetische Artbildung. Verlag CWE Gleerup, Lund, Sweden.
4. J. B. S. Haldane, 1932. The cause of evolution, p. 6.
5. G. deBeer, 1964. Atlas of evolution. Nelson, London (see my criticisms of this work in Book Review No. 142, Evolution Protest Movement, October, 1966—Atlas of evolution, A Critique by Frank W. Cousins).
6. A. Morley Davies, 1937. Evolution and its modern critics. London.
7. D. Dewar, 1931. Difficulties of the evolution theory. London, and 1937. A challenge to evolutionists.
8. R. Owen, 1841. Description of the fossil remains of a mammal *Hyracotherium lepinorum* and a bird *Lithornis culturinus* from the London clay. Translations of the Geological Society of London. 6:203-208.
9. H. Osborn, 1917. *American Journal of Science,* 46:268.
10. O. Abel, 1929. Palaebiologie und Stammesgeschichte. Jena, pp. 286, 294, 285.
11. Davies, *op. cit.,* p. 54.
12. Abel, *op. cit.,* p. 288.
13. C. Forster Cooper, 1932. The genus *Hyracotherium,* Philosophical Transactions of the Royal Society of London, Series B, p. 221.
14. Abel, *op. cit.,* p. 286.

V

FOSSIL MAN: ANCESTOR OR DESCENDANT OF ADAM?*

R. Daniel Shaw**

Introduction

For well over a century, men have been discovering, examining, and naming fossils that appear to be linked to "modern man." These analyses have resulted in a confusing mass of taxonomic terms and hypotheses, drawing a heavy cloak of false validity around evolutionary theories. In recent years, a welcome trend toward synthesis has developed; a trend that has not only made the literature more readable but has helped pinpoint problematic areas toward which future work must be directed.

A primary factor in any consideration of the fossil record (or anything else for that matter) is the attitude from which the subject is approached. Over twenty years ago Professor Portmann of Vienna noted that, if we take a palaeontological versus a historical view toward the fossil record, we will arrive at wholly divergent results: "One and the same piece of evidence will assume totally different aspects according to the angle—palaeontological or historical—from which we look at it."[1]

Chittick graphically shows the effect of viewpoint through his "facts box," arriving at the same conclusion.[2] Let me clearly state at the outset that the approach taken here is historical, with an observation of facts and a discussion of how those facts fit into a coherent view of man's history.

---

*This article appeared in *Symposium on Creation* III, Baker Book House, Grand Rapids, Michigan, edited by Donald W. Patten, pp. 119-141. 1971.
**R. Daniel Shaw is a translator with Wycliffe Bible Translators. He holds the M.A. degree in anthropology.

The Prevailing View

In viewing the fossil record of man, authors of current literature tend to arrive at four major levels or stages of Hominid development; the Australopithecine, the Pithecanthropine, the Neanderthal, and the Modern.[3] From a uniformitarian or evolutionary viewpoint, these stages generally are cast in an orthogenetic line of progression upward through the Pleistocene. Correlations of morphology, stratigraphy, and "absolute date" are the main criteria of such a scheme (see Table 1).

Morphologically, there is considerable agreement that those fossils, apart from the Australopithecine stage, belong in the genus *Homo*. Controversy continues to rage over the placement of Australopithecines inside or outside the range of the genus *Homo*. The Pithecanthropine material is seen by some as *Homo erectus,* and the

Geologic Epoch		Fossil Stage	Years from Present
RECENT		Modern	30,000
PLEISTOCENE	Upper	Neanderthal	180,000
	Middle	Pithecanthropine	500,000
	Lower	Australopithecine	1,750,000

Table 1. An evolutionary, uniformitarian time column for the fossil stages.

Neanderthal and above are assigned to *Homo sapiens*,[4] although a few workers question the authenticity of Pithecantropine remains, as we shall see shortly. Doubt also remains in some minds about the status of Neanderthal as a species or simply a racial difference.[5]

There appears to be increased pressure to place the entire fossil record within a single species and view the whole matter as a racial diversification. Indeed, Stewart pointed out before the present trends began: "Like Dobzhansky, therefore, I can see no reason at present to suppose that more than a single hominid species has existed on any time level in the Pleistocene."[6]

Hemmer,[7] using allometric measurements of the skull, recently included all fossils above the Australopithecine stage within the range of *Homo sapiens*. This, of course, in no way reduces the presumed amount of evolutionary change but merely enlarges the meaning of "species" to include a wider range of variation for hominid remains.

It must be made clear at the outset that in discussing the fossil record we are concerned with populations rather than individuals. It is true that the specific fossil represents an individual, but it in turn is but one member of a population and therefore only representative. There can, however, be considerable variation expressed in any population, thus requiring extreme caution when drawing conclusions about the appearance of "prehistoric" populations from the individuals discovered. With such considerations in mind I would like to turn to an analysis of the distribution of fossil finds throughout the Old World.

The Australopithecine Stage

Beginning with the Australopithecines (the most "primitive" in the evolutionary framework), we find that sites containing their remains appear primarily in South Africa. Here, the sites consist largely of limestone caves, with the fossils firmly cemented into the breccia. Many of the fossils show the effect of considerable pressure which may have occurred during or after deposition.

East Africa is involved also in the Australopithecine story because of the finds by L. S. B. Leakey, particularly those of *Zinjanthropus*

FOSSIL MAN: ANCESTOR OR DESCENDANT OF ADAM? 107

and *Homo habilis*.[8] Olduvai Gorge, where Leakey faithfully labored for over 30 years, has been a virtual "gold mine" of fossil material, yielding many forms, both osteological and cultural.

The stratigraphy is probably one of the clearest for the Pleistocene of anywhere in the world, enabling palaeontologists and anthropologists alike to reconstruct much of Pleistocene ecology and culture history. Since the uniformitarian time concept is built on as yet unproved assumptions, however, the "time significance" of these stratified series is presently rejected by this author.

Leaving Africa, we pick up the Australopithicine story again in Java where a lonely and hotly debated fossil *(Meganthropus)* has been found without tools, stratigraphically below the Pithecantro-

1. Taung
2. Sterkfontein
3. Swartkrans
4. Kromdraai
5. Makapansgat
6. Olduvai Gorge
7. Garusi
8. Djetis Beds (Java)
9. China

Map 1. Distribution of Australopithecine Sites.

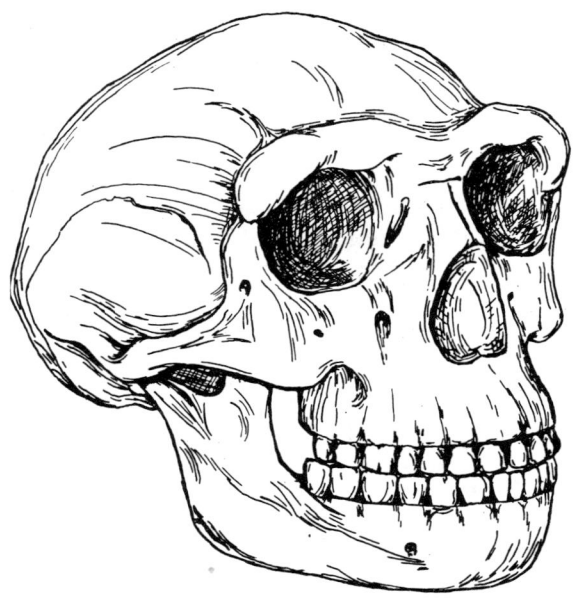

A composite reconstruction made under the direction of Franz Weidenreich and based upon the Pithecanthropine fragments found at Choukoutein, near Pekin. Originally called Sinanthropus pekinensis.

Figure 1. From C. Loring Brace, THE STAGES OF HUMAN EVOLUTION: Human and Cultural Origins, (C) 1967. Reprinted by permission of Prentice-Hall, Inc., Englewood Cliffs, New Jersey.

pine stage. Another cousin of the Java find was identified in the form of a group of isolated teeth from China. Tobias[9] would like to see these last two finds attributed to Leakey's Habiline stage, thus being somewhat intermediate between the Australopithecines and the Pithecanthropines. This may be so on morphological grounds alone, but for the present I will join with Brace and others who consider them all to be Australopithecine.

Viewing the location of these sites, we find them scattered in a peripheral area of the Old World, buried in the last outpost, so to speak. Statistically, most of Australopithecines come from South

Africa, furthest away from the center of the Old World (Map 1).

We should indicate here that certain workers regard the Australopithicine stage as a group of great-apes in no direct sense related to man. They maintain that the small brain capacity, the lack of tools, and the apparent specialization suggest that these beings were simply extinct ape-like animals.[10] It is noteworthy that Dr. Leakey himself has all but abandoned *Zinjanthropus* as a likely human ancestor.[11]

The Pithecanthropine Stage

The Pithecanthropines (Figure 1) were made famous by a young Dutch doctor exploring in Java during the 1890's. Java continues to be an area of considerable interest for the remains of *Pithecanthropus,* the sites being well described by Coon.[12] These fossils have estimated brain capacities of approximately 950 cc, nearly double that of the Australopithecines. As might be expected, we also find Pithecanthropine material in China, which von Koenigswald[13] maintains is closely related to, though somewhat more refined than, the Java material.

Turning to other areas of the world, we note that Africa again comes into the picture with sites this time being prominent in North Africa at Ternefine and Rabat. South of the Sahara the Koro Toro fossil remains in some dispute. Chellean man was found in the Olduvai Gorge, and a single jaw and a few teeth comprise the total of the Pithecanthropine stage found in South Africa.

The Pithecanthropines are also found in Europe. The still mysterious and not unanimously accepted Heidelberg jaw, an occipital and a few teeth from Verteszollos (Hungary), and a tooth fragment from Brezletice (Czechoslovakia), believed by some to be the earliest of human remains in Europe,[14] are all included in the Pithecanthropine story. The above mentioned fossil finds have been well documented and described elsewhere; the geographic location is the interest for this paper.

The Pithecanthropines are widely separated and still peripheral to Eurasia, but there appears to be a somewhat closer statistical distribution around the center of the Old World, than for the Australo-

1. Baksoka (Java)
2. Choukoutien
3. Verteszollos
4. Heidelberg
5. Prezletice
6. Ternefine
7. Rabat
8. Koro Toro
9. Ouduvai Gorge
10. Swartkrans

Map 2. Distribution of Pithecanthropine Sites.

pithecines. The Pithecanthropine material has a more even distribution than the Australopithecines, being found on all the large land masses of the Old World except Australia (Map 2). This more even distribution, plus the wide distribution of cultural debris throughout Asia, Europe, and Africa, attest to the presence of Pithecanthropine individuals throughout the Old World. Technologically they were advanced enough to penetrate nearly all ecological zones and, based on stratigraphic evidence, apparently displaced the Australopithecines in many areas.

While discussing the Java and China evidences of the Pithecan-

FOSSIL MAN: ANCESTOR OR DESCENDANT OF ADAM? 111

thropine stage, some mention should be made of the questions surrounding the finds. According to Rev. O'Connell's well-documented review,[15] it is not possible to be certain that the human femur found by Dr. Dubois bore any real connection to the skull cap situated in the same bed. It is possible that the femur was from a human, while the skull cap may have come from an ape. There was no sure way to estimate the cranial capacity of this first skull cap or of those later discovered by Dr. von Konigswald as in each instance the brain case was missing.

It is somewhat more distressing to note that for 30 years Dr. Dubois concealed the truly human Wadjak skulls that he had also found in Java! Such conflicting evidence has led certain authorities such as Dr. W. R. Thompson[16] and Rev. O'Connell to go so far as to conclude that Java man was a fraud. Rev. O'Connell cites the famous Marcellin Boule as rejecting the Java Man and shows that Dr. Dubois admitted before his death that it was actually the skull of a gibbon.

Concerning the China finds, Rev. O'Connell[17] points to the fact that all the Pithecanthropine skulls collected in China at the Choukoutien site have disappeared in some unexplained manner. Some casts or models of the *Sinanthropus* specimens were supposedly made from the original finds and these models exist; but the models differ in several ways from eye-witness descriptions of the missing skulls! As in Java, skulls and other remains of truly human forms were discovered—this time in the same deposit as the reputed Pithecanthropine type. Such information has led O'Connell to conclude that the missing *Sinanthropus* skulls were really fossil remains of large baboons or of macaques and that the tool industry in that region (including an efficient lime-burning operation) was attributable to the humans recovered at the same location.

The Neanderthal Stage

The Neanderthals (Figure 2) are well represented by a large number of finds that are centered in the Levant and Europe. This is the burly, "cave man" type fellow who appears to be responsible for a rather elaborate and refined tool kit, and apparently pushed

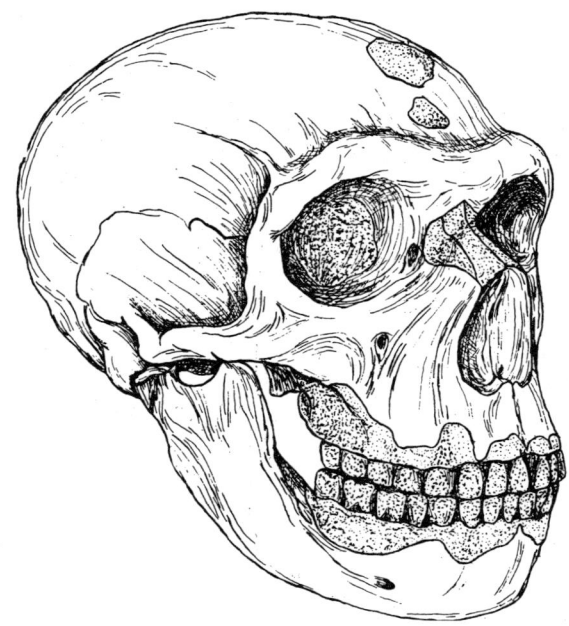

The "Old Man" from La Chapelle-aux-Saints, Correze, southwestern France. An extreme example of the "classic" Neanderthals.

Figure 2. From C. Loring Brace, THE STAGES OF HUMAN EVOLUTION: Human and Cultural Origins, (C) 1967. Reprinted by permission of Prentice-Hall, Inc., Englewood Cliffs, New Jersey.

other races further to the periphery. Morphologically, the great difference between the Neanderthals and the "lower" fossils, is the cranial capacity which averages over 1500 cc.[18]

Turning to the distribution of the Neanderthals, specimens have been found in Africa at Saldanha and Broken Hill. As with the previous stages, some material has been found in Java and China, thus allowing for some very interesting comparisons. In Central Asia, we find a child's remains at Teshik Tash, made famous by a ring of goat horns presumably used in some form of burial ceremony. Possibly our first record of care for the sick and aged was found in Shanidar in the remains of a crippled old man and his family. The Mt. Carmel finds at the caves of Skhul and Tabun provide physical anthropologists with what appears to be fossilized races.[10]

Debate over the so-called "progressive" and "classical" Neanderthals has created great interest. The more progressive forms tend to be found in the East, while classical forms are found mostly in Western Europe. This variation, however, appears to be no different than that between *Australopithecus* and *Paranthropus* (from South Africa) that are both now classed as Australopithecine, and *Sinan-*

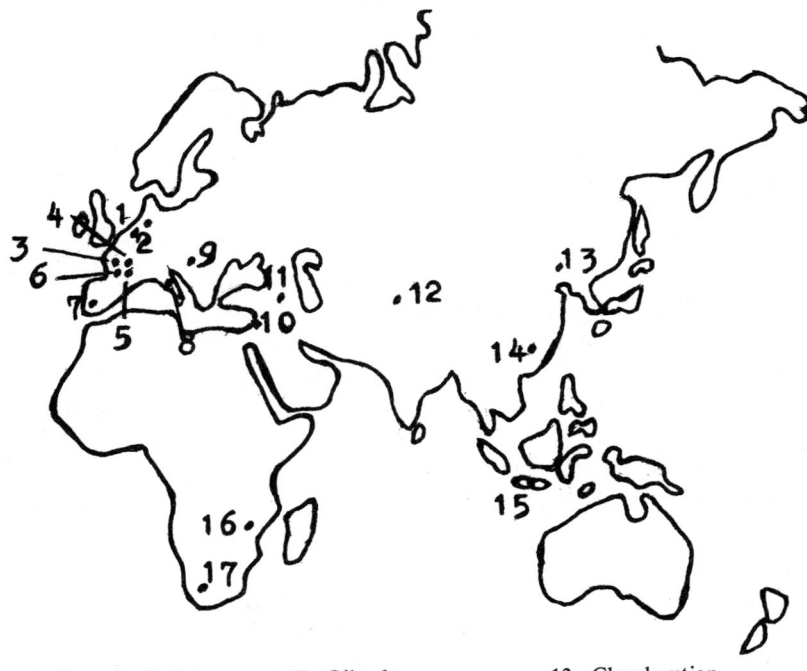

1. Neanderthal
2. Spy
3. La Chapelle
4. Le Moustier
5. La Ferrassie
6. La Quina
7. Gibraltar
8. Saccopastore
9. Krapina
10. Mt. Carmel
11. Shanidar
12. Teshik Tash
13. Choukoutien
14. Ma-Pa
15. Solo
16. Broken Hill
17. Saldanha

Map 3. **Distribution of Neanderthal Sites.**

thropus and *Pithecanthropus* (China and Java respectively) of the Pithecanthropine group.

Viewing the Neanderthal distribution statistically, we find them clustered to the west and to the north of Mesopotamia and in Europe, with more isolated finds toward the periphery (Map 3). Though the cultural distribution of the Neanderthals is considerably more widespread, the evidence still supports the contention that their primary distribution was much closer to the center of the Old World than the Australopithecines and Pithecanthropines.

Fossil Distributions: Region of Origin

This brief analysis of the distribution of the three stages of fossils for the Pleistocene points out that what appears to be the most primitive or degenerate forms of man are found in the most peripheral position, while the more advanced forms usually appear much closer to the center of the Old World. This suggests, as Custance[20] has pointed out, that man may have migrated from a point close to the center of the Old World, and what appears to be "primitive" forms at the periphery may, in fact, be descendants of the more "modern" forms that appear at the center.

Other factors may be involved which could lead to such a distribution: (1) physical conditions, i.e., soil types, caves, etc., conducive to fossilization and preservation of fossils, (2) accessibility of fossils for discovery, and (3) orientation of the discoverer, i.e., Dubois in one case, Leakey in another, each convinced that he should find fossils of early man. When, however, fossils are found, explanations for their presence in such a location must be considered.

It is possible, as pointed out previously, that this whole problem of the three "stages" is solved in a different manner. If the Australopithicines were in fact ape-like animals (as some authorities believe), then there is no question as to whether they were man's ancestors or his descendants. According to that view, they were simply not related to man in any way.

Also, if the existence of a Pithecanthropine stage is indeed questionable, then it too would be of no real concern in man's origin.

If the Java form was indeed a gibbon (as Dubois finally believed and as certain others now agree), and if the evidence for a Pithecanthropine stage in China is also highly questionable, these forms simply "evaporate" from the arena of serious scientific dialogue about man's origin. More evidence and thorough study of both the Australopithine and Pithecanthropine finds is essential.

Meanwhile, many students of anthropology do indeed consider the Australopithicines and the Pithecanthropines as valid links in man's ancestry. Recognizing that both forms may be "disqualified" on the other grounds mentioned, it is still of interest to the author here to see if another model or view of these types is possible—assuming that they are valid, and assuming that they are indeed related to man—assumptions which are in themselves questionable.

Using these two assumptions, however, it is my intent to see if another point of view is possible regarding the fossil record. The migration theory presented here conforms with the evidence and provides a possible basis for coordination with Scripture. In considering the distance of migration and its relation to "degeneracy" Custance has noted three factors which affect variability:[21]

> (a) a new species is more variable when it first appears; (b) a small population is more variable than a large one; (c) when a species shifts (or a few members of it) into a new environment, wide varieties again appear which only become stable with time. . . .
>
> Fossil remains constantly bear witness to the reality of these factors, but the witness has meaning only, and the facts are best accounted for only, if we assume that a small population began at the centre and, as it became firmly established there, sent out successive waves of migrants usually numbering very few persons in any one group, who thereafter established a further succession of centres. . . . Each new centre at the first showed great diversity of physical type, but as the population multiplied locally a greater physical uniformity was achieved in the course of time.

Before considering this in more detail, I would like to take a look at where the original center may have been.

There are, in the Old World, two areas which have a conspicuous lack of fossils, India and the Mesopotamian region. Both areas have been studied extensively by archaeologists and many ancient sites have been uncovered, but all that is found is what man left, never man himself.

In India, we find a tool kit which corresponds well with Pithecanthropine material in Africa and Java, leading one to believe that Pithecanthropine races inhabited the Sub-Continent regardless of the fact that we are unable to find their actual remains.

In Mesopotamia, however, though Neanderthal type culture assemblages appear in the Iraq foot hills, nothing earlier than the Jarmo phase of incipient agriculture can be found.[22] This seems to coincide well with the lack of any "prehistoric" fossils in the area.

It would appear then that the Mesopotamian region could well be considered the center from which man originally migrated to the ends of the earth. In this view, the Neanderthals, Pithecanthropines, and perhaps the Australopithecines represent degenerate desendants of that migration.

Genetic Action on Small Populations

The genetic aspects of such a distribution emanating from a point of common origin must now be brought into full focus. Custance has pointed out the effects of genetic drift acting on small populations (as these migrating peoples certainly must have been). Geographical isolation is also a vital consideration when discussing the movement of small populations.

As people migrated, they would gradually become separated by natural geographical barriers. Such separation would involve a reduction of gene flow which would ultimately result in an isolated homogeneous population. Genetic change under such conditions can be quite rapid, with natural selection, mutation (to a lesser extent), and genetic drift acting upon the small population "with much greater speed and effectiveness than earlier evolutionists dreamed."[23]

Such genetic change could effect significant racial differences, within a few generations. Continued inbreeding, migration, and genetic isolation could produce some of the drastic variation we find in the fossil record. The degrees of variation within the various stages appear very similar to what we observe today as racial differentiation. The variation between stages, though appearing to be greater than racial diversification today, is certainly not in the range of taxonomic difference if we deal with morphology (shape) alone. Consider the many varieties of dog, all members of the same species.

It appears to me then, upon a consideration of morphology, associated culture, and stratigraphy, that *Zinjanthropus* and *Homo habilis* are of the same species,[24] especially when these are compared with the Java and China material. Morphologically they probably stood erect and had essentially the same skeletal anatomy as present populations. Thus they had virtually the same structural relationship to most of the Pithecantrophines as the latter group had to the Neanderthals.[25]

Therefore, on genetic and morphological grounds, the Australopithecines could well represent the product of relatively rapid migration, and extreme inbreeding. The same degenerative process could be true, to a lesser degree, of the Pithecanthropine and Neanderthal populations.

In my opinion, all probably emerged from the Mesopotamian region, pushing earlier migrations ever further out, forcing adaptation to new conditions, and creating new physical and cultural appearances. Indeed, LeGros Clark has noted in a discussion of Australopithecines that: ". . . it would not necessarily follow that the transition occurred in South Africa. It may have occurred in some other part of the world, and the South African fossils in that case may represent but slightly modified survivors of the ancestral stock, which persisted to a much later time in the Transvaal."[26]

Yet in all fairness we should state, as earlier, that certain investigators, who view the fossil hominids from the creation standpoint, suggest that the Australopithicines in general were not actually human, but represent the remains of large extinct, ape-like animals. More data are necessary to settle the question with finality.

Besides the effects of genetic and geographical diversification, there are other physical factors to be considered. The function of the endocrine glands may have had an effect. Some authors have made a point of the similarity between persons suffering from acromegaly and Neanderthal fossils.[27] Sir Arthur Keith has suggested that endocrinology may be a key to understanding the formation of race.

Though this appears to be an oversimplification of the problem, glandular function has possibly had some effect. In small, rapidly changing populations that are not in genetic equilibrium, it could have an even greater effect, resulting in forms similar to those found in the fossil record. Both prenatal and postnatal development is dictated by the genes, but organized by hormones. A hormonal imbalance could result in a malformation of the skeletal system (the area of greatest concern so far as fossilization is concerned) producing such specimens as are found.

Although many of the fossil finds do not derive from aged specimens, old age might have been a factor of considerable effect upon a particular skeleton. Effects included in the process of aging are an increase in calcification, brittleness of the bones, closing of skull sutures and other points of ossification, and possible deformation through thickening of the bones and disease. The "Old Man" of La Chapelle-aux-Saints (a Neanderthal) is a prime example of the effects of arthritis upon the skeletal structure.

A Historic Model Best

Observation of the life processes, as well as study of radioactive decay, has led investigators to an understanding of what has been called the "decay curve." This simply indicates that all that starts ultimately stops. The process and time involved can be computed and, with sufficient experimentation, predicted.

The laws of thermodynamics: (1) the conservation of energy, and (2) the increase of entropy, bring out the same point, and necessitate that randomization increases rather than decreases.[28] This, in effect, "reverses" the so-called process of organic evolution forcing a historic model of man's origin and life upon earth into a new dimension.

Applying the decay curve and the second law of thermodynamics to genetic considerations leads to the conclusion that the basic building block of life and the carrier of all genetic quality, deoxyribose nucleic acid (DNA), must, in fact, be decreasing in efficiency rather than increasing.

Mutational changes in DNA are shown to cause defects of more or less serious nature. Changed nucleotide bases, additions, or losses (as Crick has indicated[29]) all yield defective results. If this is so, then the first or original man must have possessed the ultimate in genetic quality, with decreasing potential being expressed in subsequent generations.

Returning to the question of the origin of the Australopithecines, we note that, since so little is known about the behavior and nature of the Australopithecines, little can be said of great certainty about their origin or their position. Some creationists may regard *Zinjanthropus* in particular and the Australopithecines in general not as part of the genus *Homo,* but (as Leakey now asserts) as a very distinct genus quite unrelated to man.

Strong inbreeding, however, accompanied by conditions that must have been encountered by people migrating from the point of human origin, could have lead to an accumulation of changes in the DNA code and therefore the appearance of the individuals as well as the population pools so involved. As previously indicated, I believe there is considerable evidence for placing the Australopithecines within the range of human diversity so that they could accordingly represent a degenerate form of the first human being.

In that case, the fossil record would be best understood by reversing the heretofore *evolutionary* scheme, and replacing it with a historically and scientifically coherent *devolutionary* scheme.

Fossils As Adam's Descendants

The question of this paper thus reduces to who the ancestors of the fossils are. Custance, as previously noted,[30] believes that through biological processes and culture history, he can account for all the necessary changes since the time of Noah, dating from approximately 3000 B.C. Though this is indeed a possibility, and as noted, genetic change can be effected very rapidly, nevertheless, I believe it may be more profitable to view the fossil record as Adam's descendants, and assign the present racial diversification as a result of the dispersion following Noah.

A number of works in recent years have linked the Pleistocene Ice Ages with the Noachian flood.[31] These works point to the catastrophic view traceable to the 19th century French scholar Georges Cuvier. This hardly means, however, that the status of recent catastrophic work is retrogressive. Rather it simply points to the great effect that evolutionary theory has had in leading scientific thought down a blind alley for well over a century. A wealth of material has been published in recent years that supports catastrophism. The great need at present is for a reevaluation and reinterpretation of the facts.

Apart from the mechanical approach taken with respect to the Biblical flood, its direct cause, and presumably what happened during it, many agree that it was an event which left an indelible mark upon both earth landforms and survival patterns, and hence has had a great effect on subsequent history. Place Adam in a preflood environment[37] and project a migration from him, as has been described, with the resulting geographical dispersion and genetic degradation: then bring about a catastrophe such as the Noachian flood, and I believe the result would be a large portion of the fossil evidence which we observe today.

The conditions under which fossils are generally found, and the condition of the fossils when found, strongly support the implication that death and deposition were due to catastrophe. Indeed, at Shanidar and Choukoutien, there is considerable evidence for cave fall and burial of individuals as a direct result. What caused the cave fall? Both caves, at opposite ends of Asia, experienced some kind of catastrophe at about the same time. It is no secret that many fossils are found in caves, rock shelters and other types of natural protection (recall the Australopithecines crushed in limestone caves of South Africa), leading to the popular view of the "prehistoric cave man."

The caves, however, could be the result of the flood, and because of their preservative nature we find the fossils there today. The so called "cave man" may never have lived extensively in caves at all. On the other hand, caves could have well resulted from the creative process which brought the world into being initially. As men moved out into the world, caves would have afforded a natural protection from the elements and wild beasts. The question of the origin of the caves is beyond the scope of the present paper. The fact remains that the caves and other types of natural protection contain fossils.

Those fossils that are not deposited in natural protection often show signs of sudden burial. If this were not so, there would be little chance for fossilization, as the organic matter of the body would be subject to carnivores, weathering, decomposition and subsequent obliteration. Therefore, a model that accounts for sudden burial, better accounts for the majority of fossils, because it removes them from the effects of weathering, and aids in their preservation. As Cook[33] notes:

> Paradoxically, while the fossil record is considered to be one of the most compelling arguments in favor of the evolution of the species, there is every reason to believe that fossilization itself is critically dependent upon catastrophism.

Where did Adam originate? This question has long been the subject of much speculation. If one accepts the present evidence concerning the distribution of the fossils, with the more primitive types pushed to the periphery by their more refined cousins, a projection to the center of this dispersion brings one to the heartland of the Old World, the Mesopotamian region.

It appears that Mesopotamia was the general region where the second dispersion of peoples commenced.[34] Whether one accepts Cook's model of continental drift,[35] or other models which project orogeny and other geographical alternations based on the present distribution of continents,[36] the center from which migration occurred remains the general area of the Middle East.

Morphology Not of Prime Concern

Looking again at the distribution of fossils throughout the Old World, it is not difficult to notice that morphology has possibly been emphasized too greatly in analysis, while genetics, endocrinology, and the aging factor and disease have not been given enough consideration. Comparing individuals found within the same site often forces the investigator to recognize the great variation within a population.

An example is Weidenrich's now famous description, on morphological grounds alone, of what appears to be four racial classifications for seven individuals in the upper cave at Choukoutien, all presumably from the same family.[37] Such variation may be explained if one takes into account relatively rapid migration and severe inbreeding. Under these conditions it would no longer be possible to assume that the people were adapted to the area in which they are found.

Palaeontologists have usually assumed that by sampling the fauna and flora of the area associated with the fossil, the conditions under which the fossil lived could be reconstructed and knowledge gained concerning the necessary adaptations. Undoubtedly many fossils have been "adapted" by their discoverer when, in fact, the fossil was more adapted to another area, but forced to move and died as

Biblical Period	Fossil Stage	Years before Present
Christ		2000
Noachian Flood	Racial diversification from Noah and his sons	5000±
	Australopithecine	
Result of wide dispersion from Adam	Pithecanthropine	
	Neanderthal	
Creation	Man Created in Perfection (Gen. 1:27)	7000±

Table 2. **A catastrophic model of fossil stages showing morphological variation as a result of dispersion before the flood, and racial variation following the flood.**

a relatively newcomer to the area in which it is found. This would help explain the variations noted between populations of the same geologic strata and would be the expected in such a model as that presented here.

This model would also help explain such confusing relationships as Leakey found at Olduvai where the morphologically superior *Homo habilis* occurs stratigraphically below *Zinjanthropus* in Bed I, and yet Habiline type material appears almost contiguous with Pithecanthropine in Bed II.[38]

In general, a progressive increase in complexity upwards would be the expected, the earliest individuals to migrate being pushed further to the periphery and stratigraphically below the later. In those cases where two waves of migration were in association at the time of the flood, a very confusing state of relationships would result.

Conclusion

I have presented here a picture of the distribution of hominid fossils as found throughout the Old World including a majority of the major finds, though by no means a complete inventory. That distribution has been interpreted as the result of movement of peoples from a center out to the periphery. The geographical and biological factors involved in such a proposed dispersion lead one to recognize the possibility of great variation morphologically not only between populations but also within populations.

The conditions under which the fossils are found may be used to argue strongly that the individuals met with severe upheaval. This, as well as the environmental conditions associated with the fossils, leads me to suggest that these fossils were the descendants of Adam, the upheaval being the Noachian flood. Regardless of the mechanics of the flood event, the point from which the migrations emanated appears to be the Mesopotamian region.

The creation-dispersion model presented here stresses morphological variation as a result of the dispersion of peoples. As small groups moved out from the original gene pool, they were subjected to conditions, both environmental and physical, that affected their appearance. The Biblical flood captured these people under conditions that further changed their structural appearance resulting in what we view as the fossil record. Table 2 is presented as a tentative reconstruction and time table of these events as they might be corrolated with Scriptural events.

Coupled with this dispersion-degeneration model, the author recognizes the distinct possibility that the Australopithecines may not have been human beings at all, but simply extinct ape-like creatures. And it is also possible that the Pithecanthropines likewise represent fossils of other animal types, distinct from man. If both of these ideas should prove to be valid, the dispersion model proposed here would be a simpler one and the creationist interpretation of the fossils would also be less complex.

This presentation is by no means exhaustive. Even as it attempts to answer a number of questions, so it raises a number of others. If however, I have managed to present evidence for a historic approach to the fossil record, and if I have managed to create a better climate to more fully comprehend the implications of such a model, I will have been fully successful. Quoting Cook, we must realize the importance of the approach taken in viewing the evidence.

> These sequences and many like them exist and, to be sure, carry a strong implication concerning relationships . . . what remains in question is whether these relationships are ancestor-descendant ones or the result of a particular background of the *Engineer* [italics his].[39]

I believe the "Engineer," God, created man, who ultimately dispersed throughout the earth. As a result of disobedience and sin, man as he existed was destroyed and the earth drastically changed. The flood which brought about this change left an intriguing record of "relationships" which continue to both baffle and fascinate modern men of science.

REFERENCES

1. A. Portmann, 1947, Das ursprungsproblem, Eranos-Yahrbuck, p. 11.
2. Donald Chittick, 1966. Fact, logic, and faith. *Bueerman-Champion Lectureship*. Western Conservative Baptist Theological Seminary, Portland.

3. C. Loring Brace, 1967. The stages of human evolution. Prentice-Hall, Inc., Englewood Cliffs. In this book Brace discusses in considerable detail each of the "levels of hominid development." He considers the fossil evidence, its apparent meaning, and the relation of the fossil levels to each other.

4. *Ibid.*, p. 96.

5. Frederick S. Hulse, 1963. The human species. Random House, Inc., New York, p. 216.

6. T. D. Stewart, 1950. Origin and evolution of man, *Cold Springs Harbor Symposium on Quantitative Biology*, 15:105.

7. Helmut Hemmer, 1969. A new view of the evolution of man. *Current Anthropology*, 10:179-180.

8. L. S. B. Leakey, 1966. *Homo habilis, Homo erectus,* and the Australopithicines. *Nature,* 209, pp. 1279-1281.

9. Phillip V. Tobias, 1965. Early man in East Africa. *Science,* vol. 149, pp. 22-33.

10. Patrick O'Connell, 1969. The science of today and the problems of Genesis. Second edition. Christian Book Club of America. Hawthorne, Calif., pp. 143-150.

11. Louis S. B. Leakey, P. V. Tobias, and J. R. Napier, 1964. A new species of the genus *Homo* from Olduvai Gorge. *Nature,* 202 (4927): p. 9.

12. Carleton S. Coon, 1962. The origin of races. Alfred A. Knopf, Inc., New York.

13. G. H. R. von Koenigswald, 1949. The discovery of early man in Java and Southern China (in) Early Man in the Far East, ed. by W. E. Howells. *Studies in Physical Anthropology,* No. 1.

14. Oldrich Fejfar, 1969. Human remains from the early Pleistocene in Czechoslovakia, *Current Anthropology,* 10:pp. 170-173.

15. O'Connell, *op. cit.,* pp. 139-142.

16. W. R. Thompson, 1956. Introduction to Everyman's Library Issue of Darwin's *The Origin of Species* (No. 811). E. P. Dutton and Co., Inc., New York.

17. O'Connell, *op. cit.,* pp. 108-138.

18. Brace, *op. cit.,* pp. 95-96.

19. Hulse, *op. cit.,* p. 223.

20. Arthur C. Custance, 1968. Fossil man in the light of the record in Genesis, *Creation Research Society Annual,* 5, No. 1:5-22.

21. *Ibid.,* pp. 14-15.

22. Robert J. Braidwood and Bruce Howe, 1960. Studies in ancient oriental civilization. No. 31. The University of Chicago Press, Chicago.

23. Ralph L. Beals and Harry Hoijer, 1965. An introduction to anthropology. The Macmillan Company, New York, p. 261.

24. Hemmer, *op. cit.,* p. 179.

25. Brace, *op. cit.* Note especially chapters 9, 10, and 11.

26. W. E. LeGros Clark, 1955. The fossil evidence of human evolution. The University of Chicago Press, Chicago, p. 160.

27. John W. Klotz, 1955. Genes, Genesis and evolution. Concordia Publishing House. St. Louis, pp. 198, 386. Also Donald W. Patten, 1966. The

Biblical flood and the ice epoch. Pacific Meridian Publishing Co., Seattle, pp. 249-258.

28. Henry Morris, 1969. The Bible and thermodynamics. *Bible Science News Letter,* 7, No. 3:1-3.

29. F. H. C. Crick, 1962. The genetic code, *Scientific American,* 207, No. 4:66-74.

30. Custance, *op. cit.,* p. 10.

31. John C. Whitcomb, Jr., and Henry Morris, 1961. The Genesis flood. Presbyterian and Reformed Publishing Co., Philadelphia. Also, Melvin A. Cook, 1966. Prehistory and earth models. Max Parrish and Co., Ltd., London. Also Patten, *op. cit.*

32. Patten, *op. cit.,* p. 201. He speculates on pre-flood conditions in considerable detail. Global temperatures were more evenly distributed in the period before the Flood, a water vapor canopy greatly reducing temperature differentials on the earth's surface (Genesis 1:6, 7; 2:5, 6). Tropical and subtropical conditions have been recorded in both Arctic and Antarctic regions. This warmer, less variable temperature, combined with different atmospheric gas mixtures, notably a greater percentage of water vapor and carbon dioxide, resulted in a luxuriant growth. Giganticism and longevity appear to be closely associated with such environmental conditions, producing the great variety of fossil material available in the "flood alluvium" (strata) of present-day geology. Thus Patten associates antediluvian conditions with a global greenhouse effect as very similar to what is usually pictured by uniformitarians prior to the Pleistocene.

33. Cook, *op. cit.,* pp. 330-332.

34. Custance, *op. cit.,* p. 10. Also Genesis chap. 10.

35. Cook, *op. cit.*

36. Patten, *op. cit.*

37. Franz Weidenrich, 1939. Homo sapiens at Choukoutien, *Antiquity,* 13, No. 50:242-244.

38. Leakey, *op. cit.,* p. 1281.

39. Cook, *op. cit.,* p. 329.

VI

DISCOVERY OF HUMAN SKELETONS IN CRETACEOUS FORMATION

CLIFFORD L. BURDICK*

Introduction

Moab, Utah is located in eastern Utah on the Colorado River, not far from the state line. The rock outcrops there are mostly Mesozoic, ranging from the lower Triassic, or Moenkopi, up through the Jurassic to the Cretaceous, with exposures of Dakota sandstone, Mancos shale, and the Mesa Verde. Some of these formations are well mineralized, with uranium, copper and associated minerals.

The Big Indian copper mine was located on the Cretaceous Dakota sandstone of the Lisbon Valley about 35 miles south of Moab, Utah. The strata there are poorly cemented, or possibly being in the oxidized zone are weathered. The top strata of the hill were discolored a dark brown from the iron in the formation, but the lower strata where the bones were found was of a natural sandy color, whitish.

The Ottinger Find

One side of the Dakota sandstone hill had been dug away by means of bulldozers, since the rock was soft enough for that type of excavation. Apparently the quality of the ore had decreased to the point where it did not pay to dig deeper, so the digging was stopped about 15 feet below the surface of the hill. The mine super-

---

*Clifford L. Burdick, M.S., Hon. Ph.D., is a consulting geologist, Tucson, Arizona.

intendent stated that at least six feet had become hard rock, though still soft enough to bulldoze.

Mr. Lin Ottinger, a friend of the mine superintendent, and some Ohio visitors were given permission to dig for artifacts and azurite specimens. They soon found a tooth and bone fragments both obviously human, and Ottinger traced the bone fragments to their source, uncovering at least one whole skelton. Without further disturbing the find, he then notified Dr. W. Lee Stokes, head of the geology department of the University of Utah, who sent Dr. J. P. Marwitt, anthropologist, to investigate.

With the cooperation of the mine officials, Dr. Marwitt and Lin Ottinger carefully removed the sandstone surrounding the bones, and discovered two human skeletons rather than one. Meanwhile volunteers were screening the loose sand near the site to recover small pieces such as teeth and finger and toe digits.

Because the bones were: (1) in place where buried and undis-

Figure 1. **The mining company pit where human skeletons were found south of Moab, Utah, in Cretaceous rock, Dakota sandstone containing oxidized copper minerals.**

turbed, (2) still articulated or joined together naturally, indicative of no pronounced earth movement, and (3) green from copper carbonate solution (of malachite), Dr. Marwitt considered them "highly interesting and unusual." He had unearthed many Indian and other skeletons but never had found one so stained by the surrounding minerals.

Although definitely *Homo sapiens,* this staining gave a suggestion of antiquity to the find. The homogeneous character of the enclosing rock appeared to rule out the possibility of prospectors being buried by a cave in.

Dr. Marwitt moved the skeletons to his laboratory for further study, but later returned them to Mr. Ottinger, not appearing to have much interest in them for a museum display. Could it be that their association with the Cretaceous rock, presumed to be very old, could be the reason? In any event this discovery is reported for what it may be worth.

(Editor's Note: Admittedly this discovery offers as much of a problem for Flood geologists as for those of the orthodox point of view. For it is difficult to explain how two men could still be alive after such a depth of strata had been deposited. And if already drowned, why were they not buried later in the Mesa Verde formation? A more detailed and clear cut concept of just how the Flood accomplished its work is badly needed in order to be able to see how such finds as these fit into theoretical expectations, or creationists will be guilty of the same ad hoc explanations as evolutionary minded colleagues.—W. E. Lammerts, *Research* Editor)

Conclusions

(1) The bones were definitely "in place." There was no evidence of the surrounding rock having been disturbed, as I dug a foot deep at the site.

(2) The skeleton was pronounced by the University of Utah as definitely *Homo sapiens.*

(3) The deep staining of the bones with malachite attest to their age.

(4) It was evident from the location of the find deep within the man-made pit that the bodies were buried at the time of the emplacement of the sandstone rock.

(5) The type of mineral alteration suggests greater age than 100 years as suggested by the mine superintendent. Black bits of chalococite, a primary type of copper ore, are still in place. Chemical alteration changes this to blue azurite or green malachite, both carbonate minerals formed in the near surface or oxidized areas of the earth's crust. This diagenesis takes time.

(6) If this were one isolated instance of such an anomaly, one might be tempted to disregard it completely; however, other similar so called anomalous discoveries have recently come to light involving fossil remains of recently extinct mammals, even human beings, in Cretaceous rocks.

(7) These and other evidences seem to suggest that much of the geologic column has been "built" on too meager and perhaps even a "flimsy" foundation. One solution would seem to be reduction of some of the time element associated with the geologic column.

Added Note by Author

The University of Arizona personnel performed the Micro K Jeli Dahl or nitrogen retention test on the bones, and found them comparatively recent in origin, that is well within biblical time limits. The result cannot be interpreted accurately in terms of years.

VII

HUMAN FOOTPRINTS IN ROCKS

WILBERT H. RUSCH, SR.*

Introduction

I suppose Robinson Crusoe's reaction to Friday's footprint in the sand is comparable to the feeling of mystery and conjecture that takes hold of our minds at the sight of footprints from the distant past. A perusal of geological literature indicates an acceptance of footprints of various animals as evidence of their existence contemporaneously with the time of the laying down of the strata in which they are found. So we find frequent references to the three-toed dinosaur prints in the Triassic rocks of the Connecticut Valley. Many geology texts have used the photograph of a child splashing in the twenty-gallon pool of water held by a dinosaur footprint in the Cretaceous limestone of Texas.

However, there is no mention of any human footprints in any rocks. When the subject is mentioned in scientific circles, it causes raised eyebrows, general skepticism that such things can be, or a statement that these items are of no scientific value and hence of no interest. On the other hand, in creationist groups there is often considerable misplaced enthusiasm on the subject, with too great a willingness to jump to unjustified conclusions.

When one "digs" into this subject, one might wonder how much valuable evidence has been discarded or destroyed through ignorance and carelessness. An interesting case comes to my mind.

Some years ago Dr. Frank L. Marsh of Andrews University, Berrien Springs, Michigan, showed me a photograph of an iron pot. The story behind it is as follows:

---

*Wilbert H. Rusch, Sr., is professor of biology, Concordia College, Ann Arbor, Michigan 48104.

Figure 1. Iron Pot from Lump of Coal. From a letter dated January 18, 1949, Brandon, Minnesota, to Dr. Frank Marsh comes the following excerpt:

> During Christmas vacation I visited a friend's museum in southern Missouri. Among his curios, he had the iron cup pictured on the enclosed snapshot. You can probably read the letter in back of the cup.
>
> At any rate, the letter states that this cup fell from a lump of coal and left the imprint in the coal. To me it obviously suggests further evidence of a flood and of a civilization prior to the flood. . . .
>
> Letter signed by Robert Nordling;

In a letter dated February 3, 1966, to Wilbert H. Rusch, Sr., Dr. Marsh made the following statements regarding the pot and the writing on the affidavit:

> Enclosed is the letter and snap sent me by Robert Nordling some 17 years ago. When I got interested enough in this "pot" (the size of which can be gotten at somewhat by comparing it with the seat of the straight chair it is resting on) a year or two later I learned that this "friend" of Nordling's had died and his little museum was scattered. Nordling knew nothing of the whereabouts of the iron cup. It would challenge the most alert sleuth to see if he could run it down. If the cup could be found it seems to me that coal would still be present in minute quantities in spots. I don't know the geologic age of the Wilburton Mines' coal. If this cup is what it is sworn to be, it is truly a most significant artifact.

As carefully as can be determined the affidavit reads as follows:

> Sulphur Springs, Arkansas   Nov. 27, 1948
> While I was working in the Municipal Electric Plant in Thomas, Okla. in 1912, I came upon a solid chunk of coal which was too large to use. I

HUMAN FOOTPRINTS IN ROCKS

It would seem that about 1915, a fireman in a power plant in Oklahoma was shoveling native coal into the boiler. Upon reaching an overly large chunk, he had to break it with a sledge, and out of the resulting two pieces fell an iron pot (see Figure 1). He threw the two pieces of coal into the fire, but passed on to others the pot, which ultimately wound up in the private collection of an individual in Missouri. It was photographed at the time, and the picture and the story came into Dr. Marsh's possession some years ago. He personally saw the pot, and examination of it indicated nothing that would contradict the story. Since then, the owner died and the pot has been lost.

Assuming that the story is true, and if the fireman had saved the two parts of coal as well as the pot, I wonder what explanation coal geologists would have come up with to explain the presence of a fashioned iron pot *in situ* in a coal bed! One wonders how many times this same sort of thing has happened in the past several hundred years.

When one attempts a systematic study of the subject of human footprints in rock layers the evidence can be considered in three categories: (1) One finds that there really are undisputed human footprints preserved in rock. (2) There are also documented examples of footprints having been drawn or carved by various human beings in the past. (3) Finally there are examples that would seem to fall into the open, unresolved category.

Human Footprints in Rock

In 1940, Mr. F. B. Richardson of the Carnegie Institution, Washington, D.C., discovered a series of footprints in rock which

---

broke it with a sledge hammer. This iron pot fell from the center, leaving the impression or mould of the pot in the piece of coal.

Jim Stall (an employee of the company) witnessed the breaking of the coal, and saw the pot fall out.

I traced the source of the coal, and found that it came from the Wilburton, Oklahoma, Mines.

Frank J. Kenwood(?)

Sworn to before me, in Sulphur Springs, Arkansas this 27th day of November, 1948.

Julia L (?)　　　N.P.

Figure 2. Footprints of people fleeing volcanic eruption. Photographs of footprints and quarrying operation, Managua, Nicaragua.

were made by people fleeing from a volcanic eruption. The footprints were uncovered during a quarrying operation on the outskirts of the city of Managua, Nicaragua. Previously, Dr. Earl Flint of the Peabody Museum had found similar footprints and collected several samples. However, since most archaeologists were firm believers in the recency of man in the Americas, the evidence was set aside and no further investigations were made at that time.

The rock setting in Nicaragua is as follows. Over a deposit of volcanic ash, there is a deposit of volcanic mud that is about six inches deep. The footprints seem to have been made by two people walking on fairly firm material. Other people walking to their right were in material so soft that their feet sank into it. There also are footprints of a deer crossing this area. The assumption is that the footprints were made shortly after the volcanic mud had covered the area.

Dr. Howel Williams of the University of California examined the prints and considered the circumstances to be such that there can be no question of the authenticity of the footprints (see Figure 2). They are not carvings, but are definitely the impressions of human feet. The individuals are considered to be fairly small people with apparently no children, since all the prints are about the same size. Quarry workers reported that additional footprints, destroyed as a result of the quarrying operations, all pointed in the same direction as those observed.

The beds underlying the footprints are made up of hundreds of feet of ash. The geological setting suggests that neighboring volcanic craters erupted, causing mud flows which are considered to be remarkably like those that buried Herculaneum, Italy. Shortly after the footprints were made, a thin layer of black cinders covered them (see Figure 3). This was followed by another mudflow followed by more cinders interspersed with large numbers of mud flows. In a quiet interval, a river cut a channel into the underlying ash. This was followed by another eruption and pumice covered the area to a depth of more than a foot. In the succeeding quiet period, rivers cut new channels. Then top soil to a depth of three feet developed. Renewed eruptions covered this soil with ash. In

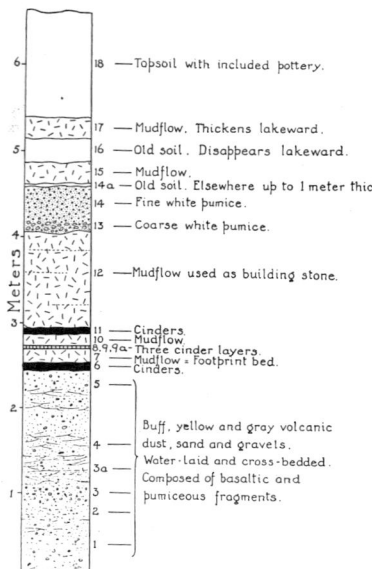

Figure 3. Principal geologic section of area near Managua, Nicaragua. Section shows pumice and ash deposits lying several meters thick above the footprint bed.

the next quiet interval, ten inches of soil developed. Apparently, four layers of soil, including the present top soil, have developed in addition to the river channels that have been cut.[1]

Thus, there is undisputed evidence of human fossil footprints being preserved in, of all things, igneous rock. So the possibility of human footprints in rock strata has to be taken seriously.

Natural "Footprint" in Rock

On the other side of the coin, it must be recognized that natural formations can be quite strange in appearance. I had the opportunity to observe this directly on April 29, 1970, during a physical geology field trip to observe evidence indicating glaciation near Ann Arbor, Michigan, when a small sandstone boulder was found on the discard pile of a gravel pit in the interlobate region known as the Waterloo Recreation Area. It was probably derived from the Marshall sandstone which outcrops to the north and west of Ann Arbor.

The boulder was apparently a concretion which had weathered

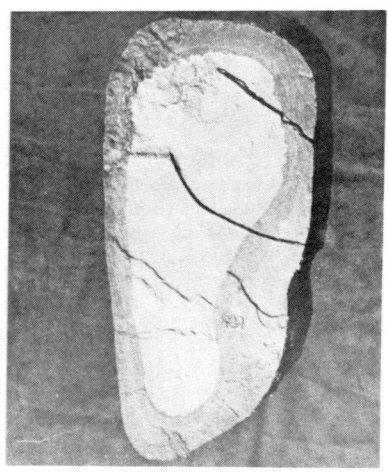

Figure 4. Natural "footprint" in sandstone boulder, found near Ann Arbor, Michigan. Despite the apparent "human" shape, this "print" was formed otherwise inside a sandstone boulder.

out and had then been ice and/or water transported to the site. As frequently happens to such sandstone boulders and cobbles, weathering had caused it to separate as if run through a bread slicer. To the astonishment of all present, one of the slices showed a gray sandstone "footprint" roughly "human" in outline against the red sandstone margin (see Figure 4). (Note: The lighting angle resulted in shadows that overemphasized the elevation differences. Careful trimming could be done to eliminate the step differences.)

As can be seen from the picture of another slice (see Figure 5), this is a three dimensional core of gray sandstone within the maroon sandstone outer surface (see Figure 6). The gray core changes shape at different surfaces on different slices. But one slice shows an astonishing resemblance to the outline of a human sandal print. In fact the average person who sees it calls it a human

Figure 5. "Footprint" in a sandstone boulder. This view of the "footprint" shows that the elevation differences (see Figure 4) are not great.

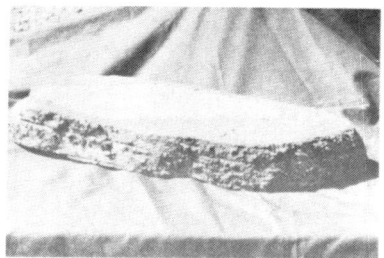

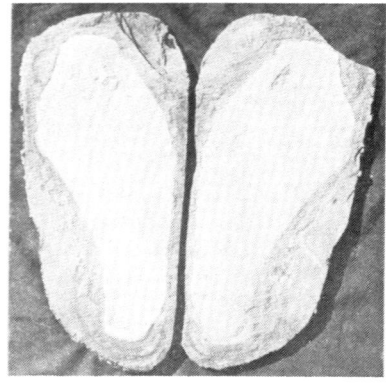

Figure 6. "Footprint" in sandstone boulder. A gray sandstone core is surrounded by maroon sandstone. Note the astonishing resemblance to a human footprint in a naturally formed rock substance.

footprint. The probability of such a "sport of nature" must therefore be borne in mind when considering the problem of human footprints in rock.

Footprint Reports in Literature

Research into old volumes of *American Journal of Science* yields a surprising number of references in rock. The following is a survey of my library research for reputable references to footprints in rock.

In 1817, at Herculaneum, Missouri, two tracks were found in a quarry, which were taken and placed in the back wall of a chimney. There was also a report of tracks having existed upon rocks between Esopers Landing and Kingston, N.Y., on the banks of the Hudson. No information is available as to the present whereabouts of these specimens.

The first detailed record of human imprints in the United States is found in *The American Journal of Science* for 1822.[2] Henry Schoolcraft noted the presence of some human footprints in a limestone slab located in a paved area between a house and garden in New Harmony, Posey County, Indiana. At the request of the Rev. Frederick Rappe, the rock bearing these prints had been transported from limestone layers on the west bank of the Mississippi River at St. Louis, Missouri. Apparently there were large numbers of these prints at the waterfront which already had been noted by the French when they first arrived at the site of St. Louis.

The footprints were found in a crinoidal limestone. The prints were those of a man standing erect in a natural position. The toes were spread as if not used to the confinement of shoes. The feet were spread so that heel to heel measurements were 6¼ inches, while the toe to toe spread was 13½ inches.

Schoolcraft described the prints as "strikingly natural, exhibiting every muscular impression, and the swell of heel and toes, with a precision and faithfulness to nature which I have not been able to copy." The foot length was 10½ inches; the width across the spread toes, 4 inches; and across the heel, 2½ inches. Schoolcraft also reported a faint outline of a sort of scroll, 2½ feet in length, placed ahead of the prints as if a man were idly doodling with a smooth stick while standing. The dimensional figures given were taken by Schoolcraft on July 19, 1821.

Schoolcraft corresponded with Col. Thomas Benton on this subject. Benton considered the tracks that were moved to Indiana to be carvings for the following reasons:

1. the hardness of the limestone;
2. there were no other prints visible leading to and from the two prints on the block (this is difficult to ascertain owing to a lack of any positive information as to where the tracks had originally been located); and,
3. the difficulty of supposing a change so instantaneous and apropos, as must have taken place in the formation of the rock, if the prints were impressed when soft enough to receive such deep and distinct tracks.

Interestingly enough, other footprints carved by Indians were known to Schoolcraft, and he refers to the grotesqueness of these in contrast to the striking naturalness of the prints under discussion.

The source of the prints was a rock that was uncovered for a distance of three miles in front of St. Louis during low water stages, and the outcrop varied from one to 200 feet in width. The prints "looked" as old as the rock, that is they showed the same fine polish which the action of sand and water produced on the rest of the rock. Schoolcraft considered them to be exquisitely natural.

In *The American Encyclopedia*,[3] reference is made to a mountain about two miles south of Brasstown, which is famed for the curiosities in its rocks. There are on several rocks a number of impressions resembling the tracks of turkeys, bears, horses and human beings, as visible and perfect as if they were made on snow or sand.

Sir Woodbine Parrish, the discoverer of *Megatherium*, told a correspondent (identifiable as the first systematic researcher in ripple marks in sandstone and referred to in Jameson's *Edinburg Journal*, issue unknown) that human impressions had been seen in various locations in South America. The Catholic laity there believed them to be the feet of the Apostles.[4]

Evidences of Stone Carvings

A Prof. W. A. Adams noted in a letter to the *American Journal of Science*[5] that he was surprised to see in a previous issue that so many respectable authorities could be found who would support the idea of genuine human footprints in rocks. He seemed to feel differently due to encountering some carved prints in a canal embankment that were uncovered when the Muskingum River broke out of its banks and removed the overburden. But these prints were an entirely different matter from Schoolcraft's. Adams described them as two human footprints, natural size, accurately drawn, outlined as if by pointed chisel and mallet, with an intaglio effect worked in. They were accompanied by many gigantic turkey tracks whose form seemed to have been made by a series of dots. Unfortunately the rock was quarried and broken up.

The difficulty is that these tracks do not seem to be available for study today. As seems to be the case in so many instances, no attempt has been made to preserve such items. There is even a reluctance to objectively discuss them, to examine them for genuineness. Rather, the usual reaction is to avoid discussion. Attempts at preservation are found only in cases where recent carving seems certain as their source.

An exception, up to at least 1961, was a block of limestone in the basement of the geology building of Washington University in St. Louis, Missouri. When I photographed this block, it had the following legend attached:

INDIAN TRAIL-END MARKER

Footprints carved in rock to mark trail end at springs and river crossings. Common in Missouri and the Southwest. Probably from Ste. Genevieve County, Mo. Formerly in the garden of Firmin Desloge at Potosi, Mo., up to his death in 1856. Loaned by his daughter Clara Desloge Pike to Washington University.

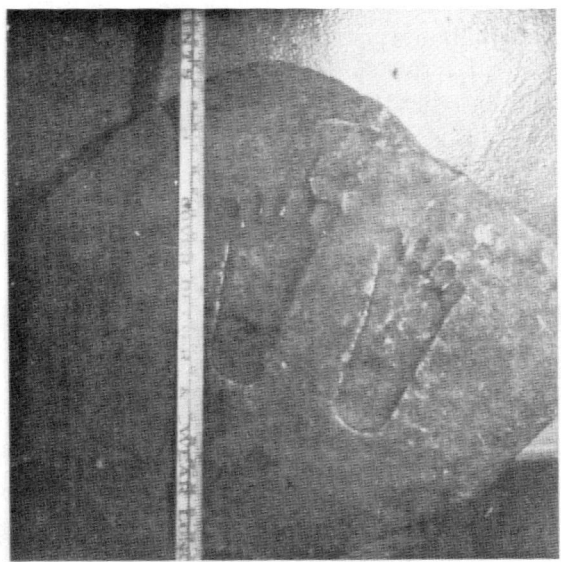

Figure 7. Footprints in Washington State Park, St. Louis, Missouri.

The accompanying photograph (Figure 7) shows the prints with a ruler to show size. The prints could have been carved, but there was a total lack of chisel marks. There was an elliptical depression just forward of the heel in each print. D. K. Greger, deceased, of the Washington University Department of Geology and a serious student of Indian cultures, reportedly said that the Indians had the custom of placing carved footprints at the end of a trail or at the site of a portage.

There is no denying the fact that there were Indians in the past who drew and carved various signs, including human footprints. One clear example that I had opportunity to observe first hand is located in Washington State Park, south of St. Louis, Missouri (see Figures 8-9). These carvings are outlined in white and protected from the wear of people walking on them. The sign at the beginning of the trail leading to the prints proclaims them as petroglyphs, and it is assumed that Indians used them as trail markers. This is probably so, since the carvings include such well-known Indian signs as thunderbird, reverse swastika, etc. The human footprints are four-toed and resemble the drawings in a comic strip, some even like those of a child (see Figure 10).

Inscription Rock is on Kelley's Island in Lake Erie off Marblehead Peninsula, Ohio, about a mile east from the ferry landing. Faintly visible on this large limestone boulder are the carvings of Indians, very similar to those at St. Louis. Erosional agents, and

Figure 8. Footprints at Washington State Park, St. Louis, Missouri. The footprints and other carvings are outlined in white.

Figure 9. Footprints at Washington State Park, St. Louis, Missouri, are apparently carvings, as they are found with petroglyphs.

possibly vandalism, have all but obliterated them. By reading a marker, one can still identify and locate these carvings, at least faint outlines can still be seen. In recent years a shelter has been erected over the rock.

Another possible example of Indian carving may be found on a glacial granite boulder on the University of Nebraska campus just north of 11th and R Streets in Lincoln, Nebraska. It weighs approximately four tons and was found in Cedar County, Nebraska, between Hartington and Coleridge, Nebraska. This boulder is covered with writing that resembles ancient Hebrew, Runic and Mexican symbols, but the most outstanding item is a human footprint.

The boulder was discovered in its original location by Prof. Samuel Aughe of the Nebraska State Department of Geology in 1869. In the following 23 years various scholars examined the boulder, endeavoring to solve the mystery of the carvings. It was

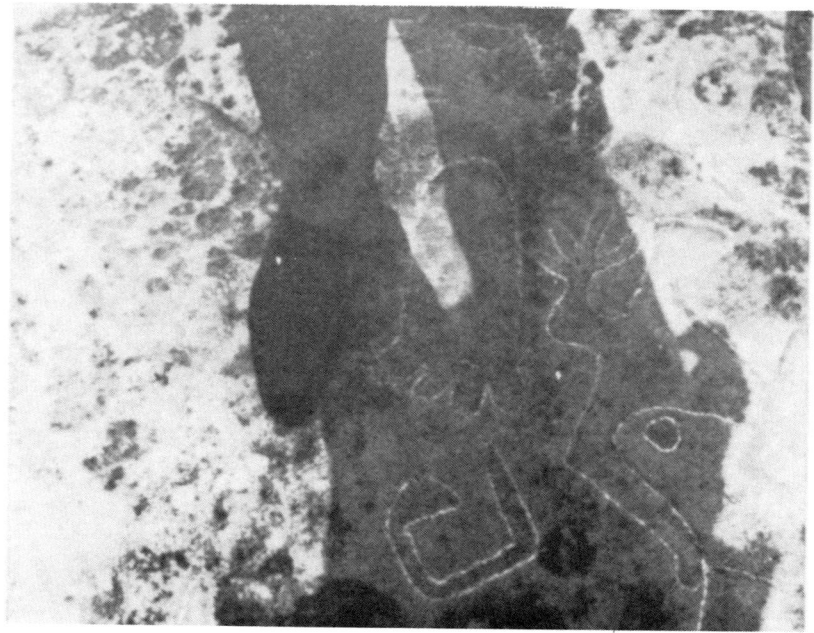

Figure 10. Four-toed footprint at Washington State Park, St. Louis, Missouri, is probably carving. This four-toed foot resembles the drawings in a comic strip.

agreed that they were not accidental, nor were the carvings made where the boulder was found. There is no evidence to link the writing on the rock in any way with Nebraska Indians.

The boulder was brought to the campus by members of the University of Nebraska class of 1892. For a period of about 60 years the writings were forgotten by all concerned and the boulder lay on the campus with the inscriptions unnoticed. Then in the fall of 1961 they were "rediscovered," the carvings emphasized by whitening, and the boulder was then photographed for newspaper publicity (see Figure 11). Certainly this example, by the nature of the rock itself, must be classed with the Washington State Park exhibit as known carvings. Thus, it would seem that we have unquestioned examples of footprints that have been carved by early residents of America. Figure 12 shows this carving with a shoe nearby.

HUMAN FOOTPRINTS IN ROCKS

Some Prints: Actual or Carvings?

However, there are some examples that cannot be so simply categorized. In my opinion they cannot definitely be considered actual footprints. On the other hand, they cannot simply be dismissed as carvings. In this category would belong those located in the Pottsville sandstone outcropping at a point southeast of Berea, Kentucky.

The known history of this outcrop is rather complex. Therefore as part of an attempt to form as complete a record of these footprints as possible, the writer planned to devote two weeks to this project. Plans called for checking the area exposures of the formation containing the prints, the Pottsville sandstone, as well as attempting to pick up leads from area inhabitants, if and where possible.

A preliminary survey was made in a few days during the month of July, 1963. The site of the footprints was located and a pre-

Figure 11. Newspaper photograph of Indian carvings found on granite boulder, University of Nebraska campus. The footprint is present with mysterious symbols and is obviously carved. Lincoln Evening Journal and Nebraska State Journal, November 6, 1961, page 8.

Figure 12. Footprint on rock, University of Nebraska campus. This is an example of a known carving. Shoe added for comparison.

liminary examination was made; however, time was short and a resolve was made to spend a longer time at the site. A second trip began from Ann Arbor, Michigan, on June 20, 1964. Needed "quad" maps were picked up at the State Geological Survey, Mineral Industries Building, University of Kentucky campus, Lexington, Kentucky.

Previously, a number of inquiries had been sent to neighboring state geological offices, e.g., Kentucky, West Virginia, Pennsylvania. In the case of Kentucky, no reply was received, although a self-addressed postpaid envelope had been enclosed. Inquiries at the office in person elicited professed ignorance of any kind of footprints whatsoever, except in the case of one individual who eventually admitted that he had heard a rumor of some person who claimed to have found some prints. The consensus seemed to be that there were no such items anywhere in Kentucky, even carved ones.

A base for first operations was selected within easy radius of Rockcastle, Laurel, and adjacent counties in Kentucky. After a week of fruitless checking, decision was reached to revisit the original print site. Contact was made with Mr. William Finnell, a local furniture dealer in Berea, whose father, Ott Finnell, originally owned the farm where the prints were found. Sessions with Mr. Finnell proved very interesting and enlightening.

Mr. Ott Finnell had acquired several hundred acres in the area southwest of Berea. Although now wooded, in the late 1800's it was all under cultivation. For a good many years there was a rock known as "Bear Paws Rock" about the level of the present road which ascends to the outcrop. This had some prints on it which gave the rock its name, and no further information on this rock is available other than its destruction in 1923 by blasting operations when the aforementioned road was constructed.

About 1930, logs were cut at the top of the hill, and "snaked" over the edge to the road below. This operation uncovered the overburden from the sandstone at the top near the edge, and another set of prints was exposed. Mr. Finnell remembered well the prints for the whole of their existence. Originally he says there were 16 tracks of footprints, many arranged in a normal walking stride. He checked out a number against his own stride.

Shortly after that time, Dr. W. G. Burroughs, who was then State Geologist for Kentucky as well as geology professor at local Berea College, became interested and made extensive studies of the prints. Mrs. Burroughs is also a qualified geologist, and they studied these items together. At the time, considerable publicity was given to the find, with the result that there were many visitors to the site. Further, a natural increase in weathering due to exposure plus a good

148   SPEAK TO THE EARTH

deal of vandalism has resulted in most of the tracks becoming faint and indistinct.[6]

Attempts at preserving the tracks were complicated by a peculiar legal situation which developed. Mr. Ott Finnell believed he owned the area as part of his extensive holdings. But when the publicity broke, a Mr. Barlow Clark came forward and claimed that he had been sold that acre. A recording in the courthouse gave a semblance of truth to his claim. Mr. Ott Finnell didn't feel that the one acre was worth litigation in those days, and so ignored the whole matter. Since that time, Mr. Clark died intestate, leaving about 70 heirs to that one acre. Mr. Willian Finnell has tried to buy the acre to complete his holdings, but clear title cannot be procured, since all the heirs cannot be located. So this has become a case of a permanently clouded title.

The question of the title played into the matter of trying to preserve the prints. The fact that there is no established ownership makes difficult any attempt at protection. Photographs taken at the present time show the degree of destruction. One print was completely broken off when the edge of the sandstone was broken, since it was at the edge of the outcrop.

Figure 13. Footprints in Pottsville sandstone adjacent to Ott Finnell property near Berea, Kentucky. Shoe added for comparison. Over-all view shows several prints. Water was spilled over the outcrop to produce clarity of detail.

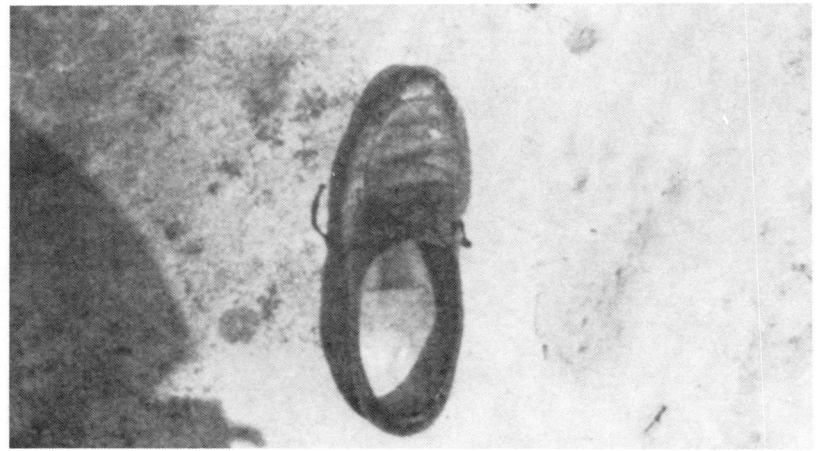

Figure 14. Footprint in Pottsville sandstone adjacent to Ott Finnell property near Berea, Kentucky.

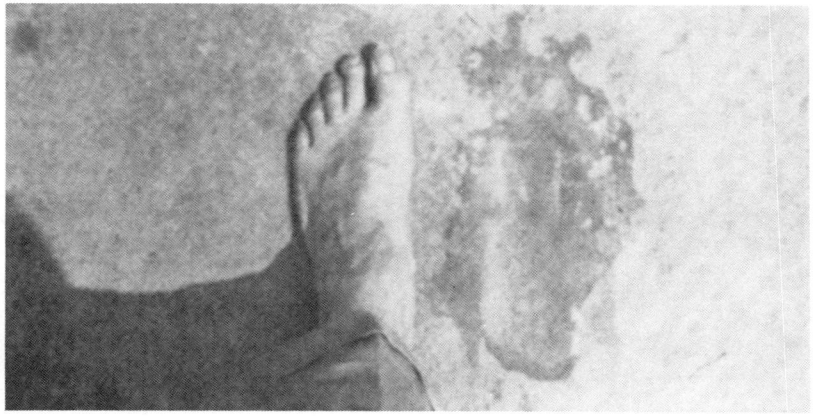

Figure 15. Footprint in Pottsville sandstone adjacent to Ott Finnell property near Berea, Kentucky. Human foot added for comparison.

A return to the site with Mr. Finnell, carrying a five gallon bucket of water to the site over rough areas, was worth the trouble. Spilling the water over the exposure, brought out items not seen before and clarified those that had been previously seen. A new set of

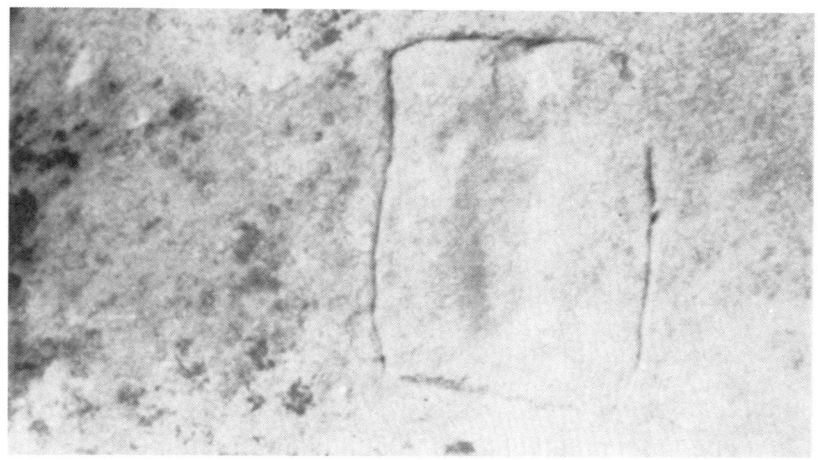

Figure 16. Footprint in Pottsville sandstone on Ott Finnell property near Berea, Kentucky. Evidence of vandalism is seen as someone attempted to remove this footprint.

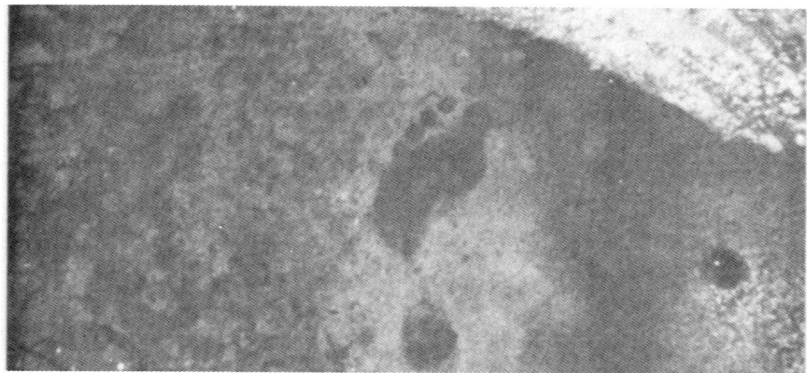

Figure 17. Photograph of author's wet footprint on rock outcrop for comparison.

photographs was taken of the prints and of the site in color and black and white.

To preserve tangible evidence of all prints remaining, plaster and water, as well as simple tools, were transported to the site. A successful procedure was found for making casts of all prints that remained in sufficient contrast. The prints were coated with detergent, plaster was dusted in, and then they were poured. These are now available.

Figures 13-18 show the footprints as photographed in 1964. Contrast in the photographs of the prints is poor because of the effects of weathering which have blurred the outlines of the prints. Evidence of vandalism is seen in the attempt to carve one footprint out (see Figure 16). For the purpose of establishing the sizes,

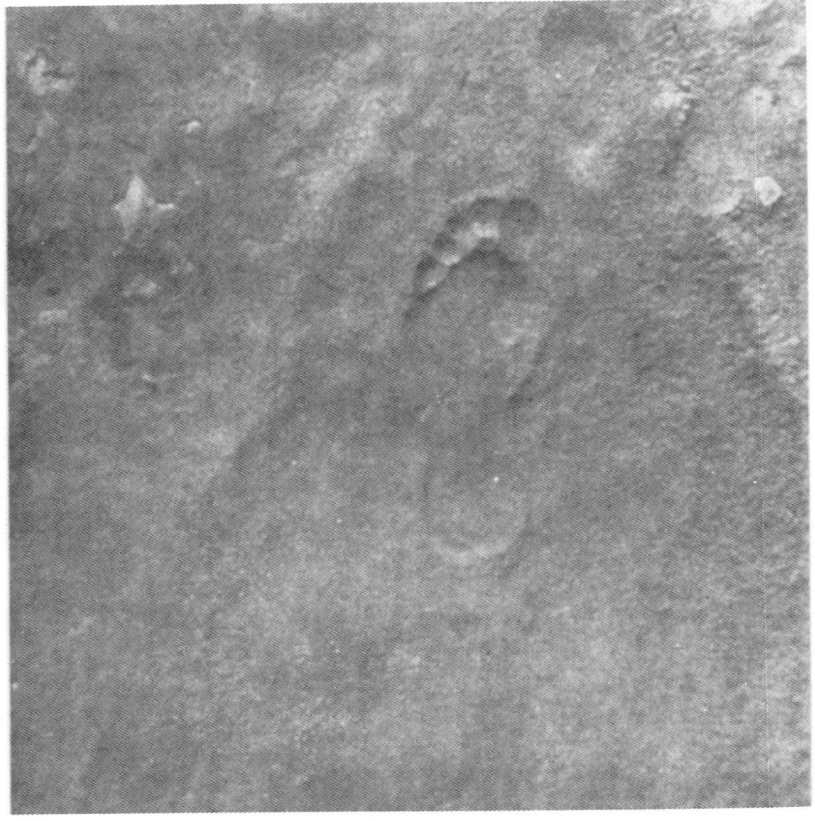

Figure 18. Photograph of author's footprint in beach sand for comparison.

either the author's foot or shoe are shown alongside the prints. Also for the sake of comparisons, I photographed my wet footprint on the outcrop as well as my footprint in beach sand (see Figures 17 and 18).

Research Report of Kentucky Prints

Correspondence with Dr. Burroughs revealed that he had carried out a unique investigation. He fitted a low power microscope with an aperture which would limit the field to a relatively small area, so that a count could be made of the grains of sand in a given area on the surface of the rock. This microscope was then set up at the footprint site. This procedure revealed a consistently greater number of grains in the soles of the prints than in the adjacent rock, which would seem to indicate that there had been compression, as for instance from the weight of an individual standing in place.

Dr. Burroughs considered these to be actual prints, based on his standgrain comparison technique. Two physicians of Berea, Drs. Baker and Cornelius, also studied the grains and reported, "the sand grains in the bottoms of the prints were much more closely packed than those in the slopes, and those in the slopes were more closely packed than those in the rocks an inch from the margins of the prints, or at any other point."[7] Dr. Burroughs referred to the prints in one article as being formed by *Phenanthropus mirabilis*,[8] organism unknown.

An original report[9] gave the following information: The Kentucky tracks are definitely not the tracks of amphibians. They were made by creatures that walked on their two hind legs and had feet strikingly like human beings who had never worn shoes. The kind of creautres that made the tracks has not been determined. Mr. Charles Gilmore of the Smithsonian Institution entered into correspondence with Dr. Burroughs on the matter. Strangely enough, Mr. Gilmore never really questioned the authenticity of the prints, but neither did he ever go to the site to observe the prints for himself, nor did he ever report them in a Smithsonian Bulletin. Dr. Burroughs reported[8] on the find directly as follows,

The footprints are sunken into the horizontal surfaces of an outcrop of hard, massive gray sandstone on the O. Finnell farm. There are three pairs of tracks showing left and right footprints. The remaining distinct impressions are single tracks, the other foot in each case not having made an impression in the sand, or if an impression was made it was washed away or has been eroded since the sand became rock. In addition to the complete footprints, parts of footprints were found. The tracks extend in various directions and bear no relation to each other, except for the left and right impressions of a pair of tracks. Each footprint has five toes and a distinct arch. The toes spread apart like those of a human being who have never worn shoes. The length of the foot from the heel to the end of the longest toe is nine and one-half inches though this length varies slightly in different tracks. The width across the ball of the foot is 4.1 inches while the width including the spread of the toes is about six inches. The foot curves back like a human foot to a human appearing heel.

The sand grains within the tracks are closer together than the sand grains of the rock just outside the tracks due to the pressure of the creatures' feet. Even the sand grains in the arch of one of the best preserved tracks are not as close together as in the heel of the same track, though closer together than the sand outside the track. This is because there was more pressure upon the heel than beneath the arch of the foot. In comparing the texture of the sandstone only the same kind of grains and combination of grains within and outside of the tracks are considered. The sandstone adjacent to many of the tracks is uprolled due to the damp, loose sand having been pushed up around the foot as the foot sank into the sand. The forward part of one track is covered by solid Pottsville sandstone only a few days or weeks younger than the sandstone in which is the track. Another track nearby is also partially covered by solid Pottsville sandstone of the Coal Age. One pair of tracks shows the left foot advanced relative to the right foot. The distance from the end of the heel of the right foot to the end of the heel of the left foot is eighteen inches. This indicates somewhat the length of legs and height of the creature that made these tracks. Thre are no indications of front feet although the rock is large enough to have recorded front feet if front feet had been used to move about. In the pair of footprints that show the left and right feet about parallel to each other, the distance between the feet is the same as that of a normal human being. Nowhere on this rock nor on another rock outcrop that also has numerous similar tracks upon its surface, is there any sign that these creatures had tails.

The *Science Newsletter* followed the original report by an article under the title, "Geology and Ethnology Disagree." In part the account[10] reads:

> So confident is Professor Burroughs that the tracks are real footprints that he has given the unknown animals a scientific name, *Phenanthropus mirabilis*. The name was suggested by Dr. Frank Thone, editor in biology of Science Service, with the concurrence of Mr. Gilmore. The first part of it translates as "looks human," and the second word simply means "remarkable."
>
> Dissent is registered by David I. Bushnell, Jr., Smithsonian Institution ethnologist. Mr. Bushnell said, in a statement issued to the press, that every print he examined was undoubtedly an Indian carving. A prehistoric tribe or tribes, he believes, attached to them some symbolic meaning.
>
> It is quite possible that the disagreement is more apparent than real. Unquestionably, many, perhaps most, of the footprint-like marks in the rocks over a wide stretch of country were carved by human sculptors. Their artificial nature is manifest at a glance, especially when they are found paired, arranged in even rows, and accompanied by other symbols such as circles and three-pronged figures like great bird tracks.
>
> It is quite as possible that other tracks are genuine footprints, especially when they are arranged quite at random, as the Berea tracks are, and where the prints vary greatly in size, as some of them do. It is this circumstance, in part, that has convinced Professor Burroughs that the Berea markings are not artificial.
>
> Dr. Alson Baker, a physician of Berea, recently wrote Science Service that he and Dr. A. F. Cornelius had made a critical examination of the tracks there, using a strong magnifier mounted on a tripod. He states:
>
>> We examined the arrangement of the sand grains in the deepest portions of the prints, with especial attention to the heels. The sand grains in the bottoms of the prints were much more closely packed than those in the slopes, and those in the slopes

were more closely packed than those in the rocks an inch from the margins of the prints, or at any other point.

Each member of the party certified and checked these findings and we all agree that the imprints were made by pressure when the sand was soft and wet.

The fact that the sand grains in the bottoms and slopes of the imprints are of exactly the same kind as those in all other parts of the rock surface examined, seems to prove conclusively that the closer arrangement observed was not due to any possible drifting in of extraneous material.

Certainly these prints should not be ignored or hidden, but should be objectively studied and reported. A creationist has the obligation to consider them as rigorously as he expects an evolutionary paleontologist to consider his fossil finds, not making them say anything further than the facts indicate. Extreme care must be taken in positively identifying the maker of a print.

At the present time I am undecided as to whether the prints are carvings or made by organisms walking. The following points would seem to favor the carving theory:

1. the great variability of the prints, namely three distinct forms.
2. the absence at present of any consistent stride pattern. This may have existed at an earlier date, before some of the prints were completely weathered away.
3. the similarity between Figure 14 and some of the Washington State Park prints from the St. Louis area.

On the other hand, the sand grain analysis would seem to support the idea that the prints were made by organisms standing or walking. In any case, it would be a mistake to make absolute statements as to the humanity of the makers of the tracks. Certainly the presence of the overburden (6 to 10 in.) on top of the prints does suggest a considerable time passage between production of the prints and their discovery. Before making a definite statement on the authenticity of the footprints, I feel the need for further study, particularly with respect to the sand grain count.

Checking all Pottsville sandstone outcrops is a monumental task, far beyond the work of a little better than a week. Several years would be needed for an exhaustive search. Dr. Burroughs said there were no other prints that he regarded as authentic anywhere in the state of Kentucky. This raises doubt as to the value of such a search.

Mr. Finnell had heard of some in the next county towards Livingston, Kentucky. Search was made for these. After a number of misdirections and wrong information, a rock was located nine miles beyond Three Links, Kentucky. This was a rock on a slope, with the surface at an angle of about 45°. On this rock are the prints of a bear(?) along with some other marks. This rock was in the center of a logging operation carried on by the land owner, Mr. Joe Daugherty. Nothing was known by anyone of the history of the rock or its markings.

I suspect that the rock has slid down from its original location further up the slope. It is sandstone, presumably Pottsville. Photos of the rock are now on file. The clearing was being done with mule and human labor, and although the owner was polite, there was an understandable impatience with the interruption of his work. It might be worthwhile to make a return trip and get plaster casts, as well as use Dr. Burroughs' technique for determining whether the mark is carved or actually an imprint in unconsolidated sediments.

It is difficult to get information from the natives of the area in an endeavor to track down some possible clues. The present generation seems to know nothing of these or any other prints, and cares less. Tracing and checking are also made difficult because ownership of the land has changed a number of times, and no one remembers readily who now owns a given farm or plot of land. Another complicating factor is that in many cases what was farm land fifty years ago, has now reverted to forest to an almost unbelieveable extent. All of this adds to the difficulty and magnitude of the task. Much of the area is being taken over by the government as part of the Cumberland National Forest.

A "lead" to the Pineville Mountain and Cumberland Gap area proved a false alarm. But in the latter area it was ascertained that a footprint had been found in Mammoth Cave (see Figure 19). A few days were spent in that area. It was hoped that additional information could be gleaned as to the survival of footprints over

Figure 19. Footprint in hardened mud floor, Mammoth Cave, Kentucky. The remains of "Lost John" (an individual believed to be contemporaneous with the maker of this print) were dated at 2470 B.C. by C-14 analysis.

long periods of time. Due to tremendous numbers of visitors, the author could not be taken to the site of the footprint in Mammoth Cave. However, through the courtesy of Chief Naturalist George Olin, files of prints were made available and permission was given to make copies of the prints; and, copies were made of prints of the Indian, Lost John, who was believed to have been contemporaneous with the makers.

A footprint can be clearly seen in the hardened mud of the cave floor as can be noted from the accompanying photo (see Figure 19). The maker of the print, and Lost John as well, penetrated great distances into the cave looking for gypsum. But no one knows why they were looking for it, or what they did with the gypsum when they found it. Lost John apparently lost his life when a block of the wall came down on him while he was underneath chipping gypsum. Lost John is only on display in the depth of the cave. Lost John has been dated by C-14 methods at 2470 B.C.

Mr. Olin also introduced me to Dr. Watson of the Cave Research Foundation. Representatives of this group were at work in the cave system under Flint Ridge in the Park adjoining Mammoth. The Cave Research Foundation had also found footprints both in dust as well as in mud, both barefoot as well as shod. These were located some 2½ to 3 miles into the cave. These prints were about as far into the cave as is the print in Mammoth Cave. Dr. Watson offered to take me down to the prints, but he also indicated that it would be dangerous and strenuous, so I politely declined, since for my purposes there was nothing to be gained by direct observation.

Postscript

As a postscript I would draw the attention of interested readers to the October-November, 1970 issue of *National Wildlife*. The pertinent article[11] is entitled "On the Trail of Bigfoot." In October 1967, Roger Patterson had encountered a large bipedal creature

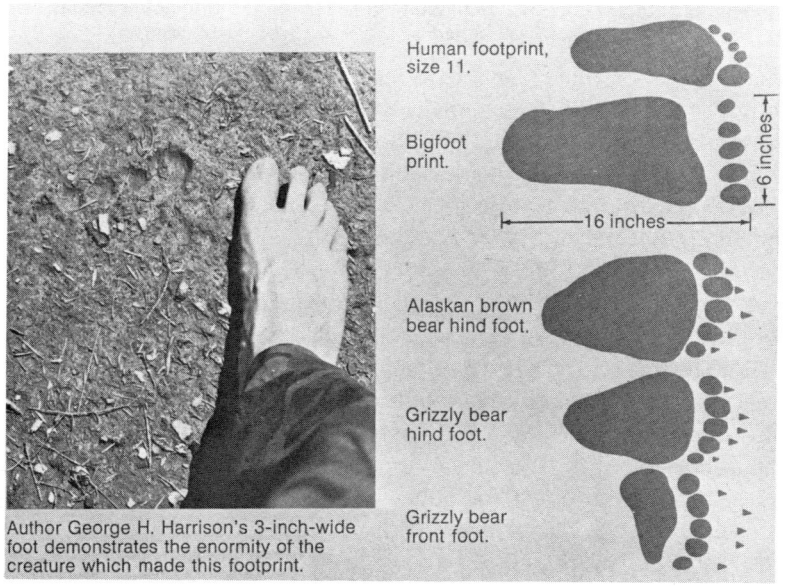

Figure 20. Impressions of Bigfoot. These photographs with accompanying captions are reproduced by permission from the article, "On the Trail of Bigfoot," by George H. Harrison, October-November issue of National Wildlife, 1970.

walking through the woods near Buff Creek, in the wilderness of northern California. His horse threw him as he was taking pictures but he did manage to shoot a few 8 mm frames of the creature. These few feet of film showed the outline of a large hairy anthropoid, about seven feet tall and weighing about 400 pounds. The idea of any creature like that loose in the California woods seemed so farfetched that Patterson was accused of fakery. He submitted to a lie detector test, which convinced the operators he was not lying. (Another article with "shots" from the film appeared in *National Wildlife,* April-May, 1968.)

In June, 1970, George H. Harrison, managing editor of *National Wildlife,* joined an expedition to the Buff Creek region, led by Robert W. Morgan of Miami, Florida. Probably the most impressive evidence they encountered was the series of tracks, ten in number that appeared fairly fresh. They were sixteen inches in length and eight inches in width (see Figure 20).

Accompanying the tracks was some strange fecal material. The latter was described by a biologist as being "not cow or elk. It has to be bear, or what we are looking for." The results of the continuing search for the American "abominable snowman," "yetti" or "big foot" will be awaited with considerable interest. Harrison indicated that before the trip he was a 50% "believer" and after the expedition he became 85% "believer." Obviously, if "big foot" is really identified, we might have a descendant of the originator of the giant footprints reported in Texas.

REFERENCES

1. Howel Williams, 1952. Geologic observations on the ancient human footprints near Managua, Nicaragua, in *Contributions to American anthropology and history,* vol. II, no. 53, Carnegie Institution. See also *Science Newsletter,* June 14, 1941, p. 382.
2. Henry Schoolcraft, 1822, Communication, *American Journal of Science,* 5:223ff.
3. *American Encyclopedia,* 1778-1803, Supp. vol. 3:344.
4. *American Journal of Science,* 1838, vol. 33:398.
5. *American Journal of Science,* 1843, vol. 44:200, April.
6. *Science Newsletter,* 1958.
7. *Science Newsletter,* December 10, 1938.

8. *Berea Alumnus,* November, 1938, pp. 46-47, "Human-like Footprints, 250 Million Years Ago."
9. *Ibid.,* pp. 46-47.
10. *Science Newsletter,* December 10, 1938.
11. George H. Harrison, 1970, On the trail of Bigfoot, *National Wildlife,* 8(6):4ff., October-November.

VIII

PALEOECOLOGY AND THE FLOOD

HAROLD W. CLARK*

History of Uniformitarianism

Modern uniformitarianism was introduced by James Hutton to the Royal Society in Edinburgh in 1785. He imagined one cycle after another, and concluded that "the result . . . of our present inquiry is, that we find no vestige of a beginning—no prospect of and end."[1]

Hutton's presentation was so difficult to follow that little attention was paid to it until John Playfair[2] published his commentary on it in 1802. He argued against a "debacle," as the Flood was generally called in those days, and proposed a purely uniformitarian theory. This idea was developed further by Charles Lyell, who in 1830 published the first textbook of geology.[3]

Lyell's *Principles of Geology* became very popular, going through several editions and being used as a text in colleges in England and America for over 50 years. It was written for the obvious purpose of establishing the uniformitarian theory of geology. Today Lyell's interpretation is almost universally accepted in scientific circles and taught in colleges and universities throughout the world.

Yet uniformitarianism was not accepted without some opposition. When Adam Sedgwick retired from the presidency of the British Geological Society, he argued[4] that the distribution of life in the ancient seas must have been similar to that of modern seas. He opposed the uniformitarian view put forward by Lyell.

---

*Harold W. Clark holds an M.A. degree in zoology. He is retired from the post of head, Department of Biology, Pacific Union College, Angwin, California. He holds an honorary degree of Doctor of Science.

The theory of regular succession of faunas and floras throughout long ages was attacked by Herbert Spencer[5] in 1859. He challenged the current "onion-coat" theory, as he called it, and argued that the fossil zones in the ancient world were distributed as they are today. Of course we must not gain the idea that Spencer was a creationist, for he was not, but he did see the flaws in the growing uniformitarianism.

These criticisms of the uniformitarianism seem to have had little effect, but they did stimulate the thinking of one young inquiring mind. In 1906, George McCready Price took up the idea under the same title used by Spencer, *Illogical Geology*.[6] Price emphasized the lack of logic in uniformitarianism, and continued to do so in his later publications. For example, we read: "How simple this problem becomes, how natural the whole phenomenon appears, when we look upon the geological series as only old-time taxonomic series of a complete world all living contemporaneously."[7] And, "They, [the geological formations] simply represent a taxonomic or classification series of the ancient world."[8]

As Price's contention became known worldwide, other scientific men who believed the Genesis record of the Flood to be that of a universal catastrophe became more and more interested in diluvial interpretation. They began to realize that stratigraphic geology should not be interpreted in terms of geological ages. The Genesis Flood interpretation may offer an explanation that encompasses all the valid data, but explains stratigraphy in terms of diluvialism.

Since Price wrote these words, some diluvialists have given considerable study to the problem of paleoecology. Several examples will be used and facts will be explained in terms of what may be called zoological provinces, life zones, habitats, or associations.

Example One: The Complex Life of the Paleozoic

Inasmuch as these rocks are at the bottom of the geological sequence, it would be expected, if evolution were true, that their fossils would be simple. But such is not the case.

The complexity of Cambrian life gives great perplexity to the paleontologists. In all of North America more than 1200 kinds of animals are found in the Cambrian strata, representing all the major phyla except the vertebrates. And they are not simple, either, but are so complex as members of their phyla found in the higher strata.

One of the most interesting of all Cambrian formations is the Burgess shale near Field, British Columbia. This formation contains the remains of many soft-bodied animals flattened like flowers in a press, and perfectly preserved. As many as 130 species have been described from a bed only a few feet thick.

In the *Olenellus* fauna, named after a trilobite, we find, distributed world wide, animals such as sponges, jellyfish, corals, starfishes, worms, brachipods, bivalves, and trilobites. How this elaborate assemblage of animals could appear so suddenly, without any evidence of ancestors in the Precambrian rocks, is a mystery.

The Ordovician strata are much like the Cambrian, with graptolites, corals, crinoids, bryozoa, and clams either new or in greatly increased numbers. In the Silurian Niagaran formation are found reefs extending from the Arctic to southern Illinois, and as far east as the mouth of the St. Lawrence River. Their average size is about one-half mile across. They are built up of corals, sponges, crinoids, bryozoans, trilobites, cystoids, and blastoids. Most of Alberta's oil comes from reefs with typical Devonian fossils.

Another peculiar feature of the lower Paleozoic strata is the occurrence in many localities of black shales. Many geologists believe them to have been formed from ancient soils. Another suggestion that has been made is that the Cambrian and Ordovician black shales appear to be similar to the black muds now being formed in depressions in the North Sea, Baltic, and other protected areas in the oceans, where fine sediments, mostly silts and clays, are known to be accumulating in basins and troughs where there is not sufficient current to disturb them.

When we take all these facts into consideration, and look at the lower Paleozoic rocks as a whole—Cambrian, Ordovician, Silurian, Devonian, and Mississippian—we can readily see how they could have been formed in deep, quiet waters, doubtless some of them before the Flood. Then when the Flood waters did begin their work, they quickly buried these deep-sea forms of life in mud and silt. Here is an example of rocks that can be explained, not by long ages of gradually accumulating sediments, but by the burial of the original habitats before and during the Flood.

Example Two: Paleozoic Exterminations

In the Cambrian rocks the trilobites are the dominant fossils. They are abundant in the lower Paleozoic, but none are known above the Permian, and even there only three species occur. Why did they "die out"? Geologic formations contain no clue to the puzzle. It is reasonable to consider these rocks as representing an ancient habitat rather than a time-span of millions of years.

The ammonites, a peculiar form of coiled mollusk, are first seen in the Pennsylvanian rocks, according to some authorities. However, their history is very peculiar. So-called "primitive" types are represented in the Devonian and Mississippian.

Then when ammonites appear in great abundance in the Permian rocks, paleontologists are puzzled because so few of the Permian species persist. New families and a great abundance of species within them are present in Triassic rocks.

Again, only a few of these persist into the Jurassic and Cretaceous, but there are hordes of new species in these rocks. In the Cretaceous many peculiar variations in shape of the coiled shells may be seen. There are none of them in the Cenozoic rocks.

This peculiar distributional pattern, while it is perplexing to evolutionists, is quite easy to explain if we understand these different groups to be simply natural ecological groups at different levels in the ancient seas, which were buried by the rising waters of the Flood.

Another fascinating problem concerns the Paleozoic fishes. Several types existed which are entirely unknown today, such as the ostracoderms or armored fishes.

The ostracoderms are abundant in Silurian and Devonian rocks. They were somewhat similar to the modern cyclostomes, or lampreys. They had no limbs, or very small ones. Their armor consisted of bony plates, especially heavy on the front of the body.

They had no jaws, and are considered to have been filter-feeders or mud-grubbers. The placoderms were much like them in appearance, though larger.

Other fishes, sharks and bony fishes, or teleosts, are found in the rocks all the way from the Devonian upwards. So abundant are they and the armored fishes in the Devonian rocks that this system has been called the "age of fishes." But the peculiar fact is that whereas the armored fishes all became extinct in the Paleozoic, the sharks and teleosts continue in the higher strata all the way up to the modern. Why should this be?

It is quite easy to imagine that the heavily armored, sluggish bottom-feeders or mud-grubbers would be overwhelmed and buried in muddy sediments, while the active fishes like the sharks and teleosts could escape, for the most part, and survive to a certain degree throughout the whole surge of Flood waters. I say "for the most part" because sharks and teleosts certainly did not escape completely. Many of their remains are found in all the stratigraphic column from the Devonian up. But the relation between sharks and teleosts on the one hand, and the armored fishes on the other, is exactly what we would expect from the Flood theory of geology.

Example Three: Burial of the Coal Forests

Popular texts on geology describe the coal beds as having been formed in great bogs, where ferns and scale-trees and many other forms of vegetation fell and were buried in the mud of the bog. But the bog theory has many inconsistencies, and it is much easier to understand the coal beds as having originated in an entirely different manner by Flood waters.

In many coal regions from 50 to 100 alternating beds of shale and silt occur between the coal beds. This would have required uplift and depression over and over again across areas of thousands of square miles in extent during millions of years. Such a phenomenon is extremely difficult to comprehend, and does not correlate with other evidences of past geological action. Furthermore, if such alterations had occurred, the whole region should show a series of sea-beaches repeatedly; yet there is no such evidence.

Another peculiar fact about the "coal age" is that it is assumed to have lasted for about 50,000,000 years, and yet during all that time, while there were quite significant differences in vegetation types, the plants in the upper beds show no changes that could be attributed to evolutionary progression.

The coal beds of Europe and America are not uniform in composition, but show differences in species composition that geologists atribute to shifting shore lines. These differences can be explained just as readily as changes in composition due to back and forth wave action. And also there are some "upland" species mixed with the "lowland" species—again an evidence of violent water action.

In the Appalachian region of North America the rocks show a very striking phenomenon. Streams rushing down from the eastern highlands, now non-existent, deposited a succession of shales, sandstones, and other materials in which much vegetation was included, but little marine material. A vast series of deltas was formed, reaching the whole length of the Appalachians, from as far down as the Devonian rocks up through the Pennsylvanian.

Coal beds in Nova Scotia and New Brunswick, where the Pennsylvanian rocks are 13,000 feet thick, are described as having been deposited in great basins between the mountains. The entire group is non-marine.

Yet in other coal regions there is a mixture of land and sea types. Shellfish of various kinds are abundant. Other marine invertebrates such as starfish form some of the most abundant marine deposits. This indicates that the sea waters were involved in forming the Pennsylvanian rocks.

All in all the Flood theory affords the most satisfactory explanation for the formation of the coal beds. It brings into reasonable correlation such apparently contradictory evidences as badly macerated material in some beds and finely preserved plant remains in others, and a mixture of marine and land forms. Wave after wave dashing on the shores would tear away the earth and carry off great masses of trees and other vegetation to be buried in layers of sand and mud. The alternation of coal with sandstone and shale and silt would be the natural result of these wave actions.

Example four: Death of the Dinosaurs

Reptiles present one of the most outstanding groups of ancient times, with great variety of types. When the term *dinosaur* is used, most people think of huge reptiles, such as carnivorous and herbivorous species, flying reptiles, fish-like reptiles, etc. Some were adapted to open plains, others to marshes and ponds and lakes. Dinosaurs were only one among many types.

In order to understand the relation between the dinosaurs and the environmental conditions, we must examine fossil botany.[9] We find that the plant life of the Triassic was similar to that of the Pennsylvanian, although the large trees do not seem to have been so abundant. It is suggested that the environment consisted of savanas at low altitudes, with valleys and swamps that harbored ferns and horsetails.

When we come to the Jurassic, where the dinosaurs are the most abundant, we find a different situation. The seed ferns persist, and so do many other ferns. But new assemblages of trees are evident, such as cycads, ginkgos, and conifers. *Araucaria* is the most prominent conifer.

The vegetation apparently consisted of widespread forests of the humid lowlands, with plants growing in and adjacent to the swamps. Above these were more or less open woodlands and plains, where the *Araucarias* and cycads grew. Ocean waters must not have been far away, for marine faunas are common. It was in this kind of surrounding that dinosaurs appear to have thrived.

Why did the luxurious "forest" growth of the Pennsylvanian vanish from the earth? And again, why did the Middle Mesozoic so quickly become replaced by modern types? Why did the dinosaurs vanish?

"The most dramatic and in many respects the most puzzling event in the history of life on the earth," says an eminent authority, was their sudden disappearance.[10] The simultaneous extinction of this great assemblage of giant forms, says the geologist Carl Dunbar,[11] is hard to explain. Edwin Colbert tells us that while they were abundant in Mesozoic "times," not one of them has ever been found in post-Cretaceous rocks. This is a big question, he declares, for which no satisfactory answer has ever been proposed.[12]

The lowlands of the earth were clothed in the peculiar vegetation which is now preserved in the coal deposits. Remains of amphibians are found among these beds, which naturally belong in the damp lowlands. There are few reptiles as might be expected. But as soon as we get into the Mesozoic rocks, particularly the Jurassic and Cretaceous, there is a great array of reptiles. Then in the Cenozoic the great reptiles have disappeared.

Why did the dinosaurs "appear" so suddenly and "disappear" so abruptly? It might be more meaningful if we asked why they disappeared at all. Why did dinosaurs not persist right on into the Cenozoic?

From all we can learn, the upper part of the Cretaceous beds have a very modern-looking assemblage of plants. There are magnolia, fir, poplar, beech, maple, oak, walnut, sequoia, and many shrubs. Grass and angiosperms are abundant. These continue throughout the whole sequence of the Tertiary. Why could the dinosaurs not have continued to live on, and to leave their remains in the rocks of the Tertiary if these represent valid time-sequences?

From the standpoint of Flood geology, the appearance of the dinosaurs in the rocks marks the rise of the Flood waters beginning to engulf their habitats. The disappearance of dinosaurs marks their extinction by catastrophic action. Perhaps this explanation appears to be too simple, but why invoke complicated ages of evolutionary progress and mysterious disappearance when the simple Flood interpretation will suffice?

In this discussion I have suggested that the Flood ended around the Cretaceous or early Tertiary. I realize that some workers think it ran clear up to the Pleistocene, while others feel that it ceased earlier, even as far back as the Permian rocks.

The Permian tectonics, however, are not great enough. Running the post-Flood period as far back as the beginning of the Mesozoic deposits would invoke too much violent action after the Flood.

In fact, the greatest of all worldwide upheavals, those of the American cordilleras, the Alps, and the Himalayas, came around the close of the Cretaceous and the early Tertiary. For this reason, I place the death of the dinosaurs there at the closing paroxysms of the Flood, in connection with these earth-shaking movements.

Further evidence for this view may be seen in the transition of climate between the beginning of the Teritary and its end. In the plant and animal life, Miocene and Pliocene deposits give evidence of being post-Flood. The whole subject is too complicated to consider fully here, but I have discussed it at quite some length in a recent treatise on the Flood.[13]

Example Five: The "Age of Mammals"

Mammals have given diluvialists much difficulty. Why, it has been asked, should mammals be found only in the Teritary rocks, if there was no succession of life throughout geological ages? Why, on the Flood theory of geology, should there be no mammals down in the Mesozoic, for example, or even in the Pennsylvanian?

It is easy to understand why mammals are not found in Pennsylvanian rocks, for these rocks show a type of environment that would not be suitable for them. In fact, about the only vertebrates found in these rocks are fishes and amphibians, and a few small reptiles. The presence of amphibia correlated with the general belief that the Pennsylvanian "coal forests" were dense, damp regions quite unlikely to shelter mammals.

But why should we not find mammals among the dinosaur remains in Jurassic and Cretaceous rocks? We do, and while it is true that the greater number of mammals are found in Cenozoic rocks, those found in Mesozoic rocks are significant, as we shall see.

The Rhaetic formation in western Europe, which is on the borderline between Triassic and Jurassic, has a few teeth of mammals in the muds and sands. In America similar remains are found up through the Jurassic, particularly in the Morrison formation, but they are small and "primitive" in structure. Simpson supplied important information on this problem.[14] In the lower Cretaceous only teeth and fragments of teeth of mammals have been discovered, but in the upper Cretaceous some marsupials and insectivores are found, such as shrews and moles.

Here the fact stands out that all the Mesozoic mammals are "primitive," or generalized. The marsupials are sluggish and stupid, and the shrews and moles are burrowing types or types that frequent low spots among masses of vegetation. They would not be able to escape the rising waters. On the other hand, the larger animals could walk away from the flooding and escape to the last.

Dunbar speaks[15] of the Cretaceous as the "time of the great dying." This has been described by some geologists as the last great overwash of oceans over the land. But if this is so, where were the mammals? We must remember that the Genesis record gives 40 days before the highest lands were covered. There was ample time for mass migration of intelligent types.

Thus it is possible that the mammals migrated upward until eventually they were overwhelmed by the waters. Their presence in the Tertiary rocks, therefore, is best viewed as resulting from their migration and final destruction rather than burial in their natural habitats.

Is there a trend toward modern types in the later Tertiary? It appears so, but these rocks are so interrupted in their distribution that it is difficult to interpret their sequential arrangement.

Sediments containing the last remnants of the antediluvian life might also contain bones of the first animals to move into the region after the Flood. There is evidence of a period of great violence for a long time after the Flood, and some of the rapidly changing deposits might easily have received recycled fossils as well as new material from the living animals.

Conclusion

In 1946 I suggested that we might interpret the fossil sequences in terms of ecological zonation rather than long ages of evolution. Then in *Fossils, Flood, and Fire,* a whole chapter was devoted to the subject. "The concept is simple, in fact so simple in its primary aspects that some may find it difficult to grasp. But its very simplicity makes it all the more reasonable. It is merely a question of *area* rather than *time*."[16]

REFERENCES

1. J. Hutton, 1785, Theory of the earth, *Transactions of the Royal Society of Edinburgh*, 1:209-314.
2. J. Playfair, 1802, Illustrations of the Huttonian theory, Edinburgh.
3. C. Lyell, 1830, Principles of geology (1938 edition by John Murray, London).
4. A. Sedgwick, 1831, Address to the geological society, *Proceedings of the Geological Society of London*, 1(20):281-315.
5. H. Spencer, 1859, Illogical geology, *Universal Review*, July.
6. George M. Price, 1906, Illogical geology, Modern Heretic Co., Los Angeles.
7. George M. Price, 1913, Fundamentals of geology, Pacific Press, Mountain View, Calif., p. 37.
8. George M. Price, 1923, The new geology, Pacific Press, Mountain View, Calif., p. 614.
9. Encyclopedia Britannica, 1966, vol. 17, pp. 97-116; article on paleobotany.
10. H. F. Osborn, 1910, The age of mammals, Macmillan, New York, p. 98.
11. C. Dunbar, 1966, Historical geology, Wiley, New York, p. 348.
12. E. H. Colbert, 1962, Dinosaurs, Hutchinson, London, pp. 249-251.
13. H. W. Clark, 1968, Fossils, flood, and fire, Outdoor Pictures, Anacortes, Washington.
14. G. G. Simpson, 1929, American Mesozoic mammals, Peabody Museum, Yale University Memoirs, vol. 3, Part 1, pp. 1-235.
15. Dunbar, *op. cit.*
16. Clark, *op. cit.*, p. 60.

IX

THE CYCLICAL BLACK SHALES

WALTER G. PETERS*

Introduction

Several Pennsylvania black shales were studied and used as the basis of a thesis submitted in partial fulfillment of the requirements for a degree of Master of Science in Education to the Geology Department and Graduate School of Northern Illinois University, DeKalb, Illinois. The research was initiated during the fall of 1968, and for purposes of the thesis was completed during the fall of 1969 and presented in 1970.[1] Since that time, all the X-Ray negatives (radiographs), samples, and notes have been rechecked and updated into a manuscript entitled, "Challenge of Black Shale Radiography."

The most significant result of the study was the establishment of the cyclical nature of black shale sedimentation. Other important observations were the sudden change from land to sea or marine-type fossils; the black-gray shale laminations indicating short-period (time duration) sediment changes; the occurrence of possible freshwater algae at the bottom and the top of the shale member; the proposed presence of soft-bodied worm-like Onychophores in Pennsylvanian rock layers; the twofold use of the X-Ray negative (radiograph) technique; and the proposal of a new "species" of conodont (small, still-puzzling toothed fossil elements).

Material and Methods

The shale studied in detail was hard, compact, sheety (fissile),

---

*Walter G. Peters, M.S.Ed. in geology, is an educator and director of the Lutheran Research Forum, 30 W. Clarendon Dr., Round Lake Beach, Ill. 60073.

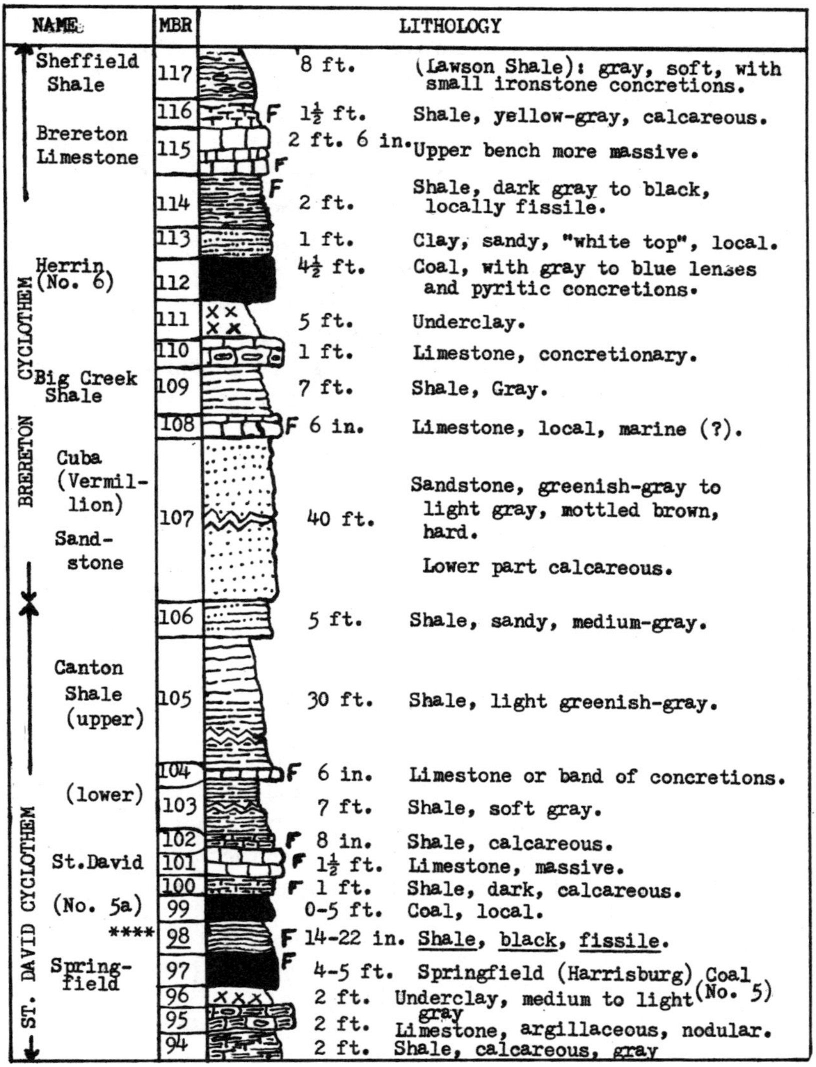

NAME	MBR	LITHOLOGY		
Sheffield Shale	117		8 ft.	(Lawson Shale): gray, soft, with small ironstone concretions.
Brereton Limestone	116	F	1½ ft.	Shale, yellow-gray, calcareous.
	115		2 ft. 6 in.	Upper bench more massive.
	114	F	2 ft.	Shale, dark gray to black, locally fissile.
	113		1 ft.	Clay, sandy, "white top", local.
Herrin (No. 6)	112		4½ ft.	Coal, with gray to blue lenses and pyritic concretions.
	111		5 ft.	Underclay.
	110		1 ft.	Limestone, concretionary.
Big Creek Shale	109		7 ft.	Shale, Gray.
	108	F	6 in.	Limestone, local, marine (?).
Cuba (Vermillion) Sandstone	107		40 ft.	Sandstone, greenish-gray to light gray, mottled brown, hard. Lower part calcareous.
	106		5 ft.	Shale, sandy, medium-gray.
Canton Shale (upper)	105		30 ft.	Shale, light greenish-gray.
(lower)	104	F	6 in.	Limestone or band of concretions.
	103		7 ft.	Shale, soft gray.
St. David	102	F	8 in.	Shale, calcareous.
	101	F	1½ ft.	Limestone, massive.
(No. 5a)	100	F	1 ft.	Shale, dark, calcareous.
	99		0-5 ft.	Coal, local.
	98	F	14-22 in.	Shale, black, fissile.
Springfield	97	F	4-5 ft.	Springfield (Harrisburg) Coal (No. 5)
	96		2 ft.	Underclay, medium to light gray
	95		2 ft.	Limestone, argillaceous, nodular.
	94		2 ft.	Shale, calcareous, gray

(Brereton Cyclothem spans members 108–117; St. David Cyclothem spans members 94–107.)

Figure 1. Generalized stratigraphic sequence of the St. David and Brereton Cyclothems in western Illinois. F: fossiliferous. Adapted from Wanless (1958, pp. 11, 12) and Kosanke, et al. (1960, pp. 65, 66).

highly carbonized, and very dark gray to black in color. Most of the samples were obtained in Fulton County, in west-central Illinois. This shale (*Member 98* of Wanless)[2] directly overlies a widely mined coal seam, the Springfield or Harrisburg (No. 5) Coal (see Figure 1). It is thought to be Unit No. 8 of the St. David Cyclothem, correlated with the middle section of the Carbondale Group (Illinois nomenclature) and with the middle-late Desmoinesian Stage of the Middle Pennsylvanian System (Period).

On a nationwide scale this shale is associated with the following deposits and geological "events": Washingtonville deposits of the Allegheny Group in the Appalachian region; Ouachita Mountain fault blocks and volcanic deposits; Uncompaghra Arch deposits from northeast Utah to north-central New Mexico; and deposits of the "uplift" of the Front Range of the Rocky Mountains (formation of some of the Hogbacks facing the Rockies) in central and northeastern Colorado and southeastern Wyoming, including the uplift of the Laramie Mountains.

Three basic techniques were used: (1) gross and macrophotography of shale at sample sites and of shale samples; (2) examination of shale samples using stereoscopic and regular microscopes; and (3) microscopic examination and photography of images in X-Ray negatives (radiographs). A fourth technique (X-Ray diffraction) was used only once to determine the principal component of the distinctly granular gray lenses, that contrasted so sharply with the black shale matrix of the lowermost and topmost layers of our black shale, Member 98. Most of the photomicrographs were taken with a Carl Zeiss Automatic Photomicroscope in the University Geology Laboratory or through a Unitron Polarizing microscope Model MPS with a SLR camera.

With a good stereo-microscope one can frequently see a three-dimensional panoramic view of the shale matrix and its imbedded microfossils. If the radiograph can be cut and taped to a 3 x 4-inch section of plate glass, it can be rotated on the stage of a polarizing microscope without scratching the X-Ray negative (radiograph). With the polarizing microscope set at or near crossed nicols; the negative can then be rotated from a position of maximum inter-

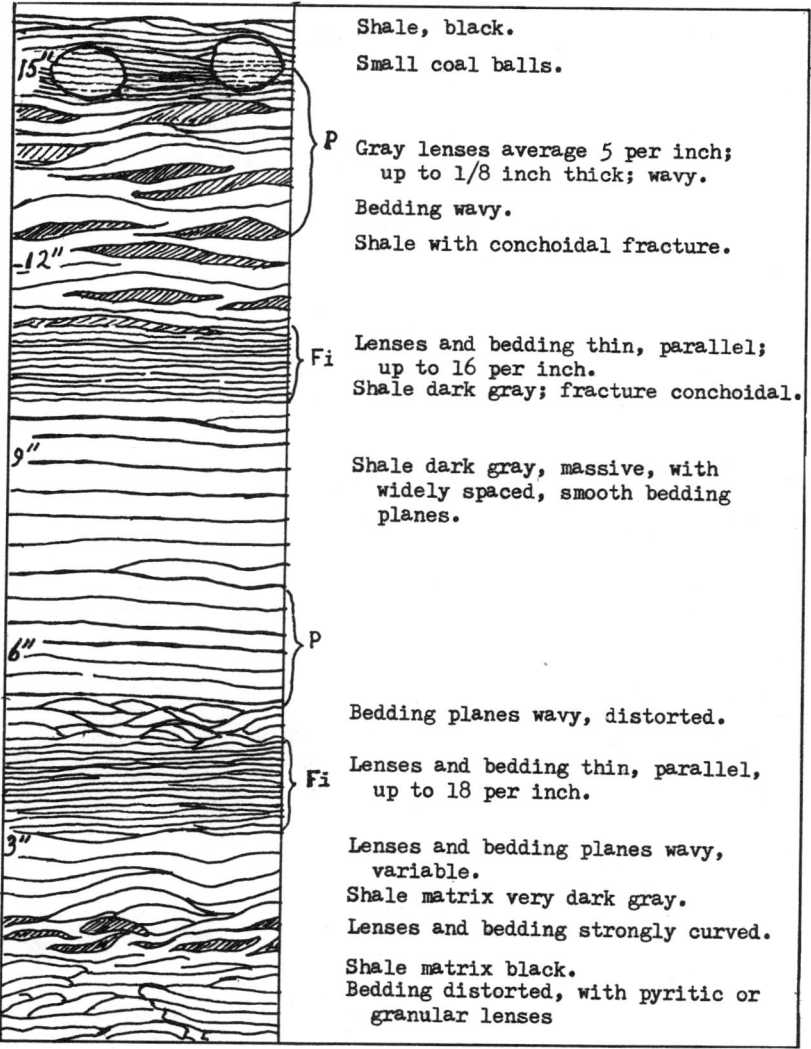

Figure 2. Composite section of black shale overlying the Springfield (No. 5) Coal, Fulton County, Illinois. P: Platform conodonts; Fi: Very fine lenses and bedding planes.

176 SPEAK TO THE EARTH

ference (brightest field) toward "extinction" (darkest field). As this is done, cellular and structural details of specimens otherwise overlooked are evident.

Massive pieces of shale about 15 to 16½ inches thick (Figure 2) and having a total area of about eight square feet were obtained *in situ* from open pits of operating coal mines. The total volume of these pieces was about 12 cubic feet. These were then chiseled into thin chips (individual samples) ⅛-inch to 1-inch thickness. Each chip was numbered and fossil elements were marked-off for more careful identification and tabulation.

Cyclical Deposition

Black shale, Member 98 of the St. David Cyclothem (Pennsylvanian System), exhibits a cyclical change in shale structure and

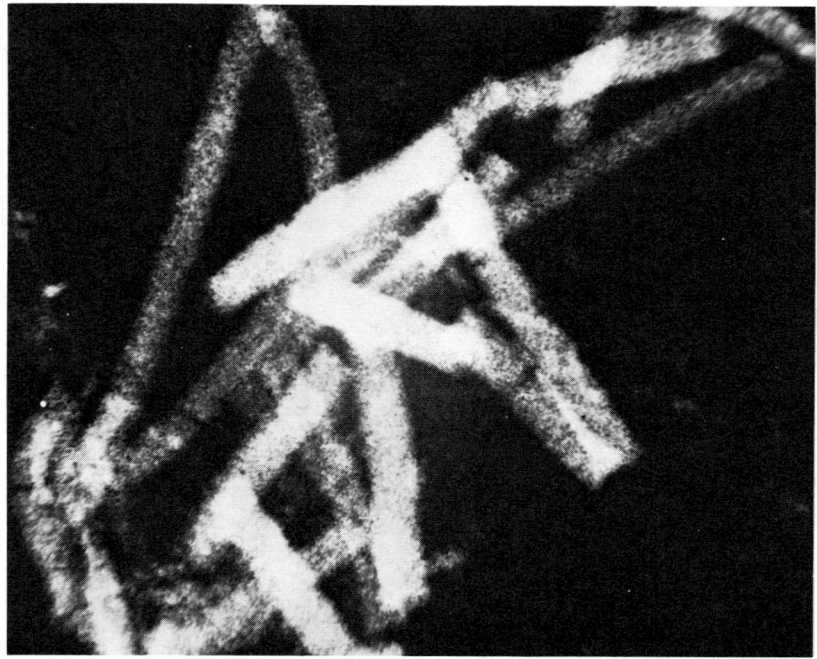

Figure 3. Cladophora. Sample 200A. 49 X magnification. Radioautograph.

THE CYCLICAL BLACK SHALES 177

fossil components. The bedding planes are most strongly distorted, the gray granular lenses are thickest and most prominent, and the black shale matrix is the darkest (blackest) at the lowermost and topmost levels (see Figure 2). The bedding planes are the straightest, the gray granular lenses and microlaminations are the thinnest, and the dark gray shale matrix layers are the thickest in the "massive" central section of the Member.

In two levels of the shale member, the 3-inch and the 10 to 11-inch levels, the lenses and bedding are thin, parallel, and up to 16 to 18 levels per inch. These microlaminations measure about 1/50 of an inch (0.5 mm) in thickness. The persistent alternation of the "black" and "gray" microlaminations strongly suggests alternating sources of sediment laden water.

This is further emphasized by the nearly complete segregation of "protozoan" foraminifera and conodonts into different layers throughout the vertical depth of the shale. Foraminifera are very small shelled protozoans and many species are used as index fossils. The exact affinities of the conodonts is still being debated. They are minute, phosphatic fossils that in general have either "toothed" bars or "blades" attached to a spoon shaped platform. The conodonts were found nearly exclusively in the black shale matrix, while the foraminifera were found nearly exclusively in the gray granular lenses, which were mainly composed of Wilkeite, an intermediate Apatite with the chemical formula $Ca_5[(P, S, Si, C)O_4]_3 \cdot OH$.

The time duration of deposition of these alternative layers, especially the microlaminations, must have been short, perhaps only hours or even minutes. This conclusion results from consideration of (1) the lack of any evidence of erosion in any of the layers, (2) lack of gradation in degree of compaction, (3) inclusions continuing through several to many layers or laminations (as with coal balls to be discussed later).

Other fossil changes as the shale increases in depth above the coal suggest a rapid change from a land environment to a marine and probably back to a nearly emerged land environment. Put another way, this might reflect a tidal sea advance and retreat. What appear to be freshwater algae (*Cladophora, Draparnaldia,* and

178 SPEAK TO THE EARTH

Oscillatoria) (see Figures 3, 4, and 5) and tissue of coal-forming trees are abundant in the lowest inch of the shale. These are mixed with marine(?) *Orbiculoidea* and *Lingula* (inarticulate brachiopod) shells.

One lens of *Orbiculoidea* shells measured nearly 1-inch in thickness, with up to 18 shells exposed per square inch of horizontal surface (sample 105.5/8). This thickness of *Orbiculoidea* shells

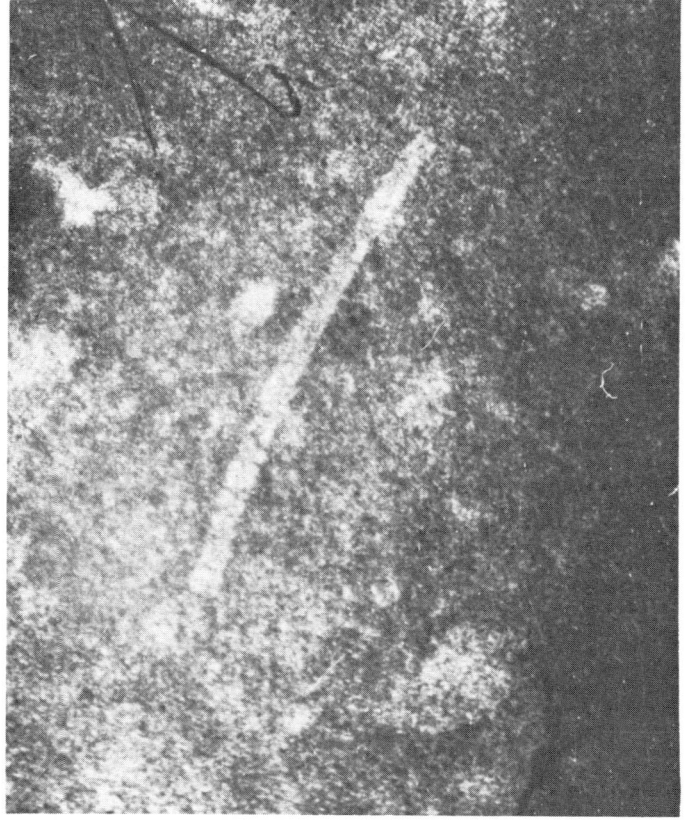

Figure 4. Drapardnaldia (?). Sample 105½. 70 X magnification. Radio-autograph.

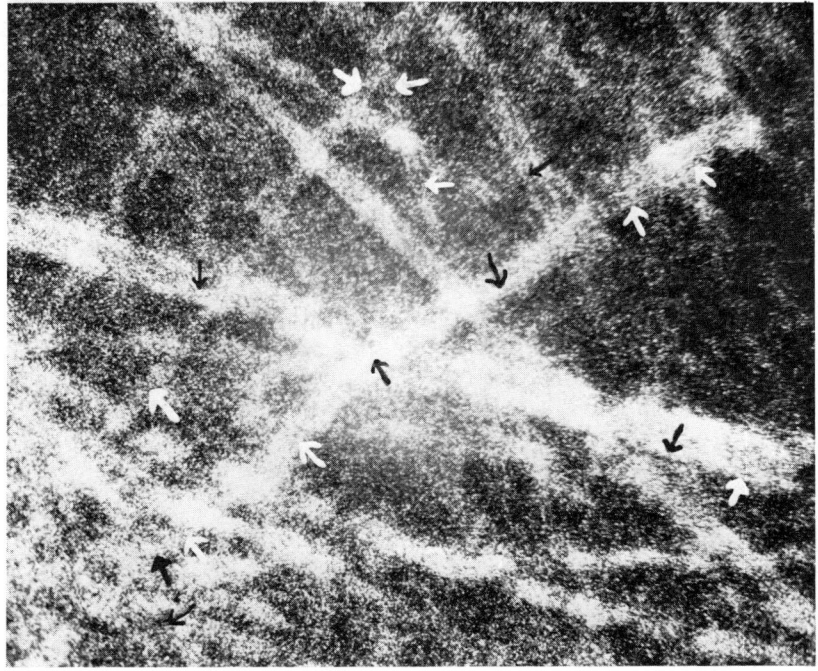

Figure 5. Possible Oscillatoria. Sample 107.1⅝. (165 X) Radioautograph.

closely packed into such a lens strongly suggests rapid transport of the shells to the burial spot (allochthanous deposition) (see Figure 6). Rapid burial is also suggested by the fine state of preservation in which the shells are found, most of them still possessing the pearly gray "mother of pearl" aragonite mantle layer.

Marine vertebrate fossil elements were not found below the 1¼-inch level of Member 98. At this level one barbed denticle of a *Listracanthus* (Elasmobranchian) shark was recorded from sample 107.1¼. All other fossil elements of marine vertebrates (sharks and fishes) were recorded from the 3-inch and higher levels of the shale. These elements included skin denticles, scales and teeth of three different groups of sharks and one group of fishes, the Paleoniscoid fish. All fossil elements, incidentally, represented small sized sharks or fish.

Paleoniscoids, with sturgeon-like beaks and tails and rhomb-shaped (ganoid) scales, were probably freshwater or brackish water fishes, two to eight or more inches in length. The scales buried in Member 98 were borne by specimens estimated probably three inches in length. The number of scales of Paleoniscoid fish rises abruptly in density-per-square-inch of exposed sample surface and in radiographs at the 13-inch level and above. This level also roughly corresponds to the level of thicker gray granular lenses and increasingly distorted and wavy micro laminations and bedding planes. It also coincides with the level in which algal and fungal filaments reoccur. Finally at this level the soft-bodied fossil thought to be an Onychophore was excavated.

Figure 6. Orbiculoidea. (3.6 X) Shells tightly packed. These number 18 to 22 per square inch of exposed surface.

THE CYCLICAL BLACK SHALES

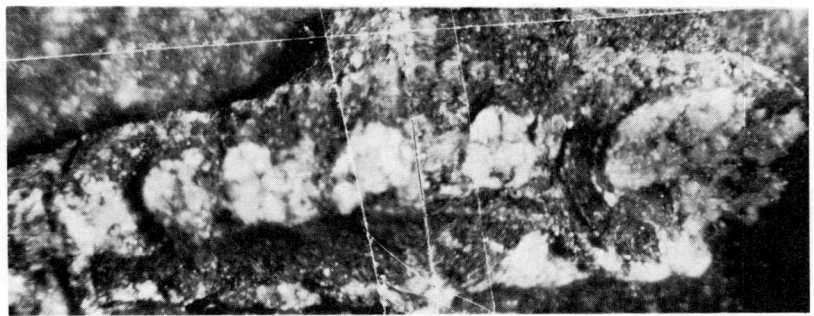

Figure 7. Onychophora. Sample 112-13.5. 16 X magnification.

The controversial fossil, the Onychophore, a wormlike Arthropod, measures only 4.5 mm long, but seems to bear at least six pairs of retractile appendages. The end of each "appendage" bears six symmetrically positioned hooks or protuberances, which surround a central projection. The *head* appears to be a contraction of several segments, with a centrally located mouth surrounded by two pairs of laterally positioned appendages and an anterior appendage. Each of these "head"-appendages appears to be similar in structure to the body or abdominal appendages. Except for its small size, the specimen fits the description of the Pararthropod, *Onychophora* (see Figures 7 and 8).

This writer does not accept the suggestion that the fossil above may be a coprolite. The hypothetical organism, in excreting the "pseudofossil" above would have required of necessity, that its cloaca symmetrically arrange in paired positions digestive residue of nearly identical food-organisms. Secondly, no illustrations of fecal material yet observed by the writer have exhibited internal or external symmetry.

A further indication of increased wave action was noted at the 15-inch level. Two small "coal balls" were recorded here (see Figure 9). One of the coal balls became dislodged exposing the inside walls of the cavity it once occupied. The bedding planes lining the cavity were essentially parallel, as they were around the

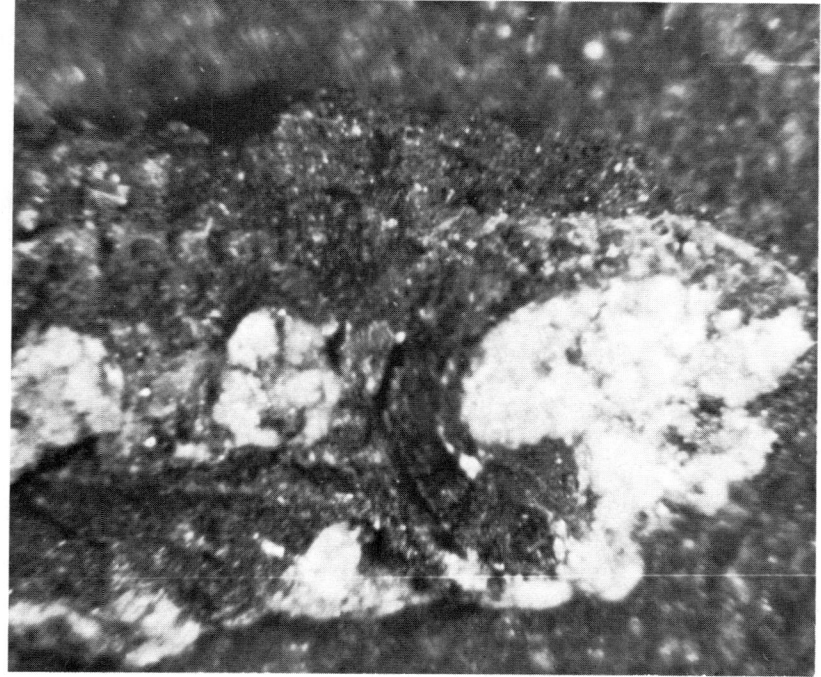

Figure 8. Onychophora. 27 X magnification.

coal ball remaining in the shale matrix. However, *all* bedding planes appeared to be distinctly interrupted by the coal balls. They did not diverge to form lenses around the coal balls as would be expected if the coal balls had originated as concretions.

The angles of the intervening and interrupted bedding planes strongly suggest that the coal balls were transported to their burial site. Their burial would therefore be allochthanous rather than autochthanous, refuting the widely taught concept that they, like the coal, are found where they were formed (or the trees grew). The rate of burial, furthermore, would be rapid rather than slow, probably within a period of minutes rather than of years, since no erosion of the coal balls was observed.

Radiographic Identification

Animal and plant fossil elements can at times be effectively identified in X-Ray negatives (radiographs). Several different kinds of conodonts, foraminifera, brachiopods, ostracods, algal filaments, (fungal hyphae?), and tissue of coal-forming trees could be more or less readily identified in the radiographs. The conodont, *Hibbardella milleri*, Rexroad, was exactly identified by rotating it 220° and reexposing the shale sample. The second radiograph clearly showed the small anterior denticle specific for *H. milleri*, Rexroad (see Figure 10). Among other conodonts identified to the species, were *Streptognathodus;* cf. *eccentricus*, Ellison, and *Polygnathus* cf. *Cristata*, Hinde.

An identification which has evoked some interest and controversy

Figure 9. Coal balls in the 15-inch level of Member 98, series 140.

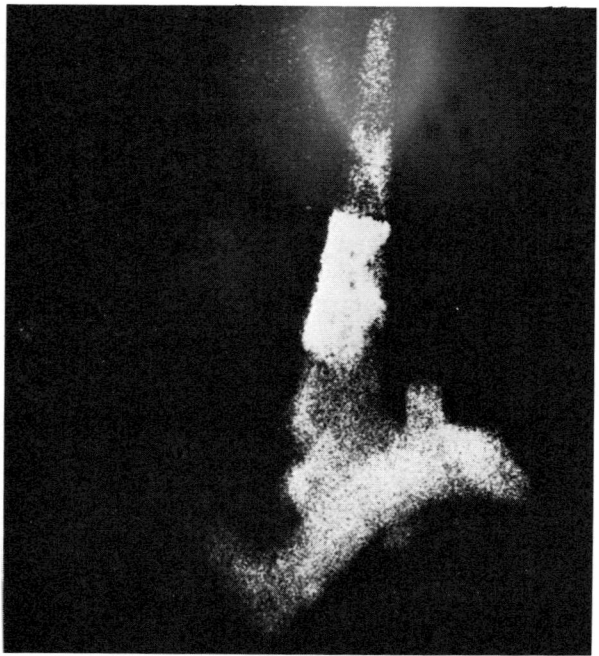

Figure 10. The conodont, Hibbardella milleri (Rexroad). Radioautograph. (46 X).

is that of the two brachiopods, *Anoplia* and *Girtyella*. The brachiopods are still hidden within the shale matrix of Sangamon County sample 330A. Adjacent to the anterior and lateral edges of the *Girtyella* shell, the radiograph is distinctly darker than it is adjacent to the other brachiopod shells. Close examination reveals the presence of many Endothyroid foraminifera crowded around the brachiopod shell. The writer proposes that they were buried while crowding around the *Girtyella*, rather than settling in this crowded, clustered arrangement as a result of random drifting during deposition. The presence and locations of the Endothyroids are therefore submitted as further evidence of rapid, allochthanous burial (tidal burial).

Perhaps the most interesting plant remains observed in shale samples and radiographs are those of freshwater green and blue-green algae. Filaments apparently displaying distinctly cellular structure resembling *Draparnaldia, Cladophora,* and *Oscillatoria* (and possible fungal hyphae) occur in shale samples and radiographs from the lowermost and topmost levels of the Black Shale Member 98 (see Figures 3-5). Their absence in the intervening central massive section of Member 98 suggests a temporary tide-like invasion or intrusion and retreat from the deposition area.

Member 98 was interpreted as a land-ward tidal intrusion of incoming ocean-water mixed with sea-ward moving freshwater causing the distorted bedding planes and microlaminations. As the seawater level increased in height, it engulfed the deposition site; the tide-like waves becoming deeper and deeper until they deposited the massive central section, and then temporarily retreated from the deposition site causing the reversal of lamination structure. The result being that the laminations and bedding planes at the top of Member 98 were distorted and wavy, as were the bottom layers of the Shale Member. The incoming sea water would engulf the land-freshwater environment causing a mixture of fauna and flora; this mixture is what we apparently observed in the fossil distribution: land-sea mixture at the bottom and at the top of the Member.

Radiographic Population Counts

Shale samples from three other Illinois counties were obtained for comparison with samples from Fulton County, mainly for radiographic studies. In several of the radiographs, the numbers of conodont specimens recorded contrasted sharply with the numbers observed visually on the sample surfaces, as follows:

(a) Hamilton County sample 700C revealed 44 *Hibbardella* specimens in the X-Ray negative and *none* visually;

(b) Sangamon County sample 300C (the shale overlying the Herrin, No. 6, coal) revealed 60 *Hibbardella* specimens in the radiograph and *only* 5 visually;

(c) Gallatin County sample 200A revealed an extensive network of algal filaments and minute (radiolarian?) organisms in the X-

Ray negative and none exposed at the surface. The algal filament in sample 200A is tentatively identified as that of *Cladophora,* a freshwater green alga (see Figure 3).

New Pennsylvanian Forms

Among animal and plant fossil elements perhaps new to the Pennsylvanian System are the Onychophore described above, freshwater green and blue-green algae, an unidentified egg or seed, and a new conodont species, *Metalonchodina magnidentatus,* Peters[3] (see Figure 11). The holotypes of the proposed new conodont species are at present in the Geology Department of Northern Illinois University. The unique feature distinguishing the proposed new species is its large first axial denticle (as opposed to the first distal—rear bar—denticle). This denticle measures 1.2 mm long, 0.1 mm longer than the main cusp, and gently diverges from the vertical axial plane of growth along an angular curvature equal to but opposite and away from the main cusp. The denticle and cusp curve gently away from each other. In other growth and structural characteristics the new proposed species corresponds to the limiting characteristics of the genus *Metalonchodina.*

Geological and Philosophical Implications

Geological and philosophical implications that can be drawn from the present study of Pennsylvanian black shales may be somewhat provocative. Among the geological implications the following may merit consideration:

1. Structural and fossil distribution similarities between the bases of Member 98 and the Francis Creek Shale suggest that both were conformably deposited directly over their respectively underlying coal seams.[4] Perhaps there was no "intervening" 6th or 7th rock (lithic) unit in the depositional history of Member 98 of Fulton County (the 8th unit of the "ideal coal cyclothem").

2. Radiography and photo-microradiography can be effectively used in a non-destructive approach to identification of fossils and for micro-fossil population counts, at least for black, carbonized shales.

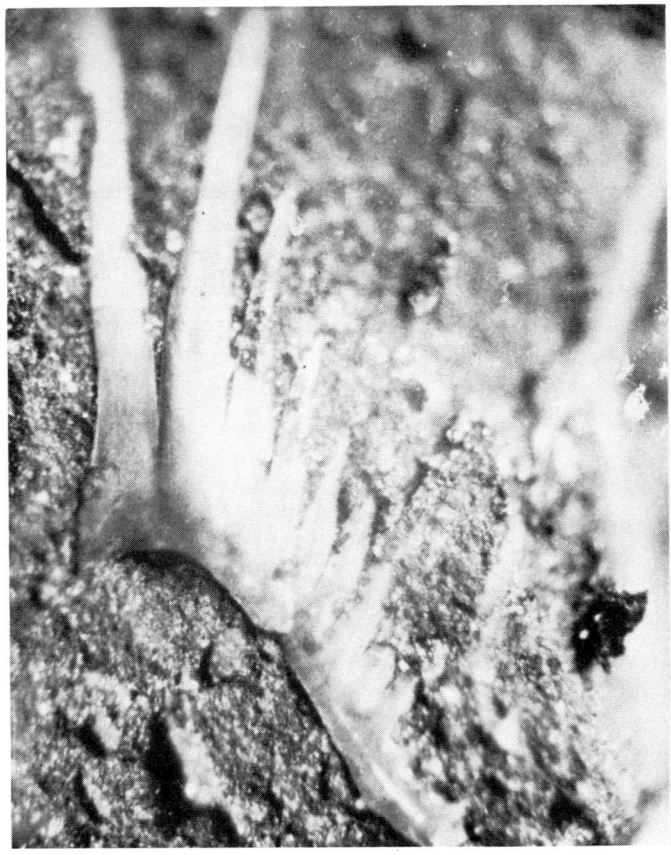

Figure 11. Metalonchodina magnidentatus, Peters. Sample 120.7. 62 X magnification.

3. Many new plant and animal fossil species and genera may be added to the fossil checklists of geological systems, series, and stages as the nondestructive X-Ray (radiographic) technique is perfected.

4. Pre-Cambrian, Paleozoic, and more "recent" shales may contain fossil elements that may radically change the interpretation of

the environment in which they were deposited. Refinement of the radiographic technique may require a restudy of such shales as the Proterozoic, the Scandanavian Pre-Cambrian, the British Columbian Cambrian Burgess Shale, the Green River Shales, and others.

5. Absence of certain fossils from the checklists of geological systems, stages, formations, or strata does not preclude their existence in some environment of the world (even nearby) during the time the rock layers in question were being deposited. The possible Onychophore, the algae, and *Metalonchodina magnidentatus* are not found in existing available Pennsylvanian checklists.

6. Member 98 exhibited a distinctly cyclical (perhaps tidal) deposition pattern. Many structural and fossil features seem to require a rapid, allochthanous interpretation of its depositional history.

From the geological observations it is obvious that the uniformitarian interpretation of long-time, slow, undisturbed sedimentation and mineralization cannot hold true for Member 98. Nearly all of the structural and fossil evidence seems to require rapid burial of sediment material transported to the burial site.

These details illustrate the kind of structural details one should expect if the earth had been subjected to a period of intense crustal disturbances and dislocations. They are what one should expect in rock layers laid down during a period of world-wide volcanism, crustal buckling, mid-ocean ridge and rift disturbances, and cloudburst type rain storms that can accompany crustal catastrophes (Furneaux, 1966, 155-165, etc.).[5]

The fossils and structure of the black shale Member 98 in Fulton County, Illinois in many aspects support rather than undermine a biblical catastrophic interpretation of Paleozoic sedimentation. The writer hopes that more high school graduates and paleontologists will take up the challenge of photomicroradiography, help refine the X-Ray (radiographic) technique, and extend the range of strata (rock layers) of geological systems examined.

It is my belief that, when all formations are studied, it will be found that the entire range of plant and animal families, genera, and species existed simultaneously. The present *apparent* paleontological segregation is attributable to lack of complex identification of all fossils in the various sedimentary rock systems.

It is not proposed that each period such as the Cambrian, Silurian, and Devonian will exhibit all the species of plants and animals, but rather that present boundaries, defined essentially by index fossils, will have to be abandoned when overlap of these fossils from one period into the other is demonstrated. Thus, eventually, vertebrates will be found in the Paleozoic and flowering plant pollen in the Cambrian system.

Acknowledgement

Without the help of my wife, Dorothy, the study reported could never have been completed within the time allotted for the completion of the thesis.

REFERENCES

1. Walter G. Peters, 1970, Masters Thesis: A paleoecological study of Pennsylvania black shales using photographic and radiographic techniques. Geology Department, Northern Illinois University, DeKalb, Illinois, 130 pp.
2. H. R. Wanless, 1958. Pennsylvanian faunas of the Beardstown, Glasford, Havana, and Vermont quadrangles, Illinois State Geological Survey, Report of Investigation 305, pp. 9, 11, 12ff.
3. Peters, *op. cit.*, pp. 31, 33, 118-120.
4. *Ibid.*, p. 24.
5. R. Furneaux, 1966, Krakatao, Prentice Hall, Inc., Englewood Cliffs, N. J., pp. 155-65ff.

X

FIELD EVIDENCE OF RAPID SEDIMENTATION

Walter G. Peters

Introduction

Authors of reports in geology are emphasizing restudy and reinterpretation of the mechanism and rates of sedimentary processes. Evolutionists are recognizing the failures and fallacies of classical uniformitarianism. They are admitting the necessity of blending catastrophism with neo-uniformitarianism. Field observations I made on camping trips together with photographs taken in the laboratory are presented to encourage more re-evaluation of geological interpretations by geologists and students.

Bentonite and Volcanism

Many visitors of the Western states have been awed by the rounded "teepees" of the Painted Desert in Arizona, and similar formations in Wyoming, and in Alberta, Canada. They marvel at the range of colors from purples, reds and yellows to greens and blues of the Mesozoic shales.

The Carlisle and Benton Shales of the Colorado Group (lower middle Cretaceous) are important sources of bentonite in northeastern Wyoming. My wife and I visited the Industrial Mineral and Chemical Corporation processing plant in June 1972, located about twenty miles west northwest of Belle Fourche, South Dakota.

These Cretaceous strata are weakly lithified. Evidence of the spongy consistency is the warped, rolling railway spur leading to the plant. A locomotive was derailed about a half mile east of the processing plant. Such derailment was a frequent occurrence according to Martin Krone, the laboratory analyst. He added that this plant has been processing gray, brown, yellow, green and blue bentonite.

Bentonite is of interest to creationists because of its origin. It is used as a Fuller's earth to plug up seepage into wells. It is rich in montmorillonite, $Al Mg)_8 (Si_4O_{10})_3 OH_{10} 12H_2O$, an expanding 2:1 layered smectite clay mineral. Deer, Howie and Zussman[1] state, "These have been formed by the alteration of eruptive igneous rocks, usually tuffs and volcanic ash . . . sodium is the naturally occurring exchange cation"; and they add:

> . . . thus montmorillonite results from the weathering of basic rocks mainly in conditions of poor drainage when magnesium is not removed . . . [and is favored by] . . . an alkaline environment, availability of calcium, and paucity of potassium.[2]

The widespread area in which these colored shales occur, the thickness of the formations, and the catastrophic implications of eruptive volcanic ash are obvious to creationists and evolutionists alike.*

Permian Conglomerates and "Talus"

The brecciated talus structure of the Permian El Capitan lime-

---

*A personal communicaiton from Donald W. Lane, Geological Survey of Wyoming, November 27, 1972, indicates that the primary source of the bentonite in the Colony, Wyoming, area is the Lower Cretaceous Mowry shale. The Geological Map of Wyoming provides the following information:

Three Upper Cretaceous shales have bentonite beds: The Monument Hill bentonite beds and the Pedro bentonite beds of the Pierre shale and the Cody shale with many bentonite beds.

There are four bentonite shales in the Lower Cretaceous beds of northeastern Wyoming:

> The Belle Foursche shale, which is black, soft with bentonite concretions.
>
> The Mowry shale, which is black, hard, siliceous and weathers to silvery gray. It has many thin bentonite beds.
>
> The Newcastle sandstone, which is gray with beds of sandy shale and some beds of bentonite and coal.
>
> The Cloverly formation, which is a light gray to brown sandstone with lenticular pebble-conglomerate, interbedded with variegated bentonite claystone.

Volcanic eruptions throughout the Lower and Upper Cretaceous were therefore significant catastrophic events accompanying the extinction of dinosaurs in an increasingly unfavorable environment.

stone mountains of New Mexico and western Texas have been well documented by Nevins.[3] Red Permian conglomerates of the same region have been associated with submarine turbidity currents and deposits.[4] Figure 1 shows a similar red, apparent Miocene-Pliocene conglomerate from about one to two miles west of Socorro, New Mexico.

Mid-continent Pennsylvanian Sediments

Pennsylvanian volcanism, mountain-forming intrusions, crustal faulting and severely disturbed and incomplete cyclothems are well established field observations. Even coal and sediment mixture was recognized by R. Feyes in 1961-1963 in explaining the distribution of illite clay. Illite is a 2:1, non-expanding clay derived from mica and feldspar minerals. Uniformitarianists recognize a "problem of illite" in the abrupt increase of illite from black shales (just above

Figure 1. Puye Conglomerate; Miocene-Pliocene, about one and a half miles west southwest of Socorro, New Mexico, at a roadcut of U.S. Highway 60.

the coal) to comprise over fifty percent of the clay minerals of the gray shales and sandy shales above them. Feyes states:

> A fraction of these illite shales may have been formed from soils (15%-50%), but in this case they do not seem to present any distinctive compositional change due to pedological action. This fact also seems to favor the action of vegetation in the hinterland also subject to seasonal climate, the *reworking and mixing of the coal measure sediments before their final deposition* in the swamp with hygrophytes having as a consequence the *spreading of illite* more or less uniformly through the succession, whether or not a soil and vegetation is preserved at *the point of final emplacement*.[5]

Creationists agree with the concept of sediment mixing, but propose *tidal rafting* as the method of accumulation of coal-forming plants and shale-forming clays. Even the black carbonaceous Pennsylvanian shale was deposited under disturbed environmental conditions. This is also recognized by Zangerl and Richardson[6]:

> The onset of the [ocean] transgressions produced an extremely sharp depositional change. Quite clearly this was not a gradual seeping of marine waters over the peat swamp, except along the most landward fringe, but very probably a sudden event accompanied with some degree of violence.

Then Zangerl and Richardson comment further:

> . . . This marine flooding was not merely the result of a major storm, although a storm or seiche may have accompanied the initial transgression thrust; we must assume that a sudden settling of the basin took place, caused most likely by increased tectonic activity. . . .[7]

The cyclical and rapid deposition of Member 98 of the St. David Cyclothem of the upper middle Pennsylvanian System has been demonstrated by the writter.[8, 9, 10]

The tectonic agencies of catastrophic deposition are recognized by Moore,[11] Dunbar and Waage,[12] and in Kummel's second edition of *History of the Earth*.[13] These include volcanism, block faulting, crustal sinking, folding, and intrusions. Moore recognized at least twelve episodes of crustal disturbances for the Pennsylvanian System alone.[14] These are reflected by the occurrence of over 100 incomplete cyclothems[15] in Illinois alone.

H. G. Coffin[16] very ably documented the catastrophic deposition of the polystrate Joggins tree trunks in the Nova Scotia sea cliff outcrops. Dunbar and Waage exhibit a photograph of these tree trunks in the 1969 edition of their *Historical Geology*. Kay and Colbert[17] speculated on the entrapment of salamanders within the hollow trunks of some of the trees. Even the Illinois Pennsylvanian limestones record rapid sedimentation. The Lonsdale Limestone of the lower McLeansboro Group (upper Pennsylvanian System) in western Peoria County, Illinois (Figure 2) shows distorted and randomly packed brachiopods.

Fossils are found in black shales of the Pennsylvanian series that should "not be there." For instance, the radiolarian, *Anthocyrtium* (Miocene protozoan); the protozoan foraminifera, *Nodosaria* (Triassic to recent), *Lituotuba* (Cretaceous), *Lagena, Bolovinina,* and

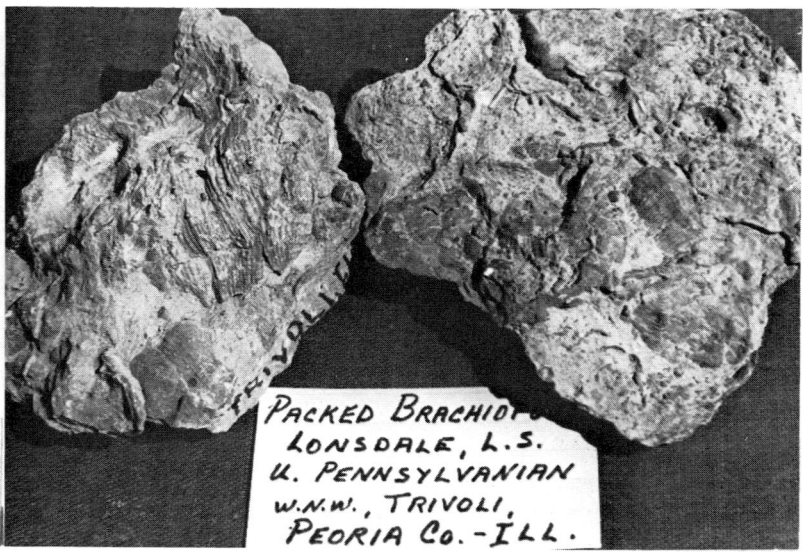

Figure 2. Randomly packed and distorted brachiopods in Lonsdale Limestone, Upper Pennsylvania; west northwest of Trivoli, Illinois.

Figure 3. Brecciated St. Louis Limestone, Middle Mississippian, east of Augusta, Hancock County, Illinois.

Hyperamminoides (Jurassic to recent); and the Conodonts, *Rhipidognathus*(?), and *Lonchodus* (Ordovician); *Trichonodella* (Devonian) and *Siphonodella* (Lower Mississippian) were reported as observed in Member 98 of the St. David Cyclothem.[18]

[Note: Photographs of the foraminiferan, *Lituotuba* (Figure 29; p. 43), the radiolarian, *Anthocyrtium* (Figure 91; p. 81) and the Conodonts, *Rhipidognathus* (Figure 35; p. 48) and *Lonchodus* (*Centrodus*) (Figure 76; p. 70) were presented as part of the Masters Thesis.]

The writer was advised at that time that even the *Treatise of Invertebrate Paleontology*[19] should not be considered the last word in paleontology. Yet each new secular biology, earth science, or geology textbook author treats as fact that animals and plants appeared in the geological time scale as specific succeeding "ages."

Mid-continent Mississippian Limestones

Mid-continent Mississippian limestones in Illinois exhibit rapid tectonic disturbances. The St. Louis Limestone (Figure 3) in a quarry east of Augusta in Hancock County contains several brecciated members. Northwest of Colchester, west central McDonough County, a fifteen-foot member of the Burlington Limestone (lower Mississippian) in the Colchester Stone Co. quarry is severely conglomerated (Figures 4 and 5). Many of the clastics in this member are fifteen to twenty inches and probably more in diameter. This limestone member was definitely fractured and recemented in a watery environment in a slurried condition.

Devonian Limestones

Strata of the Devonian System are well exposed in central western

Figure 4. Fifteen-foot-outcrop of slurried Burlington Limestone, Lower Mississippian; west of Colchester, McDonough County, Illinois.

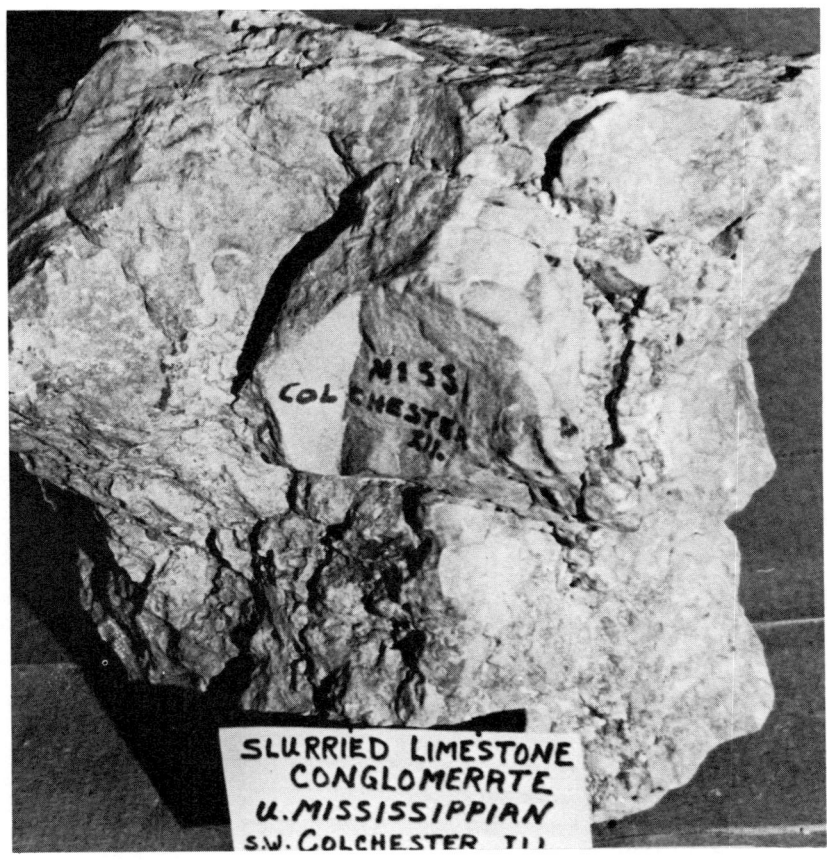

Figure 5. Closeup of slurried Burlington Limestone from outcrop west of Colchester, Illinois.

Illinois. They are referred to later in the discussion on the Ordovician.

Silurian "Polystrate" Fossils

After reading a fascinating article on Canadian Cambrian fossils by H. B. Whittington (see Reference No. 34 below) I examined several classroom specimens of Silurian Lockport dolomite. These rocks form spectacular cliffs east of Grafton in Jersey County, Illi-

Figure 6. Trilobite, Calamene, in Lockport Dolomite, Silurian; three darker layers, A, B, and C. Fossil extends from layer D into layer C.

Figure 7 Trilobite, Calamene in Lockport Dolomite, Silurian; trilobite extends through at least four microlaminations, some of which are traced with dark ink to the left of the trilobite.

nois and overlook the Mississippi River. The trilobite, *Calamene,* is common in the lower portion of the outcrop. Figures 6 and 7 show specimens of the trilobite exposed in the dolomite samples. Three darker layers and a light layer below the fossil are labelled A, B, C, and D respectively.

Microlaminations were traced laterally from each of the fossils. Notice that the microlaminations truncate against the fossils, indicating a rapid sedimentation. Figure 6 shows two darker layers

200 SPEAK TO THE EARTH

above the trilobite, which extends from a lighter layer D into the lowest darker layer C. Lines of other fine cavities (see arrow marks) seem to suggest cross-bedding, another suggestion of rapid sedimentation. In Figure 7, laminations traced by lighter colored microbedding planes have been traced with dark ink. These were traced

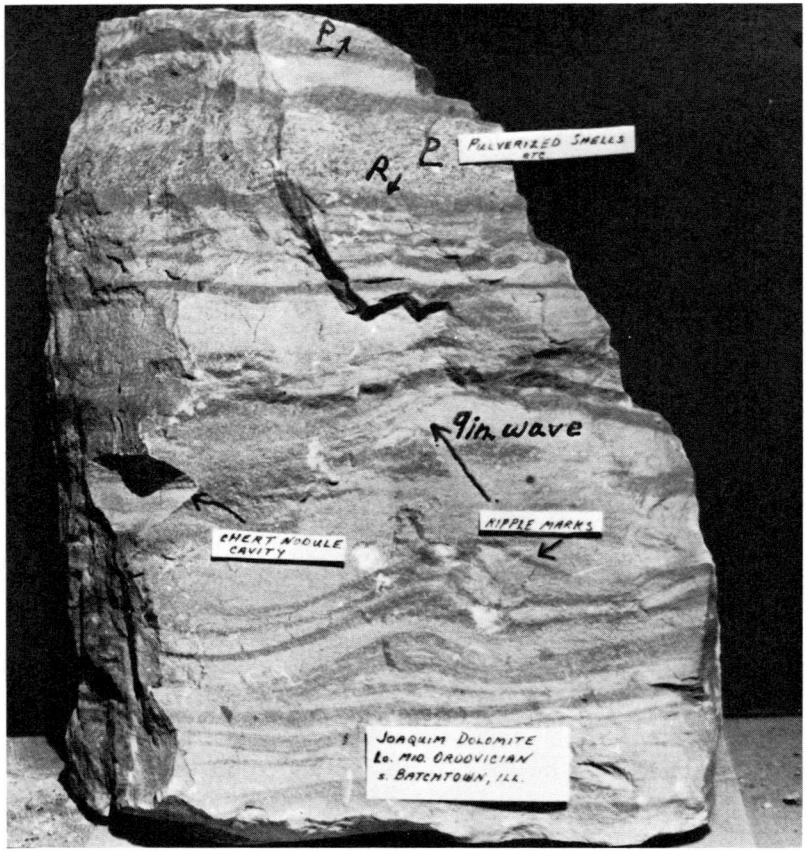

Figure 8. Joachim Dolomite, lower middle Ordovician; south of Batchtown, Calhoun County, Ill. Pulverized shells at P. Layers, nine inch and five and one-half inch wavemarks; and microlaminations truncated at chert nodule cavity.

around to the left face of the dolomite sample. The trilobite interrupts at least four microlaminations of solid dolomite. In the light of the later discussion of the Burgess Shale, catastrophic sedimentation of the Silurian Dolomite certainly seems warranted.

Catastrophic Ordovician Sedimentation

Ordovician limestones, dolomites, conglomerates, sandstones and folded rocks are directly associated with severe worldwide volcanism and crustal disruptions. Kay and Colbert in their textbook, *Stratigraphy and Life History* (Reference No. 17), display photographs of field evidence of catastrophism on pages 133, 135, 138, 139, 149, 159, 167, 168, 175, 176, and 179 related to the Ordovician System. In Illinois the Ordovician sediments also exhibit visible evidence of rapid sedimentation.

A large display sample (Figure 8) of Joachim Dolomite, lower middle Ordovician, from Batchtown, Calhoun County, Illinois, clearly shows wave-marks. The lower ripple mark had a wave length of about five and one-half inches and was apparently moving toward the right. The upper wave-mark has a wave length of about nine inches and was apparently moving toward the left.

The trough of the upper wave-mark is distorted where the slurry flowed against and over a chert nodule. Notice that the cavity of the chert nodule (left side of Figure 8) shows microlaminations truncated at the edge of the cavity, which suggests that the chert nodule might have been transported to the deposition site.

Near the top of the dolomite section are at least two distinct layers of pulverized shells and calcite crystals. The base of the thicker layer of pulverized shells covered the finely rippled surface of buff dolomite (labelled R). The ripple wave length at this interface varies from half an inch to one inch, indicating a short period of settling and fine vibration. This was followed by several flows of pulverized shells. The cyclical series of dolomite and limestone is clearly visible on the highwall of the quarry.

Cycles of (a) silicon and magnesium or dolomite(?) alternating with (b) calcite or limestone are discussed in Narin[20] on page 468 of *Problems in Paleoclimatology*. And R. W. Fairbridge[21] cited examples in the Appalachian Ordovician, mid-west Devonian, Belgium Devonian and Carboniferous, and Tertiary strata of Cuba and Jamaica. Further, Fairbridge quoted Landes' suggestion[22] of a ". . . rhythm of a sudden retreat and slow transgression of sea water," and also Rutten's suggestion[23] of a rhythmic sequence of ". . . alternation between storminess and calm sea conditions."

Significant criticism of orthodox uniformitarianism is published in the work edited by Nairn.[24] Bucher used four paragraphs to describe alternating shales and limestones in the Cincinnatian Series, Upper Ordovician. Bucher described both, a thin limestone-thicker shale formation and a thin limestone formation as ". . . formed by violent stirring up of the shale" (p. 595) and ". . . formed by exceptionally high storm-strengthened tidal currents and promptly covered by stirred-up shale settling on them." (p. 596).

All five series of strata of the Ordovician System are associated with volcanism, conglomerates, and catastrophic deposition. It is therefore not surprising that the formation of dolomite itself is apparently far from settled. Donald H. Zenger of Pomona College stated recently that, in view of the many inconsistencies and disagreements between researchers, much work needs to be done concerning:

> . . . ordered dolomite versus protodolomite versus magnesium calcites; carbon and oxygen isotopes of dolomite crystals and their relation to primary or replacement dolomites; dolomite synthesis . . . kinetics of dolomite formation. . . .[25]

Widespread, violent volcanic eruptions and settling of dust rich in ferro-magnesians could supply the magnesium, and plagioclases could supply the calcium or sodium. Plagioclase feldspars supply both calcium and sodium: anorthite, ninety per cent calcium; bytownite, seventy, eighty per cent calcium; labradorite, fifty, seventy percent calcium; and andesine, oligoclase, and albite supply increasingly larger per cents of sodium.

World-circling, continent covering gigantic tides could produce the cyclical sedimentary sequences and wave marks observed in the rock outcrops and quarries. Irregular seismic shock waves associated with crustal faulting could induce and accelerate differential compaction of freshly deposited sediments. All of these could contribute to the forces that induced continental drift as outlined by M. A. Cook[26] and could have accompanied the highest water levels of the Noachian Flood and its aftermath, as the waters receded and the Pleistocene ice age developed.

The deposition and composition of Paleozoic dolomites and limestones neatly coincide with the highest water levels of the Noachin Flood. Zenger cites the Ca-Mg ratios charted by Chilinger[27] as follows:

Age	No. of Samples Analyzed	Average Ca/Mg Ratio
Precambrian	70	4.0/1
Cambrian	40	4.2/1
Ordovician	100	3.5/1
Silurian	250	3.0/1
Devonian	160	7.0/1
Late Paleozoic	400	16/1
Cretaceous	85	56/1
Tertiary	50	53/1
Quaternary and Holocene	250	40/1

Table 1. Ca/Mg Ratios of Carbonate Rocks and Sediments vs. Geological Age after Chilinger, 1956.

Sandstones, shales, and conglomerates dominate the Triassic and Jurassic sediments. If laboratory analysis bears out the same marked increase as in the Cretaceous, it would only emphasize more dramatically the radical change from Paleozoic sediments to those of the Mesozoic System; from Flood Epoch to Post-Flood aftermath, the "Age of Reptiles."

Such analysis would serve to reinforce the climatic suggestions of Northrup[28]: that the environment during the recession of the Flood was wind-blown, drying, and sandy in some regions, while receding tidal invasions still deposited limestones and chalks in others. There is evidence of "Triassic" subaerial lava flows with dinosaur prints between them and other differences contrasting Paleozoic with Mesozoic strata (personal communication from S. E. Nevins, Dec. 9, 1972).

The Ubiquitous Cambrian

Bernard Kummel[29] describes the Early Cambrian as follows:

> The miogeosynclines of the western and eastern sides of the continent were sites of extensive deposition of quartz sand derived in part from the central region, and since Middle Cambrian from areas on the seaward side of the troughs. In the eugeosynclines of eastern North America we find Lower Cambrian shales, graywackes, and conglomerates.

The Mt. Simon in Illinois; the Marquette in Michigan, the McNaughton and Gog in British Columbia are the typical lowest Cambrian deposits in the "mid-continent." The Tapeats Sandstone marks the base of the Cambrian in Arizona. They form the Great Erosional Unconformity above the red sandstones, siltstones, and shales of the Nankoweap formation of the "Lipallian Interval."

Beneath these are the greenish gray sills and dikes of the Rama diabase intruding through and above the bright red siltstones and shales of the Docks formation. Beneath are the other Precambrian metamorphics, conglomerates, and igneous crystallines. Above are the basal sandstones of the Cambrian system.

From a biblical perspective it is significant that the Precambrian "era" was buried under red shales, siltstones, and sandstones, marking the end of a period of volcanic eruptions, igneous intrusions, volcanic sills, block faulting, rapid mountain forming, and crustal rupture, the deposition of conglomerates and basaltic and felsic lavas. This seems logical because, on the day Noah and his family entered the ark: ". . . on that very day all the fountains of the great deep burst forth and the windows of heaven were opened."[30]

Perhaps it is more than coincidental that most of the early Cambrian deposits are sandstones. Only after the rains had carried the continental sandstones to the "outer edges of the central continental cratons" (platforms), would the waters of the Flood rise high enough to carry and deposit the dolomites, limestones and shales in gigantic slurries borne within ever-deepening tidal swells and waves over successively higher elevations until all the continents were submerged.

Cambrian Fossil Deposition

The presence of seedferns (Lepidophytes), horsetail trees (Calamites) and mosses (Bryophytes) and fragments of woody stems in the Cambrian have been discussed earlier by Rusch.[31] Pollen of evergreens (Conifers) and flowering plants (Angiosperms) in Cambrian and Precambrian deposits have been isolated evidently by Burdick and Loma Linda University workers.[32] However, another restudy project on the mode of sedimentation of Middle Cambrian deposits will be of special interest to C. R. S. *Quarterly* readers.

Figure 9. Burgess Shale, lower middle Cambrian from Mt. Stephens, Yoho National Park, south of Field, British Columbia, Canada. Point at whcih fossil, Olenoides (trilobite) extends from one lamination to another, marked A; Trilobite, Ogygopsis, above and to the left.

I was afforded a unique opportunity and pleasure on July 6, 1972, to photograph specimens on 12 slabs of the famous Burgess Shales, Yoho National Park, British Columbia. Dave Nielsen, Park Naturalist, also gave me copies of three complete articles authored by Canadian and British geologists dealing with the tectonic and sedimentary aspects of the formation of the Middle Cambrian Burgess Shale at Field, British Columbia.

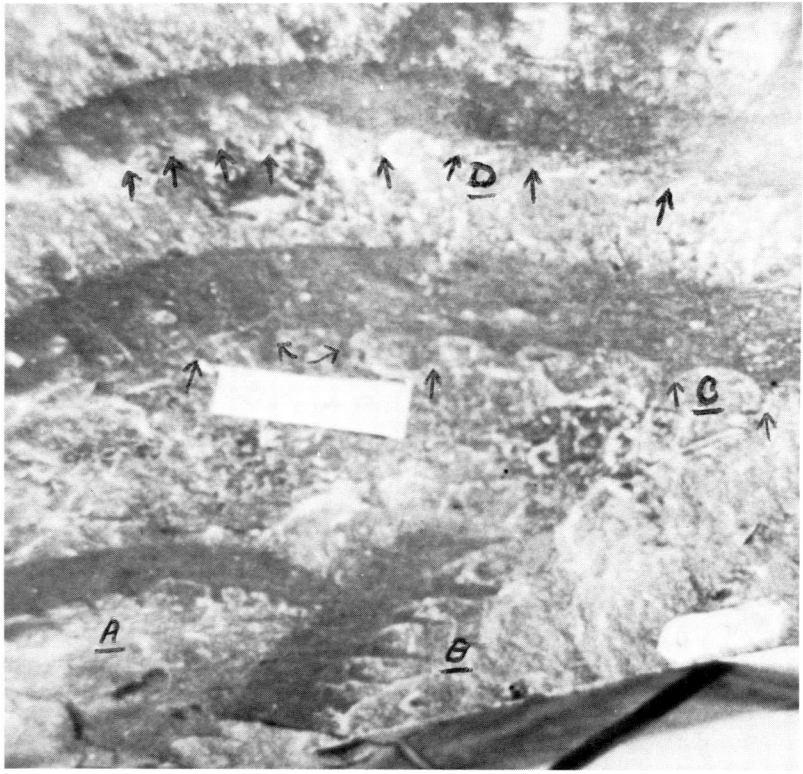

Figure 10. Portions of four polychete worms (Annelida) in Burgess Shale from Mt. Stephens, Yoho National Park, British Columbia. Worms buried lateral to bedding plane. Microbedding lamination (solid shale) separates paired appendages, covering buried member of pairs (A, C, and D).

Photographs made from 35 mm color transparencies still illustrate the polystrate nature of the fossils in the Stephens Formation, *Ogygopsis* Shale of the lower middle Cambrian System from Mt. Stephen and Mt. Wapta.

Figure 9 shows *Ogygopsis* trilobite above and *Olenoides* below and to the right. *Olenoides* clearly interrupts a microbedding plane at point A. Figure 10 shows several sea worms (Polychetes) partially exposed. Notice that the lower (right or left hand) member of the paired appendages of the worms A and B are buried in the next lower bedding layer of shale and not visible.

H. B. Whittington of Sedgwick Museum, Cambridge, England, has presented[33] detailed microlamination and photographic studies of fossils in Burgess Shale. He has described carefully the orientation of the fossils, which extended through several bedding planes. None were within single laminations.[34]

Six to thirty-nine percent of the fossils were buried at angles oblique to the bedding planes. Five to thirteen percent ". . . of the individuals in the five samples taken from the 'Phyllopod bed' are compacted in an attitude approximately lateral to the bedding."[35] Whereas fifty-six to eighty-one percent of the specimens were parallel to the bedding planes:

> . . . It may be observed that the appendages do not lie in exactly the same bedding planes as the spines of the cephalic shield, but that they lie on different levels. The gill branches overlap one over the other, are inclined downward and forward relative to the cephalic spines, and there is a thin layer of rock separating them from the gill branches (Figures 8 and 9).[36]

Whittington used eighteen photographs and six drawings to document his observations.

The mode of deposition suggested by Whittington is presented in several paragraphs.[37] In the first paragraph he states:

> A benthic population could have been catastrophically overwhelmed by a moving cloud of suspended sediment, the animals being entombed in a wide variety of orientations as the sediment settled. The delicate animals were not torn apart, but were buried with appendages such as gill branches and walking legs in natural relative positions, not twisted or disoriented.

He then suggests that they were buried only a short distance from where they lived by a slow moving current of sediment. However in the second paragraph he continues:

> A series of such catastrophic burials at irregular intervals could have produced the present fossiliferous layers [Figure 5]. The chemical conditions that obtained in this sediment during diagenesis are problematical. Presumably the relatively rapid burial preserved the animals from predation, and there was little or no decomposition nor are signs of burrowing infauna.

In the third paragraph he suggests that the waters were relatively deep: ". . . (several hundred feet) off a limestone bank, an environment where a thick shale sequence was accumulating rapidly." Finally Whittington states:

> If the rare Burgess fauna and flora were a single community: . . . why are tracks, trails and burrows absent? . . . Favorable conditions for its burial and preservation occurred for only a short interval during the accumulation of a thick shale sequence.[38]

S. E. Nevins (in the same personal communication cited above) states that rapid burial such as this requires that the shale be formed from *flocculated* clay particles, distinctly unlike the deposition of modern red clays in ocean deeps from unflocculated clay suspensions. And Whittington re-emphasized his assertion of extremely rapid burial of the Burgess fauna in his 1971 report.[39]

Soft-bodied worms (Annelids and Polychetes), medusae of coelenterates, Arthropods including trilobites and sponges are among the 150 species found in the Burgess Shales. This unique formation is located on Mt. Stephens and Mt. Wapta, south and north (respectively) from Field, British Columbia in Yoho National Park. I climbed to the *Ogygopsis* shale on Mt. Stephen in July, 1972, but snow on the paths prevented any further hike to the Mt. Wapta outcrops.

Conclusions

The Paleozoic field evidence is found in quarries, erosion, outcrops, fault-block mountains, folded metamorphic rock series, and volcanic features. There are repeated evidences of cataclysmic forces and events. Integrated with the Genesis account of the Flood, they can provide very good visible evidence. Even the rocks "speak out" in testimony to the everlasting truth and veracity of the Bible. They can be used to form a firm foundation for the believer, and a formidable challenge to the unbiased scientist.

REFERENCES

1. W. A. Deer, R. A. Howie, and J. Zussman, 1966. An introduction to the rock-forming minerals. John Wiley and Sons, Inc., New York, p. 268.
2. *Ibid.,* p. 269.
3. S. E. Nevins, 1972. Is the Capitan limestone a fossil reef?, *Creation Research Society Quarterly,* 8(4): pp. 231-248.
4. N. D. Newell, 1957. Supposed Permian tillites in northern Mexico are submarine slide deposites, *Bulletin of the Geological Survey of America,* 68 (11): p. 1569. Quoted by J. C. Whitcomb and H. M. Morris, 1962. The Genesis Flood. Presbyterian and Reformed Publishing Co., Philadelphia, p. 249.
5. R. Feys, 1964. The palaeopedology of coal basins, in Problems in paleoclimatology. A. E. M. Nairn, ed. Interscience Publishers, Division of John Wiley and Sons, Ltd., New York, p. 70 (hereinafter referred to as Nairn, Problems in paleoclimatology).
6. R. Zangerl and E. S. Richardson, Jr., 1963. The paleoecological history of two Pennsylvanian black shales. Chicago Natural History Museum, Chicago, p. 217.
7. *Ibid.,* paragraph 3, p. 217.
8. W. G. Peters, 1970 (Masters thesis). A paleoecological study of Pennsylvanian black shales using radiographic and photographic techniques. 130 pp.
9. W. G. Peters, August, 1970. The challenge of black shale radiography (an updated restudy of shale specimens and radiographs with implications bearing on the environment and rate of sedimentation). Unpublished, 79 pp.
10. W. G. Peters, 1971. The cyclical black shales, *Creation Research Society Quarterly,* 7(4):193-200.
11. R. C. Moore, 1958. Introduction to historical geology. McGraw Hill Book Co., Inc., New York, pp. 240, 241.
12. C. O. Dunbar and K. M. Waage, 1969. Historical geology. John Wiley and Sons, Inc., New York, p. 258.
13. B. Kummel, 1970. History of the earth. Second edition. W. H. Freeman and Co., San Francisco, pp. 144-170.
14. Moore, 1958, *op. cit.,* pp. 240-242.
15. Dunbar and Waage, *op. cit.,* p. 264.
16. H. G. Coffin, 1969. Research on the classic Joggins petrified trees, *Creation Research Society Quarterly,* 6(1):35-44.
17. M. Kay and E. H. Colbert, 1965. Stratigraphy and life history. John Wiley and Sons, Inc., New York, pp. 259, 261.
18. Peters, Masters Thesis, pp. 43, 81, 48, 70, respectively.

19. R. C. Moore, ed., 1969. Treatise of invertebrate paleontology, Geological Society of America, Boulder, Colorado.

20. Nairn, Problems in palaeoclimatology (see Reference no. 5).

21. R. W. Fairbridge, 1964. The importance of limestone and its Ca/Mg content to palaeoclimatology, in Nairn, Problems in palaeoclimatology, p. 468.

22. K. K. Landes, 1957. Chemical unconformities, *Bulletin of the Geological Society of America*, 68:12, p. 1759. Quoted by Fairbridge (1964). *Ibid.*, p. 468.

23. M. G. Rutten, 1956. Les calcares bein lités et les ouragans. *Compt. Rend. Soc. Geol. France*, No. 2, 15.

24. Nairn, Problems in palaeoclimatology, pp. 594-596.

25. D. H. Zenger, 1972. Dolomitization and uniformitarianism, *Journal of Geological Education* 20(3):107-124 (see especially p. 122).

26. M. A. Cook, 1966. Prehistory and earth models. Max Parrish Publ., London, 353 pp.

27. G. V. Chilingar, 1956. Relationship between Ca-Mg ratio and geological age, *American Association of Petroleum Geologists Bulletin*, 40, pp. 2256-2266. Quoted by Zenger, *op. cit.*, p. 108.

28. B. E. Northrup, 1972. Dunes, dinosaurs and death, in Challenge to education. Walter Lang, ed., Bible-Science Association, Caldwell, Idaho, pp. 72-76.

29. Kummel, *op. cit.*, p. 120.

30. Genesis 7:11. The Holy Bible, George M. Lamsa, ed. A. J. Holman Co., Philadelphia. 1957. Complete translation of the Holy Bible from the Peshitta, the authorized Bible of the Church of the East.

31. W. H. Rusch, Sr., 1966. Analysis of so-called evidences of evolution, *Creation Research Society Quarterly*, 3(1):4-15. See also by same author, 1968, The revelation of palynology, *Creation Research Society Quarterly*, 5(3):103-105.

32. C. L. Burdick, 1966. Microflora of the Grand Canyon, *Creation Research Society Quarterly*, 3(1):38-50. See also by the same author, 1972, Progress report on Grand Canyon palynology, *Creation Research Society Quarterly*, 9(1):25-30.

33. H. B. Whittington, 1969. The Burgess shale: history of research and preservation of fossils, *Proceedings of the North American Paleontological Convention*, pp. 1170-1201.

34. *Ibid.*, pp. 1180-1199.

35. *Ibid.*, p. 1185.

36. *Ibid.*, pp. 1184-1185.

37. *Ibid.*, p. 1197.

38. *Ibid.*, p. 1199.

39. H. B. Whittington, 1971. Redescription of *Marella splendens* (Trilobitoidea) from the Burgess shale, Middle Cambrian, British Columbia, *Geological Survey of Canada*, Ottawa, Canada. Bulletin 209. 23 pp. and 26 plates.

XI

THE MESA BASALT OF THE NORTHWESTERN UNITED STATES

STUART E. NEVINS*

Introduction

The late Cenozoic geologic history of the northwestern United States was rather violent. From innumerable fissures and craters enormous quantities of molten rock and ash spewed forth. The dark, fine grained rock called basalt, which is composed mainly of minerals called feldspars, $(Na,Ca)Al(Si,Al)Si_2O_8$, cooled from molten lava.

The Columbia Plateau in Washington, Oregon, Idaho, and California is built of volcanic material in some places over five thousand feet thick dominated by basalt flows each about ten to fifteen feet thick, with an occasional one of greater thickness.

The most common topographic features of the Columbia Plateau are buttes, mesas, and plateaus capped by resistant "rim-rock" (commonly basalt) over less resistant rock (commonly volcanic ash) which is easily eroded by wind and rain.

The Cascade Mountains in Washington, Oregon, and California contain a series of volcanoes, the best known of which are Mount Baker, Mount Rainer, Mount St. Helens, Mount Hood, Mount Jefferson, Mount Shasta, and Mount Lassen, each over 10,000 feet high.

Recognition of Mesa Basalt

Two professors of geology at the University of Washington in Seattle, Washington, Dr. Henry E. Wheeler and Dr. Howard A.

---

*For author information, see Article II.

Coombs, have each spent forty years carefully studying the late Cenozoic volcanic rocks of the Northwest. Dr. Wheeler's specialized field is the analysis of the regional patterns of stratified rocks. Dr. Coombs, who was head of the department of geology at the University of Washington, is a specialist in volcanology. Both are recognized worldwide as authorities in their fields.

About ten years ago Wheeler and Coombs noticed that one particular type of Pliocene or Pleistocene basalt was widespread east of the Cascade Mountains in Oregon, California, Idaho, and Nevada, forming the rim-rock of many of the buttes, mesas, and plateaus. This characteristic type of basalt is usually medium to light gray in color and differs from other basalts which are usually black.

Wherever Wheeler and Coombs found this distinctive type of basalt, it was always coarse-textured with visible crystals of olivine, a green mineral, $(Mg,Fe)_2SiO_4$, protruding into many fine pores. (The texture is technically known as *diktytaxitic*.) Upon close inspection of unweathered samples one can distinguish what appears to be a "jumble of minute jackstraws." Wheeler and Coombs have named this peculiar layer of rock the *Mesa basalt* according to the first description made by the University of California Professor J. C. Merriam in northwestern Nevada in 1910.

After recognizing the vast distribution, the thickness which averages only thirty feet, and the singular stratigraphic occurrence in any locality of the *Mesa basalt,* Wheeler and Coombs asked,

> Could this layer of "jackstraw" rock, vestiges of which were scattered over parts of four states, conceivably be the remains of a single sheet? Could such a sheet have been laid down during one enormous volcanic eruption? After initially dismissing the idea as preposterous, we later evaluated it as belonging somewhere between the improbable and the impossible. A number of lava flows had been known to travel tens of miles from their sources. J. W. Bingham and M. J. Grolier of the U.S. Geological Survey recently showed that one flow of the Columbia River Basalt succession covered at least 20,000 square miles of southeastern Washington and northeastern Oregon. However, to assign the *Mesa basalt* layer to a solitary eruptive event (even if two or three outbursts in rapid succession were assumed)

would be equivalent to saying that the flow was so gigantic that portions of it had to come to rest, cooled, and solidified no less than a few hundred miles from the place of eruption. How could any one outpouring of molten rock traverse such a distance before cooling?[1]

Subsequent mapping by Wheeler and Coombs has shown the extremely vast distribution of the *Mesa basalt* (see Figure 1).

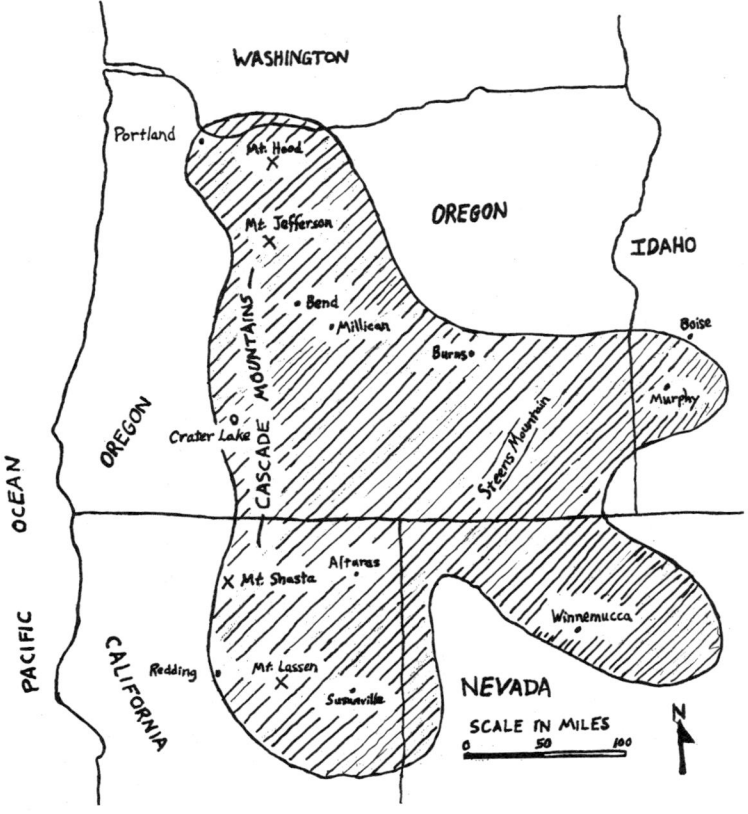

Figure 1. The world's largest known lava flow. The area of this lava is shaded on the map. It covered an estimated 100,000 square miles in Oregon, Idaho, California, and Nevada.

Although some of the earlier correlations tentatively proposed in the literature suggested a possible original continuity of *Mesa basalt* considerably in excess of 100 miles, there was no appreciation of the total sweep of the erosionally reduced remnants our everwidening search has uncovered during the last five years. Our recently completed geologic mapping in Oregon reveals at least two areas, each with continuous exposures for more than 100 linear miles. In central Oregon, the *Mesa* sheet may be kept either under-foot or in virtually continuous view for 150 miles from southwestern Wasco County on the east slope of the Cascades to Wright's Point Mesa southeast of Burns in north-central Harney County. *Mesa basalt* exposures are equally continuous from near the southeastern base of Mount Shasta in Siskyou County, California, for a distance of 90 miles southeast across the low crest of the southern Cascades to Susanville in Lassen County. If one will allow five erosional separations of present flow remnants (in which the two largest gaps are only ten and twelve miles), a minimum lateral extent of 250 miles is clearly evident. . . . We are now convinced that what we see of the *Mesa basalt* layer today is only a modest fraction of the original sheet of lava. The major portion of the sheet has been eroded away. The remnants are distributed from near Portland, Oregon, southeasterly to beyond Winnemucca, Nevada, a distance of more than 450 miles. In the northeast-southwesterly direction they occur from near Murphy in the Snake River Valley (south of Boise), Idaho, to near Redding in the northern Sacramento Valley of California. The minimum region encompassed is conservatively estimated at 100,000 square miles.[2]

Near Portland, Oregon, the *Mesa basalt* is over sixty feet thick; in central Oregon near Bend about thirty-five feet; in Modoc County, California, about twenty-nine feet; in southern Lassen County, California, about twenty-two feet; near Winnemucca, Nevada, a little over ten feet; in western Idaho about sixteen feet thick. The regional thickness gradation of the *Mesa basalt* from thickest in the northwestern most portion (near Portland, Oregon) to thinnest in the southeastern most portion of the sheet (near Winnemucca, Nevada) suggests that the fissure which fed the lava layer was located to the northwest of the entire sheet.

To support their interpretation of the *Mesa basalt* as a single, vast basalt flow, Wheeler and Coombs have also noted similarities in chemical composition, resemblances among volcanic structures, and regionally associated stratigraphic relationships. After mentioning several physically associated characteristics of the *Mesa basalt,* Wheeler and Coombs correctly claim, ". . . these are immediately recognized as the diagnostic physical criteria for the identity, original continuity, and genetic unity of any lithostratigraphic unit (sedimentary or volcanic)...."[3]

Many geologists today use fossils or radiometric methods to demonstrate stratigraphic equivalence of layered rocks in separate localities and have relatively ignored the most conclusive method, that of physical stratigraphic similarity. This incredible oversight by geologists during the last sixty years is one of the main reasons why the vast distribution of the *Mesa basalt* has only been recently appreciated.

Special Problems Presented by Mesa Basalt

Since the entire sheet of *Mesa basalt* cooled from a lake of molten lava at roughly the same moment, it is a convenient time datum to check the accuracy of potassium-argon dating. Two U.S. Geological Survey geologists, G. W. Walker and D. A. Swanson, have mentioned several dates which were made before the widespread nature of the *Mesa basalt* was recognized.[4]

In northern Nevada where the *Mesa* was first described by Merriam, the potassium-argon method dated the basalt at 1.2 million years. A date of 7.2 million years came from the basalt near Alturas, California. Near Millican, Oregon, the basalt dated at slightly over 6 million years. An occurrence of diktytaxitic olivine basalt not originally recognized by Wheeler and Coombs as part of the *Mesa basalt* on Steens Mountain in southern Oregon was dated at 14.5 million years.

In view of these and other widely divergent potassium-argon dates and the more conclusive evidence of Wheeler and Coombs for a single *Mesa basalt* flow, we must conclude that the potassium-argon dating method is unreliable.

Walker and Swanson, however, place their faith in the potassium-argon method and believe that the various occurrences of diktytaxitic basalt mentioned by Wheeler and Coombs represent dozens of smaller, individual lava flows separated by millions of years of time. Walker and Swanson claim that the supposed evolutionary order of vertebrate fossils confirms potassium-argon dating, and conclude (erroneously) that Wheeler and Coombs are in serious error concerning the existence of their regionally extensive *Mesa basalt*.

Not only are potassium-argon dating and evolutionary interpretations of late Cenozoic fossils in grave difficulty, but the basic popular assumption in historical geology is in serious question. The *Mesa basalt* is an outright contradiction of the so-called Principle of Uniformity.[5] The flowage of the *Mesa basalt* represents the largest lava flow known and far exceeds any of the present. The catastrophic outpouring of the *Mesa basalt* very possibly took only a few days.

One of the most perplexing difficulties presented by the *Mesa basalt* is its horizontal extent compared to thickness. As an illustration of the remarkable thinness of the *Mesa* compared to its widespread flow, imagine that the actual thickness of the flow were reduced in scale to the thickness of a page of this *book*. In order to represent to scale the maximum horizontal dimension of the flow, the page would have to be twenty feet long! Wheeler and Coombs write,

> We confess ourselves no better prepared than Merriam was to explain the mode of long-distance transport of the *Mesa basalt*. We still must ask how (or whether) any lava flow (in the *normal* sense of the term) can remain sufficiently hot and fluid while being spread so widely—especially across a terrain with appreciable topographic relief. . . . It seems only logical to speculate that the *Mesa basalt* also may not have been a lava flow in the completely conventional sense.[6]

In their recent geology textbook Dunbar and Waage report,

> One very destructive flow, the Mesa Basalt, so called because it caps so many of the mesas in parts of 3 states, has recently been stated to have covered approximately 100,000 square miles, although it is generally less than 40 feet thick. The

mechanism by which it was able to spread so widely before congealing is unknown, but as a molten lake of this size it must have presented a lurid scene such as the earth has seldom seen.[7]

The rock just below the *Mesa basalt* is remarkable because it must have formed a nearly level planar surface of at least 100,000 square miles over which the lava could have flowed. If any considerable topography existed in the 100,000-square-mile area, the molten lava would have "pooled" or been deflected and drained off, and would not have spread so evenly over such a broad surface. The vast plane of flow we imagine for the *Mesa basalt* is in striking contrast to the *present* mountainous topography of the region.

The vast planar surface can be explained best by the ash beds which lie immediately below the *Mesa*. Enormous volcanic eruptions seemed to have blanketed the entire area with ash filling in the topography which existed previous to the flow of the *Mesa basalt*. Then, almost immediately, before streams had eroded canyons in the ash, the molten lava blanketed the vast area.

While most of the outcrops of *Mesa basalt* occur east of the Cascade Mountains, some outcrops are found west of the Cascades near Portland, Oregon, and near Redding, California. These facts can only mean that the Cascade Mountains have been uplifted *after* the flowage of the *Mesa basalt!* Thus, the Cascades, contrary to what many geologists have supposed, are among the most recent geologic features and probably were uplifted just prior to the glaciation of the Northwest.

Mesa Basalt and Noachian Flood

It is the opinion of the author that the *Mesa basalt* as well as many other Cenozoic basalts flowed *after* the Noachian Flood. The *Mesa basalt* could not have flowed *during* the flood otherwise it would have been "quenched" by the waters and could not have spread so broadly.

Other Cenozoic basalts that the author has inspected show various evidences of subaerial accumulation such as widespread flow, development of columnar structures which is an evidence of slower cooling, and lack of rounded masses called pillow structures caused by rapid cooling in water. Included in the author's study are the widespread Columbia River basalts (Miocene), the basalts of the John Day formation (Oligo-Miocene) and those of the Clarno formation (Eocene).

Certain types of Cenozoic ash deposits also could not have accumulated in the waters of the flood. The best example is welded tuff. Some of these deposits which are over sixty feet thick were amassed so rapidly that the ash at the top of the deposits has trapped the heat and gases of the ash below and have flattened and "welded" fragments of pumice at the base. If these ash deposits had accumulated underwater the heat and gases could not be retained and the fragments would not be welded.

In the opinion of the author many of the Precambrian, Paleozoic and Mesozoic volcanics, which were deposited before the Cenozoic volcanics, show many evidences of accumulation simultaneous with flood conditions. These pre-Cenozoic volcanics in many cases have lava which has been extruded underwater and has quickly cooled forming pillow structure. Dunbar and Waage in their historical geology text comment on the Precambrian metamorphosed volcanics of the Canadian Shield, as follows:

> Metamorphosed lavas take on a greenish color from certain minerals produced in their alteration and are commonly called greenstones. Alteration, however, has not completely obliterated the structure that proves they were surface flows. Pillow structure, formed by sudden chilling where viscous lava flows into standing water, is a common feature. . . . The frequency with which pillow structure occurs in the greenstones of the shield indicates that these enormous masses of lava were extruded into water, presumably into the seas of the time.[8]

In the northeastern United States and in New Brunswick and Newfoundland, Paleozoic volcanic rocks are common. Dunbar and Waage say,

> In a local basin about Westport, Maine, layered volcanics have the impressive thickness of some 10,000 feet. In part these were submarine, for interbedded lenses of sediments include marine fossils. These date the volcanics as Silurian. Farther to

the northeast, about Black Cape on the New Brunswick coast of Chaleur Bay, the Silurian sedimentary formations have a thickness of about 8000 feet, all exposed in the sea cliffs, and in the midst of the Middle Silurian beds is a thickness of about 4000 feet of black lava flows (whence the name Black Cape). The basal flow poured out over the sea floor engulfing corals and brachiopods which are still well preserved. Here a geologist may have the unusual experience of collecting marine fossils in igneous rock. In north central Newfoundland, where the Silurian section is very thick and is all detrital, it includes some 1600 feet of rhyolitic and andesitic lava flows.[9]

The Mesozoic Franciscan formation of western California has volcanic rocks all of which are claimed to have been deposited in a submarine environment at great depth. The catastrophic significance of the volcanics, sandstones, and precipitates of the Franciscan formation was discussed by Dr. Bernard E. Northrup.[10] Also, the Metchosin volcanics of Olympic National Park, Washington, which are thought to have been deposited during the Paleocene early in the Cenozoic Era, were extruded under water.

Sedimentary rocks associated with many of these water-laid Precambrian, Paleozoic and Mesozoic volcanics show abundant evidences of catastrophic deposition under flood conditions. Commonly encountered Precambrian, Paleozoic and Mesozoic rocks such as widespread dolostone, bedded chert, black shale, coal, and graywacke can be best explained in most cases by flood deposition.[11] The pan-continental distribution of some sandstone, limestone, and shale beds is a striking feature of the Paleozoic and can be most simply accounted for by flood deposition. In terms of our thinking that many of the Cenozoic rocks were deposited *after* the flood, it is noteworthy that in late and middle Cenozoic strata widespread dolostone, bedded chert, black shale, coal, and graywacke are rare. This agrees with our original observation that pre-Cenozoic lava flows are generally submarine while late and middle Cenozoic flows are commonly subaerial.

Summary

Important events in the geologic history of the northwestern United states include:

First, the Noachian Flood which deposited great thicknesses of pre-Cenozoic sedimentary rocks;

Second, the building of the Columbia Plateau by a series of Cenozoic basalt flows and ash falls after the flood waters had subsided;

Third, an enormous volcanic eruption spread a layer of molten rock (the *Mesa basalt*) averaging 30 feet thick over parts of Oregon, Idaho, California, and Nevada, covering an estimated 100,000 square miles.

Fourth, the uplift of the Cascade Mountains occurred;

Fifth, volcanoes developed on the crests of the Cascades, glaciers covered much of the region, and flooding streams quickly carved canyons leaving buttes and mesas.

Many questions about the *Mesa basalt* still remain unanswered. How did the *Mesa basalt* spread so widely? How many years after the flood did the flow of the *Mesa* occur? Further investigation may supply the answers.

REFERENCES

1. Harry E. Wheeler and Howard A. Coombs, 1968. 100,000 square miles of burning rock. *Saturday Review*: 60-61. October 5.

2. *Ibid.,* pp. 61-62.

3. Harry E. Wheeler and Howard A. Coombs, 1967. Late Cenozoic mesa basalt sheet in northwestern United States. Bulletin Volcanologique 31:23.

4. D. W. Walker and D. A. Swanson, 1969. Discussion of paper by H. E. Wheeler and H. A. Coombs, Late Cenozoic mesa basalt sheet in northwestern United States. Bulletin Volcanologique 32:582.

5. The principle of uniformity specifies the uniformity of process rates or material conditions through geologic time, and the invariance of natural laws in space and time.

6. Wheeler and Coombs, *op. cit.,* p. 62.

7. Carl O. Dunbar and Karl M. Waage, 1969. Historical geology. John Wiley & Sons, Inc., New York, p. 425.

8. *Ibid.,* p. 137.

9. *Ibid.,* p. 223.

10. Bernard E. Northrup, 1970. Book review: Franciscan and related rocks and their significance in the geology of western California. *Creation Research Society Quarterly* 6(4):161-171. March.

11. Stuart E. Nevins, Stratigraphic evidence of the flood (in) Symposium on creation III. Edited by Donald Patten. Baker Book House, Grand Rapids, Michigan.

XII

POST-FLOOD STRATA OF THE JOHN DAY COUNTRY, NORTHEASTERN OREGON

STUART E. NEVINS*

Introduction

Sedimentary strata containing abundant mammal fossils (commonly referred to as "Cenozoic strata" by many geologists) reveal data of utmost importance to the timing of the Noachian Flood. Among members of the Creation Research Society two general views concerning the significance of such strata have prevailed.

The first and original view is that most of these mammal-bearing strata were deposited during the last stages of the Noachian Flood, and that the conclusion of the Flood initiated the recent glacial period. John C. Whitcomb and Henry M. Morris in *The Genesis Flood*[1] hold this view and suggest that the peculiar association of fossil mammals (and lack of dinosaurs, trilobites, etc.) resulted from "hydrodynamic sorting" where the creatures of similar specific gravity were deposited in the same strata by the waters of the Flood. The Flood view is promoted also by Harold W. Clark[2] who suggests that some of these mammal-bearing strata resulted from "ecological zonation" because the mammals were more agile and mobile, and were able to flee, and thus be the last creatures to be buried by the Flood.

William Springstead,[3] Reginald Daly,[4] and Donald Patten[5] maintain that the recent glacial period set in *during* the Noachian Flood. Thus, many mammoths were supposed to have been drowned in the waters of the Flood and speedily frozen in muck deposits in Siberia and Alaska. Most of the Cenozoic mammal-bearing deposits, in

---

*For author information, see Article II.

this view, were accumulated *during* the Flood. Many of the human fossils found in glacial sediments have been credited by some to be relics of the Flood.[6]

The second and more recent view proposed by a few members of the Creation Research Society is that many of the mammal-bearing strata were deposited rapidly *after* the Noachian Flood. According to this idea many mammals were born, lived, and later died *after* the Flood. Therefore, proponents of this view postulate an interval of up to many hundreds of years between the Flood and the recent glacial period.

Bernard Northrup, professor of Old Testament at Baptist Bible School of Theology, was an early advocate of the existence of considerable thickness of post-Flood strata. He interpreted diatomite fossil beds[7] and the well-known Franciscan Sequence[8] of California to be due to catastrophic sedimentation during continental movement after the Flood.

Harold G. Coffin, professor of paleontology at Andrews University, suggested a post-Flood origin for Cenozoic volcanic layers in the Pacific Northwest.[9] He noted that upright trees in basalt and volcanic breccia may be in original position of growth, and therefore, are not Flood deposits.

One of the earliest creationist articles on the Cenozoic strata in Oregon was by Ernest S. Booth.[10] He attributed the mammal fossils of the "Oligocene" John Day Formation to the last stages of the Flood, while the overlying "Miocene" Columbia River Basalt he considered to have flowed from cracks in the earth many years after the Flood. By this interpretation he supposed that the Cenozoic strata of Oregon are about half Flood strata and half post-Flood strata!

The previous discussion shows that there has been no uniformity of opinion among creationists regarding the time of origin of mammal-bearing, Cenozoic strata. There is a critical need for creationists to do more study on this problem of post-Flood strata. Field research is especially needed from creationist geologists.

This paper includes original geologic research conducted in the John Day Country of Oregon during the spring of 1970. The geologic evidences when properly interpreted indicate that the strata of this region were accumulated *after* the Noachian Flood. The study provides a basis for estimating the significance of other mammal-bearing strata of the world.

General Geology

The "John Day Country," named after a native Virginian who

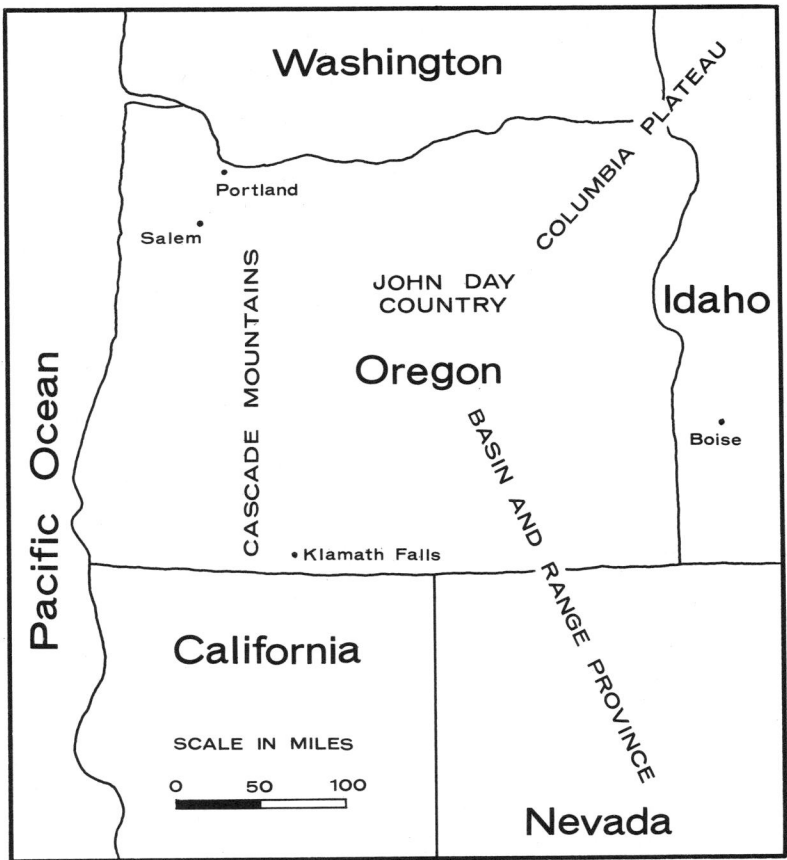

Figure 1. Location map of the John Day Country in northeastern Oregon.

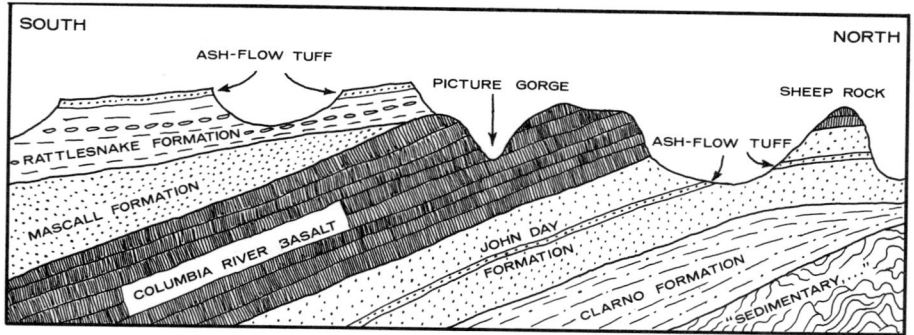

FORMATION	THICKNESS	LITHOLOGIC DESCRIPTION	FOSSILS
GLACIAL AND ALLUVIAL SEDIMENTS	THIN AND VARIABLE	LOCAL LAVA FLOWS, ALLUVIAL DEPOSITS, GLACIAL DEPOSITS, LANDSLIDES	MAMMALS INCLUDING MAMMOTHS
RATTLESNAKE FORMATION	800 FT.	GRAVEL, SAND, SILT, ASH-FLOW TUFF	MAMMALS INCLUDING PLIOHIPPUS AND NEOHIPPARION
MASCALL FORMATION	1,000 FT.	WHITE VOLCANIC ASH AND TUFF, SAND AND SILT	MAMMALS INCLUDING MIOHIPPUS AND MERYCHIPPUS
COLUMBIA RIVER BASALT	1,500 FT.	NUMEROUS BASALT FLOWS	----------
JOHN DAY FORMATION	1,000 FT.	VOLCANIC SILTSTONE AND SANDSTONE, SUBAERIAL BASALT FLOWS, ASH-FLOW TUFF, TUFF-BRECCIA	MIOHIPPUS AND MANY OTHER MAMMALS; SUBTROPICAL PLANTS
CLARNO FORMATION	UP TO 3,000 FT.	SUBAERIAL BASALT FLOWS, BOULDER BRECCIA, TUFF, TUFF-BRECCIA	EOHIPPUS; RARE LARGE MAMMALS; TROPICAL AND SUBTROPICAL PLANTS
"SEDIMENTERY, METASEDIMENTARY, METAVOLCANIC AND INTRUSIVE ROCKS"	?	VOLCANIC ASH, SUBMARINE BASALT FLOWS, SHALE, SILTSTONE, THIN LENSES OF LIMESTONE, CONGLOMERATE	RARE MARINE INVERTEBRATES

Figure 2. Generalized north-south cross section through the John Day River Valley at Sheep Rock and Picture Gorge in Grant County, Oregon. The horizontal dimension of diagram is approximately six miles, while the maximum vertical thickness is about 3,000 feet. (Note the use of vertical exaggeration.) The stratigraphy, lithology, and paleontology are summarized.

explored Oregon in the spring of 1812, is in the southwestern portion of the Blue Mountain region in northeastern Oregon and covers 5,000 square miles (see the location map in Figure 1). The John Day Country forms the borderland between the basalt flows covering 100,000 square miles of the Columbia Plateau to the northeast, and the folded and faulted rocks of the Basin and Range Province to the south. Few areas of the earth's crust provide such manifold evidences of volcanic catastrophism.

We begin our study of the strata of the John Day Country with a general description of the strata followed by a detailed field investigation of a particular location. Important geologic terms are defined in the Appendix of this paper.

A schematic cross section through the earth's crust to expose various strata is shown in Figure 2. Also in Figure 2 is a general description of rock types and associated fossils. The superposition of these rocks is determined by field investigation and by no means are fossils used to suggest which strata are older. The order of strata thus shows the chronology of the geologic history.

"Sedimentary, Metasedimentary, Metavolcanic, and Intrusive Rocks." The oldest rocks of the John Day Country make up what has been referred to in Figure 2 as "sedimentary, metasedimentary, metavolcanic, and intrusive rocks." These rocks are steeply folded, faulted, and metamorphosed by molten rock within the earth which had forced its way toward the surface.

The oldest of the sedimentary rocks are assigned by modern geologists to the "Permian System" and consist of marine volcanic sandstone, shale, siltstone, volcanic ash, and thin lenses of limestone. Lava frequently flowed over the bottom of the sea as evidenced by distinctive types of basalt. The volcanic history continued with further deposition of thousands of feet of volcanic ash, submarine lava, sandstone, and mudstone. Fossils are extremely rare.

These earliest rocks in the John Day Country in my opinion were deposited either immediately after the Noachian Floods or during the last stages of the Flood.

Strata which bear very good evidences of Flood deposition are not found in the John Day Country but are common a few miles to the south, where abundant limestone, sandstone, conglomerate, and chert are found with common marine fossils. Volcanic debris is rare. These strata, which are interpreted to be Flood rock, are older than the marine volcanic and sedimentary rocks found in the John Day Country.

Clarno Formation. The earliest rocks in the John Day Country with manifold evidences of post-Flood deposition belong to the Clarno Formation. A typical outcrop of the Clarno Formation is shown in Figure 3. This formation consists of subaerial basalt flows, volcanic breccias, terrestrial tuffs, and muds, sands, and gravels reworked by streams. Locally, giant mud flows deposited coarse gravel and boulders over several square miles. At least on one occasion between volcanic eruptions an interval of time existed of long enough duration with suitable environment for various types of trees to grow and for animals to thrive.

The climate was warm and humid as evidenced by the variety of tropical and subtropical plants (palm, breadfruit, cinnamon, sycamore, magnolia, avocado, walnut, fern, horse tail, etc.).[11] Rare herbivorous mammal fossils are found in the Clarno Formation and include rhinos, giant pig-like creatures, and *Eohippus* (a small mam-

Figure 3. Typical view of Clarno Formation in the John Day Country. Rocky meadows make agriculture difficult.

mal very much like a modern daman—thought by some to be an early ancestor in a series of supposed connecting links in the evolution of modern horses).

Subsequent to the mud flows and plant growth, the region was buried under volcanic extrusions. In some places the volcanic rocks of the Clarno Formation attain thicknesses of 3,000 to 5,000 feet.

John Day Formation. The John Day Formation, which lies immediately on top of the Clarno Formation, is readily identified by its brightly colored beds, fine-grained tuffaceous texture, and distinctively eroded appearance. Explosive volcanoes ejected vast quantities of rhyolitic ash over broad areas making the characteristic beds of tuff and volcanic siltstone. Occasionally a terrestrial lava flow inundated the country when molten rock forced its way to the surface. The John Day Formation in some places is over 4,000 feet thick. A typical exposure is shown in Figure 4.

The lower portion of the John Day Formation is generally red, and plant fossils (*Metasequoia,* birch, and alder) are common in some places. The middle, greenish portion, and the upper, buff-colored portion contain an exotic assemblage of mammal fossils which have made the John Day Formation world famous. These animals include saber-toothed cats, large dogs, camels, llamas, rhinoceroses, oreodonts (giant pig-like mammals having cud-chewing teeth), rabbits, and oppossums.

One of the most talked about fossils from the John Day Formation is the three-toed *Miohippus,* a mammal the size of a sheep with teeth equipped for browsing, thought by many paleontologists to be an evolutionary ancestor of the modern horse. At a few intervals between ash falls enough time elapsed for plant and animal life to become re-established.

The hardships encountered due to volcanic eruptions must have been extreme in those days, and there is little evidence that only the fittest survived. The entire population was buried. Volcanism also must have had a profound effect on the climate which was ideal being very warm and humid, but not as warm and humid as during the accumulation of the Clarno Formation. The large amount of volcanic dust in the atmosphere evidently served to shield some of the sun's heat.

In the western outcrops of the John Day Formation, tuff beds frequently contain pumice fragments over one centimeter in length. It is difficult to imagine how large pumice fragments could accumulate with volcanic ash during a flood. Water would readily separate the sinking volcanic ash from the floating pumice fragments.

The facts seem to require direct air-fall from exploding volcanoes as the mode of accumulation of most of the John Day tuffs. We are not surprised to find an amazing textural similarity between the tuffs and siltstones of the John Day Formation and modern loess and volcanic ash.[12] However, it is certainly possible that some beds of the John Day siltstones may be water deposited.

The most remarkable feature of the John Day Formation is the common occurrence of ash-flow tuff. This type of tuff is composed of particles of ash which have been "fused" or "welded" by great temperatures. It appears that each ash-flow tuff bed was accumulated during a single, gigantic explosion. The stratum formed while the ash particles were still hot and semi-plastic. The weight of overlying ash fused the stratum into a hard and compact mass. Such welding of particles must have occurred on the earth's surface when exposed to air, but could not have occurred in water. Accumulation of each stratum must have been very rapid.

Between Ashwood and Willowdale, Oregon, the geologist Dallas L. Peck[13] described seven different ash-flow tuff beds, each from fifty to four hundred feet in thickness, in a vertical section of the John Day Formation. These ash-flow tuffs comprise nearly one-fourth of the John Day Formation in that area! Many of these sheets of tuff are continuous over hundreds of square miles!

No portion of the John Day Country is known to have been spared these recurring inundations of hot volcanic ash. The base of the John Day Formation over much of its western exposure is marked by an ash-flow tuff sheet averaging one hundred feet in thickness. The middle portion of the John Day is distinguished by an extremely widespread sheet of welded ash averaging about one hundred and twenty feet in thickness. An excellent exposure of the middle ash-flow tuff is at Sheep Rock along the John Day River (see Figures 2 and 5).

Columbia River Basalt. After the deposition of the John Day Formation, the Pacific Northwest became the site of one of the most extensive accumulations of basalt in the world.[14] The John Day Country became a wasteland as molten lava gushed from numerous fissures in the earth's crust, while flow upon flow extended laterally for miles over Washington, Oregon, and Idaho. The flows covered an area of 100,000 square miles (250,000 square kilometers). The resultant rock is a dense, fine-grained, black basalt (called the Columbia River Basalt) which filled in irregularities in the topography of preceding strata.

Individual flows have been traced for over one hundred miles. The flows were definitely not submarine but represent a post-Flood volcanic catastrophe. Basalt when chilled under water forms characteristic pillow-like structures and cannot extend laterally great distances.

At least fourteen different flows can be recognized at Picture Gorge along the John Day River where the basalt has a thickness of 1,500 feet. In other areas of northeastern Oregon the Columbia River Basalt reaches a thickness of more than 5,000 feet. The entire basalt sequence does not represent a long history as well-developed soils and extensive fossils are not present between individual flows.

Due to its hardness and resistance to erosion, the Columbia River Basalt forms the region's dominant topographic features. Sheep Rock in Figure 5 is capped with Columbia River Basalt. The basalt forms mesas above the John Day Formation in Figure 4.

What effect would the extrusion of tremendous volumes of Columbia River Basalt (estimated volume is 1.5×10^5 km.^{3}) have had on the climate? My calculations show that 1.5×10^5 cubic kilometers of molten basaltic lava at $1100°$ C. cooling to surface temperature would yield 1.4×10^{23} calories of heat, most of which would pass into the atmosphere. This vast quantity of heat is more than 340 times the yearly amount of heat now received

Figure 4. The steeply tilted strata of the middle, greenish-colored John Day Formation (center) are present below flat-lying strata of Columbia River Basalt which form mesas on the left.

Figure 5. Sheep Rock along the John Day River, Grant County. A thick, well-exposed section of John Day Formation is present below a thin cap of Columbia River Basalt. Separating the middle, greenish-colored, from upper, buff-colored John Day is a 100-foot-thick bed of ash-flow tuff that is offset by a small normal fault dipping forty-five degrees to the left. (Sketch from pamphlet, The Geologic Setting of the John Day Country, U.S. Geological Survey, Washington, D.C., 1970, p. 14.)

from the sun at the earth's surface over the 250,000 square kilometer area of flow of the Columbia River Basalt.

It is most reasonable to conclude that rapid atmospheric cooling of the Columbia River Basalt flows had profound effects on the earth's climate, probably on a global or subglobal scale.

Mascall Formation. As the Columbia River Basalt flowed, volcanoes spewed white ash over the surface and streams distributed sediments. The resulting deposits, which are up to 1,000 feet thick, lie on the basalt and are called the Mascall Formation. That the climate was not as warm and not as humid as at earlier times is evidenced by the changed vegetation (cypress, beech, and oak are common) and presence of both browsing and grazing mammals.

In the Mascall Formation browsing mammals similar to *Miohippus* of the John Day Formation are present *with Merychippus* which is thought to be a grazer. *Miohippus* is thought by many paleontologists to have evolved into *Merychippus* but transitional forms have not been found in the John Day Country. There is a great difference between the teeth of the two mammals. The formation of *Merychippus* marks one of the big gaps in the supposed evolutionary "family tree" of the horse.[15]

Rattlesnake Formation. Tilting and faulting of the strata of the John Day Country after the accumulation of the Mascall Formation caused resedimentation of nearly 800 feet of gravel, sand and silt over the Mascall. These alluvial deposits are called the Rattlesnake Formation. The climate seems to have been considerably cooler and more arid than during the time of accumulation of the John Day Formation. Fossils of browsing creatures are not as prominent as in the Mascall Formation.

In the Rattlesnake Formation, *Neohipparion* (a three-toed grazer —very similar to *Merychippus* of the earlier Mascall beds) is found *with Pliohippus* (a very horse-like grazer with a hoof and no side toes). *No transition between the three-toed and single-hoofed forms has been found!* While the evolutionary "family tree" of the horse may appear *on paper* like one of the most compelling arguments for the general theory of evolution, under scrutiny one wonders if some other explanation might be more credible.

The uppermost portion of the Rattlesnake Formation is a single ash-flow tuff bed over one hundred feet thick which is known to extend laterally about seventy miles. The tuff bears flow structures and flattened pumice fragments in a welded ash matrix. This tuff is a grim reminder of the volcanic catastrophes so common to the John Day Country. Concerning the accumulation of this tuff layer Margaret L. Steere, a geologist of uniformitarian persuasion for the State of Oregon admits:

> The origin of this peculiar tuff was for many years a matter of considerable speculation, but was generally regarded as a flow

of rhyolite. In recent years observations of extrusions from active volcanoes have given rise to the theory that this is a form of *nuée ardents* (fiery cloud). Such volcanic outbursts are erupted as a glowing gaseous cloud of incandescent particles, the whole mass moving at great speed. The entire phenomenon is one of exceedingly short duration, perhaps only a matter of a few days. After extrusion the hot plastic particles adhere to one another till they are welded together, while the larger fragments are flattened under the weight of the mass.[16]

The suggestion that the entire tuff bed was deposited from a rapidly moving incandescent cloud seems plausible, even though nothing on such a scale is going on at the present.

The major problem in explaining the origin of ash-flow tuff is how the heat was conserved which welded and flattened particles. In order to conserve heat two United States Geological Survey geologists have suggested that the incandescent particles which form the welded ash-flow tuff were not extruded high into the air, but traveled rapidly over the ground surface. They propose an "ash-flow" origin for this welded variety of tuff. They define "ash-flow" as: A turbulent mixture of gas and pyroclastic materials of high temperature, ejected explosively from a crater or fissure, that travels swiftly down the slopes of a volcano or along the ground surface.[17]

About the same time as this remarkable ash-flow tuff bed of the Rattlesnake Formation was being deposited, an extremely widespread flow of basaltic lava (called the Mesa Basalt) occurred in central and southern Oregon, northern California, northwestern Nevada, and western Idaho.[18] This basalt flow inundated about 100,000 square miles, yet the layer averages only 30 feet in thickness.

Following the deposition of the Mesa Basalt and the Rattlesnake Formation, extensive uplifting occurred in the western United States. The Cascade Mountains in western Oregon were uplifted along with the Sierra Nevada Mountains of California. The major uplift of the Blue Mountains in the John Day Country had already been accomplished.

Glacial and Alluvial Sediments. After the deposition of the Rattlesnake Formation, local folding and faulting occurred in the

John Day Country. Minor lava flows after this time were from local vents. The climate was cold and humid as evidenced by glacial deposits found at elevations over 5,000 feet. Runoff from these glaciers carved the canyons.

Where the bedrock was hard (commonly basalt) the river canyons are very narrow, but where the rock is soft (commonly tuff) the canyons are wide. Valleys commonly are filled with alluvial sediments and the older terrace deposits often contain bones of mammoths. Recent landslides are numerous in the John Day Country.

Field Study

During the Spring of 1970, the author had the opportunity to perform field research in the John Day Country. The area studied extensively lies two miles east of the Clarno Ferry on the John Day River in Wheeler County, Oregon. Specifically, the area studied was Hancock Canyon, Indian Canyon, and "The Cove" north of Oregon State Highway 218. A nine square mile area was mapped geologically and copious field notes were recorded. The study included the upper portion of the Clarno Formation, the entire John Day Formation, and the lowest portion of the Columbia River Basalt. Only a summary of the investigation can be presented here.

Terminology used has been simplified and important geologic nomenclature is defined in the Appendix.

A generalized composite columnar section of the strata studied is presented in Figure 6. It represents a vertical thickness of over 2,000 feet. The assigned order of strata, which does not depend on correlation by fossils, has been established by careful field study of the superposition of strata. Twenty intervals will be described. The order shows the sequence of events during a portion of the area's geologic history. The significance of the various strata will become apparent during the discussion.

(1) *Black Coarse-Grained Basalt.* We begin our study arbitrarily at a hard, cliff-forming basalt stratum midway in the Clarno Formation exposed at the mouth of Hancock Canyon along Highway 218. The thickness of this basalt was not apparent because

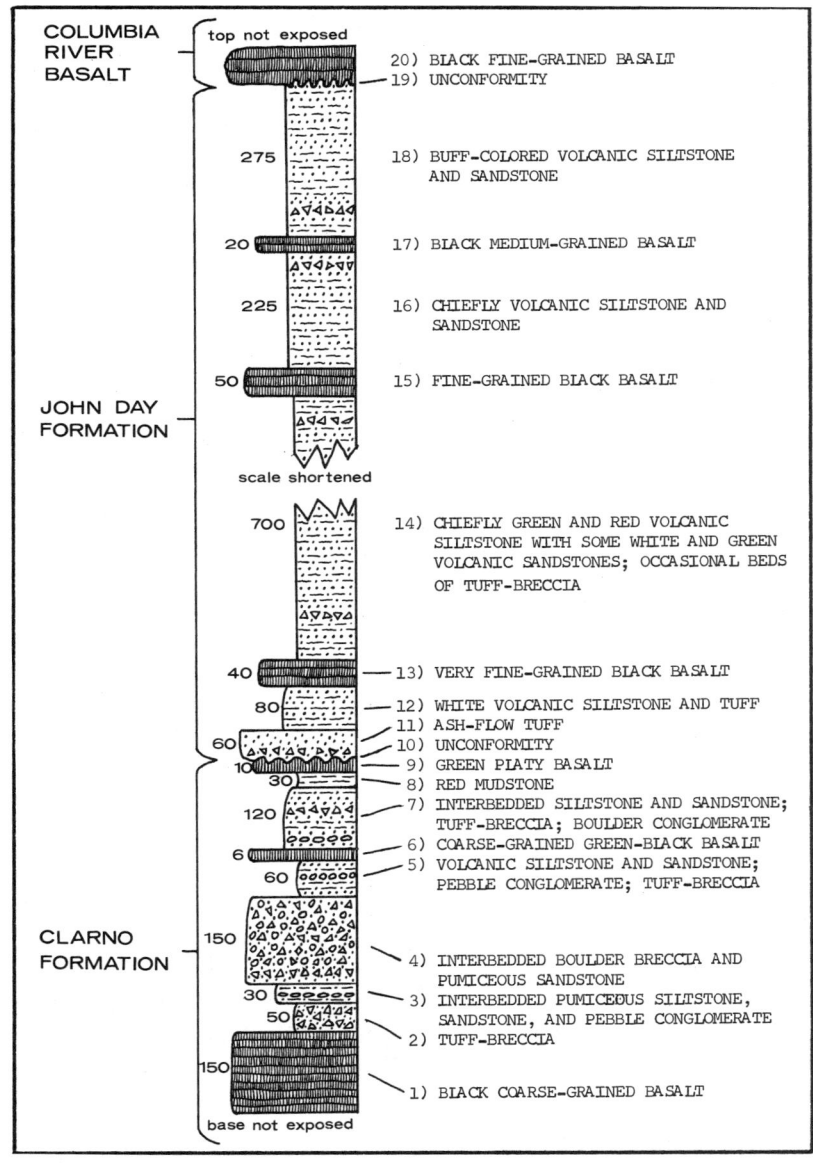

Figure 6. Composite columnar section of over 2,000 feet of strata in Hancock Canyon, Indian Canyon, and "The Cove," Wheeler County, Oregon. Thicknesses are in feet.

only the upper one hundred fifty feet was exposed. Also lateral extent was not determined because it extended out of the mapped area. At least one mile of flow was demonstrated with the probability of much more. The basalt represents a single subaerial lava flow.

(2) *Tuff-Breccia.* On top of the basalt is a fifty-foot-thick bed of distinctive tuff-breccia. The tuff-breccia matrix is white pumice containing large, angular, brick-red breccia fragments. This unit represents a very explosive stage in volcanism.

Because of the unique red breccia fragments the entire unit seems to represent a single volcanic occurrence of short duration from a single vent. Due to its softness the rock is not well exposed.

(3) *Interbedded Pumiceous Siltstone, Sandstone, and Pebble Conglomerates.* This thirty-foot-thick unit lying over the tuff-breccia represents an interval of stream deposition probably in a vast flood plain. There is little evidence of a time interval between the underlying unit where erosion of the preceding tuff-breccia or basalt could occur.

(4) *Interbedded Boulder Breccia and Pumiceous Sandstone.* This remarkable unit is composed of large boulders (many more than three feet in diameter) cemented in a matrix of sand. Thin lenses of sandstone sometimes are present between thick beds of boulders.

The middle of this unit contains a seventy-foot-thick bed of boulders some of which are over ten feet in diameter! The boulder beds are shown in Figure 7. The boulder layer can be traced as a planar stratum over two miles through the mapped area.

The boulders have different degrees of roundness but most of the larger boulders have fair rounding while the pebbles tend to be quite angular. Nearly all of the boulders and pebbles are a peculiar type of violet andesite. (Andesite, like basalt, is extruded as a molten mass, but due to the higher viscosity of andesite it cannot usually flow like basalt and tends to fracture into blocks and spheres.) Boulder and pebble sources for this unusual andesite are known in Hancock Canyon and vicinity.

Conventional stream processes could not transport boulders of this size. Some catastrophic or semi-catastrophic mechanism such

Figure 7. The Clarno Formation at "The Palisades" exposed along Oregon State Highway 218 at the mouth of Indian Canyon. The strata, which are up to 150 feet thick, consist of boulder breccia (with some boulders over 10 feet in diameter), evidently representing a series of catastrophic mud flows.

as tremendous sheet floods (as could occur by the breaching of a natural dam) or huge mud flows seems necessary. The mud flow hypothesis seems to fit the data best. No great time span was required to accumulate these strata. The unit is up to one hundred fifty feet thick.

(5) *Volcanic Siltstone and Sandstone; Pebble Conglomerate; Tuff-Breccia.* Frequent explosive eruptions deposited beds of siltstone, sandstone, and tuff-breccia, while streams distributed sand in layers. When volcanism was particularly explosive, beds of tuff-breccia were deposited, but as each episode subsided fine silt- and sand-sized particles of pumice were deposited. The resulting unit, which has widely differing characteristics when followed laterally, is about sixty feet thick.

(6) *Coarse-Grained Green-Black Basalt.* Upon the fairly gentle topography which existed after the ash falls of the preceding unit a coarse-grained basalt flowed. The basalt, which was a very local flow, is a convenient datum in many places for locating the fossil beds, which are found several feet above. It is about six feet thick.

(7) *Interbedded Volcanic Siltstone and Sandstone; Tuff-Breccia; Boulder Conglomerate.* This unit like other units below it is composed of a wide variety of volcanic materials. Boulder beds composed of the distinctive andesite boulders are common (see Figure 8). These evidently formed from mud flows created by upwarping of strata around volcanic vents. The entire unit is poorly consolidated and is about one hundred twenty feet thick.

At a horizon in the middle of this unit deposition of volcanics ceased for a long enough period of time for a remarkable array of

Figure 8. Boulder conglomerate of the Clarno Formation in Hancock Canyon containing distinctive andesite cobbles and boulders. The presence of sand and silt with cobbles and boulders is one evidence indicating mud flows.

flora and fauna to thrive. While the preceding units are notably void of fossils, this single horizon has them in abundance.

The late Paleontologist A. W. Hancock spent many years exhuming fossils from a *single* quarry only a few tens of yards wide on the western side of Hancock Canyon. The Oregon Museum of Science and Industry now operates Camp Hancock for the purpose of collecting various fossil vertebrates from the site. This peculiar vertebrate locality in the upper portion of the Clarno Formation has yielded crocodile, fish, *Eohippus,* tapir, large swamp dwelling rhinoceros, small running rhinoceros, oreodont (extinct mammal combining certain characteristics of pig, deer, and camel), and titanotothere (extinct mammal combining certain characteristics of horse and rhinoceros). There are very few animals present.

It is not hard to imagine how this fossil bed was formed. For instruction one recalls the apparently inactive, vine-covered Mt. Vesuvius in A.D. 79, which suddenly inundated Pompeii and another city in volcanic ash. It must have been much the same near the Clarno vertebrate locality when the ash began to rain down. The smaller animals were quickly overcome, while the larger, more mobile animals probably ran to the cool water of the nearest water hole before being buried. This seems to explain the odd association of both terrestrial and aquatic animals.

Southwest of the vertebrate locality in Hancock Canyon and apparently at the same stratigraphic horizon occur the famous "Clarno Nut Beds." This is one of the world's best localities to collect fossil fruits and nuts! A fossil tree seen in Figure 9 in upright (growth) position was found in volcanic sandstone at another site in Hancock Canyon. Also, leaves of various tropical and subtropical trees are found at other locations.

The presence of so many fossils at one horizon within the Clarno Formation and lack of fossils in other horizons is evidence that can be used to argue for rapid accumulation of the upper portion of the formation. The only interval of sufficient duration for various forms of life to have become established appears to be at the horizon stated above.

(8) *Red Mudstone.* Wind-blown volcanic dust accumulated

Figure 9. Upright fossil tree penetrating a visible distance of ten feet stratigraphically through volcanic sandstone of the Clarno Formation, Hancock Canyon. Rapid burial was necessary to cover the tree before it could rot and fall down.

mostly in depressions in the topography. The red coloration is due to oxidation of iron in various clay minerals. While this unit is not usually more than thirty feet thick, slopes hundreds of feet in height have been stained by the eroding mudstone (see Figure 10).

(9) *Green Platy Basalt.* A green basalt with a distinctive platy fracture flowed in a local area around Hancock Canyon. This basalt, which is over ten feet thick in some places, marks the uppermost known deposits of the Clarno Formation in Hancock and Indian canyons.

(10) *Unconformity.* Following the deposition of the volcanics of the Clarno Formation an interval of erosion occurred. During this time on a local scale several feet of the Clarno Formation was removed by wind and water. This erosion is due evidently to local uplifting on the order of a few tens of feet in one area and downwarping of another area. This is possibly due to disequilibrium

Figure 10. The red mudstone unit in the upper Clarno Formation of Hancock Canyon. John Day Formation below Columbia River Basalt is visible in the background.

caused by molten rock evacuating certain zones within the earth. The higher areas were beveled, and sediments such as the red mudstone unit were deposited in lower areas.

According to evolutionary paleontologists the upper portion of the Clarno Formation seen in Hancock Canyon is thought to have accumulated during the latest part of the "Eocene Period," an interval claimed to be about 100 million years in duration, which is supposed to have *concluded* approximately 40 million years ago.[19]

The deposition of the following John Day Formation is presumed to have *begun* about 35 million years ago near the middle portion of the "Oligocene Period." An interval of about 5 million years is thought to exist between the two formations. This vast interval of 5 million years is conveniently placed at the unconformity by many geologists.

At modern rates of erosion an entire mountain range could be washed to the sea in 5 million years. If the popular time conception is correct one would expect the soft material of the Clarno Formation to be deeply canyoned, or, most likely, totally removed. (Remember that the tropical vegetation of the Clarno should have thrived in a climate ideal for accelerated erosion.)

In actuality the erosion which occurred at the unconformity is rather minimal and therefore does not need to represent a vast hiatus of millions of years. Fossils were not found at this interval in the mapped area.

(11) *Ash-Flow Tuff*. Following the deposition of the Clarno Formation and brief interval of non-deposition, the first beds of the John Day Formation accumulated. In the Hancock Canyon area the John Day begins with a volcanic catastrophe par excellence.

As elaborated earlier, an ash-flow tuff bed seems to have accumulated from a single explosive event which expels a gigantic mass of incandescent particles. The cloud must have moved rapidly over the ground surface and deposited debris which was still very hot and semi-plastic. The resulting deposit has particles which are fused ("welded") together.

Due to the weight and heat of the single thick bed, fragments of pumice at the base of the deposit are squashed into coin-like shapes.

This type of tuff could not accumulate in water. Because of the welding of the ash particles the bed is very hard in comparison to the more common, very soft unwelded tuff beds. Due to its hardness ash-flow tuff is a common ridge former.

The ash-flow tuff bed in the lower portion of the John Day Formation in Hancock Canyon is about sixty feet thick. D. A. Swanson and P. T. Robinson[20] found nearly continuous exposures of this ash-flow tuff up to 100 feet in thickness extending a distance of forty-five miles to the southwest from Hancock Canyon! This tuff was also observed by R. L. Hay[21] about fifteen miles southeast of Hancock Canyon.

One is impressed by the widespread nature of this remarkable tuff bed. It is difficult to visualize such an enormous and short-lived volcanic event. Nothing in our day to day experience is anything like it.

(12) *White Volcanic Siltstone and Tuff.* This unit which follows the ash-flow tuff is up to eighty feet thick. Volcanic debris accumulated more slowly than the preceding unit and streams distributed sediments. This white ash unit is very widespread and was noted by Peck over twenty-five miles southwest of Hancock Canyon.

At one interval in this unit in the eastern portion of the mapped area leaf fossils of *Metasequoia* (a genus of evergreen tree which grows in modern forests in China) are fairly common. At other distant locations the white tuff in the lower portion of the John Day Formation contains abundant *Metasequoia* leaf fossils, along with pine, sycamore, birch, and alder. It seems necessary that another interval of time be added of sufficient duration for plants to become reestablished.

The climate was evidently a little cooler than during the Clarno deposits and may be due to the tremendous increase in amounts of volcanic dust in the atmosphere which tended to shield the sun's heat from the surface of the earth. Also, during Clarno time the hot climate was maintained by cooling lava flows, while during the John Day interval lava flows were not as common and did not have such a profound effect on the climate.

(13) *Very Fine-Grained Black Basalt.* At one location in Indian

Canyon a local basalt flow up to forty feet thick is present.

(14) *Chiefly Green and Red Volcanic Siltstone with Some White and Green Volcanic Sandstones; Occasional Beds of Tuff-Breccia.* The middle portion of the John Day Formation is composed of a monotonous succession of volcanic siltstones with occasional beds of volcanic sandstone and tuff-breccia. While most of this unit is aeolian ash which accumulated on the earth's surface, some of the beds may have been deposited in a large, shallow lake. The sequence is about seven hundred feet thick!

Green and red volcanic siltstone comprises the bulk of the unit with individual beds being from four to forty feet thick. Beds of volcanic sandstone and tuff-breccia are only a few feet thick and represent more explosive volcanic events. Due to their poor consolidation beds of this unit are not well exposed.

(15) *Fine-Grained Black Basalt.* A single fifty-foot-thick, very widespread lava flow spread over the very level surface. That this basalt represents a terrestrial flow (not a subaqueous flow) is proved by well-developed columnar jointing (a distinctive feature in many terrestrial flows), its broad distance of flow, and the lack of pillow-like structures which would be formed by cooling in water.

(16) *Chiefly Greenish Volcanic Siltstone and Sandstone.* This unit which is 225 feet thick is composed mainly of volcanic siltstone. Tuff-breccia beds show that more explosive volcanism prevailed than during the preceding siltstone unit. Fossils were not found in these beds in the mapped area, but mammals have been reported from the same unit in other locations.

(17) *Black Medium-grained Basalt.* Another widespread lava flow accumulated to a thickness of twenty feet. The basalt extended outside the mapped area and its flow dimensions are unknown.

(18) *Buff-colored Volcanic Siltstone and Sandstone.* Further volcanic activity deposited these beds which comprise the uppermost unit of the John Day Formation to a thickness of 275 feet. Due to their very poor consolidation they are not well exposed.

(19) *Unconformity.* Following the deposition of the John Day Formation slight warping of strata occurred on a regional scale

and another short interval of erosion prevailed. Locally several feet of the John Day Formation were removed by wind and water. Canyons in the soft siltstone were carved to a depth of almost one hundred feet in some places. There is little evidence of a hiatus of millions of years at this unconformity. The slight regional tilting and wet climate were ideal for quickly forming limited topographic features.

(20) *Black Fine-grained Basalt (Columbia River Basalt).* This vast basalt flow which overlies the John Day Formation is the well-known Columbia River Basalt. It was not extensively studied in the mapped area but was used to locate the uppermost portion of the John Day Formation.

Fallacies in K-Ar Dating

Over one hundred potassium-argon dates have been made on the Columbia River Basalt. The actual ratios of potassium to argon do not present a coherent estimate of age, having many samples giving far too great an age. The divergent ratios must be "corrected" to allow for the contamination from atmospheric argon. The corrected ratios give an age range between 14 million and 18 million years.[22] Can the range in age also be explained by errors due to atmospheric argon? Are there other factors which influence these age ratios, making them appear too old?

According to potassium-argon dates from the University of California, Berkeley, the uppermost portion of the John Day Formation is 24.4 million years old.[23] University of California potassium-argon dates on the earliest Columbia River Basalt flows indicate an age of 18 million years.[24] Thus, if this method is correct an interval of about six million years is present at the unconformity between the two formations. Yet, as suggested above there is little stratigraphic evidence of such a vast interval of time at the unconformity. How was the volcanism which was so omnipresent in both preceding and succeeding strata arrested for six million years?

Potassium-argon dates on the lower portion of the John Day Formation indicate an age of 31.1 to 31.5 million years.[25] Using the previous date on the upper portion of the John Day (24.4 million years), the potassium-argon method here indicates that the John Day Formation represents an interval of at least seven million years of deposition. (This estimated interval is very conservative among those proposed by uniformitarian geologists.) Since the John Day Formation averages 1,000 feet in thickness, the average annual amount of accumulation using these dates is 1.0×10^3 feet divided by 7.0×10^6 years giving an average of 1.4×10^{-4} foot per year or 4.2×10^{-2} mm. per year.

If uniformitarian geologists who have proposed these dates are correct, the average annual thickness of accumulation of the volcanics of the John Day Formation is approximately the thickness of a page of this *book! But such an average is verily contradicted by the strata themselves and by everything we know about the rates of volcanic processes!* There is little stratigraphic evidence of a vast hiatus of "paraconformity" *within* the John Day Formation. It is here submitted that the duration of deposition has been grossly overestimated by uniformitarian geologists.

While the fossils of the upper Clarno Formation in Hancock Canyon are dated as late Eocene by many modern evolutionary paleontologists, potassium-argon dates do not relate the Hancock Canyon strata to other late Eocene fossil deposits. Thus, the "Clarno Nut Beds" in Hancock Canyon dated as 34.5 million years[26] by potassium-argon while other late Eocene strata commonly date *older* than 40 million years. Is there an explanation for such anomalous dates?

Summary of Post-Flood Evidences

The suggestion developed in this paper, namely the presence of many thousands of feet of post-Flood strata in Oregon, needs further elaboration. The idea will no doubt be a subject of lively debate among members of the Creation Research Society. My reasons for post-Flood strata are summarized below.

First, the numerous basalt flows of the John Day Country provide one of the most obvious evidences of post-Flood catastrophism. These basalts almost always show evidences of subaerial extrusion (columnar joints, widespread flow, lack of pillow structures), which are unlike lavas which would have been extruded into water during a widespread flood.

Second, the ash-flow tuffs of the John Day Country seem to demand subaerial accumulation. How were these tuffs welded into compact and resistant layers if accumulated in water?

Third, the large fragments of pumice in fine ash require subaerial accumulation. Water readily separates the floating pumice fragments from the sinking ash.

Fourth, the poor textural sorting of the tuffs is remarkably similar to modern air-fall tuffs and windblown ash. Water, however, tends to remove fine particles from coarse particles leaving deposits which have good to fair sorting.

Fifth, many of the pebbles, cobbles, and boulders are from local sources and have not been transported any great distance. If a universal flood was responsible for depositing these strata, we would expect the pebbles, cobbles, and bouldlers to be of very distant and untraceable origin.

Sixth, the abrupt lateral variation in lithologic composition in many of the water-accumulated strata can be used to suggest that the depositional agent was local and not widespread. The most laterally extensive rock units in the John Day Country are of volcanic origin, not flood origin. If the strata of the John Day Country were partially of flood origin, we would expect widespread sedimentary, water-deposited layers.

Seventh, the fossils of terrestrial animals and plants with absence of marine creatures indicates post-Flood conditions. The occurrence of fossils on specific, widespread horizons (and absence at other levels) along with upright trees (apparently in growth position) can be used to argue for *in situ* origin, not transportation from a distant region by the waters of the Flood.

Thus, the strata of the John Day Country bear abundant testimony of volcanic catastrophism. The evidences for flood catastrophism are very meager. Since there are no good evidences of the universal Flood in any of the Cenozoic strata of the John Day Country, the Flood must precede the formation of these strata.

The amount of time between the close of Noah's Flood and the onset of the recent glacial period is not known. How long did it take for the plants to grow on the different fossil horizons? How much time elapsed during the unconformities between formations? How long did it take for a lava flow to cool before a second flow occurred? It is estimated that an interval of many hundreds of years may have existed between the close of the Flood and the beginning of the ice age. More research needs to be done on this topic.

The strict-chronology interpretation of Genesis chapter 11 would establish the date of Noah's Flood about 2,400 B.C., a date which is inconsistent with the geologic data presented in this paper. The Flood must have occurred before this date. Concerning the date of the Flood, Whitcomb and Morris say:

> A careful study of the Biblical evidence leads us to the conclusion that the Flood may have occurred as much as three to five thousand years before Abraham.[27]

If the Flood occurred about 5000 to 7000 B.C. and if the ice age is assumed to have been between 3000 and 4000 B.C., an interval of 1,000 to 3,000 years existed between the close of the Flood and the onset of glaciation. This period of time seems adequate for accumulation of the strata of the John Day Country.

Conclusion

In this paper we have presented a general overview of the strata of the John Day Country as well as a detailed field investigation of a particular locality. The Clarno Formation (lava flows, volcanic ash, boulder breccia), John Day Formation (chiefly volcanic ash), Mascall Formation (volcanic ash), Rattlesnake Formation (stream sediments and ash-flow tuff), and recent alluvial and glacial deposits according to many geologists accumulated over a period of about 60 million years. The strata, however, contain little convincing evidence of such a vast interval of time. Internal evidence within the strata (lava flows, ash-flow tuff beds, mud flow deposits, etc.) demands catastrophic deposition of thousands of feet of rock.

Fossils when found occur on particular horizons and suggest that only at rare occasions of quiescence between volcanic eruptions was life able to become re-established. The so-called evolutionary "family tree" of the horse, which is well represented in the John Day Country, is by no means a continuous transformation of species, but is very artificial, having several large gaps in the series. The climate was originally tropical in Clarno time, changing to cold and humid during accumulation of the recent glacial deposits.

Intensive field investigation in the vicinity of Hancock Canyon in Wheeler County assembled a composite columnar section of strata over 2,000 feet in thickness. According to many geologists the section represents about 25 million years of earth history. Yet, study of the strata and intervals of nondeposition suggests that the time span has been greatly overestimated. There is little evidence to refute the proposal that the strata of the columnar section represent a history of only a few thousand years or less.

It is proposed that the strata of the John Day Country accumulated after the Noachian Flood. Lava flows and ash-flow tuff beds prove subaerial extrusion and these strata could not be deposited during the Noachian Flood. The study suggests that other mammal-bearing rocks of what geologists have called "Cenozoic strata" are also post-Flood deposits.

It is therefore necessary to postulate a post-Flood era probably of many hundreds of years duration between the close of the Flood and the initiation of the recent continental glaciation. Theories which postulate the recent glacial period as being simultaneous with or very shortly after the Flood need to be modified.

APPENDIX: TERMINOLOGY

Basalt: dark-colored, generally fine-grained igneous rock extruded as molten lava of great fluidity. Minerals composing basalt include calcium-rich feldspars and pyroxene, with a characteristic lack of quartz. When basalt is extruded under water it tends to form rounded pillow-like structures and cannot flow great distances. Subaerial basalt flows tend to be very widespread and form columnar joints perpendicular to cooling surfaces.

Rhyolite: fine-grained, usually pinkish-colored extrusive igneous rock corresponding in composition to granite (containing potassium-rich feldspars, biotite, and quartz). Due to its high silica content rhyolite tends to be very viscous and cannot flow great distances. Rhyolite volcanism tends to be extremely explosive.

Andesite: fine-grained, usually gray, extrusive igneous rock having a silica content lower than rhyolite but greater than basalt. Due to its intermediate silica content andesite flows tend to be fairly viscous and do not spread widely. Common minerals in andesite include sodium-rich feldspars, hornblende, and some quartz.

Pumice: volcanic rock usually rich in silica containing numerous, fine air cells. Pumice floats in water.

Volcanic ash: fine (particles less than 4 mm. diameter), poorly consolidated, fragmental debris commonly the product of explosive eruptions of viscous lava rhyolite and andesite).

Tuff: rock composed of compacted volcanic ash. Tuff can be referred to as volcanic mudstone, siltstone, or sandstone, depending on the characteristics of the particles forming it.

Ash-flow tuff: rock closely resembling rhyolite formed from ash ejected in enormous incandescent clouds which travel rapidly over the ground and are deposited, compacted, and welded by the heat and weight of the entire stratum.

Breccia: rock composed of coarse, angular rock fragments larger than 4 mm. in diameter. Volcanic breccia (usually containing fragments of rhyolite, andesite, or pumice) indicates a very explosive stage of volcanism. Mud flow breccia is caused by collapse and fracturing of rock or mass movement of volcanic breccia.

Tuff-breccia: rock containing coarse, angular volcanic fragments in a matrix of ash.

Conglomerate: cemented gravel, pebbles, cobbles, or boulders which do not tend to be very angular.

Intrusive rock: igneous rock formed by cooling of magma which has displaced other rock within the earth.

Dike: igneous, intrusive body of rock forced into fissures which cut across stratified rocks.

Columnar section: graphic representation of strata in a particular area plotted in vertical order with the thickness drawn to scale.

Unconformity: contact between two strata with evidence of a prolonged interval of nondeposition where erosion of underlying strata occurred. The terms "paraconformity" and "diastem" are used by many geologists to denote an unconformity which shows little evidence of erosion but appears to represent a continuous, uninterrupted period of deposition.

REFERENCES

1. John C. Whitcomb, Jr., and Henry M. Morris, 1961. The Genesis flood. Presbyterian and Reformed Publishing Co., Philadelphia, p. 283. Whitcomb and Morris recognize that many of the details of the significance of mammal-bearing deposits remain to be worked out. On page 312 they say: ". . . this makes it very difficult to determine precisely which deposits were laid down in

the Deluge proper and which are attributable to the disturbed centuries after the Flood." On page 419 they say: "Extensive volcanism was undoubtedly associated with the Deluge and such volcanic deposits are only to be expected in the Deluge strata. These in the Pacific northwest are mostly attributable to the latter stages of the Deluge and perhaps post-Deluge events, since they are commonly dated at Tertiary or even sometimes Quaternary."

2. Harold W. Clark, 1971. Paleoecology and the flood, *Creation Research Society Quarterly,* 8(1):23. On page 22 Clark says, "In this discussion I have suggested that the Flood ended around the Cretaceous or early Tertiary."

3. W. A. Springstead, 1973. The creationist and the continental glaciation, *Creation Research Society Quarterly,* 10(1):50. "The Flood itself was accompanied by overwhelming turbidity mud flows which both drowned and covered the mammoths and other life in the North. This was soon followed by an extreme drop in temperature and winds of great force. The winds caused the flood waters to subside and in turn froze the mud with its vast animal remains."

4. Reginald Daly, 1972. Earth's most challenging mysteries. Craig Press, Nutley, N. J., p. 237. "That the collapse in temperature occurred, and the ice age began, exactly at the time of the flood when the canopy collapsed is proved by the frozen mammoths."

5. Donald W. Patten, 1966. The Biblical flood and the ice epoch. Pacific Meridian Publishing Co., Seattle, Washington. 336 pp.

6. See R. Daniel Shaw, 1970. Fossil man: ancestor or descendant of Adam? *Creation Research Society Quarterly,* 6(4):172-181.

7. Bernard E. Northrup, 1969. The Sisquoc diatomite fossils beds, *Creation Research Society Quarterly,* 6(3):129-135.

8. Bernard E. Northrup, 1970. Book review: Franciscan and related rocks, and their significance in the geology of western California, *Creation Research Society Quarterly,* 6(4):161-170.

9. Harold G. Coffin, 1969. Creation—accident or design? Review and Herald Publishing Association, Washington, D. C., pp. 138-139.

10. Ernest S. Booth, 1949. The little horses of John Day. *The Naturalist,* 8(2):2-8.

11. Herbert L. Hergert, 1961. Plant fossils in the Clarno formation, Oregon. *The Ore-Bin.,* State of Oregon, Dept. of Geology and Mineral Industries, 23(6):55-62.

12. Richard V. Fisher, 1966. Textural comparison of John Day volcanic siltstone with loess and volcanic ash, *Journal of Sedimentary Petrology,* 36(3): 706-718.

13. Dallas L. Peck, 1964. Geologic reconnaissance of the Antelope-Ashwood area, north-central Oregon, with emphasis on the John Day formation of late oligocene and early miocene age. U.S. Geological Survey Bulletin 1161-D, p. D7.

14. There are other examples of widespread post-Flood basalts. The enormous Triassic or Jurassic lava flows of the Parana Basin of Brazil probably covered at least 375,000 square miles to a depth of up to 2,000 feet (C. L. Baker, 1923. The lava field of the Parana Basin, South America, *Journal of*

Geology, 31:66-79). The Deccan basalts of India must have had an original extent of not much less than half a million square miles with an average thickness of about 2,000 feet (D. N. Wadia, 1953. Geology of India. Third edition. Macmillan & Co., London, pp. 291, 292.

15. For a discussion of fossil "horses" see Frank W. Cousins, 1971. A note on the unsatisfactory nature of the horse series of fossils as evidence for evolution, *Creation Research Society Quarterly,* 8(2):99-108.

16. Margaret L. Steere, 1954. Geology of the John Day Country, Oregon, *The Ore.-Bin.,* State of Oregon, Dept. of Geology and Mineral Industries, 16(7):46.

17. Clarence S. Ross and Robert L. Smith, 1961. Ash-flow tuffs: their origin, geologic relations and identification. U.S. Geological Survey Professional Paper 366, p. 3.

18. Stuart E. Nevins, 1971. The Mesa Basalt of the northwestern United States, *Creation Research Society Quarterly,* 7(4):222-226.

19. The paleontological dates given here do not agree with potassium-argon age dates given later in the text.

20. D. A. Swanson and Paul T. Robinson, 1968. Base of the John Day formation in and near the Horse Haven mining district, north-central Oregon. U.S. Geological Survey Professional Paper No. 600-D, p. D155.

21. Richard L. Hay, 1963. Stratigraphy and zeolite diagenesis of the John Day formation of Oregon, *Calif. Univ. Pubs., Geol. Sci.,* 42(5):205.

22. Derek York, Norman D. Watkins, and Ajoy K. Baksi, 1971. The Columbia volcanic episode: evidence for major volcanism during a limited part of the middle Miocene, *EOS* (American Geophysical Union Transactions), 52(4):383.

23. Ewart M. Baldwin, 1964. Geology of Oregon. Second edition. University of Oregon Cooperative Bookstore, Eugene, Oregon, p. 99.

24. *Ibid.*
25. *Ibid.*
26. *Ibid.*
27. Whitcomb and Morris, *op. cit.,* p. 489.

XIII

FRANCISCAN AND RELATED ROCKS, AND THEIR SIGNIFICANCE IN THE GEOLOGY OF WESTERN CALIFORNIA

By Edgar H. Bailey, William P. Irwin, and David L. Jones. Bulletin 183. San Francisco, California Division of Mines and Geology, 1964. ($2.50).

A Book Review by BERNARD E. NORTHRUP*

Introduction

Seldom has a book been written within the interpretative framework of evolutionary macrochronological geology that has so effectively demonstrated the inadequacy of that framework to explain the facts found in field research.

The bulletin *Franciscan and Related Rocks, and Their Significance in the Geology of Western California* is a volume of great consequence to all interested in catastrophic geology. The authors enumerate (obliquely, to be sure) more than a score of reasons for turning to a catastrophic format in search of a plausible explanation of the remarkable assemblage of rock structures that dominate western California, and apparently the entire West Coast.

A very dear Christian geologist friend, earnestly troubled about the relationships of Genesis and geology, once asked me, "But where did all of the sands come from?" This is the key question in the evaluation of Bulletin 183. The answer is found within the Bulletin.

In the case of the Franciscan assemblage of rocks this question

---

*For author information on Bernard Northrup, see Article No. 1.

is not one that is insoluble to the Christian geologist. To the uniformitarian geologist, however, it cannot but be confounding if the facts are considered squarely. For concerning the content of the graywacke alone (this is a very fine grained, dirty, unsorted, high matrix sandstone), the Bulletin reports the startling fact that there is "sufficient sand to cover the State of California to a depth of 10,000 feet" (p. 21) in this formation.

While this might appear an overwhelming argument for uniformitarian geology, because of the supposed vast amount of time required for the gradual reduction of earth's rocks to produce this amount of sand in this limited area, the facts concerning these sands powerfully controvert this approach. Rather, each truth about the Franciscan assemblage of rocks contained in this Bulletin may be used to argue that no vast amount of time was involved at all in the production of these sands, but that they were instead the product of extremely catastrophic, violent processes occurring abruptly in time and involving the degrading of basement and continental shelf materials into rock paste and sands that were redeposited almost as rapidly. Concerning the graywacke alone the authors admit,

> The vast volume of terrigenous material, as well as the great thickness locally of individual beds and the presence of a high matrix-content, points to a very rapid deposition or "pouring in" of the sedimentary material. (pp. 35-36)

The book might well have been titled more accurately, "Evidences of Franciscan Catastrophism," for the many forceful arguments presented that require a catastrophic model for consistent interpretation would make this title appropriate.

But what is the Franciscan assembly? It is a heterogeneous assemblage of rocks, predominantly graywacke, but including chert, shale, greenstone, some limestone of precipitate origins, blueschist, and other minor elements. The group of rocks clearly was deposited in one or more deep marine troughs.

The dominant rock, graywacke (so called because at least ten percent consists of a pulverized, crushed matrix) is a sandstone of medium to fine grain with very irregular bedding. Its grains are remarkably angular, with very little indication of transportation or of any kind of weathering. The cement which bonds it is normally a very fine paste of well ground rock flour. All of its physical features indicate "rapid deposition of unsorted material, presumably by turbidity or fluxoturbidity currents" (p. 5).

This would not be a surprising geological find, except for the unbelievable quantity of these sands, which are undoubtedly the product of extremely extensive mechanical abrasion in a submarine environment. That this was accompanied very possibly by violent submarine volcanic action (p. 6), which was a critical factor in the chemical precipitation of the small belts of limestones and cherts, is also significant as will be seen.

A large proportion of the book being reviewed is devoted to a description of the remarkable features of the Franciscan assemblage. Since the mere cataloging of these features under logical headings might fail to demonstrate clearly their significance to the biblical geologist, a brief evaluation of these features will be made. The headings are largely derived from the text, although the order has been elected by the reviewer to demonstrate the impact of the evidence more clearly.

1. *Proofs of Rapid, Continuous Deposition*

A. *Vast Volume of Terrigenous Material* (pp. 20, 21, 35). Though normal stratigraphic methods cannot be applied directly, a number of significant evidences are marshalled to show that the assemblage called Franciscan is over 50,000 feet thick, an estimate all the more remarkable in the light of the clearly defined Great Valley Sequence to the east, which may be measured stratigraphically at 40,000 feet in thickness. While both of these figures are admittedly estimates, it becomes apparent at any rate that the Franciscan assemblage is exceedingly thick.

This Franciscan assemblage parallels the Great Valley Sequence and lifts it, shearing its westward slopes into gigantic hogbacks most clearly seen to the north and south of Winters, California. Bounded on the west by the Pacific (though underlying it extensively also) and by the San Andreas and Nacimiento faults, it extends south into

Baja California and north an undefined extent into Oregon, Washington, Canada, and Alaska (although usually limited for discussion by the northern boundary of the Klamath Mountains). This vast bed of Mesozoic materials is of such a nature and consistency as to require "a rapid deposition or 'pouring in' of the sedimentary material" (p. 36). The significance of this striking statement is breathtaking in the light of the following paragraph on the size of this deposit:

> By far the most abundant rock of the Franciscan is graywacke, which has a truly astonishing volume. Even if the average thickness of the Franciscan is regarded as only 25,000 feet, and the depositional area in California and offshore is about 75,000 square miles, the total volume of the Franciscan graywacke is more than *350,000 cubic miles* [italics supplied]. To make this large figure more meaningful we might point out that this is sufficient sand to cover the State of California to a depth of 10,000 feet or the entire coterminus United States to a depth of 600 feet. (p. 21)

Thus this area, up to 70 miles across and at least 1,500 miles long, with no exposed basement and few younger rocks, is filled with finely ground debris consisting of rock flour and fragments, including an unusual abundance of minerals derived from metamorphic and igneous rocks (p. 22). This gains significance when studied in the light of the many other remarkable factors that are also present in the assemblage.

B. *Great Thickness of Local Beds* (pp. 22-23). When the four- to six-mile-thick (30,000 + ft.) beds that are discernible on Pacheco Pass are added to 18,000 feet found farther west to the north of the Bay, it may be seen that 30,000 feet, and indeed even 50,000 feet may be conservative as an estimate for the Jurassic and Cretaceous beds. Almost a total absence of macrofossils hinders the normal approach to correlation of beds by the historical geologist, but in any case, they can be described as tremendous in size. That this is not simply a wild correlation is possibly supported by the depth-pressure-temperature requirements of the blueschists for their metamorphosing.

C. *Presence of High Matrix Content.* This factor, which requires rapid deposition, is found in the microscopic examination of a thin section. In the graywacke the materials are often so well cemented that samples will break across many of the grains. Surrounding these sharp clasts and grains lies the matrix which acts as a superb cement. "Most of the Franciscan graywacke has a matrix content of at least 10 percent . . ." (p. 27). In some cases this rock paste is found to compose up to fifty percent of the stone (p. 32). (What a marvelous grinder is this that has deposited such a remarkable pile of grindings at the foot of the Workman!)

This rock paste acts as the cement for particles of all sizes. It is clear that between the grindings of this paste and the deposition of the crushed and pulverized materials little sorting action has occurred. The continuous nature of and the extreme rapidity of the action producing this sandy clastic material is certainly very strongly suggested.

D. *Absence of Interlayered Limestone or Calcareous Cements.* Consider this sentence in the Bulletin: "The absence of interlayered limestone or calcareous cement in most of the Franciscan also suggests continuous and rapid deposition" (p. 36). While this idea is not developed further in the text, the point is clear that a slow deposition of these materials in the clearly established marine environment would have left significant limestone deposits of those materials gathered by calcium accumulating creatures. The almost total absence of this kind of material in these beds may be used to argue strongly for extremely rapid, uninterrupted deposition. Is this acknowledgement without further discussion in the text not a significant indication of the ineffectiveness of uniformitarianism to cope with the evidence?

2. *Other Proofs of Rapid Mechanical Erosion*

A. *Lack of Rounded Quartz and Feldspar Grains.* While quartz grains average about 30 percent of the graywacke, feldspar may amount to 60 percent of it. Much may be learned from microscopic examination of a thin section. Several fine slide views in the text confirm the following statement from the text:

The predominant features seen in thin section are the general lack of abrasion and the lack of sorting of the grains of the rock. Most of the grains are angular, and this is especially true for the monomineralic grains. Rock fragments tend to be subangular or subrounded, but in many sections the compaction of the rock has led to a modification of the shape of the softer composite rock fragments by their yielding to fit between the monomineralic grains. (p. 27)

The very angularity of these grains opposes the view of slow decay, for these grains have apparently not been blown, tumbled, rolled, or washed on the beach (p. 27). Other broken rock fragments, varying in quantity from two to fifty percent, are found with these monomineralic grains. Sometimes they are from sources indicating reworked volcanic materials, sometimes reworked materials from the same beds, and at times the clasts indicate a large intake of basement rock. These angular grains appear to have an average size of one-half millimeter to microscopic size, depending upon the quantity of matrix present.

To the present reviewer, this factor requires a vast "mill," powered by a tremendous force, supplied perhaps by an enormous block of raw materials which was being processed and redeposited at the site of the operation during continental movement. This left a massive dump now called the Franciscan assemblage. At any rate, it can be seen that the interpretive system espoused in the Bulletin is wholly inadequate since the nature of such a mechanism is not suggested.

B. *High Percentage of Rock Fragments.* These rock fragments that accompany the rock paste and mineral grains demonstrate that some type of crushing action was working in massive scale in a marine environment, and that so little time passed between the "milling" action and the deposit that there was no time for rearrangement of the grains according to size. That the milling action was utterly nonselective is demonstrated by the variety of possible sources mentioned in the previous section.

The only logical conclusion that can be drawn from this remarkable situation is that the mill that ground this unbelievable quantity of sand was a moving section of the continent below the continental shelf, and that the deposit of the freshly ground materials took place almost simultaneously as currents swept them against the shelf, depositing them amidst boiling volcanic eruptions that brought the chemical precipitations that are also found embedded in the deposits. A further telling blow against the macrochronological approach is found in the next observation on the rapidity of this vast action.

C. *Low Fe_2O_3/FeO Ratio Indicating Little Chemical Weathering* (p. 32). One of the excellent characteristics of the Bulletin is that the sections are developed in graded order of difficulty, climaxing in a discussion of the chemical features of the particular rock under consideration. This allows the casual reader to handle the more easily read sections without completely bogging down. But no part of this significant Bulletin should be neglected because of difficulty. This simple chemical ratio is a most significant clue that much Californian rock solidified catastrophically! Again it is best simply to quote a section:

> Lack of rounded quartz and feldspar grains, as well as the high percentage of liabile rock fragments, indicates rapid mechanical erosion of a nearby source area. The low Fe_2O_3/FeO ratio and paucity of interlayered clay beds also indicate the lack of chemical weathering in the source area. (p. 36)

It must be added that no weathering took place in the transportation cycle or in the depositional area either. It seems that no other method of mechanical erosion and pulverization of these materials than the one suggested above can supply a meaningful model to explain this factor. Exposure of the iron particles to the atmosphere, even for a short time, would result in a totally different oxide ratio in these formations if the temperature and humidity were also conducive to Fe_2O_3 formation.

D. *Absence of Weathered Clay Beds.* As suggested above, the lack of normal weathering cycles is also displayed in the absence of evidences of the normal transformation of certain of these materials into clays. This indicates that the processes of chemical weathering were almost totally forestalled by the marine conditions which brought the particles and their deposits into existence. While admitting that "the reason for the low K_2O/Na_2O ratio, both in the Franciscan and similar units, is not understood . . ." (p. 36), the authors do give a possible explanation in the discounted argument, "Incomplete Weatherings of Source Rocks" (p. 36). This is surely the understatement of the fact.

It is the reviewer's opinion that there simply was no weathering of the material before it was immediately redeposited after being ground to dust particle size. That the reader may understand the reason for this position and its ultimate significance, the next series of evidences in the Franciscan must now be considered.

3. *Proofs of Turbid Marine Deposition*

Apparently marine conditions prevailed throughout the deposition of Franciscan rocks, and, although graded beds and sole markings are not commonly seen, the standstone textures, the lack of a large-scale crossbedding and ripple marks, as well as the absence of an indigenous shelly fauna, point to turbidity current and fluxo-turbidity current deposition in a deepwater environment. (p. 36)

In this splendid, concise fashion the Bulletin authors summarized the evidences of a deep submarine environment as the location of the deposit of the Franciscan beds. The precise location of the pulverized debris dump and the manner of its deposit both support the contention that the mill that produced these materials was located there also.

A. *The Sandstone Textures.* Examination of the assemblage provides convincing data that it is not at all the work of wind. This has been supported by the discussion under Section 2. The absence of aeolian crossbedding further confirms this. This is an interesting fact in the light of the vast wind deposits of this very same presumed time that are found widely distributed throughout the far western interior of our continent. Indeed, sand dunes are a dominant factor in the Mesozoic materials found in several of the mountain states.

Neither is the assemblage the result of stream erosion nor of marine shoreline erosion. This contrasts with the Great Valley Sequence on which it borders on the east. That formation series was surely the result of coastal erosion and deposit in gigantic magnitude. All of the characteristic signs of continental marine deposits are found.

But for the Franciscan, all of the evidences point to a deepwater environment. The very texture of the sands deposited, in that they are fine grained, practically unreworked by transportation and thus sharp edged, correlates well with the concept of abrupt deposition. This requirement is difficult to adapt to any other than an unexpanded chronology. Catastrophic events that the author presumed have produced the remarkable field evidences are distorted and stretched until almost unrecognizable when approached by the macrochronological system of interpretation.

B. *Lack of Large Scale Crossbedding* (p. 22). A characteristic of shallow water marine or lake deposits is the regularity of bedding planes. These are beautifully illustrated by the evenness of the extensive Eocene deposits of western Utah. The Roan and Book Cliffs which lie above the great dune sands show that after a temporary exposure of the land and its subjection to great winds that went to and fro, the area was again submerged as an inland sea where waters were relatively quiet until its sudden drainage wrought havoc with the present Colorado Plateau.

In the Franciscan, however, the bedding is best characterized by great "irregularity in the thickness of the beds and the unusually great thickness of some of them" (p. 22). A single section may vary from one-half inch to ten feet, although hundreds of feet are found. The observer must be careful to avoid mistaking shale which has been plastically injected into fractures for actual bedding planes. This is a common phenomenon both in the Franciscan assemblage and in the titled Great Valley Sequence.

The massiveness of these Franciscan beds, with the absence of reciprocating current patterns of shallow water, require a steady flow of heavy, load-filled currents of such vast proportions that they defy uniformitarian imagination. Time alone cannot satisfy here.

C. *Lack of Ripple Marks* (p. 24). Though both wind and water oscillations have ripple marks, their absence in massive deposits is properly used to signify a turbid deepwater deposit. Now these marks of oscillation can be located quickly in the Great Valley Sequence where its layers are exposed on Highway 16. Their absence in the Franciscan which borders it only a very few miles to the west is indeed significant.

D. *Presence of Groove and Flute Casts* (p. 24). Grooves and flute casts are characteristic of deepwater current deposits. These sole markings are depositional patterns oriented in the direction of current flows. They are occasionally found between beds of graywacke. They indicate deepwater turbidity currents as they are not produced by shallow water agitation.

The little ridges and valleys left by the currents lie in fluted patterns which enable the geologist to reconstruct the direction of current flow before the next bed was deposited swiftly to cover the patterns. These may be observed nicely in an exposure of the Great Valley Sequence just north of Rumsey, California, on Highway 16. This is only a few miles from the line of contact with the Franciscan. These patterns must not be confused with wind or water ripple marks, superficially like them, but oriented ninety degrees to the currents producing them.

The occasional presence of these adds further evidence that the massive milling action producing the assemblage occurred below the continental shelf under rare hydraulic circumstances. That this work was not accomplished on the shelf is apparent from a number of factors that have been mentioned already. Now any single factor or group of factors here could be observed today, but the multiplicity of evidences pointing to catastrophism is truly significant.

E. *Absence of Indigenous Shelly Fauna* (p. 36). The offshore depositional environment of the Franciscan is remarkably correlated by fossil information. The Bulletin authors note:

> Megafossils are remarkably rare in the Franciscan, and in spite of the wide distribution and the great thickness of the unit, they have been found in only about a dozen localities. On the other hand, microfossils, including Foarminifera in limestone and Radiolaria in chert, are locally very abundant. (p. 115)

This contrasts significantly with the Great Valley deposits, particularly on its eastern margin of shallow water origin (p. 135).

This factor could only mean that the great Franciscan deposition took place well offshore in an area that had never been a shallow water deposit area.

It does not even contain extensive megafossils in fragments that would indicate a composition of shoreline materials which had been reworked and redeposited. Their scarcity indicates that only rarely were shoreline materials transported by the violence of the coastal waters so as to intrude into this deepwater collection of materials. That such currents were present, however, is supported by the following factor.

F. *Presence of Large Conglomerate Lenses* (p. 39). Extraformational deposits provide significant clues to the violently catastrophic times of the Mesozoic "era." Lenses of conglomerate cobbles and pebbles, while usually covering a small area, may be found as large as 2,000 feet long (p. 39). While it has graywacke as its matrix, this conglomerate clearly has origin outside the formation. These cobbles are thoroughly rounded by tumbling action in transport.

These lenses of conglomerate are a common phenomenon around the Livermore Valley in the Great Valley Sequence. At times they form rounded knolls that are a part of the unique contouring of the area. These materials appear to have been swept offshore to be deposited in the Franciscan that was being formed simultaneously in deepwater.

It is the reviewer's opinion that this could have been done only in an extremely abrupt fashion. To be included in the graywacke deposit and mingled with it while it was being ground and "poured in" to form its massive offshore beds, these conglomerates from the shoreline area near the foot of the present Sierra Mountains were evidently transported by jet streams of submarine currents. Possibly massive rip tides swept them offshore before they could fall on the continental shelf. It was indeed a catastrophic time.

In no other way can one account for deposits that include quartzite, chert, and granite materials in sizes extending from one inch pebbles to boulders as large as two and one-half feet in diameter, all well-ground by tumbling, intruded into these massive beds of clastic and powdered materials. Some of these conglomerates appear to have originated as far away as the Paleozoic and lower Mesozoic materials of the western Sierra Nevada and the Klamath Mountains (p. 41). And yet they seem scattered in current deposited lenses throughout the abyssal offshore structures that were being rapidly built from materials even then being aggraded from basement and ocean floor.

That these factors require a more rapid framing sequence or "film speed" than that considered "normal" to properly project the history of the leading edge of the continent is obvious. Simply stated, this indicates abrupt continental separation and movement with the geological catastrophism which would accompany such an event. There is one Bible text with which this event could be identified. It is the post-flood text so often overlooked, Genesis 10:25, ". . . In his days was the earth divided."

G. *Presence of Massive Submarine Intrusion Evidences* (pp. 41-55). Erratically disturbed throughout the Franciscan assemblage and its evidences of massive grinding and redeposition are also found great beds of volcanic intrusives that comprise approximately 10 percent of the assemblage (p. 41). In places these have been shattered and ground up to form a considerable part of the graywacke.

In other places there is no evidence of milling action. Rather they are often found in a remarkable "pillow" structure that could only be formed by the extrusion of molten materials as blobs into a deepwater basin. While "all the extrusive volcanic rocks appear to have been deposited in a submarine environment" (p. 43), not all of these extrusions take the unique rounded form called pillows. These structures seem best explained as follows:

> A mechanism that might account for these piles of separate pillows is a *violent* [italics added] jet eruption of highly fluid lava on the sea floor. The breaking up of this jet stream of lava into large drops or blobs, which are chilled as they fall back about the vent, then builds up a pile of pillows. As a drop of magma, forming a pillow, falls through the water its surface solidifies but remains thin enough to yield under the weight of

the drop to conform to the shapes of the earlier pillows onto which it settles to rest. (p. 51)

Laboratory analysis of these pillows confirms this view that the surface of the pillow is suddenly chilled and indicates that the varying chemical makeup of the surfaces and interior of the pillow is the result of the various rates of cooling experienced by the outer shell in contrast with the inner core (pp. 53-54).

It is not difficult to see that these forms are also a significant factor pointing to a catastrophism ignored by the field geologist today. While underwater volcanoes are not unknown today, the extensiveness of the evidence of submarine volcanism here requires an unretarded chronological approach to a very chaotic period to account for its presence in large quantities among "rapidly deposited" materials that have been "poured in" to form these beds.

H. *Presence of Cherts Volcanically formed in Deepwater* (pp. 55-68). One of the most remarkable evidences for a catastrophic model of interpretation is the Franciscan chert. While it composes less than one-half of a percent of the assemblage, it is "of special interest, because it provides information on the depth of deposition of some parts of the eugeosynclinal assemblage" (p. 55). (Eugeosynclinal deposits differ from miogeosynclinal deposits chiefly in their inclusion of major volcanic activities—p. 13.)

The cherts involved are very "fine-grained, hard, highly siliceous rocks" that are loaded with extremely fine particles of iron oxides or hydroxides. For this reason they are usually red, brown, buff, or green (p. 55). The chert is finely bedded in layers up to four inches thick, often intermingled with a shale of the same color.

Careful study of the brilliant, often violently folded, layers reveals that these are not actually normal sedimentary bedding planes at all, but rather lenses that grade off into nothing in a short distance (p. 62). They are characteristically filled with the microfossil, *Radiolaria,* which may compose as much as fifty percent of the rock (p. 64).

And how is this an evidence of catastrophism? The text of the Bulletin is rather clear on the subject:

Chert and a distinctive shale occurring with it . . . are believed to be chemical precipitates formed by the reaction of magma and sea water under considerable hydrostatic pressure. They are important as indicators of the oceanic depth in which part of the Franciscan was deposited. Rhythmically interlayered red or green chert and shale form lenses less than 50 feet thick and less than a mile in extent, generally with and above greenstones. . . . This association of chert-shale lenses with greenstone suggests a genetic relation. The lenses may represent silica, alumnia, and iron released by submarine volcanic rocks at the time of volcanic eruption, the eruption occurring at a depth great enough for sea water at the reactive interface to be heated to a temperature of about 350°C without boiling. At this temperature and at a pressure equal to that of oceanic depths of 13,000 feet, water can dissolve over 1,000 p.p.m. of silica. Such heated, silica-enriched water would rise, be cooled, and quickly become oversaturated with respect to silica. Silica would then be polymerized and precipitated as a gel, apparently along with aluminum and ferrous hydroxide, and it would rain down onto the sea floor forming a mass of impure silica gel. Subsequently, by a process of diffusion and crystalization, layers that superficially resemble normal sedimentary beds would form. . . . This postulated origin for the chert-shale lenses seems to be the only one compatible with all their unusual structural and chemical features, and it implies that deposition of some Franciscan rocks must have been at a depth nearly equivalent to or greater than the average of the Pacific Ocean. (p. 6)

When considered in the light of the series of evidences already examined, this complex bit of abyssal chemistry is indeed significant. It is another piece in the mounting evidence which requires the rejection of any macrochronological explanation of California geology. Here is highly significant support for the imagined great depth involved in the assembly of the Franciscan. Here also is support for the massiveness of the violently turbulent, explosively heated marine environment in which the precipitation of these silica beds took place.

An examination of the striking chevron-folds of red chert on the heights northwest of Golden Gate Bridge shows this apparent relationship between the chert and the large beds of pillows that lie along Highway 101 just north of the bridge below these chert beds. The fantastic rapidity of deposition proposed for this relationship scarcely appears to fall within the realms of uniformitarian concepts. The rapid sequence of deposition of the pillows required by their very nature has already been discussed.

It appears that it was this same volcanic intrusion that precipitated the massive chert beds at the same time. The astounding folds that are found in these chert beds apparently indicate the extreme rapidity of the movement of the crust in the area of the precipitation.

Conceivably, long before these layers of silica had hardened, they were compressed violently by lateral compressions which left them folded upon themselves like the folds of an accordion. The frequency of exposure of these beds throughout the state of California provides abundant evidence of utterly catastrophic, disruptive chaos that is best considered under a nonextended chronological model.

It is interesting to note that this intense concentration of silica at the foot of the continental shelf has a counterpart in the exceedingly extensive blanket of oxide-stained silicates which cover much of Utah, Arizona, New Mexico, and Colorado during this same Mesozoic "era." There may be an unobserved relationship which has resulted in the silica enrichment of these waters even before the precipitation of the cherts and shales took place. In any case, the deposition of these cherts requires the offshore submarine explosions of volcanic activity in a deepwater environment that certainly would have accompanied abrupt continental movement. This is further corroborated by the following evidences.

I. *The Presence and Nature of the Precipitate Limestones* (pp. 68-77). As should be expected, limestone is not a significant part of the eugeosynclinal assemblage which is being considered, for the deposit is clearly not one made in quiet shallow waters commonly associated with limestone. Indeed, these limestones are of quite a different origin, since in places they are mingled with and blended into the chert.

Now the deposition of chert has already been interpreted to be of a violently different nature than that imagined for organic sedimentary limestone. This mingling of the two materials wherein chert may amount to as much as thirty percent of the material (and up to forty percent iron) leaves only one conclusion.

This is precipitate limestone, except for very minor deposits of organic detrital materials abraded from shelly materials. While the microfossil, *Globigerina,* may be massively present, evidences require rejection of the idea that this is simply a deep sea deposit of ooze. Indeed, evidences are conclusive that this was no normal deposit at all.

> The scarcity of terrigenous material in the Franciscan limestone indicates either that the currents responsible for the deposition of graywacke and shale were prohibited from reaching sites of limestone deposition, or that limestone deposition *was so extremely rapid as to mask the terrigenous increment* [italics added]. (p. 76)

This certainly suggests that the rapidity of the deposit far exceeded any present rate of accumulation of oceanic oozes.

> These differences between Franciscan limestone deposits and recent *Globigerina* ooze deposits are sufficient to suggest that the Franciscan limestone may have had a different mode of origin. Judging from its extremely fine grain size, its sporadic distribution in lens-shaped rocks, as well as the variable abundance and seemingly random distribution of Foraminifera, the typical Franciscan limestone may have been a result of volcanic activity and formed by direct chemical precipitation of calcite with concomitant accumulation of minor amounts of organic shell material, mainly foraminiferal tests. (pp. 76-77)

All of this is quite contrary to the "normal" mode of explanation of the origin of limestones, and is quite suggestive of the very unorthodox environment in which these materials were precipitated. It is an environment unlike any found in the world today. The past obviously cannot be judged correctly by the present.

J. *Presence of Blueschists* (p. 111). The Franciscan rocks are for the most part unchanged by heat and pressure factors. Within the assemblage, however, a group of metamorphic rocks is found that are called the blueschists, which exhibit isochemical recrystal-

BOOK REVIEW: FRANCISCAN . . . RELATED ROCKS— 269

lization. There are other groups, but for the sake of simplicity, discussion will be limited to this group. They exhibit signs of exceedingly significant geological conditions from the catastrophist's point of view. Simply stated, for the metamorphism exhibited in the blueschists to have taken place they must have been placed under remarkable pressure-temperature circumstances for a relatively brief period of time.

> Considerations of the probable pressure-temperature field of formation of the blueschists indicate that pressures were abnormally high (>5Kb) relative to the temperature (<300°C). *If* the metamorphism of the broader areas is due to *load* [italics added], the rocks must have reached a depth of about 70,000 feet, through downwarping and accumulation, *so rapidly* [italics added] that a normal thermal gradient was not established. In addition they must have been uplifted soon after their depression and metamorphism, so as to prohibit the establishment of a normal thermal gradient that would have raised the temperature sufficiently to convert the blueschists to greenschists or a higher grade facies. (p. 7)

In other words, a unique combination of enormous pressure and unexpectedly low temperature accompanied by an unexplainably brief period of exposure to the environment was required for the limited metamorphosing exhibited in the blueschists. The blueschists are basic to the idea that these amazing circumstances were found in California in the middle of the Mesozoic "era."

Now the reviewer knows of no place on the earth where sedimentary materials are expected to be found at a depth of 70,000 feet. Using a uniformitarian argument, admittedly, it seems best to reject the suggestion that load is the agent which supplied the pressures involved and required. The abrupt removal of that load to meet the time requirement, of course, obviates a uniformitarian explanation. It might be explained otherwise.

Reviewer Supplies Model

The model suggested by the reviewer which involves the abrupt movement of the continental mass appears to supply the threefold requirements for metamorphism of this type satisfactorily. There are evidences which appear to require that the entire phenomenon cannot be extended beyond the limits of 500 years.

This model considers the mid-Atlantic ridge to be the point of departure from which the dividing single continent of preflood times moved. The fracture is viewed as an abrupt phenomenon supplementing the linguistic division of Babel, but accomplished late enough to actually provide the method of transportation which scattered mankind. The animals which had already moved away from the ark undoubtedly sought ecological zones hospitable to their own physical makeup. Division of the land mass isolated these for the most part in the general areas of the continental fragments where they are now found.

Mechanisms proposed to produce such profound and abrupt movement of the crust after the flood are discussed by Cook[1] and Kelly.[2] It is the reviewer's opinion that Cook is correct that the Noahic Flood massively weighted the polar regions of the single continent with the ice sheets of the Paleozoic "era," and that the relieving of these pressures produced the rifting and movement after the Flood's subsidence had largely taken place.

However, Kelly may be right that meteoritic or cometary impact in the northern ice cap was involved to the extent that it acted as a trigger to allow the sudden release of the massive ice load on the paleopolar regions.[3]

A recent suggestion remarkably parallel to the reviewer's model (except for uniformitarian framework) appeared in a newspaper release on the views of UCLA professor W. Gary Ernst. He postulated a Franciscan trench, once lying where western California extends today, filled with sediments from the overriding "continental plate," later elevated to become the coastal ranges.[4]

The structure which produced, apparently simultaneously, the Franciscan assemblage and the Great Valley Sequence requires a coastal model something on the order of the following: (a) The Great Valley Sequence was deposited of continental materials massively eroded by seismic tidal waves. (b) The continental shelf, well over a thousand feet deep through most of the deposition, was very nearly rimmed by a submarine ridge lying along the edge of

BOOK REVIEW: FRANCISCAN ... RELATED ROCKS— 271

the shelf. (c) This allowed only minor exchange of materials from within the basin and from the deepwater site of the Franciscan. (d) The latter was deposited by the grinding action of the overriding thrust fault in an extensive trench along the coast and against the continental shelf itself. (e) Apparently this action was also accompanied by lateral northward movement of the Nacimiento fault block, so the picture must not be over-simplified (see Figure 1).

Thus there would be no time for the increasing thermal gradient to be produced by heat generated by radioactivity within the crust. The pressures involved in the movement of a portion of the crust as massive as the continent, and the resistance met in its overriding of the oceanic basic floor might very well have provided the pressure requirements without the enormous depth of load suggested in the Bulletin. Also, according to the continental movement model, the Franciscan assemblage was almost entirely (apart from offshore materials) lifted above sea level to its present position by that same movement as pressures were relieved by the upwarping of the coast range.

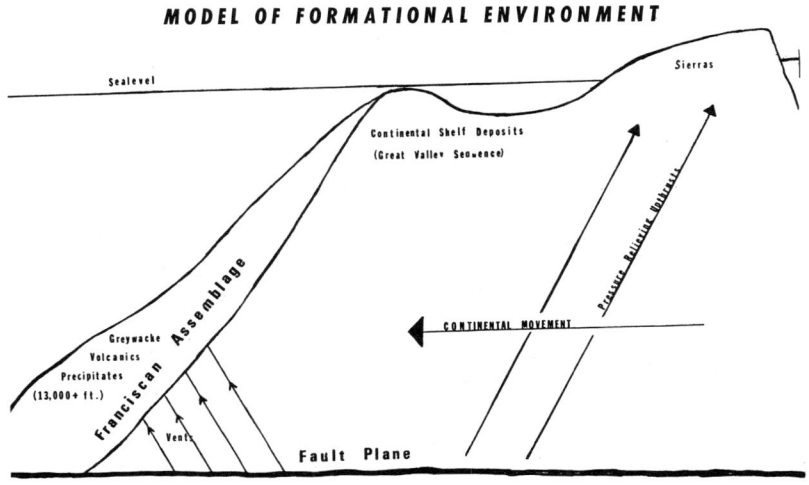

Figure 1. Stationary basement rocks and the asthenosphere.

This uplift was very possibly only a minor part of the great series of vertical pressures which relieved the lateral pressures generated by this movement. This type of pressure relief can be illustrated by attempting to push a small throw rug ahead of oneself on a cement floor. As friction builds up horizontal pressures, these tend to be relieved by vertical buckling.

Recognizing that the undersurface of the postulated moving continental platform would be in a semifluid state under greatly increased temperature and pressure factors would account for the massive batholiths that are postulated as intruding the Rockies from the Cretaceous "period" on. These masses ruptured Paleozoic and early Mesozoic "era" materials of the receding flood along the Denver Front Range, leaving their shattered ends exposed majestically at the base of the great granite intrustions of the Rockies.

They also may have produced massive, extensive volcanic flows which dominate the Tertiary "period" deposits in the Pacific Northwest. These latter materials cover the extension of the Franciscan along the Oregon coast. The intrusive magma masses produced the final elevation of the Sierras and Cascades in the Pleistocene "epoch." Titanic erosion of these great masses to their present configuration within the limitations of perhaps 5,000 years at the most (from the Flood to the present) would have been involved in the traumatic violence of the hydraulic activity postulated as an important part of this disturbed period when Noahic Flood waters were yet retreating from the present continental masses.

Uplift of the great ranges of North and South America can be accounted for by this same mode. Through this means the Paleozoic (Noahic Flood) materials were violently uplifted and distorted, broken and tilted, eroded, and redeposited all over the continent.

That this denuding largely affected the Franciscan assemblage after its deposition seems immediately evident in the field. These Mesozoic materials have been subjected to violent attack by seismic wave action. It is the reviewer's opinion that this action is largely responsible for the present contouring of these structures, for they exhibit, with the Great Valley Sequence on the eastern fringe, a surprising lack of precipitation erosion evidences.

While precipitation erosion evidences are actually present in places, they often can and should be largely recognized to be the result of wave runoff during the time of elevation. The latter is supported by massive evidences of marine erosion and deposition throughout the mountain valleys of the area. These are almost certainly playas, the result of agitated waters that were being temporarily trapped in these basins.

While the term "playa" is reserved for desert basins, they are not inappropriate here, for one may reason that those desert basins received their flat floors in the same way as a result of trapped, violently agitated basin waters which have usually left their marks on the walls of the basins as well. The fans and terraces of the Great Valley have their counterpart in many regions throughout the Western interior in its basins.

This remarkable absence of precipitation erosion is exhibited in the strikingly contoured hills of the Livermore and Amador Valleys. All of these factors fit with the suggested model that the California coast was heaved up out of the ocean even while it was being subjected to titanic attack by gigantic ocean waves. Whether this happened after the Franciscan had been deposited or during the process is not known. If the latter is true, then it may be expected that the Franciscan assemblage will be found to continue far offshore, and perhaps even down the continental shelf.

Thus it is suggested that the presence of blueschists in an environment of submarine volcanic explosions, of massive aggradation and redeposition, and also of enormous pressures and uplifts, is certainly a significant evidence of biblical catastrophism that must be given more adequate consideration in properly oriented research. It must not be forgotten, however, that this is far from the viewpoint presented in the Bulletin. While the authors are at times catastrophic in their language, they are uniformitarian in their interpretation, as may be seen from the following significant conclusions:

> As Franciscan blueschists do not normally show any sign of having been in the greenschist environment, we may infer that they not only reached considerable depths *rapidly* [italics added]

but also were subsequently uplifted to higher levels before a normal thermal gradient was established. The fact that aragonite is present and has not inverted to calcite not only indicates *very rapid subsidence* but also clearly indicates *rapid uplift and erosion* [italics added]. . . . This conclusion is compatible with what can be inferred from the geologic history of the Franciscan and its structural relation to other units. (p. 112)

That this "catastrophism" found in the Bulletin was not stated in accordance with the violence required by the reviewer is apparent from the following:

For such a curve to approximate the actual thermal gradient in the Franciscan requires the sedimentation and downwarping to have taken place in a period of a few million to a few tens of millions of years . . . , though *just how brief the period must be depends on what assumptions are made* [italics added] regarding heat flow into the pile, heat generated within the pile, and heat gains or losses due to metamorphic reactions. (p. 111)

Since the actual time structure suggested herein is entirely based upon assumptions, it is evident that it may involve a "macro-error," if the word may be coined.

4. *Proofs of Violently Disruptive Crustal Movements During Deposition*

For the sake of completeness and to show the dual role of some evidences, the following clues of abrupt movement suggested in the Bulletin are now repeated from other sections. They supplement their role there when viewed from a new perspective.

A. *Presence of Pillow Lavas and Submarine Eruptions.* Only disruptive crustal movement in the deepwater environment could be the cause of these extensive deposits. Recognition that this disturbance resulted in massive extrusions of magma along the entire West Coast in this environment presents a historical situation inexplicable in uniformitarian terms.

Consider the *Largo danse macabre* required for bubbles of magma to be extruded in grotesque, macrochronological movement, slowly rising from their spewing volcanic jet, being deposited by gravity in millennial slowness amidst the gradually growing pile of continental grindings now called graywacke!

No, the remarkable conformity of these pillows requires that they were mass produced and that they fell tumbling in semifluid state upon each other in great profusion, each shaping itself to those beneath, each having only sufficient moments of time for cooling before its successor fell for its own upper crust to gain supporting strength. Though difficult to picture, this deepwater marine environment which was also convulsively heated enough to precipitate highly concentrated silicates and calciums, seemingly was achieved by crustal movements unparalleled today.

B. *Presence of Mixed Crystalline and Sedimentary Terrain.* The fact that the sedimentary materials in the Franciscan assemblage contain unsorted mixtures of materials from original basement rock, from reworked, extruded rock, and from reworked sedimentary materials (both intraformational and extraformational), strongly supports the thesis of massive disruption. That it was a problem to the writers is evident:

> The nature of the source area from which the Franciscan sediments were derived is imperfectly understood. The lithic fragments indicate a mixed crystalline and sedimentary terrain, and the presence locally of volcanically rich graywacke and tuffaceous beds points to a volcanic source for some of the sediments. Much of the latter material, however, may have been derived from penecontemporaneous, intra-Franciscan volcanism. . . .
>
> Middleton . . . concludes that . . . the peculiar characteristics of high-rank graywackes are the result of a partial volcanic (spilitic) provenance, combined with rapid erosion and little chemical weathering. (p. 36)

This unique combination of materials, difficult to explain as is evident in the above, nicely fits the catastrophic model. It solves the problems of the intraformational volcanism, of the "rapid erosion and little chemical weathering" and the "very rapid deposition or 'pouring in' of the sedimentary material" (p. 36).

C. *Presence of Locally Volcanically Rich Graywacke and Tuffs.*

While sufficiently discussed above, the individual impact of this evidence in the reconstruction of the tumultuous time of deposit must not be overlooked. The action was taking place in an environment shattered by massive aeolian as well as submarine eruptions. The implications regarding crustal upheaval and movement staggers the imagination but helps to complete the picture of the time of deposit of the Franciscan.

D. *Presence of Greenschists.* While it has been indicated that large quantities of the blueschists "escaped" complete metamorphism into green schists, it is also true that some of these materials did not. Through contact metamorphism by intrusions, some of them became subject to the higher temperatures apparently necessary for the conversion (p. 112). This fact gives something of a check on the pressure-temperature requirements for the blueschist, since the extra heat of a volcanic intrusion was necessary for full metamorphism. Furthermore, this item confirms the view that the crust was shattered in another way.

E. *Presence of Intruded Belts of Serpentine.* Between the Franciscan and the Great Valley Sequence lies a large intrusive mass of serpentine that is at least seventy miles long and up to three miles across. A "plastic intrusion" of materials well below the melting point into the fracture between these two masses that represent offshore abyssal deposits and offshore continental shelf deposits is very evident. That serpentine might be involved in this type of flow under pressure is well known (p. 87). The points of contact are remarkably sharp. The serpentine separates the huge hogbacks representing the ends of the Great Valley Sequence from the Franciscan graywackes and shales of the area.

It is the reviewer's opinion that the serpentine mass represents an intrusion in a major fault which now separates once united structures, and that this intrusion took place at the time of the final elevation of the Franciscan to its position dominating the western horizon beyond the Great Valley. This intrusion of serpentine may be considered, of course, another indication of extreme catastrophism, abrupt diastrophism. The broken roots of the Great Valley

Sequence lie shattered, folded and upended against the serpentine mass.

It is difficult to avoid the implications that the world's most catastrophic crust-shattering series of faults and mass movements ever known occurred during the Mesozoic "era." These movements resulted in the present configuration of the continents as they were massively restructured and resurfaced during the long period of the retreat of the Noahic Flood. Thus the present reviewer attributes "Mesozoic" catastrophism to the years after the Noachian deluge.

V. *Conclusion*

More than a score of evidences of geological upheaval and tectonic disturbance set forth in the Bulletin, *Franciscan and Related Rocks and Their Significance in the Geology of Western California,* have been examined. An extensive weakness in the macrochronological interpretative framework by which these structures have been explained in this remarkable and valuable book has been identified. While the contribution of the Bulletin to one's knowledge of California is beyond reproach, for it is a superbly collected and edited work, the startling "significance" of the Franciscan assemblage is obscured.

It is the conviction of the reviewer that many of the standard works in the field of geology, while on the surface appearing to be destructive to our faith, would actually prove to be of keen interest and of great significance to the flood geologist after a careful removal of their "outer husk" of uniformitarianism. It will be seen that many of the facts contained therein (and even the arguments for erroneous views) are in reality consistent with the accurate biblical account.

The Christian geologist must never retreat from such a question as, "But where did all of the sands come from?" Rather, he should grasp the occasion and turn the attack with a question that should prove quite embarrassing to the uniformitarian: "Yes, where indeed did all of the sands come from? Have you ever noticed the problem in the Franciscan assemblage?"

REFERENCES

1. Melvin Cook, 1966. Prehistory and earth models. Max Parrish, London.
2. Allan O. Kelly, 1966. Continental drift: is it a cometary impact phenomenon? Carlsbad, California: Published by the author. 100 pp.
3. *Ibid.*, pp. 60-61.
4. W. Gary Ernst, 1969. California scientist says trench 100 million years old, *San Fernando Valley Times,* Saturday, Oct. 25, p. 5.

XIV

THE CREATIONIST AND CONTINENTAL GLACIATION

WILLIAM A. SPRINGSTEAD*

Introduction

The biblically oriented creationist espouses catastrophism. Recognizing the present process rates in their relationship to part of earth's previous history, he is also convinced that there is evidence of global catastrophes in the past. As a biblical literalist he holds a devastating flood of global proportions made radical changes in earth's biotic life and crust. Similarly he holds that glaciation produced by catastrophic agencies also occurred, drastically changing parts of the earth.

Frequent criticisms of doctrinaire uniformitarianism have been published in recent years. Articles have appeared in scholarly journals and from the pens of competent scientists calling for new and modified definitions.[1] A new school of geological thinking, termed neo-catastrophism, has risen. Its proponents recognize evidence for unprecedented process rates in the past.[2] It may be predicted that the adherents of this school will increase in numbers as scholarly research continues to uncover new evidences of catastrophism.

In appraising creationist views on continental glaciation numerous treatments will unfortunately be overlooked. Secular treatments of the subject alone are voluminous. Perhaps more articles have been written on Ice Age geology than on all the other geological ages combined. The reviewer trusts that creationists will therefore take a sympathetic position relative to the task undertaken. He further

---

*William Springstead is pastor of the First Baptist Church of Pinedale, Wyoming. He holds the A.B. degree and has undertaken graduate study in history.

trusts that readers will make note of any articles overlooked and make them known by subsequent correspondence to the editor and this author.

A major difference between creationists and secular scientists lies in their interpretation of the extent, time, and duration of the ice age. Many creationists subscribe to only one major glaciation, rather than to the classic view of four glaciations. They associate the time of the continental glaciation as being either concurrent with or following the time of the global flood.

Creationists themselves differ as to the causes, extent, and effect of the ice caps. Some hold to the theory that the ice was introduced by either an astral dump or the breaking up of an ice canopy encircling the earth. Still others hold to glaciation being produced by cold following collapse of a water canopy. Other creationists believe the causes may be found in the study of climatological and geological phenomena. Glacialists have advanced around sixty explanations for the appearance of ice caps. None of these explanations to date has received general acceptance. It is this reviewer's opinion that creationists should therefore be both cautious and nondogmatic as to the cause. Neither Scripture nor scientific investigation has revealed the exact cause of this remarkable period.

Many creationists believe that continental glaciation followed the Flood. Whitcomb and Morris, Harold Armstrong,[3] and this reviewer are among those who do. Donald Patten is an exception. He writes, "It is here proposed that the cause or causes of the Ice Epoch did not follow the Flood. They were one and the same catastrophe."[4] Those who espouse the theory of an ice canopy encircling the earth, also believe that its breaking up occurred simultaneously with the Flood.

A. *The History of Modern Glaciology*

As a result of studying the movements of glaciers in the Alps, Swiss born Louis Agassiz wrote two books projecting a startling new concept to the then current geological thinking. The books were entitled, *Studies of Glaciers* and *The Glacial System*. In these works, appearing in the middle of the 19th century, Agassiz propounded the theory of continental ice caps in which he envisioned "great sheets of ice, resembling those now existing in Greenland, once covered all the countries in which stratified gravel (boulder drift) is found."[5]

Agassiz himself had formerly been a partisan of Lyell's theory of transport by icebergs and ice rafts. When Agassiz visited the British Isles in 1840, he along with William Buckland "extended the glacial doctrine to Scotland, Northern England and Ireland."[6]

The ice caps postulated by Agassiz were vast indeed. Writing of Europe he said, "We have to do with sheets of ice five to six thousand feet in thickness covering the whole continent."[7] He wrote of the ice, that it "extended at least from the North Pole to the Mediterranean and Caspian Seas."[8] Elsewhere he stated, "It extended beyond the shore lines of the Mediterranean and of the Atlantic Ocean, and even covered completely North America and Asiatic Russia."[9] Fifty years later Dawson was to appraise such a concept: "The glacier theory of Agassiz and others may be said to have grown till, like imaginary glaciers themselves, it overspread the earth."[10]

Multiple glaciation did not gain widespread acceptance until about the turn of the 20th century. Penck and Bruckner, after studying the forms and deposits of glaciation in the Bavarian Alps, wrote a three-volume work entitled, *The Alps in the Ice Ages*. In this work they popularized the concept of four phases of glaciation and labeled them Gunz, Mindel, Riss, and Wurm. The work has become a classic among proponents of polyglaciology.

Monoglaciology was the generally held view of geologists for nearly half a century. One of its most able supporters was J. W. Dawson of Canada. Clark wrote the following eulogy of this great scientist, "He did more by precept and by spoken and printed word to further the progress of geology and education in Canada during that period than did any other person."[11] Flint was to note of Dawson's view rejecting polyglaciology, "The last scientific opposition to it in North America died in 1899 with J. W. Dawson."[12]

But scientific opposition to polyglaciology did not die with Dawson. The renowned though controversial, American anthropologist, Ales Hrdlicka refused to accept geological indications for a succession of four glaciations in Europe. Alimen writes of French paleontologists, "who admit only one glaciation in the Quaternary, viz., the Wurm."[13] The late Richard Lougee contended, "Reduction of the ice age to 'unity' shortens geologic history and nullifies the meaning of the terms Nebraskan, Kansan, Illinoian, Wisconsin and the several interglacials." Lougee wrote, "Deposits formerly attributed to four or five separate Pleistocene glaciations are deposits of a single glaciation."[14] Monoglaciology still persists today. Nor is the number of glaciations completely agreed upon by those espousing polyglaciology.

B. *The Extent of Continental Glaciation*

Evidence of continental ice caps in the northern hemispheres is generally accepted today. Cornwall has summarized: "Though there are still plenty of grounds for disagreement and controversy over questions of Pleistocene geology, the glacial origin of the Drifts in the middle latitudes is fully established today."[15] There is however widespread variance of opinion as to the extent of the land glaciation. Agassiz may well have been prophetic for others when he wrote, "I am certainly far from having said the last word about glaciers."[16]

It is widely held that nearly thirty percent of the earth's surface was formerly covered by ice, and that most of this ice was in North America. Woodbury states, "In Europe the extent of the ice was no more than one-third of its extent in Canada and the United States."[17] Patten states, "The ice mass extended from Eastern Alaska to Central Europe, and from the fringes of Siberia to the central United States."[18] A high school science text specifies. "In Europe the ice sheets covered most of Scandinavia, the British Isles, Denmark, Belgium, northern France, and the Baltic countries, and extended far into Germany and Russia."[19]

But creationists ought to be aware of qualifying statements. Ley has written, "In the Arctic, the last great ice sheets of the ice age never covered the North Pole at all but spread from centers hundreds of miles to the south."[20] Lindroth writes, "Alaska was little affected by the land ice, the major part of it remained ice free throughout the entire Pleistocene period (Flint, 1952) as did the opposite part of eastern Siberia."[21] Farb includes western Canada along with most of Alaska and much of Siberia as having been ice free during the last part of the last glacial advance.[22] Ewing and Donn postulate, "The facts about early man in the Americas support the idea of an ice free Arctic during Wisconsin time and hence during earlier glacial stages."[23]

The extent of glaciation in Europe is also debated. West thus writes, "The evidence suggests the survival in southern Britain during the glaciations of open vegetation with a flora of many northern and montane plants."[24] Hibben states, "A land bridge between Great Britain and the European continent existed all through the Pleistocene period."[25]

Turning to the European mainland, Alimen states, "France escaped the Pleistocene continental glaciation."[26] Flint specifies, "No part of Belgium was glaciated at any time."[27] Rankama wrote about "The continuous marine deposition in the western Netherlands."[28] Some glacial students have placed the southern edge of maximum glaciation in London and Leipzig. Can it be demonstrated that the glaciation in the Swiss Alps was any more extensive than one of a more localized nature? One thing is now quite certain, the ice caps never approached the extent postulated by Agassiz and others of his day. Creationists should be wary upon hasty acceptance of glaciation estimates.

C. *The Catastrophic Nature of Continental Glaciation*

Numerous creationists are convinced that glaciation occurred suddenly by catastrophic agencies. Agassiz had argued for this in writing, "The ground of Europe, previously covered with tropical vegetation and inhabited by herds of great elephants, enormous hippopotomi, and gigantic carnivora, became suddenly buried under a vast expanse of ice covering plains, lakes, seas, and plateaus alike."[29] Rejecting uniformitarian concepts, he said, "Therefore all the hypotheses of a gradual cooling of the earth, or of a slow variation either in the inclination, or in the position of the globe's axis are invalid."[30]

Dawson held that the rapidity of ice melt following glaciation was responsible for widespread destruction of life. He wrote, "that Postglacial flood, which must have swept away the greater part of men, and many species of great beasts, and left only a few survivors to repeople the world."[31] Perhaps the extensive fossil remains on the continental land shelves argue for rapidity of flooding due to swift ice melt.

It may be noted that a few uniformitarians are themselves using the term catastrophic, or synonyms, for glaciation. Smith writes, "The arrival of a glacial period must therefore have been a cataclysmic event."[32] Eiseley writes of the Ice Epoch, "It was a world of elemental extravagance, assigned by authorities to scarcely one percent of earth's history and labeled 'geo-catastrophic.'"[33] Asimov notes, "There were catastrophes after all."[34]

D. *The Vast Extinction of the Northern Animals*

The dramatic extinction of untold millions of animals in the frozen muck beds of Alaska and Siberia has puzzled and invited explanations from scientists beginning with Agassiz and continuing to those of the present. Hapgood writes of their great numbers, "Yet we know that along with the millions of mammoths, the northern Siberian plains supported vast numbers of rhinoceroses, antelope, horse, bison, and other herbaceous creatures, while a variety of carnivores, including the saber tooth cat, preyed upon them."[35] Resorting to a neo-catastrophist explanation Hapgood postulates the following cause of their great extinction,

> In conclusion, it appears to me that the whole mass of the evidence relative to the animal and plant remains in the Siberian tundra, interpreted in the light of the evidence from North America, sufficiently confirms the conclusion that there was a southward displacement of Siberia coincident with the southward displacement of North America at the end of the last North American ice age."[36]

Patten (a creationist) espouses a phenomenal astral ice dump as the cause of extinction. He states, "a great dump of astral ice, possibly 12,000,000 cubic miles, dumped over the magnetic poles, simultaneous in timing with the Flood, involving ice at temperatures approaching zero."[37] He then notes, "The mammoth carcases were frozen rapidly, perhaps at temperatures below $-150°$ F."[38]

The chief problem with accepting Patten's and similar views, is that the areas of the greatest extinctions in the north, were never glaciated. The remains are found in frozen muck or permafrost. Permafrost consists of deeply frozen soils and subsoils. Sanderson thus writes, "The really puzzling thing is that this permafrost in Alaska and Siberia contains enormous quantities of animal bones and flesh, half-decayed vegetation, wood, and other remains of living things that, in some areas, together constitute a sizable percentage of the whole."[39] Permafrost is quite different from either land or sea ice in composition.

Hapgood's suggestion of shifting poles poses difficulty. Such extinctions had to occur suddenly and dramatically. There had to be quick coverage along with sudden deep freezing. A pole shift occurring over several hundred years would hardly be sufficient.

Is there a possible solution to the puzzling situation? One is reminded of an excellent comment by Morris. He states, "In fact, there seems no way of accounting for most of the great fossil beds of the world, especially of vertebrate fossils, except in terms of very rapid burial and lithification, such as posited by the biblical deluge, with its accompanying volcanic and tectonic activity and its inferred subsequent glaciological phenomena."[40] The greatest cause of extinction was the Genesis Flood. Genesis 7:21 thus records, "And all flesh died that moved upon the face of the earth, both of fowl, and of cattle, and of beast, and of every creeping thing that creepeth upon the earth, and every man."

But if all life was killed by drowning, how do we account for the deep freezing of the mammoths and others animals in Alaska and Siberia? Daly offers the following explanation, "As soon as the protecting vapor canopy fell, the heat radiated into space and the mammoths froze, 'suddenly . . . as of a single winter's night', as Dana expresses it, and knew no relenting afterward."[41] Elsewhere he states, "That the collapse in temperature occurred, and the ice age began, exactly at the time of the flood when the canopy collapsed is proved by the frozen mammoths."[42] Daly then postulates extinction by freezing concurrent with the Flood.

Patten's view is that there was an astral dump of ice by reason of another planet approaching close enough to earth to empty its load. He proposes that the "mammoths were encased suddenly in ice." He holds that their frozen condition "supports the proposition that the Flood and the Ice Epoch were simultaneous global catastrophes (or rather, differing phases of the same catastrophe)."[43]

Is there any alternative to Daly's and Patten's view that the mammoths were killed by the causes they have postulated? In the first place it would be quite erroneous to think that the great beasts are usually found intact and in well-preserved condition. Often the remains are torn asunder and intermingled with wood and vegetal debris. When the remains are exposed they are often in a half decayed condition. Further, half of the remains occur in Siberia, where the permafrost is "riddled with plant and animal remains aggregating untold millions of tons."[44]

The coldest spot on earth today is in Siberia. Temperatures drop to 90° below zero. Summer temperatures in the same area may rise to 60° above. There then can result a temperature change of 150° from summer to winter. Besides this drop of temperature, there is the chill factor resulting from the wind. Author of a recent article on Alaska notes, "The sixty-mile-per-hour winds whipping across the slope's 76,000 square miles at just twenty-three degrees below would create a chill factor equal to 101 degrees below. In this environment unprotected flesh freezes in less than thirty seconds."[45] A chill factor of 150° below is not unlikely even today in either Alaska or Siberia.

Following the Flood, Genesis 8:1 informs us, "God made a wind to pass over the earth, and the waters asswaged." The nature and duration of this wind is said to have been a determinate factor in causing the flood waters to subside. Is it possible that this wind was also acompanied by a temperature drop in such places as Alaska and Siberia?

This reviewer would ask indulgence in suggesting the following cause of the vast frozen remains in these northern regions. The Flood itself was accompanied by overwhelming turbidity mud flows which both drowned and covered the mammoths and other life in the North. This was soon followed by an extreme drop in temperature and winds of great force. The winds caused the flood waters to subside and in turn deep froze the mud with its vast animal remains. The freezing was provided as a result of the chill factor produced by the winds. The effect was a vast area of permafrost which in some areas is around 1500 meters deep. The permafrost became the great graveyard for untold millions of drowned animals.

E. *The Theory of Ice Rafted Debris*

Sir Charles Lyell was among those earlier scientists who espoused ice-rafting, rather than glacial movement, to account for foreign rock debris in England and on the plains of Germany. Agassiz noted of Lyell's view, "He assumed that the transportation of angular boulders had taken place on top ice rafts carried by water currents, in the same manner as the northern ice transports boulders, which are finally deposited along the northern shores of Europe."[46] Dawson was to comment later, "His views as to the combined agency of land ice or glaciers, of floating fragments of glaciers or icebergs and of field ice are, or ought to be known; but I must say that they have been unfairly stated."[47]

Agassiz had confessed unfamiliarity with the effects of floating ice, "Also I have not had as yet a chance to examine the influence on shore lines of great bodies of water with floating ice; however I doubt that their decision should be different than that of ordinary water."[48] But Flint, a modern glacial specialist writes, "Not all striations on rocks are of glacial origin; agencies other than glacier ice makes striations. A common glacial agent in high latitudes is floating ice in rivers, lakes and the sea."[49] Daly points out, "The ice age was an age of icebergs. The oceans had not yet receded off the continent."[50]

There is accumulating evidence of broad misinterpretation of action by glacial movement. Ton-sized rocks were dropped in Missouri by means of floating icebergs. Lougee states, "Iceberg rafted erratic stones and boulders became grounded on the submerged topography of northern Kentucky, southwestern Missouri, and eastern Iowa."[51] These ice raftings would undoubtedly result in striations such as was mentioned by Flint.

Gansser points out, from personal observations, "The author has seen many desert fanglomerates which, except for the absence of clearly striated boulders, could hardly be distinguished from glacier boulder beds, and certain mud flows can have striated pebbles unrelated to glaciation."[52] Fairbridge has also pointed out, "Careful re-examination of the evidence in recent years, however, has rejected many of these ice ages; formations once identified as glacial moraines have been reinterpreted as beds laid down by mud flows, submarine landslides, and turbidity currents."[53]

F. *The Duration of the Ice Age*

Students of ice age history are aware of widespread variance and disagreement over the duration of the glacial ice. Cornwall speaks for one group when he states, "The Pleistocene period is now reckoned to be some 2-3 million years long, including a longer earlier portion known as the Villafranchian."[54] Yet such a view is by no means uniform and has no general acceptance. Gilluly points out, "One of the most controversial items in geochronology is that of the duration of the Pleistocene epoch."[55]

Haldane represents another quite prominent group when he states, "Indeed recent work suggests that the Pleistocene period only lasted for about 300,000 years.[56] The reader should note that this estimate is a mere one-tenth of Cornwall's estimate. Springstead cites estimates held by a few geologists for a duration of only 10,000; 30,000; and 100-150 thousand years.[57]

The chief method of dating the Ice Epoch has been in respect to postulated multiple glaciations and lengthy intervals. Krober has noted that the chief means of dating the Pleistocene is in terms of associated ice ages.[58] Springstead has pointed out, however, that the polyglacial view is faulty due to the lack of field evidence.[59]

Only three mountain ranges in the United States provide evidence of more than one glaciation. Evidence of only one glaciation has been found in such mountain areas as the Apennines, Sierra Nevadas, Atlas Mountains, Anatolia, and the Balkans. One glacial stage only is known for Australia, Tasmania and for the Pontic and eastern parts of Turkey. Finally, polyglaciation cannot be demonstrated for many areas of glaciated land.

It must be kept in mind that all Swiss glaciers are "valley glaciers" and are in contrast to the extensive, more stable, continental glaciers found in Greenland and Antarctica. The Penck-Bruccner formula for using Swiss glaciations to postulate glaciations elsewhere is fraught with error. Kurten has noted, "Many authors suggest that the Alpine nomenclature should not be used except in the Alps."[60]

G. *The Close of the Ice Age*

A notable breakthrough was made in estimates of the duration of the Ice Age when it was discovered that its close was much more recent than had been previously estimated. Many authors suggest that its close has been within the last ten thousand years.

According to Bryan and Gruhn, "Some geologists argue that the Wisconsin ended when the last Laurentian ice melted about 6,000-5,000 years ago; this was based on the fact that the sea level apparently stopped rising abruptly about that time. (Frye and Willman 1960)"[61] Hapgood, although a polyglacialist, writes of, "The last one, which ended only about 8,000 years ago."[62] Watson and Sisson write, "The major eustatic rise of the ocean level, which ended about 5,500 years ago (Godwin and Willis, 1961, 1962) restored the North Sea to approximately its present stage. . . ."[63] Although such estimates can be no more than relative, they point out the recency of the ice melt in the Northern Hemisphere. They are not far removed from some estimates for the Flood.

Through his study of the maps of the ancient sea kings, and through Dr. W. D. Urry's isotope core dates, Hapgood argues for a warm period in Antarctica only a little more than 6,000 years ago.[64] Artifacts found by archaeologists on the frozen shores of the Arctic argue for the recency of the Arctic ice. Both of these factors call for recency and rapidity of glaciation in those areas. In noting the rapidity of recent glacial demise in Alaska, Sanderson significantly comments, "Perhaps forty days and forty nights of snow or rainfall could bring on an 'ice age' or a flood."[65]

Conclusion

In conclusion, this reviewer would uphold the view taken by those creationists who are convinced continental glaciation followed the Genesis flood. In so doing, he would adhere to Dawson's conviction that the glaciations were smaller than those popularly conceived.[66]

While such a view dramatically reduces the duration of the ice age, and also postulates its occurrence within historic time, the reviewer sees nothing incongruous in holding such a concept. Catastrophic occurences may be reasonably demonstrated for several significant events. Only a catastrophe, covering one-fifth of the world's land area, can account for the enormous animal extinctions in Alaska and Siberia. The recency of their extinction is a matter of record. The rapidity of glaciation in the Arctic and in the Antarctic, within the last ten thousand years, also provides grounds for postulating catastrophic glacial processes elsewhere.

When the extensive field work to substantiate polyglaciology is carefully studied, the case for monoglaciology is strongly enhanced. And the duration of the Ice Age is seen to be much shorter. The Genesis Flood provided the water needed for consequent continental glaciation. The Flood, not glaciation, was the chief agent of Ice Age extinctions.

Flooding had a much more prominent place, even during the Ice Age, than students of the subject have imagined. In fact, it would be much more appropriate to designate the overall time period as the Pluvial Age, instead of the Ice Age. Glaciations were much more localized than have been generally postulated.

REFERENCES

1. James W. Valentine, 1966. The present is the key to the past, *Journal of Geological Education,* XIV (2):59. April; and Paul D. Krynine. 1956. Uniformitarianism is a dangerous doctrine, *Journal of Paleontology,* 30(2):1003-1004.

THE CREATIONIST AND CONTINENTAL GLACIATION

2. Wm. R. Corliss, 1970. Mysteries beneath the sea. Thos Y. Crowell Co., New York, pp. 135, 156, 157.
3. Harold Armstrong, 1972. Comments on scientific news and views, *Creation Research Society Quarterly,* 8(4):275. March.
4. Donald Wesley Patten, 1966. The Biblical flood and the ice epoch. Pacific Meridian Publ. Co., Seattle, p. 99.
5. Encyclopaedia Britannica, 1970. Agassiz, Jean; Louis, Rodolphe, vol. I. Encyclopaedia Britannica, Inc., Chicago, p. 320.
6. Louis Agassiz, 1967. Studies on glaciers. (Translated and edited by Albert V. Carozzi). Hafner Publishing Co., New York and London, p. xxvii.
7. *Ibid.,* p. xxxv.
8. *Ibid.,* pp. xvii-xviii.
9. *Ibid.,* p. 195.
10. J. Wm. Dawson, 1893. The Canadian ice age. Wm. V. Dawson, Montreal, p. 289.
11. T. H. Clark, 1964. Pioneers of Canadian science. R-6, Society of University of Toronto Press, p. 101.
12. Richard Foster Flint, 1957. Glacial and pleistocene geology. John Wiley and Sons, Inc., New York, p. 5.
13. Marie Henrietta Alimen, 1967. The Quaternary of France (in) The geologic systems: the quaternary, 2. Rankama, Kalervo, John Wiley, New York, p. 207.
14. Reginald Daly, 1972. Earth's most challenging mysteries. The Craig Press, Nutley, N.J., pp. 166, 149.
15. Ian Cornwall, 1970. Ice ages. Humanities Press, Inc., New York, John Baker, Ltd., London, p. 14.
16. Agassiz, *op. cit.,* p. lxxi.
17. David O. Woodbury, 1962. The great white mantle. The Viking Press, New York, p. 100.
18. Patten, *op. cit.,* p. 114.
19. Samuel N. Namowitz and Donald Stone, 1972. Earth science, 4th ed. American Book Co., New York and Cincinnati, p. 174.
20. Willy Ley, 1962, 1971. The poles. Life Nature Library, Time-Life Books, Time, Inc., New York, p. 11.
21. Carl H. Lindroth, 1957. The faunal connections between Europe and North America. John Wiley and Sons, Inc., New York; Almquist & Wiksell, Stockholm, p. 293.
22. Peter Farb, 1968. Man's rise to civilization. E. P. Dutton & Co., Inc., New York, pp. 193-194.
23. Maurice Ewing and William L. Donn, 1956. A theory of the ice ages, *Science,* 123(3207):1064. June 15.
24. R. G. West, 1967. The quaternary of the British Isles. The Quaternary, vol. 2, Kalervo Rankama, Interscience Publishing Div., John Wiley & Sons, New York, p. 66.
25. Frank C. Hibben, 1958. Prehistoric man in Europe. University of Oklahoma Press, Norman, Oklahoma, p. 19.
26. Alimen, *op. cit.,* p. 205.

27. Flint, op. cit., p. 406.
28. Jan D. deJong, 1967. The geologic systems. The Quaternary, 2, Rankama, Kalervo, John Wiley, New York, p. 317.
29. Agassiz, op. cit., p. 169.
30. Ibid., p. 168.
31. J. Wm. Dawson, 1894. Some salient points in the science of the earth. Harper and Brothers, New York, p. 465.
32. Anthony Smith, 1970. The seasons. Harcourt Brace Janovich, Inc., New York, p. 79.
33. Loren Eiseley, 1969. The unexpected universe. Harcourt, Brace & World, Inc., p. 98.
34. Isaac Asimov, 1964. A short history of biology. Natural History Press, Doubleday, p. 67.
35. Charles H. Hapgood, 1970. The path of the pole (revised ed. of *Earth's Shifting Crust*, 1958). Chilton Book Co., Philadelphia and New York, and London, p. 255.
36. Ibid., p. 279.
37. Patten, op. cit., p. 141.
38. Donald Patten, 1966. The ice age phenomena and a possible explanation. Creation Research Society Quarterly (Annual Issue), 3(1):64. May.
39. Ivan Sanderson, 1961. The continent we live on. Random House, Inc., New York, p. 52.
40. Henry M. Morris, 1971. Proposals for science framework guidelines. *Creation Research Society Quarterly*, 8(2):150. September.
41. Reginald Daly, 1972. Earth's most challenging mysteries. The Craig Press, Nutley, N. J., p. 236.
42. Ibid., p. 237. (Yet see contra, p. 142, "There could not be a universal flood without a glacial age following.")
43. Patten, 1966, op. cit., p. 63.
44. Sanderson, op. cit., p. 53.
45. Robert Hawkins, 1972. The invisible cities. The American West, American West Publishing Co., Palo Alto, Calif., p. 40.
46. Agassiz, op. cit., p. 155.
47. Dawson, op. cit., p. 3.
48. Agassiz, op. cit., p. 161.
49. Flint, 1957, op. cit., p. 57.
50. Daly, op. cit., p. 165.
51. Ibid., pp. 165-166.
52. Augusto Gansser, 1964. Geology of the Himalayas. John Wiley & Sons, New York, p. 50.
53. Rhodes W. Fairbridge, 1960. The changing level of the sea. *Scientific American*, 202(5):70. May.
54. Ian Cornwall, 1970. Ice ages, their nature and effects. Humanities Press, Inc., New York, p. 57.
55. Jas. Gilluly, Aaron C. Waters, and A. O. Woodford, 1968. Principles of geology, 3rd ed. W. H. Freeman and Co., San Francisco, p. 284.

56. J. B. S. Haldane, 1967. Quoted (in) Culture and the evolution of man. Edited by M. F. Ashley Montagu, 3rd printing. Oxford University Press, p. 71.
57. Wm. A. Springstead, 1971. The dying of the giants. *Journal of the American Scientific Affiliation,* 23(1):23. March.
58. Alfred Louis Kroeber, 1923. Anthropology. Harcourt, Brace & Co., New York, p. 648.
59. William A. Springstead, 1971. Monoglaciology and the global flood, *Creation Research Society Quarterly,* 8(3):177. December.
60. Bjorn Kurten, 1968. Pleistocene mammals of Europe. Aldine Publishing Co., Chicago, p. 19.
61. Alan Lyle Bryan and Ruth Gruhn, 1963-1964. *American Antiquity,* 29:307.
62. Charles H. Hapgood, 1966. Maps of the ancient sea kings. Chilton Books Publishing, Philadelphia and New York, p. 98.
63. J. Wreyford Watson and J. B. Sissons, 1964. The British Isles—A systematic geography. Nelson, University of Edinburgh, p. 149.
64. Hapgood, *op. cit.,* p. 98.
65. Sanderson, *op. cit.,* p. 64.
66. Springstead, *op. cit.,* p. 177 (reference no. 59).

XV

THE ARK OF NOAH

Henry M. Morris*

Purpose of the Ark

The biblical record of the great Flood is quite explicit in describing it as world-wide cataclysm. Its purpose and effect were, in God's own words, to:

> destroy man whom I have created from the face of the earth; both man, and beast, and the creeping thing, and the fowls of the air. (Gen. 6:7)

The destruction was universal, so far as land animals were concerned. "All in whose nostrils was the breath of life, of all that was in the dry land, died" (Gen. 7:22).

However, in order to preserve two of each kind of animal, with which to repopulate the earth after the Flood, as well as Noah and his family, God gave directions for the building of the Ark.

> Make thee an ark of gopher wood," He said, "rooms shalt thou make in the ark, and shalt pitch it within and without with pitch. And this is the fashion which thou shalt make it of: The length of the ark shall be three hundred cubits, the breadth of it fifty cubits, and the height of it thirty cubits. A window shalt thou make to the ark, and in a cubit shalt thou finish it above; and the door of the ark shalt thou set in the side thereof; with lower, second and third stories shalt thou make it. (Gen. 6:14-16)

Size of the Ark

The Ark was thus to be essentially a huge box (the Hebrew

---

*Henry M. Morris, Ph.D., is director of The Institute of Creation Research and academic vice-president of Christian Heritage College, 2716 Madison Avenue, San Diego, California 92116.

word itself implies this), designed essentially for stability in the waters of the Flood rather than for movement through the waters. Assuming the cubit to be 1.5 ft., which is the most likely value, the dimensions of the Ark were 45 ft. x 75 ft. x 450 ft., as sketched in Figure 1, to a scale of $1'' = 150'$.

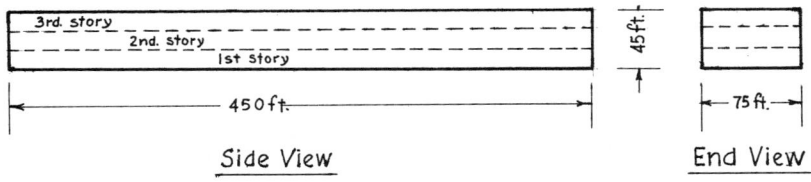

Side View   End View

Figure 1. Dimensions of Noah's Ark.

The Ark was obviously a very large structure, taller than a normal three-story building and half again as long as a football field. The total volumetric capacity was 450 x 45 x 75 = 1,518,750 cubic feet, or 56,361 cubic yards. Since the standard railroad stock car contains 2,670 cubic feet effective capacity, the Ark had a volumetric capacity equal to that of 569 standard stock cars. It obviously could have carried a tremendous number of animals, and was clearly designed to hold representatives from all kinds of animals throughout the entire world.

Stability of the Ark

In the complex of hydrodynamic and aerodynamic forces unleashed in the Flood, it was necessary that the ark remain afloat for a whole year. The gopher wood of which it was constructed was no doubt extremely strong and durable.

Timbers forming the sides and bottom, as well as the floors of the intermediate decks, were probably cut and shaped from great trees that had been growing since the world began, over 1600 years earlier. The "pitch" (Hebrew *kaphar*, meaning simply "covering") was evidently an excellent waterproofing material, though we do not now know what it was.

In addition to floating it must not capsize under the impact of the great waves and winds which might beat against it. The Scripture says the floodwaters rose at least 15 cubits above the highest mountains (Gen. 7:20), evidently to point out that the ark was floating freely wherever the waters might propel it. The height of the ark was 30 cubits, so it seems probable that the 15 cubit figure represents the draft of the ark when loaded.

When the ark was floating at this depth, Archimedes' principle tells us that its weight must have equalled the force of buoyancy, which in turn equals the weight of the equivalent amount of water displaced. The weight of the ark therefore was

$$W = 450(75) \left(\frac{45}{2}\right) (w)$$

where w is the weight of each cubic foot of water.

Fresh water weighs 62.4 lbs. and sea water 64 lbs. per cubic foot. Because of the minerals and sediments in the water, its density may well have been at least that of sea water, in which case the weight of the ark would be calculated at 48,600,000 pounds; this is close enough for practical purposes.

The average unit weight of the ark must then be half that of the water, or 32 lbs. per cubic foot. The center of gravity of the ark and its contents presumably would be close to its geometric center, with the framework, the animals, and other contents more or less uniformly and symmetrically dispersed throughout the structure.

Two Tests of Stability

The ark as designed would have been an exceptionally stable structure. Its cross-section of 30 cubits height by 50 cubits breadth, with a draft of 15 cubits, made it almost impossible to capsize, even in the midst of heavy waves and violent winds.

To illustrate this, assume the ark tipped through an angle such that the roof was actually touching the water's edge, as sketched in

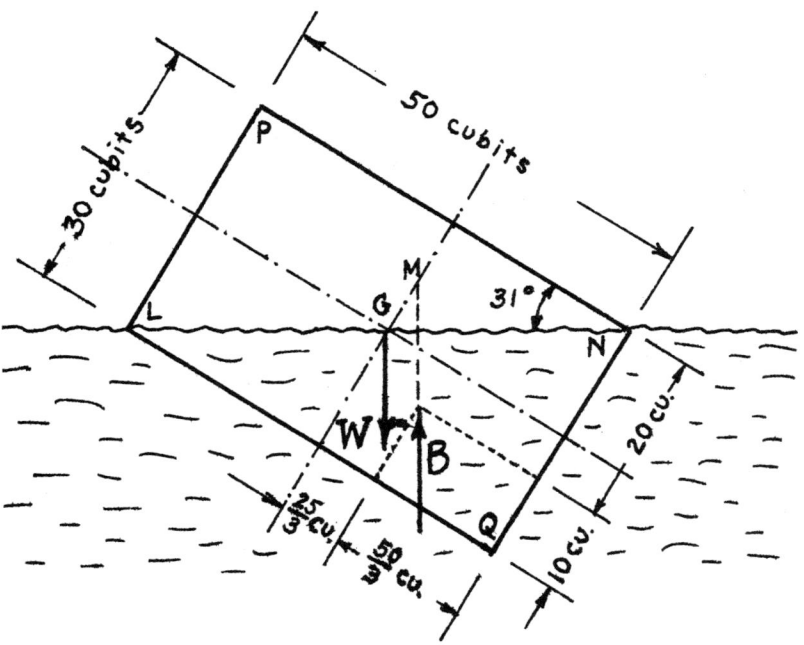

Figure 2. Stability of Ark at 31° angle of tilt.

Figure 2. This is an angle of approximately 31°, that is the angle whose tangent is 30/50. Since the weight of the ark continues unchanged, it must still displace an amount of water equal to half its cross-section. Thus the water surface coincides with the diagonal. The buoyant force B continues to equal W, the weight of the ark.

However, the two forces are not now acting in the same line. The weight W acts vertically downward through the center of the ark's cross-section. The force B acts vertically upward through the centroid of the triangle LQN, since this is the location of the center of gravity of the volume of water that has been displaced by the ark. The two forces W and B, equal in magnitude but opposite in direction, form a *couple,* of intensity equal to the product of either force times the distance between them.

As long as the line of action of B is outside that of W, in the direction toward the submerged side of the ark, the couple is a "righting couple" and would act to restore the vessel to its upright position. The magnitude of the couple is of no particular interest, but the location of M, the *metacenter,* is significant. As long as M is above G (the centroid of the entire vessel cross-section) on the axis of symmetry of the vessel, then the ship is stable.

For the condition shown, M can be calculated to be 8.9 cubits above G on the axis of symmetry (calculated, from dimensions shown on the sketch, as $\frac{25/3}{\tan 31°} - 5 = \frac{125}{9} - 5 = \frac{80}{9}$ cu.). This is almost 13.5 ft. above the centroid and indicates the ark was extremely stable, even under such a strong angle of listing. The righting couple is then equal to 8.9 (sin 31°)(W) = $\left(\frac{80/}{/(3\sqrt{34}\ )} \right)$ (48,600,000) = 222,000,000 ft.-lbs.

As a matter of fact, the *metacentric height,* as the distance GM is known, is positive for this cross-section even for much higher angles. Suppose the boat, for example, were tilted through a 60° angle, as shown in Figure 3. The centroid of the immersed area is obviously to the right of the line of action of G, and thus there is a righting couple and the metacentric height GM is positive.

As a matter of fact, the ark would have to be turned completely verticle before M would coincide with G. Thus, for any angle up to 90°, the ark would right itself.

Furthermore its relatively great length (six times its width) would tend to keep it from being subjected to wave forces of equal magnitude through its whole length, since wave fields tend to occur in broken and varying patterns, rather than in a series of long uniform crest-trough sequences, and this would be particularly true in the chaotic hydrodynamic phenomena of the Flood. Any vortex action to which it might occasionally be subjected would also tend to be resisted and broken up by its large length-width ratio.

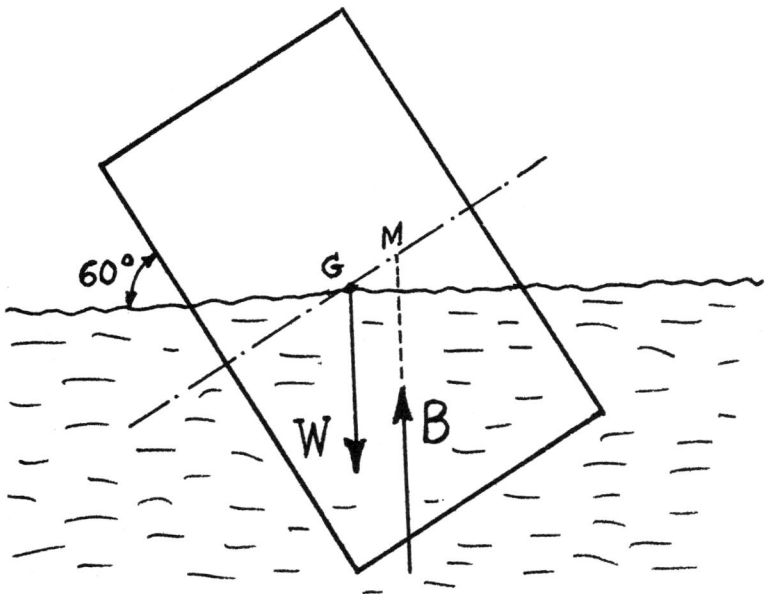

Figure 3. Stability of Ark at 60° angle of tilt.

The ark would, in fact, tend to be lined up by the spectrum of hydrodynamic forces and currents in such a direction that its long axis would be parallel to the predominant direction of wave and current movement. Thus it would act as a semi-streamlined body, and the net drag forces would usually be minimal.

In every way, therefore, the ark as designed was highly stable, admirably suited for its purpose of riding out the storms of the year of the great Flood.

XVI

DECAY OF THE EARTH'S MAGNETIC MOMENT AND THE GEOCHRONOLOGICAL IMPLICATIONS

THOMAS G. BARNES*

Magnetic Moment: Source of the Earth's Main Field

The earth's main magnetic field has been shown to be due to a *magnetic dipole*.[1] The strength of a magnetic dipole is called its *magnetic moment*. The magnetic moment is due to circulating currents.

In the case of the earth these currents probably reside in the earth's core, which is thought to consist of hot liquid metal, perhaps iron. These currents are extremely large. There is no known mechanism to sustain these currents.[2] So, as one would expect, the earth's magnetic moment is decaying.

This paper considers the experimentally determined decay of the earth's magnetic moment. It is a surprisingly large decay rate for such a large scale phenomena.

The earth's magnetic dipole (Figure 1) is located about 300 kilometers from the center of the earth with the magnetic axis making an angle of approximately 11.5° with the rotational axis of the earth.[3] The magnetic dipole moment, M, points southward, yielding a magnetic field that points *outward* at the South Magnetic Pole and *inward* at the North Magnetic Pole.

The field due to this magnetic moment is symmetrical about its axis and may be represented by two orthogonal components, $B\phi$

---

*Thomas G. Barnes, D.Sc., is professor of physics at the University of Texas at El Paso and consultant to Globe Universal Sciences, Inc., El Paso, Texas 79902.

DECAY OF THE EARTH'S MAGNETIC MOMENT

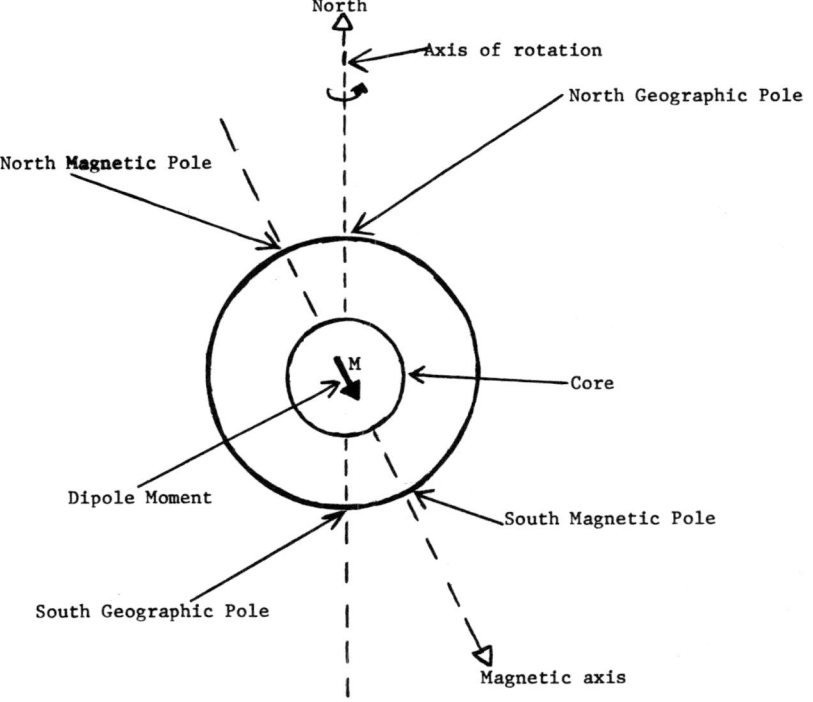

Figure 1. The earth's magnetic dipole moment, M.

and B_r, as shown in Figure 2. These components can be derived from the magnetic moment, M, by the following equations:[4]

$$B\phi = \frac{\mu M \sin \phi}{4\pi r^3} \quad (1)$$

$$B_r = \frac{\mu M \cos \phi}{2\pi r^3} \quad (2)$$

where μ is the *permeability,* a magnetic property of the medium. The value of μ is usually taken as $4\pi \times 10^{-7}$, its value in free space,

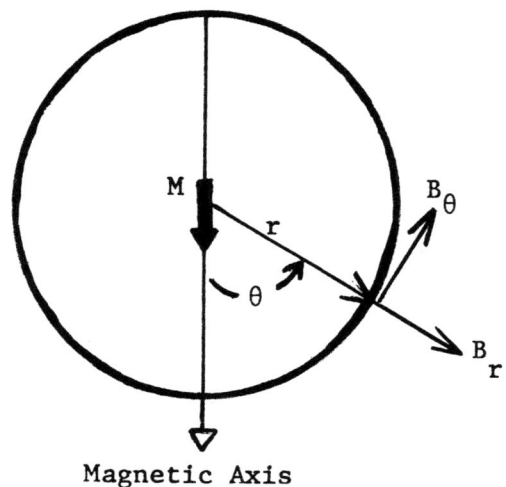

Figure 2. Field components due to the magnetic moment.

unless the medium contains an appreciable amount of magnetic material.

In order to have up-to-date units the "Systeme International d'Unites" (called SI for short) is employed. In this system the unit of B is the *tesla* (equal to 10^4 gauss, the unit most often found in the literature) and M has the units *amp meter^2* (reminding us that it consists of circulating *amperes* of current enclosing *meter^2* of area).

The net field, B_o, at any point on the magnetic equator reduces to the $B\phi$ component and may be written as

$$B_o = \frac{\mu M}{4\pi r^3} \quad (3)$$

because $\sin 90° = 1$. Letting the earth's radius $r = 6.371 \times 10^6$ meter and $\mu = 4\pi \times 10^{-7}$, the equatorial value of B at the surface is

$$B_o = 3.687 \times 10^{-28} M \quad (4)$$

Scientists	Year (Epoch)	M (amp meter^2) x 10^{22}	B$_0$ (telsa) x 10^{-5}
Gauss	1835	8.558	3.309
Adams	1845	8.488	3.282
Adams	1880	8.363	3.234
Neumayer	1880	8.336	3.224
Fritsche	1885	8.347	3.228
Schmidt	1885	8.375	3.239
Vestine, et al	1905	8.291	3.206
Vestine, et al	1915	8.225	3.181
Dyson-Furner	1922	8.165	3.157
Vestine, et al	1925	8.149	3.151
Vestine, et al	1935	8.088	3.128
Jones-Melotte	1942.5	8.009	3.097
Vestine, et al	1945	8.065	3.119
Afanasieva	1945	8.010	3.097
U.S.C. & G.S.	1945	8.066	3.119
Fanselau-Kautzleben	1945	8.090	3.128
U.S.C. & G.S.	1955	8.035	3.107
Finch-Leaton	1955	8.067	3.120
Nagata-Oguti	1958.5	8.038	3.108
Cain, et al	1959	8.086	3.127
Fougere	1960	8.053	3.114
Adam, et al	1960	8.037	3.108
Jensen-Cain	1960	8.025	3.103
Leaton, et al	1965	8.013	3.099
Hurwitz, et al	1965	8.017	3.100

Table 1. **Magnetic Moment M and Equatorial Magnetic Field B$_0$ of the Dipole. 1835 to 1965 (Earth radius = 6.371 x 10^6 meter).**

This example illustrates how Equations (1) and (2) enable one to compute the earth's main field at any point (r, $\emptyset$) on earth, or above the earth, if the earth's magnetic dipole moment is known.

Historical Values of the Earth's Magnetic Moment Indicate the Decay

The study of the earth's magnetism led Gauss to develop a magnetometer for making *absolute* measurements of B and to develop a mathematical method (spherical harmonic theory of potentials) for analyzing the magnetic surveys of the earth.[5] Gauss was then able to determine the magnetic dipole moment of the earth. His determination for the year (epoch) 1835 is $M = 8.558 \times 10^{22}$ amp meter.[2] The value of M and the date 1835 are taken as a key historical reference from which the decay in the earth's magnetic moment has been measured.

Table 1 contains the values of the earth's magnetic dipole moment, the net field value B_o, the year (epoch), and the scientists who made the determination. The source for the magnetic moment values is a recent U.S. Department of Commerce ESSA publication[6] produced by the Institute for Earth Sciences, Boulder, Colorado.

Values in that table were given in cgs units and have been converted to SI units through the conversion factor for magnetic moment, namely 1 unit of $M_{SI} = 10^3$ units of M_{cgs}.

The equatorial values for the field were computed by means of Equation (4). These computed values of B_o check with those values which are listed in an early table by Sidney Chapman[7] after application of the conversion factor between SI and cgs units, namely, 1 tesla = 10^4 gauss.

It is clear from Table 1 that *the magnetic moment and the earth's main magnetic field have been decaying relatively rapidly since 1835.* Sidney Chapman states in his monograph *The Earth's Magnetism,*[8] in which he had compiled the data up to 1945,

> these results certainly suggest a decrease of a few per cent in H_o and the earth's magnetic moment during the last century. When the great scale of the phenomenon is considered, this must seem a remarkably large and rapid secular change, not paralleled for any other worldwide geophysical property.

Chapman used the symbol H_o instead of the symbol B_o used in this paper, but it refers to the same magnetic field.

Additional confirmation of the rapid decay rate of the earth's magnetic moment can be seen in the following quote from the aforementioned ESSA publication,[9]

Since the time of Gauss' measurements the earth's dipole moment has decreased, sensibly linearly, at approximately the rate of 5% per hundred years. Assuming these rates to persist, our analysis discloses that the dipole moment will vanish in A.D. 3991.

Exponential Decay of Earth's Magnetic Moment

One would expect the magnetic moment of the earth to decay exponentially because it is produced by *real* currents that dissipate energy through Joule heating. The magnetic moment of the earth is *not* produced by *amperian currents* (dissipationless currents), such as those that exist in permanent magnetization of material.

Permanently magnetized material has been rejected as the source of the earth's magnetic moment for two reasons: (1) It would require greater intensity of magnetization than has been observed in the crust of the earth, and (2) No magnetization exists in the core material, because the high temperature there would destroy the magnetization.

The temperature of the earth increases with depth to such a degree that it has exceeded the Curie point. For example at 25 kilometers the temperature has reached the Curie point for iron, viz., 750°C, as reported by Jacobs.[10]

The earth's magnetic moment being due to a system of circulating real currents will undoubtedly have associated, with its loops of current and its imperfect conductors, an inductance, L, and a resistance, R. Since there seems to be no dynamo or other energy source in the earth that can generate these currents, the current that does exist in the core must be decaying exponentially. This means that the magnetic moment will also be decaying exponentially.

It is comparable to the freely decaying current in a simple series circuit in which the time to decay to e^{-1} of its initial value is equal to the ratio of the inductance, L, to the resistance, R. The problem is complicated by distributed inductance and resistance instead of the simple lumped elements of circuit theory, but the fundamental physics of the decay process is the same, namely exponential.

To be sure, the original magnetic energy contained in the inductive field of the earth was phenomenal to have been decaying as long as it has and still have such a sizeable amount of magnetic energy left. But, by no stretch of the imagination could it have been decaying continuously like this for billions of years.

Evolutionists will not accept this continuous decay process, because of the consequences it has on their preconceived ideas of billions of years age for the earth. But they have yet to propose any acceptable alternative explanation of the earth's magnetic field and its decay.

Note how the excellent work of Horace Lamb is rejected in a recent survey article on the Earth's Magnetic Field,[11]

> H. Lamb showed in 1883 that electric currents generated in a sphere of radius a, electrical conductivity σ and permeability μ, and left to decay freely would be reduced by electrical dissipation by Joule heating to e^{-1} of their initial strength in a time not longer than $4\sigma\mu a^2/\pi$. This time is of the order of 10^5 years, whereas the age of the earth is more than 4×10^9 years.

No other reason is given for excluding this theory. But note the futility of all other attempts to explain the earth's main magnetic field as expressed in this same article:

> There has been much speculation as to the cause of the earth's main field and no completely satisfactory explanation has as yet been given. . . .
>
> It seems that rather extreme assumptions are necessary to make any theory satisfactory—either an extreme geometry or extreme and implausible values of the physical properties of the material in the core and lower mantle.

It is this author's contention that Lamb's solution for the earth's main magnetic field is reasonable as a first approximation; that freely decaying currents are the source of the earth's main magnetic field. This makes sense because the data for the last 130 years indicate that the earth's main magnetic field is decaying at a rate that is at least as great or greater than one would predict with Lamb, that rate being dependent upon what assumption has been made for the value of the conductivity in the core—a value that is not easy to determine.

1400-Year Half-Life for the Earth's Magnetic Moment

When values of the magnetic moment, M, in Table 1 are plotted against time, t, on semi-log coordinate paper, the points lie approximately on a straight line as one would expect for an exponential decay of the earth's magnetic moment. This is also true of course for a plot of B_o against t. We therefore assume that the decay is exponential and write

$$M = M_o e^{-t/T} \quad (5)$$

Where M_o is the magnetic moment at some reference time, and M is the magnetic moment t years after that reference time. The *time constant*, T, is the time required for the magnetic moment to decay to e^{-1} of its reference value M_o.

Rearranging Equation (5) and taking the natural logarithm, the following is obtained:

$$\ln (M_o/M) = t/T \quad (6)$$

Specifying M_o at its 1835 value, M at its 1965 value, and t at 130 years (the time lapsed between these two values), we have

$$\ln (8.558/8.017) = 130/T \quad (7)$$

Solving for T, we obtain the time constant of 2000 years, the time for the earth's magnetic moment (or its main magnetic field) to decay to e^{-1} of its reference value.

To find the half-life Equation (6) is evaluated for t with the ratio M_o/M set equal to 2 and T given its value of 2000 years,

$$\ln (2) = t/2000 \quad (8)$$

This gives a rounded value of 1400 years for the half-life of the magnetic moment of the earth.

This means that in A.D. 3371 the earth's magnetic moment will be down to half of its present value, and there will be less protection from cosmic radiation.

Going backward in time, assuming this same exponential function, the earth's magnetic moment doubles every 1400 years of prior time all the way back to its origin. Table 2 gives the equatorial value of the magnetic dipole field (main field) on the surface of the earth as a function of time.

It is computed on the basis of 1400 year half-life or what amounts to the same thing, a time constant of 2000 years, with the reference value of 3.1×10^{-5} tesla (.31 gauss) in 1965. Time, t, is years backward from 1965. The exponential equation is

$$B = 3.1 \times 10^{-5} \, e^{\, t/2000} \qquad (9)$$

and for convenience in computation it is expressed in the base 10 making use of the relation $e = 10^{0.43429}$ to put it in the form

$$B = 3.1 \times 10^{-5} \times 10^{0.0002171t} \qquad (10)$$

The table is carried back one million years to show the *absurdity* of that age for the earth, if its magnetic field is assumed to be historically associated with its present processes. The value of 3×10^{215} is impossible, of course. This means that the earth is not a million years old, if its magnetic field originated at the time of the earth's origin and followed its present type of decay processes thereafter.

Date	Magnetic Field (Tesla)
1965 A.D.	3.1×10^{-5}
1000 A.D.	5.0×10^{-5}
1 A.D.	8.3×10^{-5}
1000 B.C.	1.4×10^{-4}
2000 B.C.	2.3×10^{-4}
3000 B.C.	3.7×10^{-4}
4000 B.C.	6.1×10^{-4}
5000 B.C.	1.0×10^{-3}
6000 B.C.	1.7×10^{-3}
10,000 B.C.	1.2×10^{-2}
20,000 B.C.	1.8
30,000 B.C.	2.7×10^{2}
40,000 B.C.	4.0×10^{4}
50,000 B.C.	5.9×10^{6}
100,000 B.C.	4.2×10^{17}
200,000 B.C.	2×10^{39}
1,000,000 B.C.	3×10^{215}

Table 2. Value of the Magnetic Field at the Surface of the Magnetic Equator for Various Dates in the Past as Computed from the 1400-Year Half-life Decay Rate Currently Observed.

DECAY OF THE EARTH'S MAGNETIC MOMENT

One cannot date the origin of the magnetic field because we have no way of knowing its initial value. However, it can be seen that this rapid decay process requires that it be a very "young" age. For example the magnetic field on the surface of the earth in 20,000 B.C. namely 1.8 tesla (18,000 gauss) is stronger than the field between the pole pieces of the most powerful radar magnets. It is not very plausible that the core of the earth could have stayed together with the Joule heat that would have been associated with the currents producing such a strong field.

Even now the currents in the core of the earth can be shown to exceed one billion amperes;[12] but, if the field at the surface of the earth were 1.8 tesla instead of its 3.1×10^{-5} tesla, the currents in the core of the earth would be more than 50,000 times greater than they are now. Joule heating in the earth is proportional to the square of the current. This means that the Joule heating in the core of the earth would have been 250 million times greater than it is now, a phenomenal amount of heating.

It would appear from these arguments that the origin of the earth's magnetic moment is much less than 20,000 years ago.

Secondary Magnetic Fields

It should be pointed out that there are many anomalies in the earth's magnetic field that are not associated with its dipole source. Anomalies are presumably caused by ferromagnetic deposits, telluric currents, and other more or less localized causes.

Some of the anomalies may alter the earth's field over large regions of the earth. Sometimes the anomaly may cause a magnetic field that is larger than the dipole field in that region. However, when averaged over the whole earth, these anomalies are much smaller than the dipole field, otherwise the compass would not be classified as having *north-seeking* and *south-seeking* poles.

Solar winds, charges emitted from the sun, are considered to be the source of diurnal and other fluctuations in the earth's magnetic field. But these secondary fields are usually much smaller than the earth's dipole field strength. The main field of the earth is still the dipole field produced by the magnetic moment in the core of the earth.

It is the main magnetic field of the earth, the dipole field, that shields the earth from much of the solar wind. It also "guides" much of the radiation in toward the magnetic polar regions. It is this magnetic polar effect that locates the *auroral zones.*

It is this main magnetic field that shields much of the earth from some of the cosmic radiation. We shall next consider the influence of past stronger magnetic fields upon this radiation.

Effect of Strong Magnetic Field in the Past on Radio Carbon Dating

One of the consequences of the stronger magnetic field in the past was better shielding of the earth and its atmosphere from primary cosmic rays. This also reduced the rate of production of Carbon-14 in the atmosphere.

Primary cosmic rays interact with the atmosphere to produce neutrons which in turn transmute nitrogen atoms into Carbon-14. Hence, with the lesser number of cosmic rays striking the atmosphere per second, a smaller rate of production of Carbon-14 existed in the past. A smaller production rate of Carbon-14 in the atmosphere than has previously been assumed would reduce the age of Carbon-14 dates.

Primary cosmic rays consist of high speed positively charged atomic nuclei. The earth is constantly bombarded from all directions with these charged particles. The earth's magnetic field tends to bend the path of those particles away from the earth as shown in Figure 3. This magnetic force, F, is a function of the magnetic field, B; the charge, q, the particle velocity, v; and the sine of the angle ø between v and B, that is,

$$F = qvB \sin \phi \qquad (11)$$

Note that the shielding force is greatest when the particle motion is at right angles to the direction of the field B, and decreases as this angle decreases. Hence fewer cosmic rays reach the earth's atmosphere in the lower latitudes than in the polar regions. Figure 4 shows the cosmic ray neutron intensity vs. geomagnetic latitude at 30,000 feet as determined by J. A. Simpson, Jr.[13]

DECAY OF THE EARTH'S MAGNETIC MOMENT

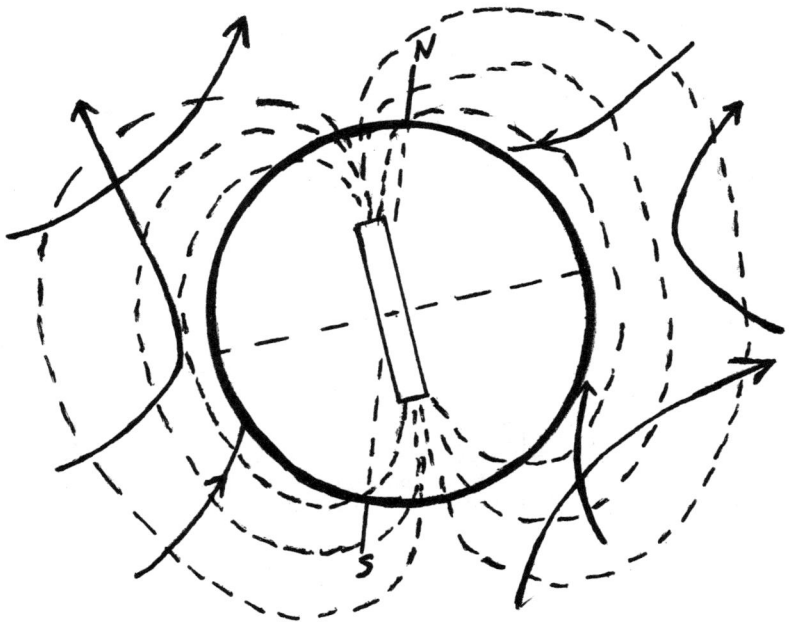

Figure 3. Earth's magnetic field tends to bend the paths of cosmic rays and to shield the earth.

The present magnetic field has already reduced the cosmic-ray neutron intensity in the equatorial region down to 22 percent of its value at 65 degrees latitude. Hence there is a limit to how much more it can be reduced by a stronger magnetic field. But the stronger field in the past must have caused some reduction in the rate of production of Carbon-14.

The total process is quite complex and will not be analyzed in this paper. However, one might make a crude estimate, on the basis of Figure 4, that the worldwide neutron intensity might have been reduced by as much as 10 percent about 2800 years ago, back when the field was four times as strong. This would affect the experimental results of radiocarbon dating by reducing the age of the sample.

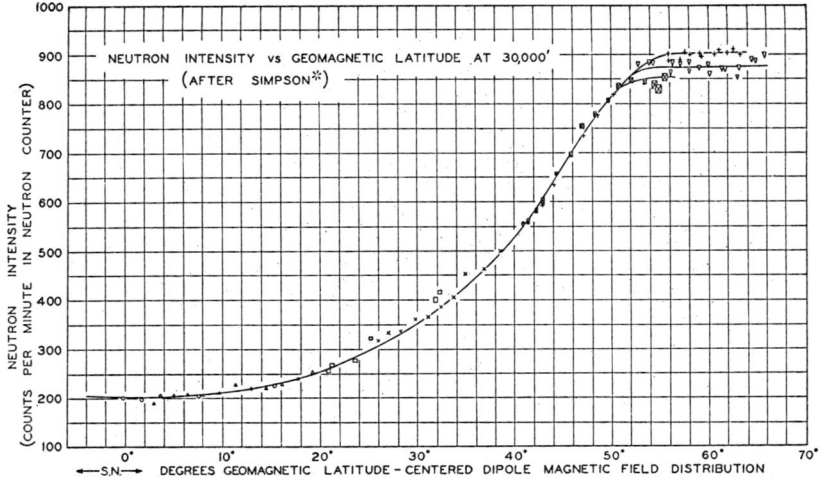

Figure 4. Variation of the cosmic ray neutron intensity vs. magnetic latitude at 30,000 feet. (Permission granted to use Figure 2 from *Radiocarbon Dating* by Willard F. Libby, 2nd ed., p. 13. University of Chicago Press, 1955.)

Melvin Cook has already pointed out that a non-equilibrium condition exists now that reduces the experimental results on radiocarbon dating. This reduction is progressively greater with the age. From his analysis he concludes that

> it reduces the computed age by an amount dependent upon the age of the sample by amounts increasing in time from about 20% in 1000 years, 30% in 4000 years and finally telescoping all the very long ages to 12,500 years or less.[14]

When the effect of the larger magnetic field in the past and the consequent lesser rate of production of Carbon-14 is included these ages will be telescoped still further.

Conclusion

The search for a physical explanation of the earth's main magnetic field and its decay rate seems to have been retarded by an evolutionary bias toward long ages. The physics seems inevitably to point to a much shorter age. It is believed that Horace Lamb's treatment of the freely decaying currents in a huge conducting sphere, such as the molten core of the earth, should be reconsidered as the source of the earth's magnetism.

REFERENCES

1. J. A. Jacobs, 1967. The earth's magnetic field, Mining geophysics, *Society of Exploration Geophysicists,* Tulsa, 2:426.
2. *Ibid.,* pp. 429-432.
3. *Ibid.,* p. 429.
4. Thomas G. Barnes, 1965. Foundations of electricity and magnetism. D. C. Heath and Co., Boston, p. 277.
5. S. K. Runcorn, 1956. The magnetism of the earth's body, *Encyclopedia of Physics.* Springer-Verlag, Berlin, p. 498.
6. Keith L. McDonald and Robert H. Gunst, July, 1967. An analysis of the earth's magnetic field from 1835 to 1965, Essa Technical Rept. IER 46-IES 1. U.S. Government Printing Office, Washington, D.C., Table 3, p. 15.
7. Sidney Chapman, 1951. The earth's magnetism. Methuen & Co., Ltd., London; John Wiley & Sons, Inc., New York, p. 23.
8. *Ibid.*
9. McDonald, *op. cit.,* p. 1.
10. Jacobs, *op. cit.,* p. 430.
11. *Ibid.*
12. Sidney Chapman and J. Bartels, 1940. Geomagnetism. Clarendon Press, Oxford, vol. 2, p. 704.
13. Willard F. Libby, 1955. Radiocarbon dating, 2nd edition, University of Chicago Press, Figure 2, p. 13.
14. Melvin A. Cook, 1966. Prehistory and earth models. Max Parrish and Co., Ltd., London, p. 8.

1971. 8(1):50-54. June.

XVII

ON THE RECENT ORIGIN OF THE PACIFIC SOUTHWEST DESERTS

WALTER E. LAMMERTS*

Introduction

My interest in the question of how recently the Pacific Southwestern part of the United States became a desert was first awakened by a visit to the Bandelier National Monument near Los Alamos,

Figure 1. Tyuonyi apartment house type of pueblo. Photograph reprinted by permission from the publication, "This Enchanted Land," University of California, Los Alamos Scientific Laboratory, P.O. Box 1663, Los Alamos, New Mexico 87544.

*Walter E. Lammerts, Ph.D., Hybridization Gardens, P.O. Box 496, Freedom, Calif. 95019.

New Mexico. On October 28, 1970, my daughter took me down to the Park Headquarters in Frijoles Canyon and we looked at the many foundations of former Indian dwellings and ceremonial caves. Some of these have been reconstructed.

One of the most remarkable is Tyuonyi, a semi-circular apartment-house group of former Indian homes. Only the foundations now remain and indicate that each apartment was only 5 feet by 5 feet (Figure 1). The Pueblo Indians must have been very short people indeed! Archeologists have concluded that they lived in these apartments until about A.D. 1550.

Large caves were dug into the sides of the steep cliffs. One very large one, called the Ceremonial cave, contains ruins of a large religious ceremonial room or Kiva. Most of the dwellings were built right up against the steep cliffs, as shown in Figure 2. All of this building indicates a long period of canyon occupancy. The questions as to when they arrived, and why they left their cliff homes, began to

Figure 2. Typical ruins of former cliff dwellings of the Pueblo Indians. Photograph reprinted by permission from the publication, "This Enchanted Land," University of California, Los Alamos Scientific Laboratory, P. O. Box 1663, Los Alamos, New Mexico 87544.

interest me and the following is a rather well authenticated history, the dates estimated by pottery association and tree ring counting.

Pueblo Indians from 1100 to 1580

The golden age of the Pueblo Indians was from 1100-1300 when they lived on the Colorado Plateau. Cotton woven into textiles and corn were their main crops. In the 1200's they began to leave and tree ring studies indicate a 200 year period of drought. The lands these people left had been their home for about 1000 years.

Some re-settled southeast in the North Rio Grande Valley, where the Bandelier National Monument is located. Others moved southwest into north-central Arizona. The Pajarito Plateau, in which Frijoles Canyon is located, was first settled in the late 1100's. At first the Indians lived on the plateau, and remains of villages having up to 800 rooms, such as Tsirege, Navawi, and Otowi, have been found. Most accessible, at the intersection of State Highway 4 and the South mesa-access road, is Tsankawi with about 350 rooms.

An ancient reservoir 75 by 130 feet has been found about 120 feet west of the pueblo called Puye. This ruin is located about ten miles west of Espanola and 140 miles northwest of Santa Fe. Edgar J. Hewett writes:

> Meagre amounts [of water] could be obtained by opening a spring in sand, but here, as on all parts of this plateau, a much more plentiful water supply than that now existing would be essential to the maintenance of such large settlements as once existed at Puye.[1]

As the plateau became increasingly dry, the Indians moved down into the various canyons, such as Frijoles, and built their cliff houses. The attraction was the stream, much larger than now, and the small flat alluvial areas beside it on which they grew their crops of corn, beans, and squash. The peak population was in the 13th, 14th, and 15th centuries and they were called the Jemez people.[2]

Then an even more serious drought, beginning in the 1500's, started driving them out and all but a few stragglers were gone by about 1580. Some of their descendents still live in Cochiti and San Ildefonso pueblos.

Even in recent years there is evidence of increasing drought. Mrs. Evelyn Frey, operator of the Frijoles Canyon Lodge, moved into the canyon with her husband, George, in 1925. She cites two great changes in the last 30 years:

> The winters used to be much colder. We were always snowbound, but it was delightful. And the Rio de los Frijoles is only about half as wide as it used to be. There are hardly any fish left. The river used to swarm with fish that would bite at anything. You didn't feel ethical fishing in those days.[3]

We may conclude that this vast area was blessed with a surprisingly high rainfall until comparatively recent times (1500-1550) and that the drought is getting worse. The former high rainfall seems correlated with much colder winters.

Portions of California Considered

Turning now to California, I was amazed to read in a Pacific Gas & Electric Progress bulletin of the recent existence of Lake Tulare.[4] Primary sources of information were history books published in the 1850's to the 1870's, such as *Resources of California* by John S. Hittel.[5] In 1875 the sidewheel steamer, *Mose Androsa,* was used to carry hogs and cattle across this lake, and it was joined in 1878 by the *Water Witch,* a shallow draft schooner used to catch terrapin.

In 1870, Lake Tulare was the largest lake west of the Rockies! Fed by the Kern and King's Rivers, it was described in 1862 as extending for 60 miles north and south, being 36 miles across at its widest, and covering 800 square miles. Nearby were three smaller sister lakes—Buena Vista, Kern, and Goose Lakes. These great shallow, inland bodies of water sheltered an abundance of aquatic life, trout that weighed up to 40 pounds, perch, salmon, and sturgeon in quantities that supported a commercial fishing industry. Ducks and geese were abundant and great herds of deer and elk grazed along the seashores.

Thousands of Yakuts Indians lived along the shores, and on the islands. They fished from rafts and canoes made of tule reeds. Canadian and American fur traders, who trapped for beaver in the tules, kept the geography of the area a trade secret. Mosquitoes and tule fogs were so bad most of the year that the area was quite uninhabitable.

Seasonal variation in rainfall caused these lakes to wax and wane. Finally, a series of dry years shrank them considerably. In 1880 the state legislature passed an act permitting settlers to buy reclaimable land for $2.50 per acre, $2.00 of which was refunded when the settler spent it on levees or other reclamation.

This touched off a land stampede. Horses were fitted with planks so they could walk in the mud, and vast areas of swampland were drained and cultivated. The lake was doomed, and when the King's and Kern Rivers were dammed, reduced to small reservoirs maintained by high levees. Yet last year the run-off from heavy snows caused this phantom lake to spread over 90,000 acres!

Great Salt Lake once had an area of 50,000 square miles, and was known as Lake Bonneville. The shrinking of this lake was more recent than usually supposed and correlated with the drought causing the decline of the Pueblo Indian civilization in the 1200's. More precise information is needed as to the exact times of greatest shrinkages. The decrease in the size of the Great Salt Lake still continues. Thus the big amusement palace built on the shore of the lake in 1925 is now over one mile from shore.

Though a detailed history of the Colorado Desert, in which the Imperial Valley, Salton Sea, and Coachella Valley are located, is beyond the scope of this paper it is of great interest to note that historian George Wharton James wrote:

> Then came a flood which broke over the channel (of the Colorado River) and formed the course of what we call the Alamo River. Year after year it flowed, and maintained the freshwater character of what had, in comparatively recent times, been an arm of the gulf, then a salt lake, then a dry basin. It was at this time that the fresh water shells were deposited, of which millions are now found. Possibly it was while the bed of the basin was dry that the aborigines first came and dwelt in it. If so this would account for their tradition that long after they occupied the region the floods came and drove them out.[6]

Considering another line of evidence, artesian wells once existed both in Santa Clara County and near the town of Artesia in Southern California. Hittel stated that there were 318 of them within a distance of six miles wide by fifteen miles long![7] The wells supplied about two million gallons in twenty-four hours. Artesia still had some functioning wells in 1918 when my family first moved into the area.

These wells ceased to be of practical value long before the population pressure became a factor. Thus again, Hittel wrote in 1863 "that many have gone dry because the soil is generally dried out." He mentioned the disappearances of Honey Lake on the plateau of the Sierra Nevada and Lake Elizabeth in the great Basin as further proof of the disappearance of surface water.[8]

A comparison of the rainfall in Northern California in the past 88 years is pertinent. In the 44 years from 1879-80 through 1922-23, the annual totals varied from 9.77 inches in 1917-18 to 43.72 inches in 1889-90 with 29 seasons having 20-37.20 inches. In contrast from 1923-24 until 1966-67 the variation was from 8.71 inches in 1923-24 to 36.59 inches in 1940-41, with only 18 seasons having a rainfall of 20 to 31.93 inches. Certainly the trend is still toward lower annual rainfall.

Relation to Biblical Statements and Flood Geology Concepts

As regards the Bible, the story of the Israelites' journey from Egypt has some statements unintelligible in terms of *present day* conditions. Thus, in Exodus 17:5-6, in response to the people chiding Moses for water, he was commanded to smite the rock at Horeb. "And there shall come water out of it, that the people might drink."

Under present conditions this would involve a double miracle, knowing where to strike the rock *and* creation of water in the rock strata. In terms of relatively recent aridity, that area still enjoyed much more rainfall than now, though *relatively* speaking it was already a desert area. Hence much more underground water and water pressure existed.

Later in the desert of Zin at Kadish in 1471 B.C. Moses was commanded to smite the rock and "with his rod he smote the rock twice: and the water came abundantly, and the congregation drank and their beasts also" (Num. 20:10).

When the spies reported on Canaan they said, "We came unto the land whither thou sentest us, and surely it floweth with milk and honey and this [bunch of grapes] is the fruit of it" (Num. 13:27). No one would describe the unirrigated part of Palestine in these terms now!

Even during the time of our Lord (4 B.C. to A.D. 33), He and His disciples were castigated for going through the grain fields and eating the grain (called corn) on the sabbath day (Matt. 12:1-2). Rainfall must have been heavier than now to cause such abundant fields of grain to grow without irrigation. It seems the decrease in rainfall has occurred since A.D. 100, but much more research is needed here to be exact.

Relative to Flood geology concepts, the decrease in rainfall seems to be correlated with two phenomena: (1) the drying up of such great lakes as Bonneville, and (2) the decrease in size of the glaciers and snowfields. Water in a sense begets water, and as the great inland lakes resulting from the Flood gradually dried up, the rain clouds generated by the moisture evaporating from inland lakes decreased, and finally were no longer formed.

Then the areas south of them no longer enjoyed rainfall from the storms generated in the vast lake and snowfield areas north of them. They became dependent on moisture from the west. This was Phase I, when the Pueblo Indians moved south from the Colorado Plateau.

Decrease in Glaciers Considered

Now the decrease in size of the glaciers is still continuing as a worldwide phenomenon. While on our vacation in 1962, I hiked up to the 9000-foot level of Mt. Rainier, Washington, and had a good look at the Nisqually Glacier. It was much smaller than even 40 years ago, according to records. Similarly the Paradise Glacier had receded a lot, as could easily be seen from the many acres of terminal and lateral moraines. And in 1963, during a trip to Alaska, I was amazed to see how far back the Mendenhal Glacier had retreated since measurements made fifty years ago.

Correlated with this decrease in the extent of the glaciers is the extent of the snowfields in the High Sierras. As may be seen from the historical records, the snowfields are not as extensive now as even in 1860. The effect on the size of the rivers of California is pronounced indeed. The King's and Kern Rivers are not nearly as wide now, each spring following the snow melt, as they were about 100 years ago. Thus Hittel mentioned in his *Resources of California* (1863) that the King's River was 80 yards wide where it left the mountains.[9]

With extensive snowfields on the High Sierras there would be much evaporation from them, in the spring and early summer, as they melted and decreased somewhat in size until replacement of snow the following winter. The prevailingly westerly winds would carry this over the areas east of them, as clouds giving rain to a limited extent in these areas.

But as the snowfields decreased in size practically no rainfall from the storms originating in the Pacific would reach the inland areas. Moisture would all be precipitated as either rain or snow as the clouds moved higher and over the Sierras, leaving little if any for the valleys and mountain ranges beyond. This was Phase II when the Pueblo Indians had to move down into the canyons and build their cliff houses, such as are found in Frijoles Canyon.

The above trend, from an abundance of water at the time of Lake Bonneville until there was so little rain that this whole area became a desert, has been known for a long time. What is remarkable is the *recency* of these events. Were it not for the biblical record, I would be inclined by a study of the trends to believe that the Flood took place about 2500 years ago instead of over 4000!

Possible Research Project Listed

This study is but one of a series that should be made by Flood geologists. Just how recently did such great areas as Egypt, the Sahara, and Arabia become deserts? Orthodox geologists interpret these trends in terms of tens of thousands of years, mostly on the basis of Carbon-14 dating. Studies by some of our members have shown that these dates are not reliable.[10]

The recency of our Pacific Southwest deserts leads one to wonder if the deserts in other parts of the world may also be more recent than usually supposed. In terms of being a witness to the continual drying up of the world from the Flood, it leads one to wonder if the whole world may eventually become a vast desert?

The remarkable adaptations of plants to the Colorado desert might well be the subject of careful study. These plants include the mesquite, creosote bush, ocatilla, desert holly, and the very unusual cactus species shown by George Wharton James in full page illustrations, facing pages 222 and 224, in his book *Wonders of the Colorado Desert,* already referred to above. Whatever the origin of such plants, they most certainly could not have "evolved" their unusual adaptations in the short time since this area became a desert.

In recent prehistoric times, an area of over three thousand square miles was included in the Gulf of California. The Colorado River then emptied near Pilot Knob, and in a few centuries formed a dam by the continual extension of its alluvial fan. The upper part of the Gulf became a great salt lake, following which it went through the stages of a dry basin, and then when the Colorado had another flood, a great fresh water lake.

The lake was 120 miles long by 30 miles wide. It was called Lake Cahuilla by W. P. Blake in his government survey report[11] of 1853. For many years the Colorado fed this lake by way of the Alamo River, but finally this ceased and the lovely lake became the desert it now is. At various times since then water has collected in this basin and lated disappeared through evaporation.

At the very most, less than a thousand years have gone by since the existence of Lake Cahuilla. Accordingly, plants of the area, which are so well adapted now, must have been carried to the basin by seeds as it dried out. The whole problem of the origin of these desert plants is a fascinating one. Presumably they once grew under conditions of plentiful moisture, possibly in salt marshes.

Thus the desert holly, *Atriplex hymenelytra,* is able to grow very well when given an abundance of water! A plant I transplanted into a pot in the desert and brought back to my greenhouse did very well when watered just as often as my regular flowering plants.

It is still alive by one wall of my greenhouse where it gets an abundance of water.

Now many *Atriplex* species are salt marsh plants or grow in alkaline flats. They do seem to thrive on a high salt content in the soil or water. Perhaps then desert plants have been catastrophically selected by the relatively rapid conversion to desert conditions. Only those *already* having the potential for growing in the desert would survive; that is, those capable of tolerating a high salt level and having a deep root system. Transplantation studies of other desert plants to see if they actually grow well at high moisture levels would be most interesting in this connection.

REFERENCES

1. Edgar J. Hewett, The Pajarito Plateau and its ancient people. University of New Mexico Press, p. 67.
2. This enchanted land—the Jemez mountain wonderland, 1966. Office of Public Relations, Los Alamos Scientific Laboratory, University of California, Los Alamos, New Mexico. See pp. 20, 21, 29.
3. *Ibid.*, p. 20.
4. Pacafic Gas and Electric Progress, October, 1970. Vol. XLVII, No. 10, p. 8. San Francisco, Calif.
5. John S. Hittel, 1863. Resources of California. A. Roman Company, San Francisco, p. 13.
6. George Wharton James, 1906. The wonders of the Colorado desert. Little, Brown and Co., Boston, pp. 30-31.
7. Hittel, *op. cit.*, p. 67.
8. *Ibid.*, p. 69.
9. *Ibid.*, p. 12. Also interesting data on the navigation of the Sacramento, Feather, and Salinas Rivers are given.
10. For example, Sydney P. Clementson, 1970. A critical examination of radioactivity dating of rocks. *Creation Research Society Quarterly,* 7(3): 137-141.
11. William P. Blake, 1853. Geological report for proposed railroad route. Referred to in the Columbia encyclopedia and in George Wharton James' book, *op. cit.*

XVIII

"CARLSBAD CAVERNS IN COLOR"

By Mason Sutherland

An article (in) *National Geographic Magazine,* CIV: 4:433-468. October, 1953.

Review by Robert Harris*

> ... The Rock of Ages is the most celebrated formation in the caverns.
>
> Because of its huge bulk this stalagmite was popularly supposed to be one of the oldest decorations. Actually there is no good way of determining its exact age; no one can tell when it grew or how fast. (p. 463)

Little seems to be known about the growth rates of dripstone; most authorities are content to indicate vaguely that the process is a slow one. Attempts to determine deposition rates through uniformitarian methods (the present is the key to the past) have been unsuccessful.

Comparing the growth of stalactites under concrete bridges with the Carlsbad formations has failed because of the highly variable conditions of deposition. Mineral concentration, speed and volume of water flow, and atmospheric conditions must be taken into account. *Encyclopedia Britannica* states:

> Conditions which favour dripstone deposition of calcium carbonates are (1) a source rock above the cavity; (2) downward percolation of water supplied from rain; (3) tight but continuous passageways for this water which determine a very slow drip; (4) adequate air space in the void to allow either (a) evaporation or (b) escape of carbon dioxide from the water which thus loses some of its solvent ability.[1]

Applying uniformitarian suppositions to the cavern formations

---

*Robert Harris holds the M.A. degree in English from Claremont Graduate School.

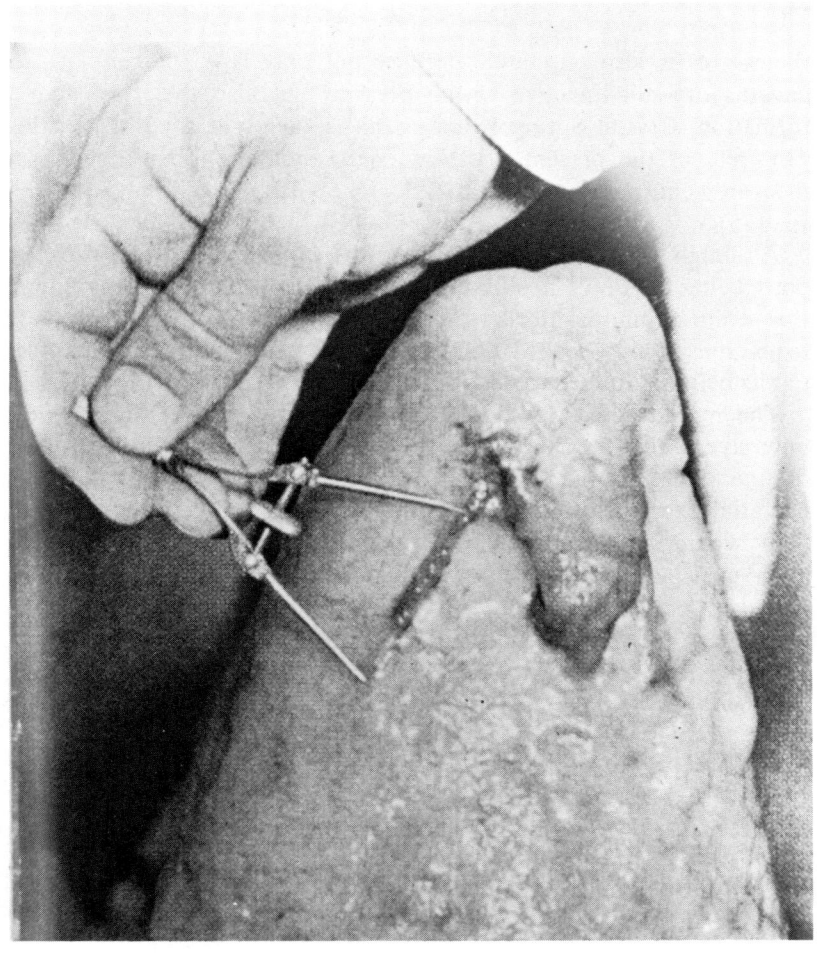

This illustration shows a bat that was cemented inside a stalagmite at Carlsbad Caverns, New Mexico. This supplies a clue to the problem of stalagmite growth rate and may be used to point out that uniformitarians are in great error to assert that stalagmite accretion requires multiple thousands of years. Evidently it occurs so rapidly that a bat can be entombed before action of bacterial decay and/or predators can take their effect. This photograph appeared in the article, "Carlsbad Caverns in Color," by Mason Sutherland, National Geographic Magazine, CIV(4):433-468, October, 1953. It is used by permission of the photographer, Mr. "Tex" Helm, of Carlsbad, New Mexico.

themselves is also unreliable because not only is 95 percent of the caverns dry and inactive at the present, but also the most active formation, Crystal Spring Dome, is not growing at a constant rate. (In spite of the present dry New Mexico desert above, one day's measurement put the rate at 2.5 cubic inches per year in 1953 [p. 455].)

Although the author muses about the possibility of a guano deposit being "perhaps a million years old" (p. 452), he does admit that even by uniformitarian dating, "Few of these . . . [dripstone] formations can exceed 100,000 years, for many rest on silt and fossils believed to be of that age" (p. 446).

The most interesting and revealing picture in the article, which may give a clue to growth rates, is on page 442, showing the clear outline of a bat cemented upside down in a stalagmite! Due to bacterial decay and scavenger attack, it seems unlikely that a bat's body would last several thousand years before entombment in calcium carbonate. Rather it would appear that very rapid growth would be required—perhaps even catastrophic growth.

Much study into cave phenomena is needed. The power of crystallization is strong enough to defy gravity, allowing helictites to grow in any direction; perhaps further research will disclose that possible growth rates are likewise amazing by virtue of rapidity.

REFERENCE

1. Encyclopedia Britannica, 1970 edition, vol. 21, p. 104.

XIX

COMETS AND A YOUNG SOLAR SYSTEM

HAROLD ARMSTRONG*

Comets cause great difficulty for any uniformitarian theory of the Solar System. This is especially true for those comets of fairly short periods, say no more than two hundreds years or so. For at each encounter with the sun the comet loses some of its material; some have broken up completely into a swarm of meteorites.

Now if the solar system were as old as the uniformitarian theorists would have it, these comets would have encountered the sun so many times that they should all have long since been destroyed. It has been suggested, to save the situation, that there is a sort of reservoir of comets somewhere out beyond the orbit of Pluto; but there is no evidence for any such thing, and some evidence against it.

Incidentally, is it not noteworthy that there are no comets, of any brilliance at all, with quite short periods, say ten years or so? Is the reason that, if there ever were any, they have been destroyed, even in a few thousand years?

This consideration might provide another argument against the "reservoir;" if comets were being brought in from storage, surely some of them would end up in orbits giving them a quite short period, and would survive long enough to have several encoutners with the sun. But nothing of the sort is observed.

There are also some comets with very long periods, as much as hundreds of thousands of years. Of course, these figures, are calculated; from the viewpoint of man these comets have not yet

---

*Harold Armstrong is a faculty member of The Queens University, Kingston, Ontario, Canada. He has been editor of the *Creation Research Society Quarterly* since June, 1974.

completed one time around. The greater the period, the greater the orbit; thus such comets have orbits extending to vast distances from the sun.

It will be recalled that the orbit of a body around the sun is a conic section, an ellipse or an hyperbola. (Or the limiting case between these is a parabola.) The ellipse is a closed curve; a comet in an ellipitical orbit would (in enough time), return to the vicinity of the sun again and again. The hyperbola, on the other hand, is an unlimited open curve; a comet in a hyperbolic orbit would approach the sun once, go around, and depart for ever.

Support for Vectorial Treatment

May I commend, at this point, the vectorial treatment of this problem of orbits, over what is usually presented in the books; especially to anyone who may want to teach it? There are several books,[1-3] none of which, I fear, is as well known as it deserves to be, in which this method is set forth.

While comets are influenced mainly by the sun, their motion is "perturbed" to a certain extent by the attraction of the planets, especially of Jupiter, the most massive planet. To a first approximation, the comet, during its encounter with the planet which perturbs its motion, can be considered as if it were moving under the influence of the planet alone.

(Just as in considering the orbit of the moon one can consider the effect only of the earth, although the attraction of the sun is easily calculated to be greater. The reason for this is that, to a good approximation, the attraction of the sun is balanced by the centrifugal effect of the motion of the planet around the sun approximately in a circle. Then the motion of the smaller body, the comet or the moon, can be considered separately with respect to the larger, as if only the two were present.)

Again, then, the comet will move in a conic section, which will be an hyperbola, with respect to the planet, during its encounter with the planet. So the comet will approach the planet, at a certain velocity relative to the planet, approximately along one asymptote of the hyperbola just mentioned. It will leave the planet, at the same velocity with respect to the planet, along the other asymptote. Thus the direction of its motion is changed.

Moreover, while the speed with respect to the planet is left the same, the speed with respect to the sun and the fixed stars, which seems to be what matters for mechanisms as expressed in Newton's laws, is changed, in general. For this velocity is the resultant, in the usual manner of vectors, of the velocity of the planet, and that of the comet with respect to the planet. While these are the same in magnitude before and after, their directions will generally be different; they might, e.g., be at right angles before, in the same direction after. The result of the change in magnitude and direction of the velocity is to give the comet a different orbit.

Comets Should Die or Disappear

Now the way in which the comet encounters the planet is a chance thing. (I am using the word as a convenient one, with no intention of thereby denying that there is purpose in the universe. It is interesting to notice, in fact, that the problem here is something like the kinetic theory of gases; but the "gas" concerned is made up of planets and comets.) It is possible to make statistical calculations (again as in kinetic theory), and the calculations show that, more often than not, the effect is to speed up the comet, and likely to make it escape from the solar system.[4]

Indeed, it would seem that no calculation is needed to show that this must happen in the long run. For an encounter either sends the comet out of the system or it does not. If it does, that is the end of the story. If not, the comet goes around again, and there will be another encounter with the planets. There can be but one ending.

It is just the same as the way in which children, splashing in a wading pool, are sure eventually to empty it. For water which is splashed out is lost. That which is splashed, but lands back in the pool, is splashed again and again, until it is thrown out.

The conclusion to be drawn from all this is plain. If the solar system were as old as it is claimed to be, how could any long-period comets be left? They would all have been thrown out of the system long ago. Again, there is no evidence for any reservoir. In fact, the very presence of comets, whatever be their periods, is thus good evidence for a young solar system.

REFERENCES

1. L. Brand, 1930. Vectorial mechanics. Wiley, New York, pp. 401-404.
2. W. J. Gibbs and E. B. Wilson, 1901 and 1929. Vector analysis. Yale University Press, pp. 135-136. (I believe that this book has been reprinted, as a paperback, by Dover.)
3. E. A. Milne, 1948. Vectorial mechanics. Methuen, London, pp. 235-240.
4. J. L. Brady, 1970. Influence of the planetary system on 143 long-period comets, *The Astronomical Journal,* 75(9):1052-1065.

XX

TIME, LIFE, AND HISTORY IN THE LIGHT OF 15,000 RADIOCARBON DATES

Robert L. Whitelaw*

Introduction

A hundred years after Darwin, the theory of total evolution appears to have swept the field of all challengers. The idea that multiform life, order, and complexity all arrived on the scene by mere chance from lifeless, lawless chaos is now accepted almost without question. Such an idea pervades the public press; it colors the teaching of history, philosophy, and science; and in the life and earth sciences it is the general premise upon which new evidence is analyzed and new research performed.

Without adducing a shred of supporting evidence, a leading scientist[1] can boldly state: "There is no need of explaining the origin of life in terms of the miraculous or the supernatural. Life occurs whenever the conditions are right. It will not only emerge but persist and evolve." Such statements are generally hailed as twentieth century wisdom, while the biblical record is relegated to folklore.

Perhaps the best expression of the modern rationale for *total* evolution comes from the pen of George Wald:

> The important point is that since the origin of life belongs in the category of at-least-once phenomena, time is on its side. However improbable we regard this event, . . . given enough time it will almost certainly happen at least once. . . . Time is in fact the hero of the plot. The time with which we have to deal is of the order of two billion years. What we regard as impossible on the basis of human experience is meaningless here.

---

*Robert L. Whitelaw is professor of nuclear and mechanical engineering, Virginia Polytechnic Institute, and State University, Blacksburg, Va. 24060.

Given so much time, the "impossible" becomes possible, the possible probable, and the probable virtually certain. One has only to wait: time itself performs miracles.²

Such an argument contains both a logical fallacy and a philosophical absurdity. If it is true, any incredible event becomes possible *at any instant*. Cinderella's pumpkin easily becomes a chariot; and the resurrection of Jesus Christ should likewise be accepted without cavil!

The argument, however, is advanced for a different purpose. It is satisfying, persuasive, and allays all doubt. And like the speculative "science" of a bygone day, it demands no evidence. Time alone —unlimited, inconceivable, unimaginable—becomes at once a fortress and a weapon with which to demolish opposition. No matter how well attested the evidence against evolution, it must crumble every time before the sweeping premise, "given enough time. . . ." For if two billion years proves not enough, who can stop one from making it ten billion? Or ten trillion, if need be!

Such is the real basis of modern evolutionary theory. No matter how disguised as mathematics or science, it is simply blind faith that given enough time a miracle will happen. And not one miracle only, but a billion miracles in succession, all in the right place and right order without a single intervening mistake. (For no less a miracle than this is required to account for even a single cell!) Intoxicated with such a faith as this, it is no wonder that evolutionists remain deaf to the best arguments from logic, from evidence and from Scripture. The hero is *time;* and so long as it is inexhaustible, evolution is secure.

Time, however, is also the hero of another plot! It is central to the meaning and validity of the biblical record. Whereas evolutionists demand immeasurable, purposeless, endless time, the Bible just as unequivocally demands acceptance of a world whose time is measured, purposeful and destined to end; and all in exact accordance with the eternal purpose of a sovereign God, "who worketh all things after the counsel of his own will." The result is that either the Bible stands and evolution falls, or evolution stands and the Bible falls. They cannot stand together.

Nor is there room for part-Bible and part-evolution with regard to concepts of time. For, if the Bible is untrustworthy when it speaks of time in Genesis 1, 5 and 11, it is equally untrustworthy when it speaks of time in Galatians 4:4, Acts 17:31, and Hebrews 1:1. The challenge of evolution thus compels every scientist and scholar to face up to biblical chronology as part of its total claim to authority. Is biblical chronology true or false?

For such a task, modern scientists bring forth a special new tool —radiocarbon dating. Fifteen thousand dates are already published, with thousands more coming in each year. With these it is now possible, as never before, to compare the time-claims of evolution with the chronology of Scripture, and discover where the truth lies.

The Radiocarbon Dating Method

The radiocarbon dating method was first proposed and worked out by Dr. Willard F. Libby for which he received a well-earned Nobel Prize. By painstaking measurements of living matter of every kind all over the world, Libby was able to show that all living cells have the same specific radioactivity by virtue of the presence of approximately 765 atoms of Carbon-14 in every billion atoms of Carbon-12.

So long as a cell lives, this ratio is maintained by the constant cycle occurring between living matter and the carbon dioxide in the air and sea, known as the "carbon exchange reservoir." He then showed by atmospheric measurements at various latitudes and altitudes that the rate at which Carbon-14 (C-14) is being replenished in this reservoir by cosmic rays from outer space is *reasonably close* to the rate at which it is decaying in living matter.

He then *assumed* that these two rates are essentially equal, and that they have been so for many years. Thereupon was "born" the radiocarbon dating method used by scientists ever since, a period now over 20 years.

The validity of the above two assumptions will be considered later. Granting them for the moment, let us see how simple and sure the method is. By measuring the radioactivity of a specimen of once-living matter found today, and comparing it to the activity it had when it died, the elapsed number of years is simple to calculate. After 5,570* years the clicks per minute on a Gieger counter would be half the value at death; after 11,140 years the count would be down to one quarter; after 22,280 years down to a sixteenth; and so on. The only requirement is a pure sample unmixed with any other living or dead matter through all the passing years, *plus* the assumption that the radioactivity the specimen possessed at death was the same as all living matter exhibits today, namely 16.0** disintegrations per minute per gram of total carbon (dpm/g.)

Among the first specimens measured by Libby and his coworkers were some tree rings and relics of "known" date from ancient Egypt. The agreement was quite satisfactory. In 1952 the method was published in book form,[3] along with some 200 dates of both archeological and geological specimens gathered from over 30 widely scattered sites. A second edition[4] was published in 1955, and special addenda to most chapters were included in a 1965 printing of the second edition.

TABLE 1

RADIOCARBON DATING LABORATORIES
(*Radiocarbon,* vol. 10, pp. 169-177, 1968)

A	Arizona	C	Chicago
ANL	Argonne National Laboratory	CT	Caltech
		D	Dublin
ANU	Australian National Univ.	DAK	Dakar
B	Bern	FR	Freiberg
BIRM	Birmingham	FSU	Florida State
BLN	Berlin	G	Goteborg
BM	British Museum	GAK	Gakushuin Univ.
BONN	Bonn	GD	Gdansk

---

*More recent analysis gives 5,730 years as a better "half-life"; a mere 3% error.

**16.2 in seashells, but 15.3 in vegetation and living tissue, due to the different ratio of C-12/C-13 in each group.

TABLE 1 (Continued)

GIF	Gif-sur-Yvette	O	Humble
GL	Geochronological Laboratory	ORINS	Oak Ridge Assoc. Univ.
		OWU	Ohio Wesleyan Univ.
GRO	Groningen	OX	U.S. Dept. of Agriculture
GRN		P	Pennsylvania
GSC	Ottawa	PI	Pisa
GSY	Gif-sur-Yvette	PR	Prague
GU	Glasgow University	Q	Cambridge
GX	Geochron Lab'y Inc.	R	Rome
H	Heidelberg	RI	Radiochemistry, Inc.
HV	Hanover	S	Saskatchewan
I	Isotopes—A Teledyne Co.	SA	Saclay
II	Isotopes, Inc.	SH	Shell
IRPA	Institut Royal Du Patrimoine Artistique	SI	Smithsonian Institution
		SL	Sharp Laboratories
ISGS	Ill. State Geol. Survey	SM	Mobil Oil Corporation
IVIC	Caracas	SR	Salisbury, Rhodesia
K	Copenhagen	ST	Stockholm
KI	Kiel	SU	Finland
KN	Koln	T	Trondheim
L	Lamont	TA	Tartu
LE	Leningrad	TAM	Texas A & M Univ.
LJ	Univ. of Calif., San Diego	TB	Tbilisi
LP	La Plata	TBNC	Kaman Nuclear
LU	Lund	TF	Tata Inst. of Fundamental Research
LV	Heverle Louvain		
LY	Univ. of Lyon	TK	University of Tokyo
M	Michigan	TX	Texas
MA	Manitoba	U	Uppsala
MC	Monaco	UCLA	Univ. of California, L.A.
ML	Miami	UW	Univ. of Washington
MO	Vernadski Inst. of Geochemistry	V	Victoria
		VRI	Vienna Radium Inst.
MP	Magnolia Petroleum	W	U.S. Geol. Survey
N	Riken (Tokyo)	WIS	Wisconsin
NPL	Nat. Physical Lab'y	WSU	Washington State Univ.
NS	Nova Scotia	X	Whitworth College
NSW	New South Wales	Y	Yale
NY	Nancy	PIC	Packard
NZ	New Zealand		

Once the new radiocarbon clock had been thus established, scientists at universities and research centers all over the world entered the new research field, setting up their own dating laboratories. By the end of 1968 almost 100 laboratories were thus engaged as listed in Table 1. C-14 was recognized widely as a valuable new tool to identify the age of ancient cultural deposits and artifacts, to date pollen, shell deposits, buried trees and vegetation, bones and relics of the past of all kinds.

TABLE 2

Distribution of Radiocarbon Specimens by Categories

ARCHEOLOGICAL SPECIMENS IN CLASS I AND II:
Occupational charcoal, middens, bones, wood and clay artifacts, furnishings, wooden tools and structures, grain, dung, canoes, nests, fossils, barrows, skin, hair, tissue, blood, tusks, shellmounds, scrolls, burial items, and such.

GEOLOGICAL SPECIMENS OF CLASS III:
Wood, such as stumps, logs, twigs, or bark, either fossilized, petrified, or natural; charcoal from fires unrelated to human occupation.

SPECIMENS PUT IN CLASS IV:
Seals, whales, fish, coral, shellfish, and all other forms of marine life; insects, pollen, calcareous deposits, marl, lacustrine, sandy loam, peat, lignite, coal, petroleum, natural gas, tufa, gyttja, moss, pingo, ferns, seeds (ungathered), caliche, sapropel, carbonate mud, ocean floor sediments, lave, fossil flora, and such.

At the same time it was understood by all concerned that the method could give measurable dates only to about 50,000 years B.P. (before present), since the radioactivity from anything older would be scarcely detectable. Most certainly it was out of the question to expect any datings of fossils, petrified matter, coal, oil, or bones of prehistoric men or animals. Using evolutionary premises, scientists had long since assigned such matter to ages well beyond 100,000, and even in the millions of years. In short, only late Pleistocene and Holocene matter was considered datable. A date from tertiary strata was absolutely unthinkable, and a large number of specimens were fully expected to give "infinite" dates, i.e., too old to be measurable.

What have been the results? In a word, astounding! Astounding

HISTORY IN LIGHT OF 15,000 RADIOCARBON DATES 337

to every investigator with evolutionary presuppositions. But even more astounding when compared with the biblical record—as we shall see.

Ten Amazing Facts Itemized

Commencing with the first group of 200 dates published in Libby's first edition, the list has now grown, and as of the end of 1969, includes over 15,000 dates of independent specimens of every kind gathered from every part of the globe by the ninety-one laboratories listed in Table 1. The wide distribution of these specimens by category and by geography is given in Tables 2 and 3.

TABLE 3

Distribution of Radiocarbon Specimens by Geography

WESTERN HEMISPHERE SPECIMENS (assigned to Class II):
United States (almost every state included, with most dates from areas of Indian and Eskimo culture), Canada (all provinces, Yukon, and N.W.T. represented), Greenland, Mexico, Cuba, and most of West Indies, Central America, Easter and Galapagos Islands, South America (all countries), Antarctica, Bermuda.

AFRO-EURASIA SPECIMENS (assigned to Class I):
Iceland, Europe (every country), Morocco, Algeria, Libya, Tunis, Egypt, Sudan, Equatorial Africa, Nigeria, Rhodesia, most regions of central and south Africa, Ethiopia, Turkey, Palestine, Mesopotamia and Arabia (especially sites of classical antiquity), Iran, Afghanistan, India, China, Indonesia and southeast Asia, almost every S.S.R. in Siberia and central Asia, Japan, Taiwan, Philippines, Korea, Madagascar and islands of Indian Ocean, S. Atlantic Islands, Australia.

SPECIMENS FROM OCEANIA (Few in number, divided between Class I and II):
New Zealand, Fiji, Tahiti, and other mid-Pacific islands.

All these dates were published, up to the year 1958, in *Science*, and thereafter in the annual journal, *Radiocarbon*, with extensive details of the subject matter and location of each specimen. In summary, the stockpile of radiocarbon dates is now so numerous and broad, as to age, location, and subject matter, that no informed scientist, nor historian, nor educator, nor publisher—no matter how dedicated to evolutionary premises—can be excused from examining them and considering their profound implications.

Upon sorting through these dates and after checking the descriptive material, one may detect at least ten amazing facts:

(1) Practically every specimen of once-living material is found to be datable within 50,000 years. Very few are listed up to 60,000, and only three—three out of 15,000—are stated as "infinite;" these being some megapod eggs from a Phillippine Islands cave.

(Note: To fully appreciate the significance of this, it must be emphasized that if Lyellian geology and evolutionary "time" are valid, if living matter has been accumulating and dying upon earth over supposed eons of time, then such a worldwide random sampling of buried organic matter should yield 20,000 undatable specimens for each one datable! Granted that many investigators were looking for specific ancient cultures, such as Indian, Mayan, Babylonian, etc. Nevertheless, all were still dated within 50,000 years *to the maximum depth of any deposit!* The great preponderance of samples, moreover, related to vegetation, shells, pollen, peat bogs, buried trees, fossiliferous clay, ocean-bottom cores, buried bones, and cultural charcoal beds—*most* of which should have been undatable. Yet, all have measurable radiocarbon activity!)

(2) Samples in strata identified by the investigator as Pleistocene, Pliocene and even Eocene (i.e., 50 million years old to an evolutionist!), and most archeologic findings identified as Paleolithic, are found with dates much younger than 40,000 years.

(3) Even coal, petroleum, natural gas, and lignite are dated within 50,000 years. Yet the accepted carboniferous period that supposedly produced them was 100,000,000 years ago!

(4) Of the most ancient dates, most belong to buried vegetation of all kinds.

(5) Over 220 dated specimens are identified as "fossil," semi-petrified matter or fossiliferous bed material.

(6) Many dates are of extinct flora, and fauna, hitherto thought

(Continued on page 343)

TABLE 4

Published Dates of Fossils, Extinct Fauna, and "Prehistoric Man"

(*Partial* list, selected from 250 specimens identified as such through 1969)

Radiocarbon, vol. 11, 1969:   *Age. yrs.*

GaK-1042: Bone of *Metacurvulus astylodon,*
Kei-jima, Ryukyu Is _____ 18,800

Gif-774: Molar of *Elephus Primigenius,*
Thonon-les-bains, Haute Savoie _____ 14,000

Tb-21: Coaly loam, Uzhgorod _____ 12,050

Y-1163: Skin of *Nothroterium Shastense,*
Aden crater, New Mexico _____ 9,840

UCLA-1325: Fossil wood from La Mirada, Cal., below extinct pleistocene animals of same species as in La Brea tarpits (see UCLA-1292) _____ 8,550

OWU-190: Spruce wood beneath partial mastodon skelton, Akron, O _____ 15,315

UCLA-1319: Mammal bones from Omo R. valley, Ethiopia (compare findings in same locality reported in reference 6 as "Australopithecus," and "dated" by K-Ar date of underlying sediments as "two to four million years old") 15,500

UCLA-1321: Mammalian bones from Bed V, Olduvai Gorge, Kenya (compare references 5 and 7 which reported similar findings in same general locality as nearly two million years old, based on K-Ar dates of sediments, findings by L. S. B. Leakey in 1959) _____ 10,100

Leakey's fossil *"Zinjanthropus"* was found in Bed I, whose rock stratum was dated by K-Ar at 2.03 million years. But *Science,* 162:559 (Nov. 1/68) contains this frank admission, "Bed V overlies with angular unconformity the older Beds I to IV in many places and occasionally even the basaltic lava underlying Bed I."

UCLA-1321 here dates the bones themselves in a horizon largely identical to that of *Zinjanthropus.**

---

*Editor's Note: Based on catastrophism, Professor Whitelaw equates Beds I and V. The original authors of the *Science* report, however, viewed the two beds as having been formed during vastly different time periods. Certainly more research on this question will be profitable.

TABLE 4 (Continued)

Age. yrs.

Obviously, the underlying lava bed, the presence of fossil-bearing strata, an angular unconformity, and gross erosion of Beds I to IV support a single catastrophe involving volcanic, hydraulic, and erosive action plus the rapid burial of life. In any case, K-Ar dating of *any* strata has been shown to be totally inconclusive in ref. 14.

* * *

Radiocarbon, vol. 10, 1968:

M-1739-1783: Mastodon ulna and tusk; tusk and skull. Michigan _____ 9,910; 9,250
NY-73: *Homo neanderthalensis* bones. Jebel Irhoud Cave, Morocco _____ >32,000
GSC-611-614: Mastodon bones. Thamesville and Chatham, Ontario _____ 11,380; 8,910
S-246: Mammoth bone, in fossiliferous Sand, Kyle, Sask. _____ 12,000
UCLA-1292: Sabre-tooth tiger, r. and l. femur, La Brea tarpits, L.A. Part of extensive analysis of Pleistocene fossil community _____ 28,000
GIN-7: Fossil bones, 1 m. deep in yellow clay. Molodova, Ukraine _____ 10,590
GIN-93: Mammoth scapula, in Cro-magnon burial site. Kosinski, Siberia _____ 11,000
TA-121: Mammoth bones. Byzovaya, Konu ASSR (pleistocene) _____ 18,320

* * *

Radiocarbon, vol. 9, 1967:

A-195-536: Mammoth vertebra, and rib. Naco, Ariz; Clovis, N.M. _____ 8,980; 6,370
ANU-9: Fossil wood, beneath tuff and lava. Auckland, N.Z. 31,000
UCLA-1069: Sloth dung. Gypsum Cave, Idaho _____ 10,455

* * *

Radiocarbon, vol. 8, 1966:

I-1149-1150: Natural Gas, in cretaceous and eocene formations. Ala. and Miss. _____ 34,000; 30,000
GIF-198-278: Fossil coal; and wood. Spain __ 5,025; 3,930; 4,250
GX-445: Fossil bone. Wadi Halfa _____ 6,485
I-622: Mammoth bones and tusks. Dent, Colo.; Rawlings, Wyo. _____ 11,200

TABLE 4 (Continued)

Age. yrs.

MO-334: Coal. Naryn R. Kirgizia _____ 1,680
MO-3: Fossil tree (salix). Taimyr L. _____ 11,700
UCLA-720-722-723: Fossil bones. Middle
    Zambezi _____ 2,520; 2,010; 960
WIS-67-85-113: Fossil sphagnum and sedge peat.
    Manitoba and NWT _____ 5,780; 5,600; 2,170
Gak-643: Penguin bone fossils. Antarctica _____ 6,100
N-141-3: Formation containing abundant mammalian fossils, including *Megaceros, Leptobison, Loxodonta,* and extinct flora inc. *Tsuga, Larix, Picea, Picea maximoviczii.*
    Hanaizumi, Japan _____ 29,300; 37,000

* * *

Radiocarbon, vol. 7, 1965:

GX-105: Jawbone of *Nototherium* sp.
    Boolcunda Cr., Australia _____ 14,000
M-1254, OWU-126: Mastodon bones, Gratiot,
    Mich., Novelty, Ohio _____ 10,700; 10,654
UCLA-630: "Broken Hill Man" Rhodesia
    (incl. animal bones) _____ 9,000
NZ-1: *Diprotodon* molar. New Zealand _____ 11,100
UCLA-705: Ilium of dwarf mammoth.
    Santa Rosa Is., Calif. _____ 8,000

* * *

Radiocarbon, vol. 6, 1964:

A-372: Mammoth fossil vertebra. Rawhide Butte, Wyo. __ 9,600
Lv-17: Fossil wood. Leopoldville, Congo _____ 7,840
Sa-170: Piston cores, 400 cm. below Mediterranean floor _ 30,000
Sa-100: Fossil bank; incl. bovines, hippo, catfish.
    Adrar Bous, Sahara _____ 5,140
Sa-49: *Mylodon manure,* Felt Cave, Chile _____ 10,200
UCLA-285: Fossil human and animal bones.
    Tabon Cave, Phil. Is. _____ 21,000

* * *

Radiocarbon, vol. 5, 1963:

NZ-7: Fossil tree-trunk, rooted. Aramaho, N.Z. _____ 2,400
NZ-206-381: *Diprotodon* jaw and molar. Orroroo,
    S. Australia _____ 6,700; 11,000
NZ-282: Fossilized herbs, interbedded in sediment.
    Ngaruawahia, N.Z. _____ 16,300

TABLE 4 (Continued)

Age. yrs.

GrN-2022: Neanderthal mandible. Haua Fteah, Libya ___ 40,700
GrN-1495: Neanderthal skelton. Shanidar I Cave, Iraq __ 50,600

* * *

Radiocarbon, vol. 4, 1962; and vol. 3, 1961:
Trondheim dates: Fossil shells in Norway.
  Ten specimens _____ 7,250 to 11,200
T-172: Wooly rhinoceros skin. Nochnoj ASSR _____ 38,000
M-1068: Fossil bone in bed of 27 extinct species.
  Muaco, Venez. _____ 14,300
L-601: Skin and flesh of baby elephant.
  Fairbanks, Alaska _____ 21,300
Pi-75: Calcareous petrified wood. Campi
  Flegrei, Italy _____ 10,090

* * *

Radiocarbon, vol. 2, 1960; and vol. 1, 1959:
A-30-31-32-33: Bones of mammoth, horse, tapir, bison, with charcoal and human implements. Lehner Mammoth
  Site _____ 6,877 to 8,330
M-569: Human bone in fossil breach. Algoma, Mich. ___ 3,170
LJ-55: Wood from tree root packed around with bones of many extinct pleistocene animals. LaBrea tarpits. Los
  Angeles _____ 14,400
LJ-82: Fossilized (phosphatized) log, 1500′ in ocean off
  Mexico _____ 28,000

* * *

Science, 1957 to 1958:
W-418: Wood, in *Megalodon* beds, with *Megalonyx,* bison, *Equus, Tapirus, Odocoileus.* Evansville, Ind. _____ 9,400
Y-103: Fossil skull, 'Florisbad Man," 19′ deep. Florisbad, S. Africa with fossil bones of many extinct species
  >35,000
L-228: Fossil wood interbedded in Miocene sandst. and
  cong. Wash. _____ >27,000
L-137: Peat and wood *under* muck of early Pleistocene fauna, incl. elephant, horse, bison. Seward Pen., Alaska
  8,800 to 10,200

* * *

Science, 1957 to 1951: *Age. yrs.*
H-145: Mammoth bone. Heidelberg, Germ.

TABLE 4 (Continued)

Age. yrs.

(Comment; incredible)	3,370
L-182: Hotu Man. Charcoal from hearth of skelton, Iran	9,500
O-235: Charcoal 20' deep, with bones of elephant, camel, horse, antelope, glyptodon, etc. Lewisville, Tex.	>37,000
W-169: "Keilor Skull" (previously believed to be oldest remains of homo sapiens) Keilor Terr., Victoria	8,500
L-127: Extinct superbison skin and tissue. Fairbanks, Alaska	>28,000

* * *

Dates in Reference 3 (1952):

C-558: Bison bone in gray sand horizon with elephant and other fossils, followed by diatomaceous earth with *extinct* bison as the most abundant fossil. Lubbock, Tex.	9,883
C-631: Crude oil. 1100' deep in Tulare form. Kern Co., Calif.	>24,000
C-632: Crude oil, upper or middle Pico form. Ventura, Calif.	>27,780
C-822: Charcoal from hearth in Sioux Co., Neb. written up in "Early Man" (Reference 12) as "Pleistocene mammals of Nebraska"	2,049
C-823: Charcoal from 9' level. Burnet Cave, N.M., associated with fossil remains of 62 diff. extinct species. incl. *Antiquus taylori, Preptoceras sinclairi,* giant bear, large horse	7,432

CONTINUED from page 338

to be early and middle Pleistocene, such as mastodon, mylodon, sabre-tooth tiger, etc. Almost all are dated between 10,000 and 30,000 years.

(7) Many "prehistoric" human remains and artifacts are datable within 30,000 years, including such famous cases as Neanderthal Man, Broken Hill Man, Florisbad Man, Heidelberg, Keilor, and Hotu. Furthermore, certain doubt is cast upon the dates of two to four million years put by Leakey *et al.,* on such forms as Olduvai Gorge *Zinjanthropus* and the Omo Valley *Australopithecus!*[5, 6, 7]

(8) Deep ocean deposits and cores from forty feet below deep

TABLE 5
Reconstruction of Biblical Chronology: Creation to Present

Eras		Time	Reference
I: ANTEDILUVIAN (Creation to Flood)		2000 yrs. (approx.)	Gen. 5 (per original and LXX texts; deduced from Mas., Sam. Pent., Modern LXX, *et al.*)
II: POSTDILUVIAN OLD TESTAMENT		3000 yrs.	
Flood to Abram	1070		Gen. 11 (as above)
Abram to Exodus	430		Ex. 12:41, Gal. 3:17
Exodus to Temple	580		Judges, I Kings 6:1 (LXX)
Temple to Captivity	363		Kings and Chronicles
Babylonian Captivity	70		Jer. 25 and Daniel 9
Emancipation to the Cross	487		Daniel 9, Ezra 1, Luke 3:1; also Josephus, *Antiq.*
III: NEW TESTAMENT (Cross to Present)		1940 yrs.	Calendar
		6940 yrs. (approx.)	

NOTE: Apart from the Bible there is *no* reliable means of dating any historical event prior to Christ. Classical dates based on Ptolemy's "canon" plus solar eclipses, and Greek olympiads are in error by about 80 years. Ancient dates based on Assyrian eponyms, Manetho, and Berosus are connected to present via Ptolemy.

---

ocean beds, supposed to contain the detritus of the most primitive forms of life, are dated within 40,000 years ago.

(9) Ancient artifacts dated by archeology (i.e., in Egypt, Syria, Iran, etc.), in general, show radiocarbon dates up to 500 years younger (according to reference 5), confirming the now recognized tendency of ancient historians to exaggerate.

(10) The most ancient dates of human culture are found in the Near East, while the oldest "human" dates in the Western Hemisphere are noticeably younger. To bear out the dramatic findings of facts in items (3), (5), (6), and (7) above, Table 4 lists seventy-five typical dates out of over 220 found in these specialists categories to date.

That these facts have already disturbed some specialists of evolutionary geology and paleontology is shown by a typical statement in *Science* (October, 1956): "as a result of radiocarbon dates, all the previous interpretations of Pleistocene lake history, depth and position in geologic time must be reassessed." (p. 669) Even more disturbing, however, are the facts that emerge from a more careful analysis of this great harvest of dates.

Here before us, gathered from all parts of the globe and covering almost every once-living form, we now have a sufficient number of death-dates to learn something from their distribution alone. If distributed by age, by location, and by type in accordance with some ancient historical record, it should not be difficult to confirm or refute such a record. Consider a chronology based on the Bible, for example. (See Table 5) It describes a creation a mere 7,000 years ago, followed some 2,000 years later by a worldwide catastrophe that all but extinguished man, animal and birds from the face of the earth. Now that we have a broad sampling of death dates back to man's earliest beginnings, surely such a strange record can be dismissed once and for all! Or is it just possible it might be confirmed?

Radiocarbon Assumptions Re-examined

First let us consider the date of biblical creation. At the outset this seems clearly refuted by a host of C-14 dates much older than 7,000 B.P. We recall, however, that the radiocarbon dating system was built on two assumptions; namely, (1) the rate of production of C-14 in the atmosphere by cosmic rays is assumed equal to its rate of decay in living matter, at a value of 16.0 dpm/gm, and (2) this equilibrium is assumed to have been reached eons ago, so that all once-living matter datable by radiocarbon possessed this same activity when it died, namely 16.0 dpm/gm.

As to the first assumption, Libby himself conceded in his first edition (and on p. 7, second edition) that whereas the specific activity (decay rate) of C-14 in living matter today is about 16.0 dpm/gm, the production rate is more like 19.0, an imbalance of

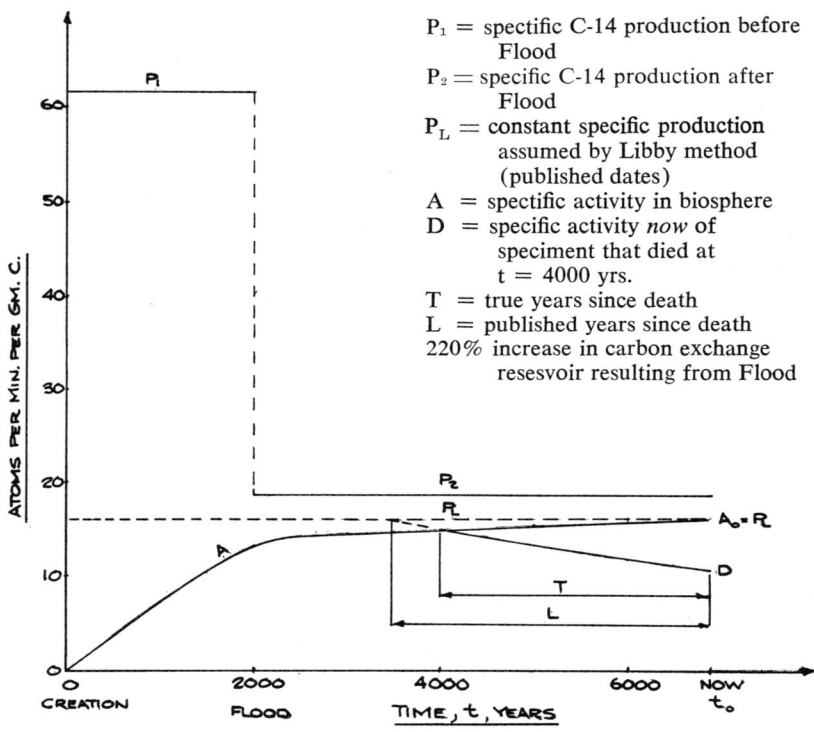

Figure 1.

almost twenty percent. This imbalance, to use Libby's own phrase, points to a recent "turning on" of cosmic radiation:

> If one were to imagine that the cosmic radiation had been turned off until a short while ago, the enormous amount of radiocarbon necessary to the equilibrium state would not have been manufactured, *and the specific radioactivity of living matter would be much less than the rate of production*. . . . (emphasis added) (p. 7, second edition)

Furthermore, a specific calculation of when this "turning on" occurred is easy to make. From the simple law of exponential build-up, $A/P = 1 - e^{(.693T/T)}$, in which we have the specific activity $A = 16.0$, the production rate $P = 19.0$, and the half-life of C-14 $T =$

5,730 yrs. The "turning on" date, T, comes out less than 16,000 years ago!

A second inescapable consequence of this imbalance is that the *true* age, T, of any specimen will always be *less than* the measured age, L, using Libby's assumptions (as published in *Radiocarbon*) since the latter is calculated as if no imbalance exists. The error $(L-T)$ is illustrated in Figure 1 and clearly becomes progressively worse as age increases. Thus the underlying data on which the radiocarbon clock is built compel us to acknowledge (1) a recent creation, and (2) a reduction in all published ages.

At this point an objector will rightly point out that the biblical creation date is by no means yet confirmed; 16,000 is certainly less than 4,000,000,000; but it is still not near enough to 7,000 to make the biblical chronology trustworthy.

The answer is not hard to find. There is good reason to believe that the production rate of C-14 has *not* been constant since creation, at Libby's value of 18.8 atoms/min-gm. Several observers[8, 9] would in fact place it higher even today—not realizing perhaps that this would make creation even more recent! But the best clue to the actual value of P in ancient times is derivable from the actual published dates.

Radiocarbon Dates Re-evaluated

First, we compute a *preliminary* set of corrections based on Libby's constant $P=18.8$ back to creation, (see appendix A), giving a preliminary true age, T, for each published age, L. Then, out of all the published dates we take the 7,318 independent dates (defined later) pertaining to man and animals and apply the appropriate correction to each. Finally, we distribute these corrected dates into 500-year "boxes" from the present back to 8,500 years, and into 1,000-year boxes from 8,500 B.P. to "tentative" creation at 15,700 B.P. When this is done, the distribution of dates appears in Table 6 (next page).

Two anomalies clearly show up in this distribution. The first anomaly is the drop-off from 127 to 51 dates shortly after 15,700 B.P. The second anomaly is the drop-off from 218 to 86 dates im-

TABLE 6

Corrected Date Span	Published Date Span	Number of Dates
	(years B.P., "before present")	
0- 500	0- 580	780
500-1,000	580- 1,160	1,174
1,000-1,500	1,160- 1,745	857
1,500-2,000	1,745- 2,340	777
2,000-2,500	2,340- 2,940	628
2,500-3,000	2,940- 3,545	538
3,000-3,500	3,545- 4,160	447
3,500-4,000	4,160- 4,780	371
4,000-4,500	4,780- 5,410	290
4,500-4,950*	5,410- 5,995	86
4,950-5,500	5,995- 6,805	218
5,500-6,000	6,805- 7,500	146
6,000-6,500	7,500- 8,215	133
6,500-7,000	8,215- 8,950	127
7,000-7,500	8,950- 9,710	107
7,500-8,000	9,710-10,500	86
8,000-8,500	10,500-11,320	66

Corrected Date Span	Published Date Mid-span	Number of Dates
	(1,000-yr. spans counted from 8,500 back)	
8,500- 9,500	12,150	72
9,500-10,500	13,990	65
10,500-11,500	16,050	52
11,500-12,500	18,500	41
12,500-13,500	21,570	39
13,500-14,500	26,180	51
14,500-15,500	33,460	127
15,500-15,700	33,460 to infinity	13

*The period 4,500 to 4,950 was arbitrarily contracted from 500 to 450 years in counting dates on grounds that, if it represents the first post-flood period, death dates in 4,950 to 5,000 are flood deaths; and if the flood is fictitious such a minor contraction should make no noticeable difference in column 3.

mediately after 4,950 B.P. followed by a steady recovery. With so much data neither drop-off can be dismissed as mere statistical randomness. For the first anomaly we will find a clue later, but reason for the second anomaly is unmistakable. We are warranted in assigning the second anomaly until proven otherwise, to the one great event in history which certainly would have caused it; and the more so when we note that its date, 5,000 B.P., is substantially in accord with the historical record of the Genesis Flood.

For no matter how ignored and dismissed by evolutionists and uniformitarian geologists during the past century, the fact of such a worldwide cataclysm at just such a time has been amply attested by many competent writers.[10, 11, 12, 13]

Method of Radiocarbon Date Correction

We see then that the radiocarbon record, using Libby's own data, gives evidence of a recent creation and of the Genesis Flood, even without knowledge of the exact variation of C-14 production with time, by which to pinpoint the date of each. In such a situation a well-established scientific method can be applied to ascertain the C-14 production rate in time past, thereby the true age of every radiocarbon specimen. The method is as follows:

(a) We state the *hypothesis* that, if the preliminary corrected dates in table 6 above reflect both biblical Creation and biblical Flood, then their *true* values would correspond precisely with creation about 7,000 B.P. and the flood close to 4,950 B.P.

(b) Assuming these two dates, we are then able to compute, by the procedure described in Appendix A, the most probable way in which C-14 production has varied.

(c) And given this C-14 production rate the relationship of true age, T, to published age, L, is shown to be as given in Table 7 (next page).

Note the close correspondence between the true versus published age shown here and the initially corrected versus published age of Table 6, as far back as 5,000 B.P. This comes from the fact that Libby's figure of C-14 production fits the hypothesis quite well back to the flood. Prior to that a radically different production

TABLE 7

True Age	Published Age	True Age	Published Age
1,000	1,155	4,000	4,725
1,500	1,730	4,500	5,350
2,000	2,310	5,000	5,990
2,500	2,900	5,500	8,860
3,000	3,500	6,000	12,530
3,500	4,110	6,500	19,100
		7,000	Infinite

(shown also graphically in Figure 2)

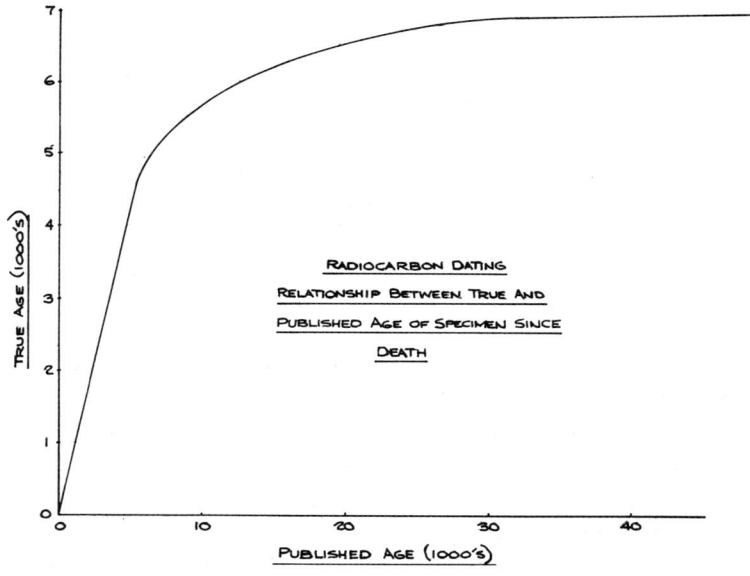

Figure 2.

rate is necessary, as presented in Appendix A, which accounts for the rapid divergence of the two tables from 5,000 B.P. back to creation.

So much for the results of the hypothesis. The important thing is to test its truth. To do this, the argument is as follows: If the

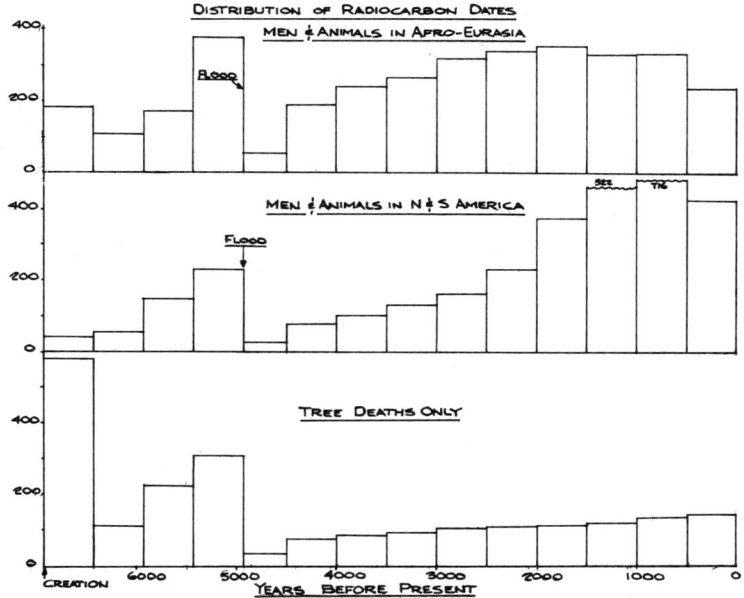

Figure 3.

accumulated radiocarbon dates, corrected to *true* dates as above, disclose details concerning flood and creation that are only found in the Bible and that are in no way implied in the hypothesis itself, it follows that the corrections to true age* in Table 7 are valid, the assumed C-14 production rate* is valid, biblical Creation and Flood are confirmed, and the hypothesis is sound. This we now proceed to show.

Date Re-valued Hypothesis Verified

All the published dates were first reduced to those that are strictly independent, by eliminating duplications, multiple specimens at the same location, etc. The dates included all lists published, first in *Science,* and since 1959, in *Radiocarbon,* through volume 11, cov-

---

*Granting any margin of error that would lead to the same conclusions.

ering the year 1969, giving a total of over 15,000 dates. These independent dates were then classified as follows:

CLASS I: Dates pertaining to human occupation and ark-borne** animals found in the Afro-Eurasia land mass (3768 dates).

CLASS II: Dates pertaining to human occupation and ark-borne** animals found in the Western hemisphere (3550 dates).

CLASS III: Dates pertaining to substantial trees (not low-lying vegetation) regardless of geographical location, but omitting wood associated with human culture, i.e., firewood, implements, etc. (2353 dates).

TABLE 8
DISTRIBUTION OF RADIOCARBON DATES IN 500-YR. AGE GROUP SINCE CREATION

PERIOD IN YEARS B.P. (Before Present)	NUMBER OF DATES IN EACH PERIOD		
	CLASS I	CLASS II	CLASS III
	Man & animals in Afro-Eurasia	Man & animals in W. Hemisphere	Tree Deaths only
0- 500	276	496*	154
500-1,000	384	803*	150
1,000-1,500	361	540*	119
1,500-2,000	357	391*	108
2,000-2,500	363	253	110
2,500-3,000	344	182	108
3,000-3,500	289	158	102
3,500-4,000	259	114	91
4,000-4,500	198	83	71
4,500-4,950 (Flood)	56	26	35
4,950-5,500	403	249	326
5,500-6,000	185	155	236
6,000-6,500	116	57	119
6,500-7,000 (Creation)	187	43	624
TOTALS	3768	3550	2353

**Ark-borne animals include all those specifically indicated by the biblical record; i.e., all except sea-life, insects, and smaller forms.

*Dates in these three periods are abnormally numerous because of concentrated research by many universities in American Indian culture.

CLASS IV: Other dates of matter not clearly affected in time or distribution by a Flood catastrophe; i.e., oceanic flora and fauna, ocean bottom sediments and detritus, marl, loam, peat, tufa, gyttja, caliche, sapropel, leaves, sedge, grass, pollen, etc. (Approx. 5300 dates).

The 9671 dates in Classes I, II, and III were then corrected from published age to true age, in accordance with Table 7, and distributed into age groups, each group spanning 500 years.

In each case the published "mean" date is used, the probable error always being equally plus or minus. Dates published as "greater than 40,000," "greater than 33,000," etc., of which most were in Class III, were put in the next older group.

Finally, since biblical chronology puts the Genesis Flood almost exactly 3,000 years before the death of Christ, or close to 4,950 years ago, all dates between 4,950 and 5,000 were arbitrarily put in the age group just preceding the flood, i.e., 5,000 to 5,500 B.P. The argument here is that,

(a) If the biblical record is true as to the flood and its date, these would be death-dates of flora and fauna killed by the flood, and should therefore appear in the age group terminating at the flood or,

(b) If the biblical record is untrue as to either the flood *or* its date, such an adjustment would be of no consequence to the results, since the deaths in such a 50-year span would be no more than in any other nearby 50 years.

Summarized Results of Data Analysis

Results of this classification are shown in Table 8, and plotted graphically in Figure 3. Even a casual study of this table and graph reveals the following significant facts:

FACT No. 1: The number of dates in *each* of the three classes shows a sudden drop from a large number in the period preceding the flood, to less than fifteen percent of this number in the period immediately following the flood.

FACT No. 2: Class I dates (man and animals in Afro-Eurasia) commence fairly large (187), fall off to 116 in the next 500 years, and then build up to a peak of 403 just before the flood. After the marked drop-off at the flood, they build up again to a similar peak within the last two millennia.

FACT No. 3: Class II dates (man and animals in the Western Hemisphere) are considerably more scarce than Class I dates immediately after both creation and flood, and are slower building up after each event. Unlike Class I dates, they show no drop-off after creation.

FACT No. 4: Class III dates (tree deaths) are by far most numerous (624) at the beginning, then drop off to twenty percent in the next period, rise again to 326 before the flood, and then drop to a mere thirty-five. After the flood, these dates slowly build up again, but never are more than twenty-five percent of their post-creation value.*

Now if we analyze the dates in the periods immediately following creation and flood we discover additional facts of even further significance:

FACT No. 5: In the first 500 years following creation the dates found in Class I break down as follows: seventy-five percent are of animal deaths, twenty-two percent are of human culture (i.e., fire-sites and tools, etc.) and only three percent are of human deaths. What is more, the oldest human dates are in the Near East.

FACT No. 6: In the first 500 years following creation, the forty-three dates in Class II are of two kinds only: ninety percent animal deaths, and ten percent human culture. There are no identifiable human death dates.

FACT No. 7: In the 450 years immediately after the flood, the fifty-six dates in Class I break down as follows: thirty-seven of animal deaths, twelve of human culture, seven of human deaths.

---

*EDITOR's NOTE: Since the publication of this 1970 research report, Professor Whitelaw has authored a paper in which he deals with radiocarbon dates of various marine specimens. In the paper he asserts that life date distributions among such marine forms stranded on land closely parallel the date distribution evident among these terrestrial samples here and hence become independent confirmatory evidence. See "Voices from the Deep That Shout Forth the Genesis Flood," by Robert L. Whitelaw, Bible-Science Newsletter, March 1974. Box 1016, Caldwell, Idaho.

Again, the earliest dates are most frequent in the Near East!

FACT No. 8: In the 450 years following the flood, the mere twenty-six dates of man and animals in the Western Hemisphere (Class II) are made up of twenty animal deaths, five cultural deposits, and 1 human death date whose margin of error could put it at the flood. (Here we see man's late arrival in the West after the flood, just as Fact No. 6 suggests his late arrival in the West after creation!)

FACT No. 9: The thirty-five tree-death dates (Class III) in the 450 years after the flood are mostly from temperate and tropical zones. Dead trees from polar regions almost exclusively date before the flood, and no redwood (sequoia) deaths are found in the first post-flood period except those associated with volcanic action or lava flow.

Comparison of Facts to Biblical Record

Against these nine facts we now compare the biblical record. We read of an original world of evident verdure, beauty and abundance; of animals and reptiles of all kinds, vegetarian in habit, populating the earth undoubtedly in ecological equilibrium; and of a human race commencing with an intelligent man and woman, somewhere in the region of Mesopotamia, to whom the animals were instinctively subservient.

We then read of a "fall" and a "curse" with three physical consequences, principally: as to fauna, some animals became carnivorous and preyed upon each other; as to flora, thorns and thistles are mentioned, suggesting possible climatic as well as ecological disturbances; and as to man, violence and greed appeared, while at the same time he lived to great age, 900 years not being uncommon, so that apart from infection and disease few deaths should appear for the first 500 years.

Over the next 2,000 years we are told particularly of violence, murder, and rapacity among mankind; yet there is equal emphasis upon the prolific growth of the human race. Whether the American continents were contiguous with Africa and Europe at this time we cannot tell. Regardless, there was ample time, intelligence, and incentive for the human race to spread to the Americas, Australia, and the islands of the Pacific, and even develop an "advanced" culture.

The record is not of ignorant or "primitive" men. We read of artificers in brass and iron, of agriculture, of animal husbandry, of tents (suggesting spinning and weaving), and of sophisticated musical instruments such as harp and organ—a far cry from African tom-toms! There is also archeological evidence of written language, numerology, and extensive libraries in clay tablets in this period.

Suddenly we are told of a worldwide cataclysm of awesome and frightful detail; a cataclysm in which all of mankind, all land animals and all birds are destroyed, save those uniquely preserved in a great ship previously built by one family at God's explicit instructions. The cataclysm is clearly described as the rapid inundation of the entire earth, probably by tectonic or volcanic upheaval of the ocean floor ("fountains of the great deep") accompanied by or causing great rain ("windows of heaven.")

Vast and violent changes of the earth's surface, stripping of the luxuriant vegetation, and sudden entombment of desperate men and animals must have occurred, all to vanish beneath strata upon strata of sediment and lava, just as the geological record attests (see References 11, 12, 13).

Only after some 375 days do the waters abate sufficiently to permit the survivors to leave their floating refuge; four men, four women, a male and female pair of each "kind" (not species!) of animal, and in a few special cases, seven of a kind. And from that spot, somewhere in the mountains of Ararat, those survivors alone repopulated the ravaged earth. At the same time vegetation slowly returned, first the grass and shrub, then the fast-growing saplings, and finally the slow oak and giant sequoia, but now in a world of vastly different climate and terrain.

All of this is a story well-known to many. Yet it bears re-telling here to bring out the dramatic way that the above details and the radiocarbon record correspond. The sophisticated modern mind, no matter how predisposed to dismiss the story as folklore and myth, is thus confronted with the inescapable fact that: (1) the biblical record is corroborated by each of the nine facts listed above discovered in the distribution of the radiocarbon dates, and (2) *not a single detail* of this record, nor even its chronology, is found in conflict with the age and distribution of the thousands of dates now available.

Further Consideration of Stated Hypothesis

We now return to the hypothesis being tested; the hypothesis that, *knowing* there has been a recent creation, it is probable it occurred when the Bible says it did, i.e., about 7,000 years ago; and secondly that, *knowing* there has been a worldwide catastrophe to man and animals, it is probable it corresponds in date with the Genesis Flood, i.e., about 4,950 years ago.

Making these two assumptions, a C-14 production rate in time past was established. With this rate, a correction from published to true radiocarbon ages was obtained; and with these true ages assigned, the distribution of radiocarbon dates disclosed nine facts. The question before us then is simple. Were the nine facts automatically predetermined regardless of what dates had been chosen for creation and flood; or do the nine facts result *only* if we assume the biblical date for each of these events?

If the former statement is true, we have merely deceived ourselves with circular reasonings—just as evolutionists have done in assuming evolution to date index fossils to date rocks to date fossils to prove evolution! But clearly this is not so in our case.

There is nothing whatsoever in the choice of the two numbers, 7,000 and 4,950, which predetermined that the radiocarbon dates would distribute themselves so as to correspond with the *details* of both biblical Creation and biblical Food. Yet unmistakably they do.

It follows then that the hypothesis is in accord with the accepted criteria of the scientific method by which one derives a general truth from a particular set of facts by testing the truth against the facts.

It follows also that the hypothesis is confirmed, along with the details of the biblical record and biblical chronology, within the limits of accuracy of the radiocarbon data.

It is granted that a variation in creation date of $\pm$ 400 years would probably not affect the distribution of dates in a manner out of harmony with the Bible. On the other hand, a variation in the flood date as much as 100 years *older* would show noticeable discrepancies between the date distribution and the details of Scripture. It is also worth noting that the flood date of 4,940 B.P. established from biblical chronology leads to a date of the Exodus at 3,240 B.P. or 1,470 B.C., agreeing with both radiocarbon dates and other investigators (see Reference 13).

It is also granted that the paucity of unambiguous radiocarbon dates in some of the groups cited in the "nine facts"—as well as the large probable error in many of the older dates—taken by themselves would make solid conclusions difficult. However, by the very laws of statistical data, this is a weakness which must diminish with time as thousands of new dates accumulate each year.

And the thesis of this paper is that the number of good dates already available is sufficient to *point to* the conclusions now to be drawn; while the number of dates with large uncertainties is insufficient to invalidate these conclusions, particularly when the Bible—a body of evidence not lightly dismissed—supports the same conclusions.

Conclusions

In the light of the above facts and reservations, it is concluded that:

1. Radiocarbon supports the idea of biblical Creation by pointing unmistakably to a recent beginning of cosmic radiation.

2. Radiocarbon supports a date of creation at approximately 7,000 B.P.

3. Radiocarbon supports the contemporaneous appearance of all forms of living matter at creation. Man and modern animals, along with extinct flora and fauna all appear equally ancient and with equal suddenness, as shown in Table 4.

4. Radiocarbon supports the beginning of the human race from a few ancestors in the vicinity of the Near East.

5. Radiocarbon, on the other hand, indicates the sudden concurrent appearance of the rest of the animal kingdom in larger numbers in every part of the world.

6. Radiocarbon clearly indicates an original world in which both trees and low-lying vegetation were profuse and widespread even throughout present polar regions and deserts. (Facts amply attested by geology and paleontology of an ancient world uniquely different in climate, in location and elevation of the very continents, and possibly even in the inclination of the earth's axis!)

7. Radiocarbon points to some drastic change, shortly after creation, which depleted both animal world and arboreal vegetation, but without noticeable effect upon the multiplication of man; just such an effect as might be deduced from Genesis 3.

8. Radiocarbon clearly points to a worldwide catastrophe destructive of man, beast, and tree, just as described in Genesis 7 and confirmed elsewhere in Scripture, in worldwide human tradition, and in worldwide geological evidence.

9. Radiocarbon supports the date of such catastrophe at about 4,950 B.P. (compare Tables 5 and 8).

10. Radiocarbon indicates a large and widespread human population in the world just before this catastrophe.

11. Radiocarbon indicates the widespread existence of now-extinct flora and fauna in the world before this catastrophe, including evidence of the gradual extinction of many forms during the two millennia between it and creation (Table 8).

12. Radiocarbon indicates that the "re-origin" of both animals and man after this catastrophe was in the vicinity of the Near East and noticeably later in the Western Hemisphere.

13. Radiocarbon supports the biblical chronology of ancient empires and of Israel and exposes suspected exaggerations in Manetho, Berosus, *et al.*

14. Finally, there is no question as to which concept of time and history is supported by the radiocarbon record. Is it the endless time and meaningless history postulated by evolution? Or is it a specific span of time marked off by the purposeful acts of a sovereign God, from creation to flood to cross to ultimate consummation, as the Bible portrays?

Fifteen thousand radiocarbon dates, dead voices from the past assembled by scientists from every kind of once-living matter and every corner of the globe, now answer the question unequivocally in favor of the Bible!

APPENDIX A

Analytic Determination of the Variation in C-14 Production Rate, and of the Relationship Between Published and True Radiocarbon Dates

In the body of the report, grounds were established for the working hypothesis that (a) cosmic radiation commenced about 7,000 B.P. (true date), and (b) the significant drop-off in specimens of man and animals at published dates about 6,000 B.P. actually occurred at a true date about 4,950 B.P. With this hypothesis it is possible to determine the most probable variation in C-14 production rate in time past; and with this variation it is possible to correct published dates to true dates. As shown in the report, the results confirmed the hypothesis.

Here it is necessary to show first the determination of the most probable specific production rate (hereafter called SPR) of C-14, in time past. Three alternatives are considered:

(1) A constant SPR throughout history, such as Libby assumed, but at a value high enough to yield the hypothetical creation date, 7,000 B.P., rather than the 15,700 B.P. which results from Libby's SPR of 18.8 atoms/min-gm. Such an SPR value comes out (using equation 1 below) at 27, for $t = 7,000$, and was proposed in 1968 by the author.[14] Such a constantly high SPR, leads to unreasonably large corrections to the published dates, as follows:

Published age:
    1,800   3,805   5,090   9,020   12,580   19,180
Corrected age:
    1,000   2,000   3,000   4,000   4,950   6,000

Equally serious is the objection that the published date corresponding to the flood date of 4,950 would be 12,580, since no noticeable drop-off in published dates of man and animals occurs at this point. Since this does not satisfy the hypothesis, this alternative must be dropped.

(2) An SPR value highest at 7,000 B.P. and decreasing either linearly or exponentially to Libby's value at present. This alternative suffers from the same objections as (1), with the additional objection that no mechanism is evident in the carbon-exchange reservoir, or in cosmic radiation, to account for such a steady decline.

(3) A two-step SPR, as shown in Figure 1, with a constant effective value of P_1 from 7,000 to 4,950 B.P., and a lower value of P_2 from 4,950 to the present.

To determine these two values we apply first the standard equation for buildup of specific activity, A_1, in the biosphere during the time from 7,000 to 4,950 B.P.:

$$A_1/P_1 = (1-e^{-\lambda t}), \text{ for } 0 < t < 2050 \qquad (1)$$

Then for the second period we apply a similar equation,

$$A_2/P_2 = (1-e^{-\lambda(t+\Delta)}), \text{ for } t > 2050 \qquad (2)$$

where λ in both equations is .693/5730, and Δ is the increment of time *before* $t=0$, that would have been needed for A_2 to build up under the influence of P_2 to the same value as A_1 at time $t=2050$, i.e., the specific activity of the biosphere at the flood (Note: A_1 and A_2 must fall on a single curve A as shown in Figure 1).

To solve equation (1) and (2) for P_2, P_1 and Δ, we need three boundary conditions which are: $A_1 = A_2$ at $t = 2050$; $A_2 = 16.0$ (today's value) at $t = 7,000$; and a final condition that the discrepancy between a published age, L, and a true age, T, should be about 1,000 years at $t = 2,050$ years, since the drop-off apparently caused by the flood (by our hypothesis) occurs in the published dates with that error. Looking again at Figure 1, the two ages, L, and T, are further defined by:

$$D/A = e^{-\lambda T} \qquad (3)$$
$$D/P_L = e^{-\lambda L} \qquad (4)$$

where D is the specific activity, dpm/gm., of a specimen today of true age; T; A is its activity when it died, lying on the A curve (Figure 1) T years ago; P_L is 16.0 at/min-gm, the SPR equal to today's specific activity which Libby and all investigators assume to be activity when a specimen died; and $\lambda_L =$ .693/5570, the original Libby decay constant, still used for dating.

Following the above procedure, the value $\triangle$ came out at 9,400 years, and the two values of SPR, $P_1 = 64.4$ and $P_2 = 18.6$ atoms/min-gm. The latter value is very close to Libby's value for the SPR today, which is as expected.

The third alternative thus fits the conditions required at creation and flood, and the $(L-T)$ corrections that result have been shown in the body of the report (Table 7) to produce remarkably satisfactory confirmation of the hypothesis. Despite this confirmation, there is still need to show what might have caused such a drastic decrease in SPR from 64.4 to 18.6, that is, from SPR of pre-flood to that of post-flood era, respectively.

To account for this decrease it is first noted that Libby determined the value of $P_2 = 18.8$ atoms/min-gm as the ratio of two other values, each determined experimentally. The numerator is neutron production, via cosmic rays, per unit area at earth's surface, on the showing that each free neutron almost certainly produces an atom of C-14. This numerator value, allowing for altitude and latitude variations, came to 156 atoms/sq. cm.-min.

The denominator of this ratio giving P_2 is the total inventory of *exchange-carbon* per unit area of earth's surface, i.e., the carbon that actively participates in the great carbon-exchange process on earth. This inventory Libby subdivided as follows:

Ocean carbonate	7.25 gm/sq. cm.
Ocean, dissolved organic	.59
Total biosphere	.33
Atmosphere	.12
Total	8.3

Now consider the principal effects of a cataclysm such as the Genesis Flood on the principal items in this inventory. Undoubtedly the Flood demolished the carbon-exchange inventory in the terrestrial biosphere. Moreover, it is clear that the continents, since the Flood, have recovered scarcely one-third the wealth of living matter they once had.

Allowing then for the less disturbed inventory of marine life, we may judge the pre-flood biosphere inventory to be .50 gm/sq. cm. Likewise the pre-flood atmospheric carbon inventory would be slightly less than now, say 0.10, due to the enormous competition of vegetation for CO_2.

We must look then for some entirely different action of the Flood which would greatly *increase* the carbon-exchange inventory of the oceans, and it is not hard to find. On the verdure-rich continents was the accumulated animal and vegetable detritus of two thousand years, over ninety-nine percent of it inert to the carbon-exchange cycle.

While much of it entered into formation of coal, peat, and oil, the greater mass by far must have been rolled and swept into the world ocean; thus, suddenly "enriching" the sea with organic detritus many times previous concentration, an inventory which in this new environment and at new temperatures could now actively participate in the carbon-exchange process to this very day.

We may thus readily postulate a pre-flood carbon-exchange inventory as follows:

Ocean carbonate	1.70
Ocean dissolved organic	.20
Biosphere	.50
Atmosphere	.10
Total	2.50

The total here of exchangeable carbon before the Flood (2.50 gm. per sq. cm.) is significantly lower than the present value indicated by Libby, 8.3 gm/sq. cm. This does not indicate that the Flood somehow increased the absolute total amount of carbon on the earth, but that it increased the *exchangeable* carbon.

As suggested previously, the flood might be expected to carry much of the accumulated vegetable matter back into the oceans and thereby increase directly the amount of carbon in the carbon cycle.

This value of 2.50 gm/sq. cm., divided into a pre-flood C-14 production rate of about 161 atoms/min-cm. (i.e., essentially the same as today) would give the SPR value of 64.4.

REFERENCES

1. Harlow Shapley, July 3, 1965. *Science News Letter,* p. 10.
2. George Wald, 1955. The origin of life, (in) The physics and chemistry of life. Simon & Shuster, New York, p. 12.
3. W. F. Libby, 1952. Radiocarbon dating. University of Chicago Press, 1st edition.
4. *Ibid.,* 1955, 2nd ed. (with enlarged list of C-14 dates in chapter 6, and addition of chapter 7 by F. Johnson, entitled: "Reflections upon the significance of radiocarbon dates").
5. L. S. B. Leakey, 1959. A new fossil skull from Olduvai, *Nature,* 184:491.
6. F. C. Howell, 1969. Remains of hominidae from pliocene pleistocene formations in the lower Omo basin, Ethiopia, *Nature,* 223:1234.
7. *Datelines in Science.* November 7, 1969, 1.5 million years are added to early hominids' age. See also *Datelines in Science,* September 17, 1917, re Olduvai Gorge skull of Reference 5.
8. W. W. Rubey, 1950. Geological evidence regarding the source of the earth's hydrosphere and atmosphere, *Science,* 112:20.
9. Minze Stuiver and Hans Suess, 1966. On the relationship between radiocarbon dates and true sample ages, *Radiocarbon,* 8:534.
10. George McCready Price, The fundamentals of geology. Pacific Press, Mountain View, Calif.
11. A. M. Rehwinkel, 1951. The flood. Concordia Publishing House, St. Louis, Mo.
12. John C. Whitcomb and Henry M. Morris, 1961. The Genesis flood. Presbyterian & Reformed Publishing Co., Philadelphia.
13. I. Velikovsky, 1965. Earth in upheaval. Dell Publishing, New York.
14. R. L. Whitelaw, 1968. Radiocarbon confirms biblical creation (and so does potassium-argon), *Creation Research Society Quarterly,* 5:78.

XXI

A CRITICAL EXAMINATION OF RADIOACTIVE DATING OF ROCKS

SIDNEY P. CLEMENTSON*

The method employed to obtain the ages of sedimentary rocks using samples containing radioactive materials, is widely known. It rests entirely upon the basic assumption that when radioactive material enters the rock it consists solely of parent element, and the object is to arrive at a theoretical date when the daughter elements in the sample would be considered to have been all parent element. This date is believed to give the age of the rock.

Calculations are made from mass ratios of parent and daughter elements. When due allowances are made for known variable factors such calculations are accurate enough to arrive at a theoretical starting point of the disintegration. But the basic assumption that this starting point corresponds to the time when the radioactive materials entered the host rock is of course fundamental, for if this is not true, then the theoretical age will bear no relationship to the age of the rock.

Facts to Be Considered

In order to establish the truth or falsity of this assumption the following facts should be considered:

Radioactive materials come originally from the crust of the earth, and with the flow of magma, sedimentary strata may be overlaid or intruded with igneous rock containing radioactive materials. No significance can be placed upon values from materials not associated

---

*Sidney P. Clementson is a consulting engineer. He resides at 15 Marshalls Rd., Sutton, Surrey, England.

with igneous rock as these must have been displaced at least once and possibly many times.

The basic assumption is built on the theory that while the radioactive material is in the earth prior to eruption, it is in a molten state. In this condition, daughter elements are constantly separated from parent elements by convection. It is also assumed that when magma flows, the parent element is separate and clean, ready to be used as a natural chronometer in regard to the rocks in which it is found. This should be carefully considered, in relation to what is known about the earth's crust and in light of the evidence of the rocks themselves.

Below the granite basement of the crust of the earth there is the mantle. The crust is solid and temperatures increase with depth. At levels of the mantle, the temperatures are considered to be so high that if it were not for the high pressure, the mantle material would be in a liquid state; "as it is, seismic evidence indicates that the mantle is solid throughout."[1]

While the mantle has been called solid, views have been expressed that, due to vast differences of temperature and pressure, there are slow but massive movements of the mantle over continental areas. This is indicative of the kind of forces necessary to move mantle material. That the slight differences in specific gravity of parent and daughter elements could cause convection currents is highly unlikely.

It is more likely that the daughter elements, born within the depths of the earth, have been held in "close custody," and when a fissure occurs in the crust, and the surrounding pressure drops, the local rock, with its minerals, becomes liquid and issues forth—parent and daughter elements together. If this conclusion is correct, then the isotope ratios will in no wise indicate the age of the host rock.

This subject should be considered also in relation to concentrations of radioactive materials at various levels of the crust. The result of tests "forces us to suppose that radioactive elements are for some reason confined solely to the comparatively thin outer layer of the crust,"[2] and that it is usually assumed that "the concentration decreases by half for each kilometer in depth."[3] On this basis we arrive at the conclusion that at a level at which magma may flow, the concentration of radioactive material may be small.

If the upper layers of the crust through which the magma may flow have considerable concentrations of radioactive material, in view of the temperature of the magma, we would expect the surrounding rocks to be fused and the magma to carry with it upper subsurface rocks, together with any radioactive elements contained in them.

Specific Problematic Issues

These considerations give rise to the following questions. Does the evidence of the rocks confirm that in magma, parent element emerges alone, without daughter elements; or, does it in fact establish the reverse, that it is accompanied by daughter elements? Does the evidence of the rocks imply that radioactive elements laid by magma are usually from one level; or, does it rather show almost invariably that the elements in the lava stream are joined and enriched by upper subsurface elements?

The effect of enrichment can be understood in relation to the normal process of decay of a radioactive series. Assuming a given point in time with a known mass of parent element, for any predetermined period the relative mass of all the isotopes in the series can be calculated. For each length of time, the series of ratios is constant.

When in a sample the ratios of the isotopes are all found to be in accord with such a series, the isotopes are said to be in equilibrium, and it is accepted that they have developed together without disturbance. Should it be found, however, that the ratios of any of the isotopes are not in accord with a series, then the isotopes are not in equilibrium, and it is known that there has been disturbance resulting in some enrichment or fractionation of the elements.

In the use of the old lead-uranium calculations any enrichment of the isotopes was not apparent for it is only when the ratios are all known that discrepancies appear. If the elements are in disequilibrium, enrichment to any extent might have taken place, and the age calculated would bear no relationship to the age of the rocks.

How many published ages of sedimentary rocks may come within this category is not known. If it were possible for research workers to make the isotope values available, there is no reason to suppose that any of the dates would stand, because (as it will be shown) there is evidence of disequilibrium and enrichment in all cases of recent research on young rocks.

Of even greater significance than the question of enrichment is the other matter raised, i.e., does disintegration commence when the minerals enter the host rock? It will be realized that if the disintegration elements are carried over into the host rock, then whether in equilibrium or not, the ratios will be in no way related to the host rock. There is one certain way of determining the truth of this matter, and this is by considering analysis of rock samples of known ages.

Research Results Analyzed

Research in the U.S.S.R. has been carried out on some eighteen samples from twelve volcanoes containing radioactive materials in the U^{238} series, and the isotopes in the chain are said to be in disequilibrium. It is stated that "since the age of the rocks is small, the daughter elements U^{234} and Io^{230} must have entered the mineral bodies at the time of their genesis instead of being formed on the decay of the parent material"[4] (see Tables 1-3).

Figures are not given for some of the isotopes in the series nor for lead, and the reference to disequilibrium appears to be based largely on the U^{234}/U^{238} and the Io/U^{238} ratios. The U^{234}/U^{238} Io/U^{238} ratios should be negligible quantities because of the relatively short half-lives for U^{234} and Io. But those ratios given are in fact appreciable. In a number of cases the U^{234}/U^{238} value is about 1.0, given in activity units. In mass units this represents approximately .000037, a ratio which would apply to an age of many millions of years (see Table 2).

Here it will be seen that the authors are viewing the question of equilibrium from the aspect of ratios assuming the commencement

Table 1. Equilibrium Tables—Uranium 238 Series

YEARS	U238	U234	I230	R226	R222	R210	Pb206
100	0.9999999	0.0000000	0.0000000	0.0000000	0.0000000	0.0000000	0.0000000
200	0.9999999	0.0000000	0.0000000	0.0000000	0.0000000	0.0000000	0.0000000
400	0.9999999	0.0000000	0.0000000	0.0000000	0.0000000	0.0000000	0.0000000
800	0.9999998	0.0000001	0.0000000	0.0000000	0.0000000	0.0000000	0.0000000
1,600	0.9999997	0.0000002	0.0000000	0.0000000	0.0000000	0.0000000	0.0000000
3,200	0.9999995	0.0000004	0.0000000	0.0000000	0.0000000	0.0000000	0.0000000
6,400	0.9999990	0.0000009	0.0000000	0.0000000	0.0000000	0.0000000	0.0000000
12,800	0.9999980	0.0000018	0.0000000	0.0000000	0.0000000	0.0000000	0.0000000
25,600	0.9999960	0.0000036	0.0000001	0.0000000	0.0000000	0.0000000	0.0000000
51,200	0.9999921	0.0000070	0.0000006	0.0000000	0.0000000	0.0000000	0.0000001
102,400	0.9999842	0.0000127	0.0000021	0.0000001	0.0000000	0.0000000	0.0000008
204,800	0.9999685	0.0000211	0.0000059	0.0000001	0.0000000	0.0000000	0.0000043
409,600	0.9999370	0.0000302	0.0000120	0.0000002	0.0000000	0.0000000	0.0000203
819,200	0.9998741	0.0000359	0.0000169	0.0000003	0.0000000	0.0000000	0.0000726
1,638,400	0.9997482	0.0000372	0.0000181	0.0000003	0.0000000	0.0000000	0.0001960
3,276,800	0.9994965	0.0000372	0.0000181	0.0000003	0.0000000	0.0000000	0.0004476
6,553,600	0.9989934	0.0000372	0.0000181	0.0000003	0.0000000	0.0000000	0.0009507
13,107,200	0.9979878	0.0000372	0.0000181	0.0000003	0.0000000	0.0000000	0.0019564
26,214,400	0.9959797	0.0000371	0.0000181	0.0000003	0.0000000	0.0000000	0.0039646
52,428,800	0.9919757	0.0000369	0.0000180	0.0000003	0.0000000	0.0000000	0.0079688
104,857,600	0.9840158	0.0000366	0.0000179	0.0000003	0.0000000	0.0000000	0.0159292
209,715,200	0.9682871	0.0000360	0.0000176	0.0000003	0.0000000	0.0000000	0.0316587
419,430,400	0.9375800	0.0000349	0.0000170	0.0000003	0.0000000	0.0000000	0.0623676
838,860,800	0.8790563	0.0000327	0.0000160	0.0000003	0.0000000	0.0000000	0.1208945
1,670,000,000	0.7727400	0.0000288	0.0000140	0.0000002	0.0000000	0.0000000	0.2272168
3,350,000,000	0.5971271	0.0000222	0.0000108	0.0000002	0.0000000	0.0000000	0.4028394

Table 1. This table contains a rundown of the Uranium 238 series on the computer. These data are useful in calculation of the equilibrium ratios—see Table 2. If a certain crystal were all U-238 at time zero (formation of the crystal), each line in Table 1 indicates the fraction of each nuclide of the U-238 decay series that would be present after the given interval of time had elapsed.

of disintegration when the minerals enter the rocks. But as these rocks are young, they cannot account for the high intermediate ratios. This is of course a plain admission that these ratios are not consistent with the known age of the rock.

Research in the U.S.A. on ten samples from Faial Azores, Tristan da Cunha, and Vesuvius supports this view. Here the question of the equilibrium of the isotopes is viewed frankly as based on an origin in the mantle before the flow of magma into the host rocks. It is said:

> If a region of the mantle has remained a closed system for a sufficient length of time, the isotopes in the Uranium decay series will be in secular equilibrium. During the melting process which produces a magma, the condition of secular equilibrium will be upset by any chemical fractionations which take place involving the members of the decay chain. If co-existing phases are in isotopic equilibrium when a magma is formed from a region in secular equilibrium prior to melting, we may use any observed radioactive disequilibrium in the resultant igneous rock to study chemical fractionations.[5]

It is clear from this that any attempt here to calculate an age of the rock from isotope ratios would result in a completely false answer. Since all radioactive materials that become involved in

TABLE 2
Equilibrium Ratios

YEARS	U^{234}/U^{238}	Pb^{206}/U^{238}	Pb^{208}/Th^{232}
100,000	.000013	.000000	.00000
410,000	.000030	.000020	.00002
1,690,000	.000037	.000200	.00008
6,550,000	.000037	.001000	.00032
26,200,000	.000037	.004000	.00130
52,400,000	.000037	.008000	.00260
104,900,000	.000037	.016000	.00520
210,000,000	.000037	.033000	.01040
420,000,000	.000037	.066000	.02070
840,000,000	.000037	.138000	.04100
1,680,000,000	.000037	.294000	.08300
3,360,000,000	.000037	.675000	.16600
6,710,000,000	.000037	1.805000	.33000

Table 2. Data such as those illustrated in Table 1 are here presented as ratios between the various nuclides in the U-238 decay series.

sedimentary rock must similarly flow with magma, the answer in all cases would be equally false.

In this research, figures are given for lead in addition to the other isotopes and consequently it is possible to calculate a theoretical age from this. From the data given, the Pb^{206}/U^{238} ratios in mass units can be obtained. The minimum value is 0.84 which represents an age of over 5,000 million years. This, it should be noted, is a calculated age for rocks which are known to be quite young. (see Tables 2 and 3).

TABLE 3
Research Figures

U.S.S.R.		U.S.A.					
Sample	U^{234}/U^{238}	Sample	Pb^{206}/Pb^{204}	Pb^{207}/Pb^{204}	U^{238}/Pb^{204}	Pb^{208}/Pb^{204}	Th^{232}/U^{238}
1	1.12	TR230	18.50	15.78	17.87	39.42	4.26
2	1.11	TR232	18.63	15.75	17.7	39.52	4.23
3	1.17	TR516	18.74	15.74	20.50	39.62	3.84
4	1.04	TR518	18.46	15.85	15.91	39.48	4.44
5	1.00	TR627	18.67	15.78	22.18	39.68	4.33
6	.91	VES	19.14	15.78	12.6	39.48	3.02
7	.49	MAF I	19.36	15.81	14.19	39.59	3.57
8	.45	MAF II	19.36	15.84	16.50	39.53	3.94
9	1.07	MAF III	19.41	15.87	15.31	39.72	3.59
10	1.0	MAF IV	19.36	15.84	13.21	39.67	4.04
11	1.35						
12	1.0						
13	1.36						
14	.97						

U^{234}/U^{238} ratio from sample 5 above calculated:

Ratio in activity units = 1.0 multiply activity units by half lives to obtain mass units.

$$1.0 \times \frac{2.5 \times 10^5}{4.5 \times 10^9} = .000054 \text{ (See Tables 1 and 2)}$$

This is higher than maximum equilibrium value at .000037 for approx. 100 million years.

Pb^{206}/U^{238} ratio from sample TR627 above calculated:

$$\frac{Pb^{206}}{Pb^{204}} \times \frac{Pb^{204}}{U^{238}} = 18.67 \times \frac{1}{22.18}$$

$\frac{18.67}{22.18} = .84$. (See equilibrium tables, Table 1 and Table 2)

Theoretical age over 5,000 million years. Minimum of all samples.

Pb^{207}/Pb^{206} ratio from sample MAF I above calculated: $\frac{Pb^{207}/Pb^{204}}{Pb^{206}/Pb^{204}}$

$15.81/19.36 = 0.81$

Theoretical age over 3,000 million years.

Pb^{208}/Th^{232} ratio from sample TR230 above calculated:

$$= \frac{Pb^{208}}{Pb^{204}} \times \frac{Pb^{204}}{U^{238}} \times \frac{U^{238}}{Th^{232}}$$

$$= \frac{39.42}{17.87} \times 4.26 = 0.52 \text{ (See Table 2)}$$

Using approx. Thorium age formula age
$$= 2.01 \times 10^{10} \times (Pb^{208}/Th^{232})$$
$$= 2.01 \times 10^{10} \times .52 = 10,500 \text{ million years.}$$

Table 3. Data are presented here from References 4 and 5. These calculations show that the radioactive materials in the U-238 series are in disequilibrium. Since these are known to be recent volcanic deposits, it is quite evident that samples may be contaminated with daughter elements from the very start and that the "ages" calculated from such ratios are open to serious question. Thus from these recent volcanic deposits one might variously calculate "ages" of anywhere from 100 million to 10,500 million years!

Values of Pb^{207} are also given and this provides the facility to obtain a theoretical concordant age, by the use of $Pb^{207/206}$ ratios. These are expected to be something like 0.05 for young rock, but to reach unity for rocks 3,000 million years old (see Table 3). In this case the values in the samples are all above 0.8, which confirms the conclusion: the ratios of the minerals are not those developed from the parent in the rock, but are the ratios of the minerals in the mantle of the earth.

Concordant Ages Misleading

Derivation of concordant ages is usually thought to be a confirmation of the reliability of the ages obtained for the host rock. But as it has been shown that the ratios are carried over from the mantle, it will be understood that instead of confirming the ages of the rocks, concordant ages provide a powerful confirmation that ratios are carried over from the mantle. Where samples are taken from common sources, the ratios of all the isotopes will of course give concordant theoretical ages.

A further theoretical age can be obtained for these young rocks with the thorium ratio, i.e., Pb^{208}/Th^{232} (see Table 3). This gives an age of a mere 10,500 million years!

The same facts are derived from attempts to date rocks by the potassium-argon method. Research in this field has been carried out in Hawaii on volcanic rocks, and a number of comments are made about what are called "old age anomalies" caused by "excess argon." It is reported that many of the samples from the Hawaiian Islands contain excess radiogenic argon, and that the ages for rocks containing them "are apparent only, and not derived from potassium *in situ*. Radiogenic argon was incorporated either during primary crystal growth, or during secondary crystallization."[6]

G. H. Curtis writing on the same problem says:

> On theoretical grounds one might expect to find many more cases of the presence of noticeable amounts of Ar^{40} in igneous rocks than so far have been detected. Magmas formed at depths of 50 to 100 kilometers are under sufficient confirming pressures to keep significant quantities of old radiogenic argon in solution.... Argon that has been formed from K^{40} decay deep within the earth. Crystals growing in this environment should incorporate some of this argon into their latices even though argon is inert.[7]

In the case of previously calculated ages, where the real ages were unknown, though presumed to be old, these anomalies apparently were not noticed. But in the case of rocks which were known to be young, it was very obvious that the ages calculated had no relationship to the true ages.

An article by P. M. Hurley[8] is important as it is still used as an argument favoring great ages for earth deposits. The paper deals with dating by radioactivity in the usual manner but the whole conception of time clocks is based upon the assumption that the parent radioactive element enters the sample rocks alone—that it is not accompanied by any of the decay elements acquired in the mantle.

Recent research upon young rocks of known ages challenges this assumption. Isotopic ratios indicated that even "young" volcanic deposits are at an advanced stage of decay, giving theoretical "ages" of thousands of millions of years (Table 3). This refutes the basic assumption of Hurley and means that the dates are not just marginally wrong, but wrong *en toto*.

Conclusion

The conclusion which can be drawn from these facts, which applies equally to dating of all mineral bearing rocks, is that calculated ages give no indication whatever of the age of the host rocks. In cases where calculated ages are millions of years, the rocks could be quite young.

Furthermore, these ages have no relationship to the age of the earth, because of course, the various ages computed have varied so widely. Consequently ratios of parent and daughter elements are merely ratios, and their use as a base for projecting "ages" of the rocks, or of the earth itself, is highly questionable and fraught with many assumptions that cannot be checked.

This conclusion would fit the concept of a young earth and a recent creation as deduced from the Bible.*

---

*EDITOR'S NOTE: The reader will find that a whole series of articles dealing with flaws in radioactive dating assumptions has been published in previous issues of *Creation Research Society Quarterlies*. D. O. Acrey dealt with basic inconsistencies and unknowns in various radioactive methods [1(3):7-9, Jan. 1965]. Problems in radiocarbon C^{14} dating have been analyzed by several authors: Harry V. Wiant, Jr. [2(4):31, Jan. 1966], Robert Wood [2(4):24-27, Jan. 1966], Harold Armstrong [2(4):28-30, Jan. 1966], R. H. Brown [5(2):65-68, Sept. 1968], and two articles by Robert L. Whitelaw [7(1):56-71, 83, June 1970 and 5(2):78-32]. In these last two articles, Robert Whitelaw establishes that radiocarbon studies actually confirm a Bible-based chronology rather than negating it. Melvin A. Cook has shown that the rate of formation of C^{14}

REFERENCES

1. Brian Mason, 1958. Principles of geochemistry. Wiley & Sons, Ltd., New York, p. 33.
2. George Gamow, 1959. Biography of the earth. Macmillan & Co., Ltd., London, p. 112.
3. Ibid., p. 114.
4. V. V. Cherdyntsev, G. I. Kislitsina, and V. L. Zverev, 1967. Isotopic composition of uranium and thorium in rocks and products of active volcanism. Geological Institute. Academy of Sciences. U.S.S.R. Earth Science Section. 172:178.
5. V. M. Oversby, and P. W. Gast, 1968. Lead isotope compositions and uranium decay series disequilibrium recent volcanic rocks. Earth and Planetary Science Letters (5). North Holland Publishing Co., Amsterdam, p. 199.
6. J. G. Funkhouser, I. L. Barnes, and J. J. Naughton, 1966. Problems of dating volcanic rocks by the potassium-argon method. Bull. Volcan., 29:709.
7. G. H. Curtis, 1966. The problem of contamination in obtaining accurate dates of young geologic rocks. Springer Verlag, Berlin, p. 155.
8. P. M. Hurley, 1949. Radioactivity and time, *Scientific American,* August.

---

is significantly greater than the rate of its decay—a disequilibrium which argues for a recent creation and a collapsed time-scale [5(2):69-77, Sept. 1968 and 7(1):53-56, June 1970]. Gross uncertainities and problems with the potassium-argon dating methods have been demonstrated by Robert L. Whitelaw [5(2): 78-83, Sept. 1968, and 6(1):71-73, June 1969]. Diligent study on the part of these and other creationists has produced much ammunition against the evolutionary time-scale which so many people believe to be factual or unassailable. Thus the present paper by Sidney P. Clementson becomes an important treatise demonstrating that radioactive "dates" bear no relationship to the ages of rocks which are known to be quite young. Readers will find that certain back volumes of C.R.S. *Quarterlies* may be purchased from the Membership Secretary—Prof. Wilbert Rusch, Sr., 2717 Cranbrook Rd., Ann Arbor, Michigan 48104.

XXII

THE EMPIRE MOUNTAINS — A THRUST FAULT?

CLIFFORD L. BURDICK* and HAROLD SLUSHER**

Introduction

The Empire Mountains occupy about thirty square miles in southeastern Pima County, Arizona, and consist of two parallel ridges trending north-northeast. They are connected with the Santa Rita Mountains to the west by low rolling foothills and are separated from the Whetstone Mountains to the east by the broad floor of Cienega Wash Valley.

Dr. F. W. Galbraith[1] gives the following description of the Empire Mountains:

> The Empire Mountains are made up of marine limestone, shale, and quartzite, of Cambrian, Devonian, Mississippian, Pennsylvanian, and Permian age, aggregating approximately 5,700 feet in thickness, and a series of Cretaceous (?) continental clastic deposits possibly 18,000 feet in thickness. The sedimentary rocks are intruded by stock-like bodies of quartz-monzonite and granodiorite and by dikes ranging in composition from rhyolite to basalt.
>
> The range has two structural parts—an underlying block of Cretaceous (?) rocks, and an overthrust block of Paleozoic and cretaceous (?) rocks which is divided into four segments by northwesterly striking tearfaults. The thrust fault is exposed along the western edge of the mountains and dips to the east at a low

---

*Clifford L. Burdick, Ph.D., is a consulting geologist of Tucson, Arizona.

**Harold Slusher is assistant professor of geophysics, University of Texas at El Paso.

Note: The authors wish to express appreciation to the Creation Research Society for a grant made in partial support of the research presented in this report.

angle. Within the overthrust block there are at least three separate imbricate thrust sheets. Domes, anticlines, and overturned folds have been formed in the Paleozoic rocks.

The central part of the Empire Mountains is occupied by the Sycamore quartz-monzonite which extends for about two miles along the trend of the range as a roughly elliptical body less than one mile wide. The quartz-monzonite is light gray and medium to coarse grained.

The Empire Mountains are divided into two structural parts, a basement block of Cretaceous rocks, in part folded into a series of broad anticlines and synclines with east-west axes, and in part dipping steeply to the east; and an overthrust block of Paleozoic strata which dip eastward. East-west and north-south faults have added to the structural complexity of the range.

Small bodies of granodiorite, rhyolite-porphyry are exposed near the Sycamore stock and small dikes of aplite, syenite, trachyte, rhyolite, diorite, andesite, and basalt occur throughout the Empire Mountains.

The purpose of the present investigation was to verify or reject the Empire overthrust hypothesis as mapped (Figure 1). This particular area was selected because the "thrust-plane" contact is especially visible in the Empire Mountains, and can be subjected to physical analysis contrasting structural interpretation with fossil evidences.

The method used in this study was that of comparing known small overthrusts in terms of amount of brecciation, gouging, slickensides, and other mechanical features proving rock movement, with the Empire "thrust" fault where rock containing fossils from the Permian clearly overlies rock having typically Cretaceous fossils.

Analysis of Known Thrust Faults

(1) *Known Thrust Fault in Santa Rita Mountains*

On the west side of the Santa Rita Mountains, in the Montosa Canyon area, Santa Cruz County, Arizona, occurs a large granite intrusive, or so-called "pluton." South of this granitic structure the Permian limestone blocks tilt away from the granite at angles be-

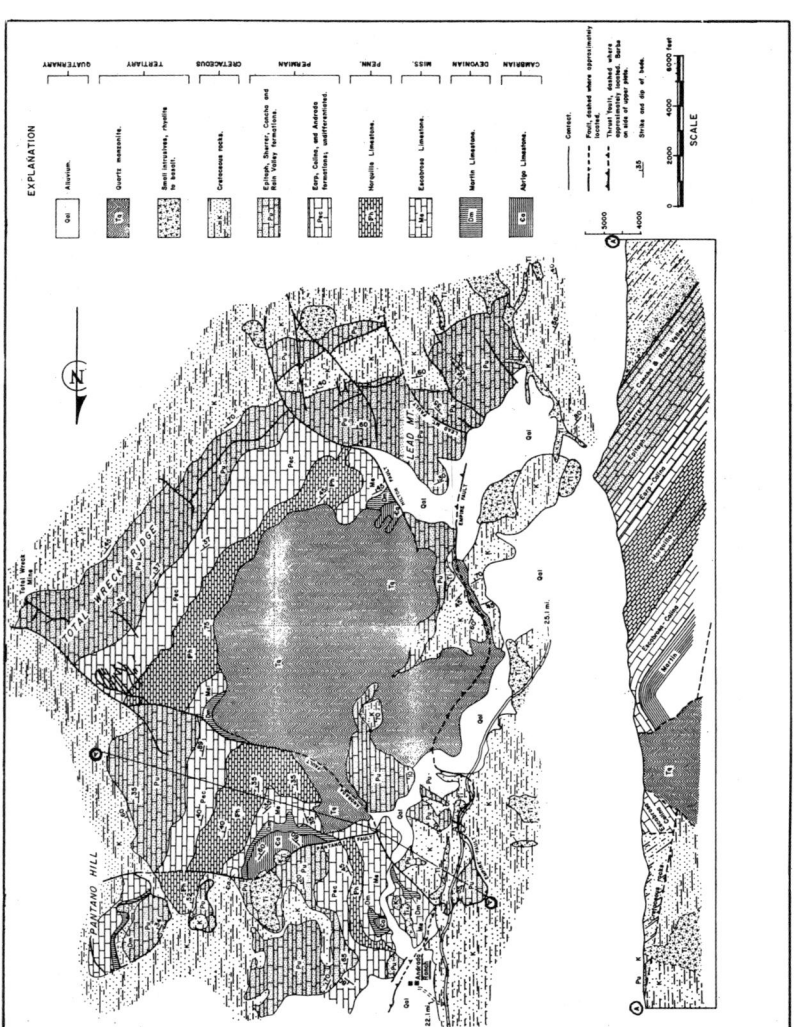

Figure 1. Generalized geologic map and cross section of the Empire Mountains, Arizona. Note location of the Andrada Ranch near the left edge of the general geologic map. The "thrust-plane" contact discussed in this paper is located at the left edge of the cross section (A to A'), where Permian (Pu) rock is found overlying Cretaceous (K) rock.

tween ten and twenty-five degrees. These blocks rest on igneous rock.

A graduate student at the University of Arizona wrote a thesis on that area, and has indicated in personal conversation that the limestone blocks had been thrust about half a mile. The blocks themselves probably average half a mile in length.

As proof of his contention, the graduate student designated a gouge layer about three feet thick composed of ground up rock powder separating the underlying igneous layer from the overlying thrust block. The authors have studied this evidence and detected indications that there was a drag of one block over the other. We feel that he proved his case for thrust-faulting in that particular instance.

(2) *Known Thrust Faults in Tortolita Mountains*

The senior author made a study of this range when preparing a thesis for the University of Arizona. The lithological type is granodiorite, diorite, monzonite, and granite. Most of the range has been subjected to regional metamorphism, forming a granite gneiss. On the north side of the mountains, where compression formed mica schist, some blocks of rhyolite were thrust southward over the underlying andesite. There is no fossil evidence here for thrusting, but very strong mechanical indication.

Between the andesite and the rhyolitic cap rock occurs a layer (from fifteen to twenty feet thick) of tectonic breccia—crushed and ground pieces of rock fragments. One notably large piece of rock, a boulder, shows marked fluting or "slickensides" much like the striae or scratches caused by glaciers (Figure 2).

Problem of Empire "Thrust Fault"

The geologic map (Figure 1) shows the outcrop of the fault plane along the western edge of the Empire Mountains, visible for about four miles. In only one or two places, however, can the contact between the Permian (Paleozoic) and the Cretaceous (Mesozoic) be seen clearly. Accompanying photographs show the contact along the wash just south of the Andrada Ranch. Here the dark,

Figure 2. A thrust block in Tortolita Mountains, Pima and Pinal Counties, Arizona. This detached rock was along the thrust plane. It shows the "slickensides grooves" which point toward previous tectonic activity. This is a close-up, showing a section about 10 by 10 feet.

blue-gray, Permian limestone caps the underlying Cretaceous (Figures 3, 4, 5, and 6).

The lithology of the Cretaceous varies from place to place, but at this point along the wash the Cretaceous has been metamorphosed. On the extreme left side of the geologic map and cross section intrusive igneous rock is shown in direct contact with the

Figure 3. Overall view of "overthrust" (near "A" in cross section in Figure 1). This picture shows the north end of the Empire Mountains looking eastward. Most of the mountain is Paleozoic (Permian). The center of the picture— light part along the wash—is the locale of the "overthrust" depicted in more detail in Figures 4, 5, and 6.

Cretaceous. This caused a "contact metamorphosis," which bleached and marbleized the limestone. Presumably then, the presence of hot intrusive igneous rock converted Cretaceous strata to a light buff colored marbleized limestone. Further south this white marble is being quarried.

Metamorphic rock is usually considered to be older than rock which has not been so altered. Since metamorphism is a more advanced stage of petrogenesis, it should normally be considered older than unaltered rock. Oddly enough, the Permian capping rock

Figure 4. "Thrust-plane" contact, Empire Mountains. A closer view of the supposed "thrust-plane" is seen above Dr. Hamara and his son. The line of "thrust," which is supposed to have traveled to the left (west) is plainly visible here.

(which is supposed to be much older) overlies the Cretaceous metamorphic limestone. Although it is slightly fractured, the Permian cap rock is not metamorphosed. From these data one can reasonably infer that the metamorphosed Cretaceous rocks beneath are indeed older than the Permian capping rock!

Other Physical Evidence Considered

But are there other lines of physical evidence to the contrary which would support the validity of the thrust idea at this Empire Mountain site? If so, one should find tectonic breccia, ground rock

Figure 5. "Thrust-plane" contact, Empire Mountains. This close-up of the supposed "thrust contact" shows the darker Permian limestone above the Cretaceous marble. Figure of young Deter Hamara gives size perspective.

powder, mylonite, gouge layers, slickensides, or striae as noted previously in references to the two known thrust fault areas.

The authors have examined the exposure of the fault contact carefully and no such evidence was located. The buff-colored bed rock had been eroded so that an angular unconformity exists between the two formations. But the capping Permian rock fits into the deep grooves eroded in the Cretaceous like a glove on a hand, or like material poured into a mold (Figures 4, 5, 6, and 7).

If the Permian cap rock had been thrust over the Cretaceous (as uniformitarian geologists assert), all sharp projections would have been planed off because they would have been directly in the line of thrust from the west! The contact appears, rather, to be a purely depositional one and would be difficult to explain otherwise.

Figure 6. "Thrust-plane" contact, Empire Mountains. Another view of the supposed "thrust contact" shows how the two layers fit nicely against each other without the usual evidences of thrust faulting. Roy Kingman is seen here.

The Permian above is apparently younger than the underlying Cretaceous material—the fossils and uniformitarian theory notwithstanding to the contrary!

Rocks Carefully Classified

With the help of Doctor Oma Hamara of the University of Arizona, and his two sons, much time has been spent verifying the classification of the "thrust block" in the Empire Mountains as Permian. We were unable to find any very large fossils, nor any complete or perfect ones, but we did find parts of brachiopods which should definitely belong to the Paleozoic Era. Fragments of coiled gastropods showed up plainly, but we were unable to name any genus.

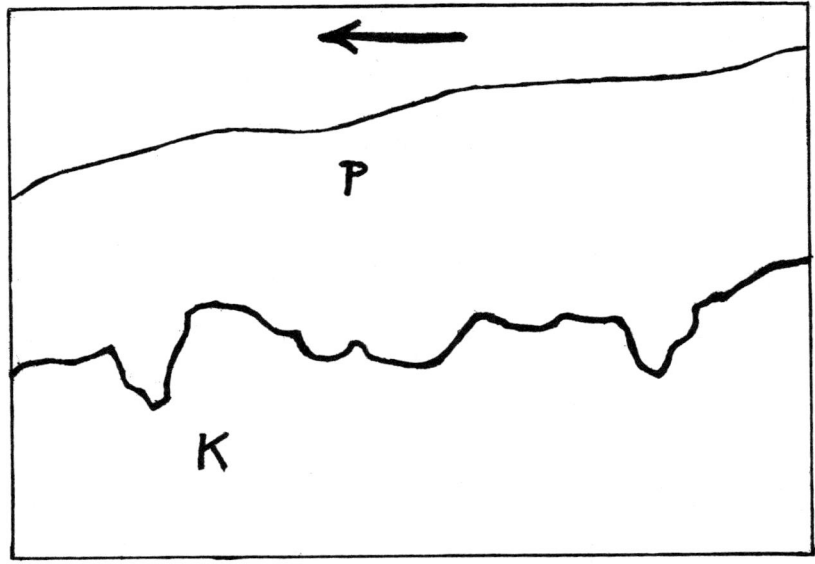

Figure 7. Cross-section of assumed Empire Mountain overthrust. This drawing of the contact shows the jagged fit between the two layers. Arrow indicates the direction that the thrust is supposed to have taken. One may wonder how the overlying Permian limestone could have been thrust over the Cretaceous without planing off the rough edges and grinding rock powder! (P—Permian blue limestone; K—Cretaceous formation, in part buff colored marble.)

We did find some beautiful specimens of tiny horn corals, perhaps too small to identify for sure but they did resemble the *Lophophyllidium,* which are typically Pennsylvanian or Permian. Some horn type corals belong to earlier periods of the Paleozoic, such as Devonian and Mississippian, but many types overlap from one period to another.

We were able to find many pieces of crinoinal stems, belonging to the attached type of Echinoderms, having a water-vascular system. These are all Paleozoic, although they could not be placed in any particular period. We found nothing that could have been classified as later than Paleozoic or Permian.

This Permian "thrust block" has a very dark gray color, indicating a large amount of organic material was buried with the fossils. We have no reason to doubt the classification of the various formations of the Empire Mountains. The only point at issue is whether there was a thrust, whether an "older" and lower stratum of rock of the Permian was raised up and thrust over the "younger" Cretaceous.

Are we to trust the evolutionary build-up of the fossils, or say that the Permian limestone was laid down later and on top of the Cretaceous? All the physical evidence would indicate the latter conclusion.

Discussion

In the past, stratigraphers have been inclined to correlate strata and formations primarily on the basis of the fossil evidence—as if that were an all-important criterion. In some instances physical evidence was ignored.

As an illustration of the supreme confidence some scientists have placed in the evolutionary order of fossils, Professor Henry A. Nicholson[2] flatly declared:

> It may be said that in any case where there should appear to be a clear and decisive discordance between the physical and the paleontological (fossil) evidence as in the age of a given series of beds, it is the former that is to be distrusted rather than the latter.

A time has arrived, however, when the physical evidence can no longer be overlooked, even if it cuts across lines of popular theory.

Validity of evolutionary geology rests upon the concept of invariableness in the fossil order. There are many places on earth, however, where fossils do not occur in the order predicted by the evolution theory. To save the theory in face of such evidence, giant overthrusts (thousands of square miles of sedimentary strata) have been postulated—often without proper regard to the physical improbability of such tectonic activity.

Sir Archibald Geike was a leading British geologist and authority on the Alps. Nappes and overthrusts had been postulated to account for the inverted order of the fossils, but Geike[3] candidly commented:

The strata could scarcely be supposed to have been really inverted, save for the evidence as to their true order of succession supplied by their enclosed fossils. . . . Portions of Carboniferous strata appear as if regularly interbedded among Jurassic rocks, and indeed could not be separated, save after a study of their enclosed organic remains.

This quotation illustrates the "reasoning in a circle" that has been prevalent from Geike's day to the present. Biology in many instances did not offer the positive proof required to substantiate the evolutionary hypothesis. Scientists looked to geology—to the order of the fossils in the strata—to furnish the essential evidence. When the strata showed a contrary order, however, they fell back upon the overthrust hypothesis to explain the embarrassing discrepancy; thus employing evolutionary concepts they hoped to demonstrate, to try actually to show the strata in the wrong order.

In this study we have not intended to present a blanket denial of all thrust faults. We have shown, however, that when such faults exist, they are accompanied with physical evidence of differential movement. In the specific case of the Empire Mountain range (where Permian rock lies atop Cretaceous) we have demonstrated the lack of any conclusive evidence for a thrust. The only conclusion we can reach from such data is that no thrust occurred. The area was once mapped as a thrust fault on paleontological evidence alone and physical data have evidently been disregarded.

The authors suggest that many such supposed "thrust faults" must be re-analyzed on the basis of physical evidence alone. The lesson seems clear enough that thrust faulting must be judged hereafter solely upon the physical criteria and aside from any evolutionary preconceptions.

REFERENCES

1. F. W. Galbraith, 1959. The Empire Mountains, Pima County, Arizona. Southern Arizona Guide Book, No. 2. Arizona Geological Society, Tucson, Arizona, p. 21f.
2. Henry Alleyne Nicholson, 1897. Ancient life history of the earth. D. Appleton and Co., New York, p. 40.
3. Sir Archibald Geike, 1903. Textbook of geology. Macmillan and Co., New York, p. 678.

XXIII

THE GLARUS OVERTHRUST

WALTER E. LAMMERTS*

Resumé of K. J. Hsu's Observations and Conclusions

K. J. Hsu[1] reported on his studies of the Glarus overthrust in 1969. He concluded that the overthrust has a dimension of thirty-five kilometers (or about twenty-one miles) in length by about five to six kilometers in thickness. It lies upon an Eocene formation and consists of Jurassic limestone at the base and Verrucano conglomerate above. The limestone above the fault line is classified as Malm, and below as probably Vanlangien (L and L-2 in Figure 1).

The overthrust took place in two phases at least. The earlier phase of main movement was related to the flowage of the Lochseitenkalk (limestone) within the thrust zone. The later phase of frictional sliding produced the thin film of fault gouge within the Lochseitenkalk.

The later movement was probably related to an uplift of the autochthonous (sediment deposited in place) massif, which caused the present ten degrees to twelve degrees northerly dip of the Glarus overthrust. If the pore pressure (in the rock) had remained abnormally high, the block would have to slide under its own weight. If the pore pressure had dropped to normal, then a push from behind would be necessary.

The earlier movement was related to a push from behind along a nearby horizontal thrust plane where the pore pressure was equal, or nearly equal to the overburden pressure.

---

*Walter E. Lammerts, Lammerts Hybridization Gardens, P. O. Box 496, Freedom, Calif. 95019

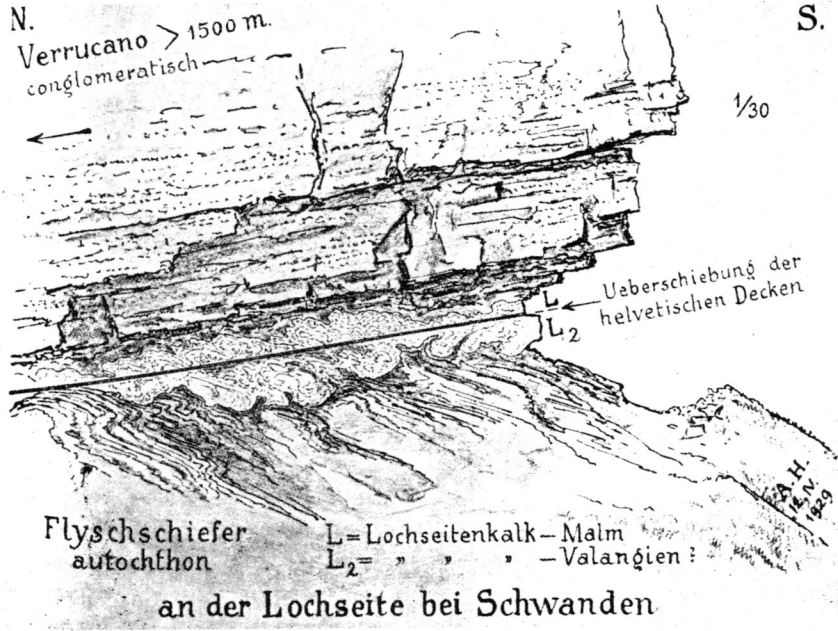

Figure 1. The thrust contact of the Glarus overthrust at Lochseite near Schwanden (Glarus), reproduced from Albert Heim, 1929, Naturforschende gesellschaft, Zurich, Viertel Jahrschrift, pp. 213-233.

The rate of the earlier displacement through the flowage of the Lochseitenkalk was estimated as ranging from .2 to 10 cm/year at a temperature of 300-400°C. at the base of the thrust, which is at about six kilometers of depth. The heat generated by overthrusting may have contributed to the steep geothermal gradient then prevailing in the Glarus region.

The rate of later displacement by frictional sliding was governed either by the rate of stress built up as a result of the push from behind by an advancing nappe, or by the rate of erosion of the toe which obstructed gravity sliding. In either case the displacement would be a jerky sliding resulting in a series of shallow earthquakes.

More precise study of strain rate, stress, and temperature, based upon experimental creep studies or tests of the Lochseitenkalk, are planned.

Critique of Earlier Studies

Hsu believes that earlier studies of overthrusting erred in that only the friction at the base was considered in estimating minimum resistance. Thus Smoluchowski[2] concluded that the friction factor alone would restrict maximum length of an overthrust to eight kilometers (about five miles). Oldham[3] suggested large overthrusts move like the crawl of a caterpillar which advances one part of its body at a time, and all parts in succession.

Hubbert and Rubey[4] substituted for the term "caterpillar crawl," the terminology "dislocation mechanism," which purportedly eliminated the cohesion strength in succession so that resistance to overthrusting was by friction only. This faulty analysis led them to greatly underestimate the shearing resistance at the base of overthrusts, and greatly overestimated their length and the ease of gravitational sliding along very gentle slopes. Hsu shows that their analysis is not applicable to those overthrusts whose movement is related to flowage of ductile materials within the thrust zone, and proposes a new treatment of the mechanism of such thrusts.

Hsu's Proposed Explanation

By a rather complicated mathematical analysis Hsu shows that brittle fracture depends on the initial shear strength or cohesive strength, and a variable friction term directly proportional to the effective normal stress. He maintains that Hubbert and Ruby erred in that they considered only the variable friction. Thrust faults as long as the Glarus cannot therefore be explained by their proposed mechanism.

Between the upper Verrucano and lower Eocene is the Lochseitenkalk, less than one meter thick. This smeared out limestone shows signs of flowage and is present practically everywhere as the lowest layer of the Glarus thrust (labeled L and L-2 in Figure 1). This Hsu considers as evidence that the upper thrust plate moved forward as the limestone *flowed*. There is in addition a fault gouge zone or a clay film, a few millimeters thick, present as a planar system within the limestone.

Now fault gouge has been produced experimentally when one block slid past another along a preexisting fracture surface as noted by Byerlee.[5] This gouge is then considered as evidence that the thrust later moved along a cohesionless plane by frictional sliding *after* the limestone had fractured with a loss of cohesion.

The main thrust was followed by uplift of the autochthonous massifs, which resulted in arching of the thrust plane and produced its present northerly dip of ten to twelve degrees. During the main phase the thrust plane was more nearly horizontal, and northerly dip not more than five degrees. Since the plane was originally dipping only about five degrees, the main movement could not have been due to gravity sliding. A push from behind must be assumed. Because of obstructions in front of such a thrust producing the so-called toe effect, the minimum angle would have to be at least 11.6 degrees and more probably twenty degrees to cause gravity sliding.

The rocks of the Glarus are re-crystallized in part. Sericite and chlorite are present in the Verrucano formation. But there is no evidence of amphibolite facies metamorphism which starts at 540°C. and two Kilobars pressure at K-1. Hence the average temperature at time of deformation and flow of the limestone could not have been more than 500°C.

A temperature of 400°C. seems to be higher than expected judging from the largely unmetamorphosed nature of the Flysch (Eocene) under the thrust. In the later phase of frictional sliding resulting in the gouge, a "stick-slip" jerky movement occurred. The stress built up and was then relieved by small slips such as those now causing earthquakes along the San Andreas fault.

Observations June, 1970

I left for Schwanden, Switzerland, by train from Zurich at 9:20 A.M. June 3, 1970. It was surprising how much open land and forests still remain. We arrived at 1:30, and after checking in at the Adler Hotel, immediately went up the Sernf River road, and after one wrong turn, soon found the little steps described by Dr. Hsu. A rather well worn pathway led to the outcrop shown in Figure 1. Unfortunately it was cloudy, so pictures could not be taken.

The following day was clearer so some pictures of the contact line were quite clear cut. The following notes are most pertinent:

(1) The broken up clay at the contact line separating L and L-2 varies from one-eighth to one inch in thickness and is mostly one-eighth to one-quarter inch thick. This layer is almost horizontal and a very straight line (Figure 2).

(2) The limestone is about six inches thick above and six to seven inches thick below the broken up clay layer.

(3) The limestone both above and below the contact is mostly very hard, though some is quite soft and does not seem metamorphosed.

Figure 2. Almost straight line of contact L and L2.

(4) The contact of the limestone with the Verrucano above is very irregular.

(5) Also the contact with the Eocene below is even more irregular.

(6) The Eocene is very hard and a type of slate formation.

(7) Toward the north end of the exposure the contact line separating L and L-2 is lying directly on the Eocene rock in places with very little of the L-2 part below it anywhere.

(8) Soft areas like the gouge layer extend down as streaks for about 4 inches into the lower Jurassic (L-2) (Figure 3).

One of the most difficult facts as regards accepting Hsu's concept of flowage of the limestone, followed by a secondary movement of frictional sliding after its fracture between L and L-2, is that the gouge layer is mostly clay instead of ground up limestone particles. If the gouge layer is actually the result of the grinding action of

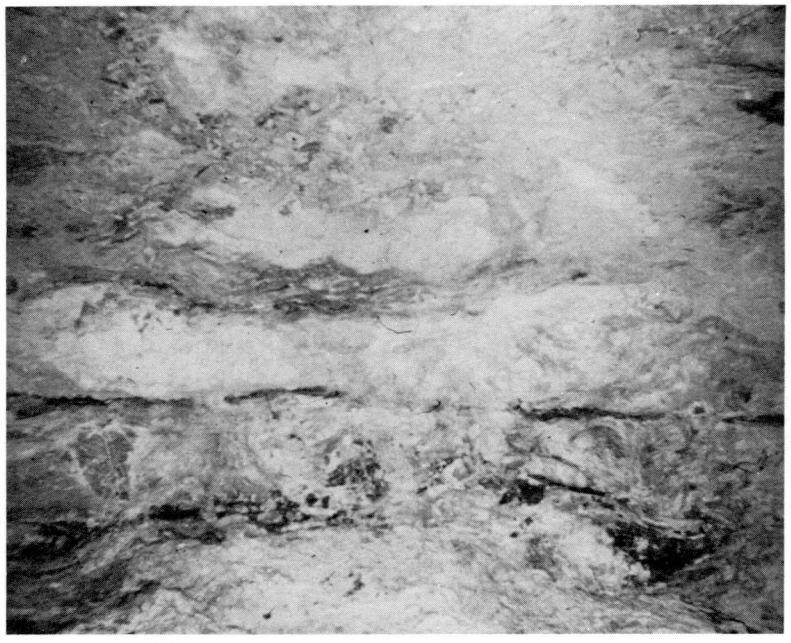

Figure 3. Shows black streaks of clay particles in L2.

the upper layer L sliding over the lower layer L-2, it would seem that a chalky, powdery type of layer would be formed. Chemical tests of this clay layer show that only about five to ten percent of it is $CaCO_3$, the rest remaining insoluble in hydrochloric acid.

Even more important is the present order of the formations. In order to have the Verrucano, a Permian formation, on top of the Jurassic, Hsu postulates a recumbent fold of these formations, or overturning of them. They were then according to his concept thrust over the Eocene by the flow type of mechanism he postulates.

Now the usual order of these formations is of course Permian, Jurassic, and then much later the Eocene. An assumed overturning would have to occur after the Eocene above the Permian and Jurassic had been eroded away in the area they *were located* before the overthrusting, but *not in the present location at the overthrust*.

The fact that the Eocene rock is very hard and slaty makes it difficult to see how this differential localized erosion could have occurred. Besides the contact line of the Jurassic with the Eocene below is very irregular. Hsu's flow concept would allow for this but as noted above some of the limestone is quite soft and does not seem to have flowed. Though there is no question as to the fact of metamorphosis it seems strange this was not complete if heated to 300-400°C. long enough to make it flow for over twenty-one miles.

Also as indicated the contact of the limestone with the Verrucano now above it is also very irregular. This indicates that considerable erosion of the Verrucano took place before the Jurassic was deposited on it. Though in itself not conflicting with the concept of overturning and then thrusting over the Eocene, this evidence of large-scale erosion would seem to fit in much better with a flood geology interpretation.

Flood Geology Interpretation

If one looks at this famous exposure of wrong order rock formations without any bias in favor of the authenticity of the geologic time table, a much simpler explanation of it can be given in terms of flood geology concepts. According to this view point the various formations have no time value in the sense of millions or even thousands of years of time, but were all deposited rather rapidly during or relatively soon after the worldwide flood action.

The Eocene formation at the bottom of L-2 was deposited, hardened or rather consolidated to some extent and then eroded into its present irregular surface. Then the Jurassic L-2 layer of almost pure limestone was deposited but not in a completely uniform manner, the amount being greater in the south end than toward the north end.

After this a change of current and a quieter deposition period led to the formation of the one-eighth to one inch deposit of mostly clay particles, though some limestone particles were still in the water. That the transition was an uneven one may be supported by the fact that the streaks of black clay particles extend down into the L-2 layer of limestone.

This was followed by a renewed current carrying limestone particles resulting in the deposition of the Jurassic L layer above the clay. No erosion took place between the deposition of L-2, the clay layer, and L, hence these layers form an almost straight line. Following the deposition of L, considerable erosion took place causing the irregular surface. This erosion was followed by a long period of deposition from a different source, thus causing the very thick Permian or Verrucano conglomerate to be formed.

Most of the deposits have been more or less metamorphosed into partly crystalline rock. This is particularly true of the Jurassic formation and it may well be, as Hsu suggests, that they were heated to a temperature of 300-400°C. and flowed into their present position. The remarkable continuity of the Jurassic into the Verrucano above and Eocene below would then be accounted for.

As may be seen by a careful study of Figure 2 these contacts are no longer depositional but the rock is actually so intimately united that it is difficult to obtain samples of one without some of the other. (Note irregular black Eocene in very close contact with the Jurassic at bottom of Figure 2.) The Eocene formation was also much hardened and, as Figure 1 shows, is now inclined and much distorted. The Verrucano above is also a very hard rock forma-mation, though relatively unaltered as compared to the Jurassic and Eocene.

The flow postulated by Hsu could hardly have resulted in a movement of over twenty-one miles since some of the Jurassic limestone has not been metamorphosed. This part is a rather loosely compacted material which can be broken off and pulverized with one's fingers. It is mostly found in the lower or L-2 layer. Both it and the crystalline metamorphic parts consist of almost pure limestone dissolving rapidly in hydrochloric acid. About one percent or even less consists of magnesium carbonate since part of it dissolves in hot hydrochloric acid, and the rest is made up of dark almost black particles and some undetermined mineral.

It is interesting to note that the upper or L layer contains no black streaks of clay particles, and is a remarkably pure limestone, dissolving completely in hydrochloric acid. Microscopic study of both L and L-2 particles indicated that they are of inorganic origin. No evidence of any even minute fossils was found.

Figure 4. Sample from upper surface of thrust plane. Jurassic L just above the layer of clay. Some of the limestone was quite soft. (Scale is in inches.) inches.)

The flow mechanism suggested by Hsu could hardly apply to such large-scale wrong-order formations as the so-called Lewis overthrust. As described by Burdick[6] the contact line shows no evidence of any gouge layer, breccia, or striation. Also the Altyn limestone above, unlike the Jurassic of the Glarus overthrust, shows no evidence of flowing and resultant metamorphosis. It is a relatively soft, sandy dolomite of light buff color.

As regards the later phase of movement, there is no question as to its occurrence leading to the thrust plane now visible. Any stress built up would be most readily relieved at this comparatively thin weak layer of clay. It is, however, difficult to see how this movement *caused* the clay layer as postulated by Hsu since movement

Figure 5. Sample from lower surface of thrust plane. L 2 surface just below the layer of clay. Some of the limestone was quite soft. (Scale is in inches.)

of two surfaces of limestone against each other would result in a gouge of limestone particles.

Clay or kaolin results from the breakdown of feldspar. As mentioned above only five to ten percent of this layer is calcium carbonate. Furthermore the upper L and lower L-2 contact surfaces of the very hard Jurassic with this clay layer are very glossy, black, and uneven. Not the slighest trace of even a striation can be seen (Figures 4 and 5).

Undoubtedly many small movements each accompanied by an earthquake have occurred. This resulted in the highly polished look of both surfaces as they moved along the comparatively soft black clay layer separating them. These "stickslip" jerky movements are the same as those now occurring along the famous San Andreas fault.

As shown by Howe[7] these result in very bad breakage and gouging when hard surfaces slide against each other, but relatively little damage if one surface is soft. Certainly phenomena such as these could never result in any major twenty-one mile movement such as is postulated at the Glarus overthrust. This part of Hsu's able analysis is undoubtedly incorrect.

Conclusions

In conclusion the following has been established:

(1) The Glarus "overthrust" is a complex one in which the formations instead of being in their correct order according to the commonly accepted geologic time table (i.e., Permian, Jurassic, Eocene) are actually Eocene, Jurassic, Permian.

(2) In order to explain this order, Hsu postulates a recumbent fold placing the Jurassic under the Permian followed by a twenty-one mile thrust over the Eocene formation.

(3) This thrust resulted from a push from behind, heating the Jurassic rocks to 300-400°C. so that they flowed into their present position.

(4) A secondary series of small movements is also postulated resulting in the gouge layer of clay from one-fourth to one inch thick.

(5) As opposed to Hsu's conclusions it is shown that the so-called gouge layer is only five to ten percent limestone, the rest being clay particles. Also the surfaces of both L and L-2 in contact with this clay layer are shiny and black, show no striations, and even their irregularities have not been worn away.

(6) The small "stick-slip" movements resulting from stress were thus rather easily made against the relatively soft clay layer.

(7) Undoubtedly a major movement such as postulated by Hsu also occurred which initiated the almost level fault line. The stress may very well have heated this rock to 300-400°C., so that it flowed into its present position physically united with the uneven Verrucano or Permian above and irregular Eocene surface below.

(8) The evidence for a *flow* of twenty-one miles is lacking since only the major part of the Jurassic limestone was metamorphosed into its present crystalline structure. Much of the limestone is quite soft and shows no evidence of metamorphoses and movement.

(9) From the view point of a worldwide flood and later resultant settling stresses there is no need to postulate a flow of twenty-one miles. It is more likely that this limestone flowed only as far as necessary to relieve stress.

(10) An outline is given as to how these deposits may have been laid down in their present order, and later subjected to pressures and vulcanism resulting in their partial metamorphoses.

(11) It is shown that the flow type of mechanism postulated by Hsu will not explain such vast wrong-order formations as the so-called Lewis overthrust since no large scale flow type of metamorphosis is found in the Altyn limestone lying immediately above the Cretaceous shales.

REFERENCES

1. K. J. Hsu, 1969. A preliminary analysis of the statics and kinetics of the Glarus overthrust. *Ecologae Geologicae Helvetiae,* 62:143-154.

2. M. S. Smoluchowski, 1909. Some remarks on the mechanics of overthrusting, *Geological Magazine,* 6:204-205.

3. R. D. Oldham, 1921. Know your faults. *Geological Society of London Quarter Journal,* 54:LXXVII-XCII.

4. M. K. Hubbert, and W. W. Rubey, 1959. Role of fluid pressure in me-

chanics of overthrust faulting, *Geological Society of America Bulletin*, 70: 115-166.

5. J. D. Byerlee, 1967. Frictional characteristics of granite under high confining pressure, *Journal of Geophysical Research*, 72:3939-3953.

6. C. L. Burdick, 1969. The Lewis overthrust, *Creation Research Society Quarterly*, 6:106-111.

7. G. F. Howe, 1972. Overthrust evidence as observed at faults caused by the San Fernando earthquake, *Creation Research Society Quarterly*, 8 (4): 256-260. March.

XXIV

SOME ASTRONOMICAL EVIDENCES FOR A YOUTHFUL SOLAR SYSTEM

HAROLD S. SLUSHER*

Introduction

Numerous arguments have centered on the age of the earth, the solar system, and the universe as a whole. Though the chronology of geological and astronomical events is based on many dubious assumptions and questionable ventures beyond the province of science, it is absolutely necessary for the evolutionists to try to establish a long chronology.

Most evolutionists believe that life began by a chance process in a shallow sea and that the world we see today came about by gradual and infinitesimal changes taking place over vast and almost limitless stretches of time. The evolutionist tries to eliminate problems which face his naturalistic scheme of origins by covering the whole issue with a veil of time.

Thus, long periods of time have become a tenet in the evolutionist's creed. For example, the physical appearance of rocks in the Franklin Mountains, El Paso, Texas, suggests the rapid deposition of sedimentary material and consequent movement of the rocks while in a somewhat unconsolidated or semi-plastic state. At one time a geophysicist of evolutionary faith viewed these rocks with me and agreed about the appearance of catastrophe. But he resisted this ultimate conclusion by pleading for long time and gradual process in their origin.

Also, time is fostered as a rationale for the missing links in the

---

*Harold Slusher, M.S., is assistant professor of geophysics at the University of Texas at El Paso.

evolutionary explanation of the fossils. While discussing the problem of missing links with an evolution-minded geologist, I asserted that the fossil links are still missing and probably were nonexistent. He reminded me that the links might have been present originally and then after subsequent erosion they are not to be found. I remarked that if the links could not be found, one could not know that they were present in the past. At this point an evolutionist places his faith in epochs of unknown time to solve his difficulties.

There are very basic difficulties and limits placed on working into the past. In the second law of thermodynamics, or law of entropy, physicists deal with the natural and continual tendency of the universe toward disorder. It is a study of deteriorative processes. The attempt to work backwards into the past where deteriorative processes have dominated is fraught with many insuperable obstacles. Entropy of the universe is increasing, chaos is gradually replacing order. One cannot measure backward to the beginning by studying the decay processes, as has been shown by authors of past articles in this publication.

One of my college professors once remarked that, even if most or nearly all mutations are harmful to the organism, during a vast period of time a few beneficial mutations would occur and these would produce the upward progress of the organism. He overlooked the effect of lethal mutations upon the organism in the meantime. Given enough time, the evolutionist believes that the improbable becomes probable.

Dr. Harold F. Blum,[1] however, points out that an increased time span for a biological system increases the probability of reaction equilibria being set up in the chain and does not increase the probability of improbable reaction products being formed. Time cannot supply what the evolutionist needs even if it existed in the quantities he demands.

Yet in spite of strong evidence to the contrary, many people feel that if the earth is very old, evolution will somehow or other be the answer to the question of the origin of the universe and life in it. Therefore it is still quite pertinent to ask if things are as old as evolutionists claim.

EVIDENCES FOR A YOUTHFUL SOLAR SYSTEM

Many telling attacks can be launched against the various methods of geochronology. Some of the very basic assumptions of these methods such as steady state existence of C-14 in the atmosphere, constancy of decay rates in the long radiological clocks, etc., seem to be erroneous. I will limit the present paper, however, to presenting several indicators which imply a rather short age for the solar system. In pointing these out, I will follow the thinking of the scheme which is the basis of any dating system, namely; the measurement of some physical quantity produced in the time associated with some event (Q), the determination of the rate at which this quantity is produced (R), and, consequently, the calculation of the time involved in the production of the quantity (T), and consequent dating of the past event, where:

$$T = \frac{Q}{R}$$

Meteoritic Dust Influx

The first of these indicators has to do with the influx of meteoric dust into the earth's atmosphere and finally down onto the earth's surface and into its oceans. This dust material is called micrometeorites since the particles are obviously very small. These particles are moving so slowly that they do not burn up with entry into the atmosphere and they settle very gradually to the ground.

The material may be collected in chemical trays, and then analyzed as to what is extraterrestrial. Only the mass of the magnetic meteoric material is used in the calculations, since stony meteoric matter cannot be clearly separated from terrestrial matter. Consequently, estimates of the influx of meteoric dust are very conservative since stony meteorites are considered far more abundant than iron meteorites.

Estimates of the influx range considerably with different investigators. The Swedish geophysicist, Petterson, estimates 14,300,000 tons of meteoric dust come onto the surface of the earth per year.[2] In five billion years there should be a layer of dust 54 feet in thickness on the earth if it were to lie undisturbed. This should, of course, put a tremendous amount of nickel (since it is a major constituent of meteorites) into the oceans.

Nickel, on the other hand, is actually a rare element in terrestrial rocks and continental sediments and is nearly nonexistent in ocean water and ocean sediments. This seems to indicate a very short age for oceans. Taking the amount of nickel in the ocean water and ocean sediments and using the rate at which nickel is being added to the water from meteoric material, the length of time of accumulation thus turns out to be *several thousand years* rather than a few billion years.

From the reports of the lunar landings the accumulation of dust on the surface of the moon is very small (not much more than one-eighth inch).[3] The moon moves through the same region of space that the earth does and consequently should have about the same influx of meteoric dust as the earth. N.A.S.A. scientists were worried that a lunar ship would sink down into the postulated huge amount of dust that should have accumulated on the surface in about 4.5 billion years of assumed time.

Also, in the "sea" areas, where the lunar ships landed, there should have accumulated more dust than elsewhere on the moon. Yet the amount of dust is amazingly small. What could have happened to all the dust?

Although more data and calculations are needed to substantiate this conclusion, from the absence of dust, we may deduce a short period of time for accumulation, and thus a young age for the moon. If the earth is about the same age as the moon (as the Scriptures assert and as some astronomers suggest), then the earth is also young.

Poynting-Robertson Effect

A second indicator of youth (low entropy state) is given by the Poynting-Robertson Effect. Solar radiation has an important influence on the orbits of small particles, which have a large ratio of surface area to mass. Several points of consideration are significant.

First, there is a simple outward force from the sun due to radia-

EVIDENCES FOR A YOUTHFUL SOLAR SYSTEM

tion pressure. For particles with diameters of a few thousand angstroms or less, this force may exceed the gravitational attraction of the sun and blow them out of the solar system.

Second, the solar radiation received by a particle is Doppler-shifted to cause an increase in radiation pressure if the particle is approaching the sun, and a decrease if it is receding; thus, changing elliptical orbits to circular ones.

Third, the angular momentum of an orbiting particle is progressively destroyed by the fact that it receives solar radiation, which has only a radial momentum from the sun, and re-radiates this energy with a forward momentum corresponding to its own motion about the sun. This produces a drag force on the particle causing it to spiral into the sun. This is called the Poynting-Robertson Effect.

The particle re-radiates energy it receives from the sun back into space as fast as it is received, thereby getting rid of momentum also. If it is radiating energy equally in all directions, this would not by itself alter either the direction or rate of its motion. After a loss of a millionth part (for example) of its mass, it would have lost a millionth part of its own momentum and the velocity of the remaining portion would be unaltered.

But during this time it would have gotten back the same amount of mass by radiation from the sun, so that its mass is the same as at the start, but its momentum is a millionth part less. Its orbital velocity will therefore be *decreased* by a millionth part. This effect is similar to that of the particle moving through a resistant medium. The orbit diminishes in radius and the particle moves into the sun along a very closely wound spiral.

Robertson found that a particle of rock (density 2.7) one centimeter in diameter started at the earth's distance would fall into the sun in 10 million years. In a time of 2 billion years any masses of rock less than six feet in diameter within the earth's orbit would be cast into the sun. This "sweeping up" process would get rid of anything less than three inches in diameter inside Jupiter's orbit, and anything less than one-tenth inch in diameter inside Neptune's orbit.

Yet significant quantities of meteoric matter are known to exist!

There are the particles grouped around the sun which reflect what is called the zodiacal light. A tremendous amount of matter is there! Although no attempt will be made here to determine a definite age for the solar system using this information, it is possible to deduce a much smaller age than the evolutionist demands, when one considers that there is much particulate matter still circulating. Such would not be true if the solar system was of great age!

Age of Comets Calculated

As comets travel around the sun, they are continually undergoing disintegration from gravitational and radiative effects of the sun and planets. This phenomenon may be taken as a third indication of young age of the solar system.

Comets have been observed to diminish in size and even to break up. Debris for meteor showers remains along their orbits. Comets are generally of two types: short-period and long-period. Certain astronomers believe that comets, and the planets, came into existence about the same time. If this is true, then the lifetime of a comet can be estimated and the age of the planets accordingly determined.

Some Russian astronomers estimate the maximum life of a short-period comet is 25,000 years. Lyttleton[4] estimates that no short-period comet can survive longer than approximately 10,000 years. Considering the "dynamical" effects of the planets in causing the long-period comets to be ejected from the solar system, Lyttleton estimates that only one in 10,000 could be left after 4.5 billion years. This does not take into account physical disruption of the comet which would further reduce this estimate.

Calculation of a short life for comets has led to a number of hypotheses to explain away the obvious corollary of a young solar system. These attempts have ranged all the way from ejections of comets from the planet Jupiter to comets coming from the galaxy outside the solar system. Certain astronomers have also suggested that there is something akin to a "deep-freeze" storage of comets outside the solar system toward the nearest star, which is continually replenishing the supply of comets to the solar system.

Numerous attempts have been made to avoid the notion of youth, but as yet there is no real substantiation for any of these suggestions. Had the age turned out rather large by this method, however, I assume that the evolutionists would have welcomed the results unquestioningly! Lyttleton makes the comment:

> In the whole age of this system, a comet with average period 100,000 years would make 4.5×10^4 returns to the sun, and if at each one of these it lost only $1/1000$ of its mass, through tail-formation and meteor stream production, the initial mass would have been more than 10^{19} times as great as the present mass—which at a minimum means several times the mass of the sun![5]

When one adopts a nautralistic explanation of origins, he is soon driven to incredible extremes!

Other Indicators of Youth

There are other indicators for a smaller age in general, such as the destruction of the spiral arms of the galaxies due to differential rotation. Objects in the galaxies rotate in Keplerian orbits where the velocity decreases outward from the center of the galaxy. This causes a winding up of the spiral arms in a short time (relatively speaking). It is believed by some that the magnetic field maintains the coherence of the arms. However, the strength of the field seems rather small. Also, there is the rapid break-up of the star clusters. The helium content of the atmosphere is yet another interesting sign pointing to young age of the earth. Helium content of the atmosphere, its exudation rate from the lithosphere, and other considerations indicate a maximum atmospheric age of around 10,000 to 100,000 years.[6]

These are a few of the signs pointing to a young age of the earth and the solar system. Much excellent work with regard to the age of the earth has been done already by Dr. Melvin A. Cook concerning the radiological "clocks." His work indicates that these clocks too may give very small ages for geological events when all external influencing factors are considered.

REFERENCES

1. Harold F. Blum, 1955. Time's arrow and evolution. Second Edition. Princeton University Press, Princeton, N.J.
2. H. Pettersson, 1960. Cosmic spherules and meteoric dust. *Scientific American*, 202:132. February.
3. El Paso *Herald-Post*, July 21, 1969.
4. R. A. Lyttleton, 1968. Mysteries of the solar system. Clarendon Press, Oxford, England, p. 110.
5. *Ibid.*, p. 147.
6. Melvin A. Cook, 1966. Prehistory and earth models. Max Parrish and Co., Ltd., London, p. 14.

XXV

CRITIQUE OF STELLAR EVOLUTION

George Mulfinger*

Today the following doctrines are taught almost universally as fact:

1. All astronomical bodies have condensed from clouds of primordial material such as hydrogen. (When this is considered in conjunction with alleged biological evolution processes, then plants, animals, and people are held to be nothing more or less than descendants of mere hydrogen gas.)

2. Such "creative" processes have been proceeding for billions of years and are still continuing today.

3. These processes are totally spontaneous and self-ordering, ruling out any need for a Creator.

4. Various types of stars such as red giants and white dwarfs are serially related, much as the larva, pupa, and adult stages of insect metamorphosis. One type is said to merge or evolve into another over millions or billions of years. The Creator is thus denied the prerogative of structuring variety or diversity into the original universe. Each star, it is claimed, started as an undifferentiated cloud and has passed inexorably through the prescribed stages.

Little spiritual perception is needed to appreciate that there is something amiss with the theory that human beings have evolved out of hydrogen gas by natural processes. Yet this is only one of the many problems, both scientific and scriptural, that must be reckoned with if the basic framework of stellar evolution is accepted. A number of these problems will be discussed in the course of this paper.

---

*George Mulfinger is a member of the Department of Physics, Bob Jones University, Greenville, South Carolina 29614.

Let us be aware of what is solid experimental evidence on the one hand, and what has been supplied by human imagination on the other. May we have the wisdom to remain firmly grounded on that which is true science.

Observation Lacking

Needless to say, no one has even watched a star traversing its "life cycle" from "birth" to "death." In fact Abell has likened our most extensive observations on an individual star to observing the aging process in a man, by studying him for only ten seconds out of his lifespan of threescore and ten.[1] The other 69 years, 364 days, 23 hours, 59 minutes, and 50 seconds would have to be inferred by guesswork.

Stuart Inglis, in his *Planets, Stars, and Galaxies,* readily admits, ". . . for any single star we cannot yet tell accurately its age, its past, and its future existence."[2] In all the heavens there is no star concerning which astronomers have detailed knowledge. Yet when they generalize about *all stars,* they appear quite certain. This is most difficult to understand. Even if far more were known, it would still behoove scientists to maintain an attitude of humility and caution. Not only are we restricted to *present* observations; we are severely limited by the fact that we can only study stars "skin deep" (we see only their surface), and we are forced to view them through interstellar material whose nature and quantity are only poorly understood.

Circular Reasoning

To one who delves into this realm in any depth, it soon becomes apparent that astronomers are guilty of the same type of circular reasoning that is practiced by geologists and pateontologists. Stellar evolution is assumed in making the age estimates of stars. But then the age estimates are used to establish a framework *for* stellar evolution. The following discourse might serve to make this more concrete:

Instructor: "Aldebaran, in the constellation Taurus, is considerably older than our sun."

Student: "How do we know that?"

Instructor: "It has obviously evolved past the Main Sequence up into the red giant region of the Hertzsprung-Russell diagram (see next section) whereas the sun is still *on* the Main Sequence. There is another category of stellar objects called the T Tauri stars that are *younger* than our sun, not having yet evolved *to* the Main Sequence."

Student: "But how do astronomers know that stellar evolution takes place at all?"

Instructor: "Because we find stars of various ages that testify to it. These are snapshots, as it were, of different stages of the process. From these we are able to piece together a logical evolutionary sequence."

Christian students of biology or geology will be only too familiar with this kind of reasoning. Evolution is assumed in establishing the "ages"; then the "ages" are used to establish evolution. Astronomers use the stars instead of the index fossils of biological evolution. Whenever a certain type of star is found, a certain history is automatically demanded. The alternative of direct creation with diversity is not even considered.

The Hertzsprung-Russell Diagram

For the stars in the spiral arms of our galaxy, if one makes a plot of the actual intrinsic brightness (absolute magnitude) versus temperature, then results similar to Figure 1 will be obtained. For most stars there is a clear-cut correlation: the hotter the star the greater its brightness. The majority of stars fall along a diagonal extending from the upper left to the lower right, called the Main Sequence. Our sun, a typical Main Sequence star, is located at "B." Other important categories are the red giants, the supergiants, and the white dwarfs.

The Hertzsprung-Russell (H-R) diagram has long served as a useful descriptive representation for stars in our galaxy. However, in recent years its use has been turned largely to tracing "evolutionary tracks." One such track is included in Figure 1. It purports to trace the life history of our sun from the time of its condensation from interstellar material at "A" to its final demise in the white dwarf "stage" at the lower part of the diagram.

Presumably the Main Sequence consists of stars whose chief energy-producing reaction is the fusion of hydrogen to form helium. The red giants are said to be stars in which all hydrogen has been consumed and only helium fusion occurs.

There are, interestingly enough, more "missing links" than stars along the "evolutionary tracks." This important fact will be discussed in a subsequent section.

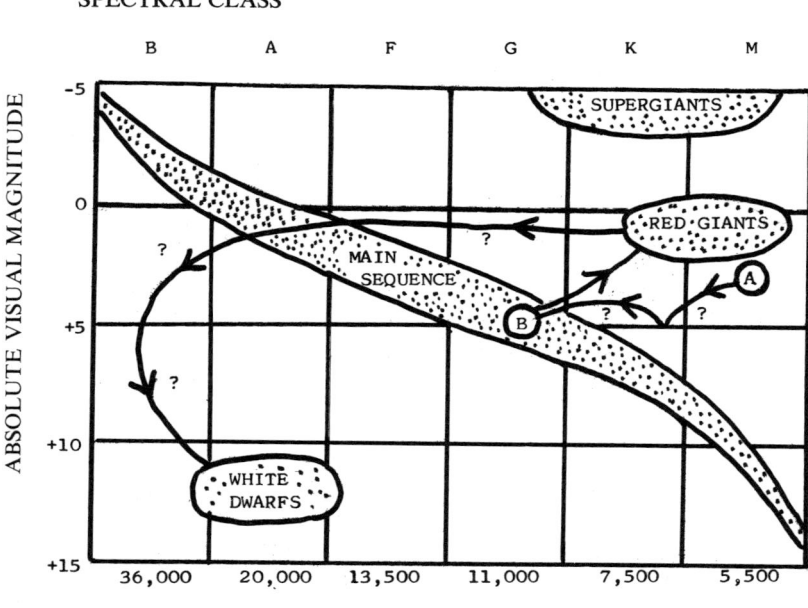

Figure 1. Hertzsprung—Russell Diagram for stars in the spiral arms of our galaxy, showing hypothetical "evolutionary track" for the sun. The track starts with the alleged condensation from interstellar material at "A" and goes through the sun's present position at "B." Eventually, it is claimed, the sun will evolve into a red giant, and finally a white dwarf.

CRITIQUE OF STELLAR EVOLUTION

The alleged directions of such tracks have been drastically altered in recent years. At one time many astronomers had envisioned evolution down the Main Sequence from left to right. Now the tracks are often at right angles to the Main Sequence. Projecting ahead into the future, we may expect many more changes, as the theories are further adjusted to conform to the whims of the times.

No star has ever been followed through such an evolutionary path observationally. Minor shifts in position on the H-R diagram *have* been observed. Cepheid variables, for example, oscillate both in brightness and in temperature. Novae and supernovae brighten up explosively, moving them upward temporarily on the H-R diagram. But never has one type of star been observed to merge or evolve into another type.

Stellar Aging

Every star is a dynamic system undergoing degenerative changes. The 'normal" degenerative processes such as fuel consumption do not produce perceptible changes on the H-R diagram during the length of time that we have been observing stars telescopically. Since only the outermost parts of a star can be observed, it is necessary to guess at the interior composition.

The theoretician therefore devises a *model* that is based on various simplifying assumptions. It is this model that is dealt with so imaginatively in projecting evolutionary processes forward or backward on a time scale that is extended many orders of magnitude beyond what is warranted by the data at hand.

Actually, we do not even vaguely comprehend the makeup of the present universe, let alone what it once was, or what it is destined to become. To extrapolate into billions of years on the basis of a few decades of observations is sheer folly. But scant as these observations may be, they should be faithfully adhered to in erecting the superstructure of the science of astronomy, rather than merely using them as a point of departure for speculation.

Concerning the terminology that is applied to changes in stars it would be far more accurate to use the term "stellar aging" rather than "stellar evolution." The latter implies that there is some kind of upgrading or improvement involved. In all the studies that have been made to date, *only downhill processes* have actually been found to occur: disruption, dissipation, and disintegration. These include:

1. Consumption of hydrogen, a high-energy content fuel, leaving as "ashes" low energy fuels such as helium. The sun, a typical star, consumes four and one half million tons of fuel per second.

2. Radiation of electromagnetic energy and neutrons into space in all directions, with no possible means of recovery.

3. Loss of material by violent disruptive events, as in novae and supernovae. (It is also suspected that planetary nebulae are formed by catastrophic eruptions in stars.)

4. Spinning off of material to form an expanding stellar atmosphere, as in shell stars.

5. Ejection of energetic particles from a star's surface by mechanisms such as solar flares.

Star Formation

As spontaneous generation is supposed to precede biological evolution, so star formation is said to precede stellar evolution. Herein lies one of the knottiest problems of all. One unusually frank astronomer states:

> Contemporary opinion on star formation holds that objects called protostars are formed as condensations from interstellar gas. This condensation process is very difficult theoretically, and no essential theoretical understanding can be claimed; in fact, some theoretical evidence argues strongly against the possibility of star formation. However, we know that stars exist, and we must do our best to account for them.[3]

The last sentence is not without humor. Stars are "there," presenting a challenge to the cosmic evolutionist, in the same sense that Mt. Everest was "there" as a challenge to Hillary. But why is it that there *are* things which exist that the evolutionist feels no need to account for—such as the primeval hydrogen and the law of gravitation? These things and many others are simply taken for granted.

Another very revealing statement, admitting that star formation

CRITIQUE OF STELLAR EVOLUTION

seems so improbable that it should never happen, comes from none others than G. R. Burbidge, a recognized authority on the "evolution of elements" in stars: "If stars did not exist, it would be easy to prove that this is what we expect."[4] The problem, simply, is that the condensation of a star from interstellar material would violate a good deal of what we know about the laws and processes of nature.

Practically all of the popular paperbacks, and 100 percent of the many textbooks that I have acquired, gloss over this problem most superficially. Implicit faith is expressed in the theory that stars condense spontaneously from interstellar clouds by gravitational attraction. As both cause and effect seem to be present, it "makes sense" to the average reader. He readily accepts the idea and reads on the next speculation. However, precise computations with available data indicate that the alleged process would fail completely.

Calculating with figures given by cosmogonists, we can estimate the entropy change for such a hypothetical condensation. If it turns out that the entropy *increases* in such a process, we must conclude that it is natural and in keeping with the "downhill" trend of nature. If, however, we find that the entropy would have to *decrease,* we have every right to be suspicious; "uphill" processes require organizing intelligence and/or energy from the outside. We would then have to examine whether such could be supplied within the scope of natural occurrences.

I will use for my calculations values suggested by Lyman Spitzer of Princeton in a paper presented at the Goddard Institute for Space Studies in New York.[5] Let us consider an interstellar cloud massive enough to form the sun, 2×10^{30} kilograms. Spitzer gives, as the temperature of the cloud, $100°$ Kelvin.[6] From a relationship that he gives, its volume can be readily determined, to 5.64×10^{47} cubic meters.[7]

By the time the radius of the cloud has supposedly shrunk to 100 times the sun's radius (stellar dimensions), its mean temperature is presumed to have risen to $100,000°$ Kelvin.[8] The volume at this stage is calculated to be 1.40×10^{33} cubic meters[9] (see Figure 2).

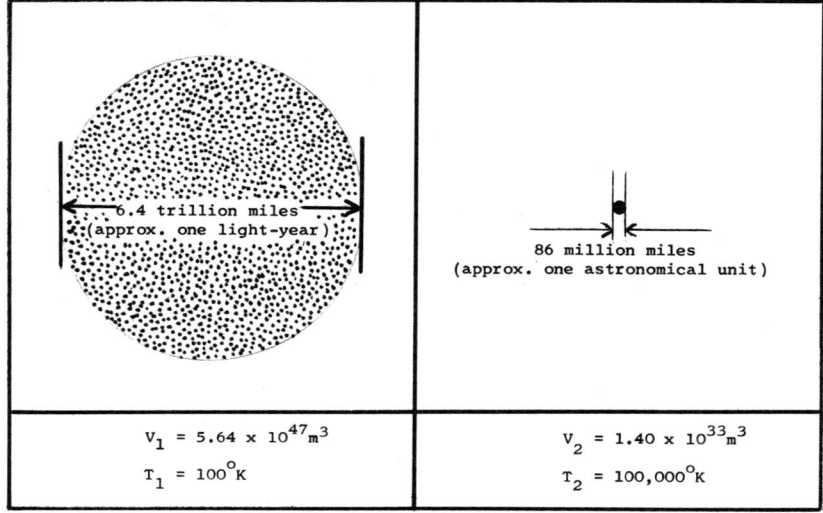

Figure 2. "Before" and "After" sketch of hypothetical condensation to form star (not drawn to scale).

We see that the volume has been reduced by a factor of 400 trillion (the diameter going from about one light-year down to about one astronomical unit) while the temperature has been increased by a factor of only 1000. We might guess already that the entropy would have to decrease in such a process.

Calculation of Entropy Change

Treating the system as an ideal gas (which is an excellent approximation because the material is so spread out) the entropy change may be computed by a well-known relationship found in any standard thermodynamics text:[10]

$$dS = Cp \frac{dT}{T} + R \frac{dV}{V} \qquad (1)$$

where S is the entropy; T, the absolute temperature; V, the volume; Cp, the molar heat capacity at constant pressure; and R is the universal gas constant. Integrating both sides, we obtain

CRITIQUE OF STELLAR EVOLUTION

$$\Delta S = Cp\ln T_2 - Cp\ln T_1 + R\ln V_2 - R\ln V_1 * \quad (2)$$

Substituting the values previously discussed for V_1, V_2, T_1, and T_2, and utilizing the ideal gas value of $(5/2)R**$ for Cp, we obtain

$$\Delta S = 5/2\ R\ln T_2 - 5/2\ R\ln T_1 + R\ln V_2 - R\ln V_1$$

Now, as mentioned above, we will call T_2 the temperature existing when the radius has shrunken to 100 times the sun's radius and its value is 100,000° or 10^5 degrees while T_1 was 100° or 10^2 degrees presumed for the interstellar cloud. The volume V_2, when shrunken, is 1.40×10^{33} cubic meters as compared to the original volume V_1 of 5.64×10^{47} cubic meters. By substitution of these values, we obtain

$$\Delta S = (5/2)\ R\ln 10^5 - (5/2)\ R\ln 10^2 + R\ln 1.4 \times 10^{33} - R\ln 5.64 \times 10^{47}$$

Temperature and volume units are dropped because a logarithm is an exponent and as such has no units. To simplify this equation we may substitute the value of 2 cal/mole°K for R and arrive at the following equation:

$$\Delta S = 5\ln 10^5 - 5\ln 10^2 + 2\ln 1.40 \times 10^{33} - 2\ln 5.64 \times 10^{47}$$

---

*The integral of dT/T equals the natural logarithm of T plus a constant. To evaluate this as a definite integral between the temperatures T_1 and T_2 we substitute T_2 into the expression (ln T+C) and from this subtract the expression with T_1 substituted into it. Thus

The constants cancel and we have
$$\ln T_2 - \ln T_1$$
Since originally dT/T was multiplied by Cp, our result is multiplied by Cp:

The same reasoning holds for transforming RdV/V into $R\ln V_2 - R\ln V_1$.

**Cp is the molar heat capacity of a gas at constant pressure. The cosmogonists generally assume that such a cloud contracts under a constant external pressure and that the gas is neutral atomic hydrogen (see Reference

We change to common logarithms or "$\log_{10}$" by multiplying each natural logarithm by 2.3. This changes the base from the natural log base "e" to base 10:

$$\Delta S = (5)(2.3)\log 10^5 - (5)(2.3)\log 10^2 + \\ (2)(2.3 \log 1.40 \times 10^{33}) - \\ (2)(2.3 \log 5.64 \times 10^{47})$$

$$\Delta S = (5)(2.3)(5) - (5)(2.3)(2) + \\ (2)(2.3)(33.146) - (2)(2.3)(47.751)$$

$$\Delta S = 57.5 - 23.0 + 152 - 220$$

$$\Delta S = -33 \text{ eu/mole}$$

The entropy must decrease 33 entropy units for every mole of material in the cloud! The fact that the derived result in negative indicates clearly that the condensation is not a spontaneous process. The temperature term makes a positive contribution, but this is more than offset by the large negative contribution of the volume term.[11] As our scientific intuition might have told us, it is more natural for the cloud to expand than to contract, since we know from laboratory observations that gases expand spontaneously but do not contract spontaneously. Anyone who has ever pumped up a tire by hand and thus concentrated a given amount of air into a smaller volume realizes how much energy goes into such an operation.

Applying the second law to the star formation process, then, we find that the *reverse* process rather than the forward process is favored. Here is just one more instance where the second law of thermodynamics points to creationism as the only realistic explanation for the origin of the universe we live in.

Calculation of Outward Push

We will also calculate the forces acting at the surface of the original cloud. It can be shown thereby that the outward push due

---

No. 12). Hydrogen in this form is a good approximation to an ideal monatomic gas, whose Cp is $(5/2)R$.

CRITIQUE OF STELLAR EVOLUTION

to thermal motion of the molecules, even at 100° Kelvin, is greater than the gravitational pull inward.

The outward push of the cloud can be calculated starting from the ideal gas law

$$PV = nRT \qquad (3)$$

where P is the pressure, V is the volume of the cloud, n is the total number of moles of material in the cloud, R is the universal gas constant, and T is the absolute temperature. Again, this is an excellent approximation because the individual particles are so far apart. Solving for pressure,

$$P = \frac{nRT}{V}$$

The total force outward over the whole surface of the cloud is simply this quantity times the surface area of the cloud.

Assuming a spherical cloud, as is customary in the literature, its area and volume would be $4\pi r^2$ and $4\pi r^3/3$ respectively. We have, therefore,

$$F = PA = \frac{nRTA}{V} \qquad (4)$$

By cancellation of $4\pi r^2$ from numerator and denominator and multiplying each by 3, we find that

$$F = \frac{nRT\,(4\pi r^2)}{4\pi r^3/3} \qquad (5)$$

where r is the radius of the cloud. The numerical value of the radius is 5.13×10^{15} meters (about 3.2 trillion miles). Assuming the material to be neutral atomic hydrogen,[12]

$$F = 3\left(\frac{2 \times 10^{33} \text{ grams}}{1 \text{ gram/mole}}\right)\left(8.31 \frac{\text{joules}}{\text{mole }^\circ\text{K}}\right)(100^\circ\text{K})$$
$$\overline{5.13 \times 10^{15} \text{ meters}}$$

$$F = 9.72 \times 10^{20} \text{ newtons}$$

The *outward push* due to thermal motion of the molecules is found to be 9.72×10^{20} newtons.

We shall now compute the *gravitational pull inward* for the whole cloud by the hydrostatic equilibrium relationship:[13]

$$\frac{dP}{dr} = \frac{-\rho GM(r)}{r^2} \tag{7}$$

where r is the radius of the cloud, P is the pressure, ρ (rho) is the density, and M(r) is the mass of the whole cloud expressed as a function of r. Assuming uniform density, M(r) may be replaced by density times volume or

$(\rho)\left(\frac{4}{3}\pi r^3\right)$ giving

$$\frac{dP}{dr} = \frac{-\frac{4}{3}\pi\rho^2 Gr^3}{r^2} = -\frac{4}{3}\pi\rho^2 Gr \tag{8}$$

Writing this in differential form,

$$dP = \frac{-4}{3}\pi\rho^2 Gr\, dr$$

Integrating from the center of the cloud to the edge,

$$\int dP = -\int_0^r \frac{4}{3}\pi\rho^2 Gr\, dr$$

$$P = \frac{-2}{3}\pi\rho^2 Gr^2 \tag{9}$$

The total force inward at the surface is this quantity times the area of the surface, which, as before, is $4\pi r^2$:

$$F = PA = (-\frac{2}{3}\pi\rho^2 Gr^2)(4\pi r^2) \tag{10}$$

which simplifies to

$$F = \frac{-8}{3}\pi^2\rho^2 Gr^4 \tag{11}$$

When we substitute $M/\frac{4}{3}\pi r^3$ for ρ, the expression reduces to

$$F = \frac{-3GM^2}{2r^2} \tag{12}$$

Substituting MKS values,

$$F = \frac{-(3)(6.67 \times 10^{-11})(2 \times 10^{30})^2}{(2)(5.13 \times 10^{15})^2}$$
$$F = -1.52 \times 10^{19} \text{ newtons}$$

The inward pull at the surface of the cloud due to gravitational attraction is found to be 1.52×10^{19} newtons.

Let us now compare the outward and inward forces at the surface of the cloud:

$$\frac{F \text{ outward}}{F \text{ inward}} = \frac{9.72 \times 10^{20}}{-1.52 \times 10^{19}} = 64$$

The cloud has 64 times as much outward force as inward; it therefore has a greater tendency to expand than to contract. Let us keep in mind that we allowed a leading cosmogonist to choose the initial conditions for the cloud. We gave him the advantage of choosing his starting materials and circumstances, but the results of the calculations are *still* seen to militate strongly against star formation.

When we apply the same equations to the condensed material (the material at V_2 and T_2 having a radius slightly less than the radius of the earth's orbit) we see that here gravitation *is* in fact causing the material to contract.[14] But how it was reduced to that volume in the first place is impossible to understand, short of direct creation.

From equations (6) and (12) used above it can readily be seen that an object which already possesses stellar dimensions will exhibit a strong gravitational pull inward, easily overcoming the thermal push outward:[15]

$$F = \frac{3nRT}{r} \quad \text{(thermal push outward)}$$

$$F = \frac{3GM^2}{2r^2} \quad \text{(gravitational pull inward)}$$

The outward force is inversely proportional to the radius, while the inward force is inversely proportional to the radius *squared*.

In general, therefore, the smaller the object the more successfully it can contract, provided equilibrium has not yet been reached. But the enormous clouds that are fashionable among theoreticians today (those that are supposed to produce stars in groups of hundreds of thousands) are extremely unfavorable for contraction. *Gravitation avails little at such a radius.*

More Speculation Introduced

How, then, do they propose to make the star formation process "work"? With the second law of thermodynamics working against them, and gravitation failing to overcome the thermal force outward, are they not ready to concede defeat? Never!˙

Some fertile mind can always concoct a scheme to get around the laws of nature—at least on paper. The scheme that is invoked here is simply this: surround the cloud you wish to compress with a *hotter* cloud, so that the molecules at the surface of the inner cloud will be bombarded by the faster moving molecules of the outer cloud and pushed inward. By stacking the deck in this manner, enough brute force can allegedly be mustered to render the impossible possible.

As Spitzer describes it, the 100°K cloud we wish to compress must be surrounded by a second cloud having a temperature of

10,000°K, the inner cloud being neutral hydrogen, the outer, ionized hydrogen (HI and HII regions, respectively, in astronomical parlance).[16] Unfortunately for the theory, however, it is questionable whether HI regions occur in such pockets surrounded by HII regions.

The realistic situation appears to be just the opposite. According to Bart Bok, HII regions are generated by very hot O or B class stars,* and expand against the surrounding HI region.[17] But in order to make the above-mentioned scheme work, an HI region would have to be providentially enclosed within an HII region, over 4π stearadians of solid angle, *contrary to observation*.

By rigging the starting conditions in this manner Spitzer leaps over a number of problems without ever facing them. The inner cloud being 100 times cooler than the outer, is already much more condensed than its surroundings at the very outset. How did it get that way?

The 10,000°K that Spitzer postulates for the outer cloud is more than half again as hot as the sun's surface. How could an extended region of interstellar material attain such a temperature? Heating by nearby stars? How, then, did the first stars condense before there were other stars present to heat up the gas? It is reminiscent of the chicken-versus-egg dilemma encountered in Whipple's Dust Cloud Hypothesis discussed in an earlier paper.[18] In that instance, light pressure from other stars was imagined to concentrate the material into a smaller volume.

Perhaps the most ludicrous part of the whole hypothesis is the cosmogonists' naive faith that the hot and cold clouds will remain unmixed over many millions of years (Herbig gives a figure of 50 million years!) while the condensation process is in progress! But an avid pantheist credits "Nature" with many great and mighty powers, including the ability to violate its own laws.

---

*Stars are classified according to their spectra into seven major divisions: O, B, A, F, G, K, and M. The class O and B are bluish-white stars possessing unusually high surface temperatures—greater than 25,000° K for the class O and 11,000-25,000 for the class B. (This is considerably hotter than the sun, which has a surface temperature of about 6,000°K.)

Other Star Formation Difficulties

Turning now to other types of difficulties connected with star formation, we note that there is a serious angular momentum problem. The original cloud would be rotating slightly, due to differential galactic rotation (a surface velocity of about 100 meters per second).[19] If the cloud were to contract to a star with strict conservation of angular momentum, the surface velocity of the star would be greater than the speed of light![20] Thus the cosmogonist finds himself embarrassed by too much angular momentum and he is forced to imagine mechanisms for disposing of the excess. So far, the schemes that have been proposed have been notably lacking in credibility.

Still another big question mark concerns the strength and topography of the magnetic field throughout the galaxy. If the field intensity as high as 2×10^{-5} gauss, star formation will be "in difficulty."[21] One widely held view is that the field is parallel to the spiral arms of the galaxy, and is indeed as strong as 2×10^{-5} gauss.

However, whenever a question exists due to lack of experimental evidence, the cosmogonists have a habit of giving themselves the benefit of that doubt.

All in all, Spitzer does not seem completely sold on the scheme that he outlines. This is evidenced by statements such as the following: "It should be emphasized that all this discussion is quite tentative and serves principally to point out some of the problems involved."[22] After listing the hypothetical stages in star formation he states, "As one indication of the many uncertainties in star formation theory, it should be noted that possibly some of these stages do not even arise during the actual process of star birth."[23] Thus the man, who is probably the leading authority on the subject, appears to have numerous reservations concerning the details of the process. Yet faith abounds that the process does in fact take place, and that it is a common everyday phenomenon throughout space and time.

Journalists are always anxious to produce sensationalistic copy bearing a headline such as "A Star Is Born," or "Birth of Star Appears Imminent." A UPI release of October 2, 1967, declared that mankind may be treated to the grand spectacle of the birth of a star within the next 20 years. Based on a somewhat misquoted *Scientific American* article by George Herbig,[24] the release stated that the Orion Nebula (Figure 3) is being watched closely in hopes that the "gestation period" of some "protostar" will soon be completed.

There is one serious problem concerning observational verification when studying such a nebula. If a "new" star is seen, it could simply be due to the thinning of interstellar dust in front of a star that was already there. This fact has been soberly admitted in the

Figure 3. Great Nebula in Orion (M42). Astronomers are watching this nebula closely in hopes of seeing "the birth of a star" in the next few years. However, even if such a process were theoretically possible, such an event could never be definitely verified. If a "new" star is seen, it could simply be due to the thinning of interstellar dust in front of a star that was already there.

literature but has yet to find its way into the news media.

Scripture seems clear on the fact that the heavens were fully structured at the end of the creation week. Genesis 2:1 declares "Thus the heavens and the earth were *finished,* and *all the host of them.*" The 33rd Psalm also conveys the impression of a divine fiat that brought the stars suddenly into existence: "By the word of the Lord were the heavens made; and all the host of them by the breath of his mouth. . . . For he spake, and it was done; he commanded, and it stood fast" (Ps. 33:6, 9). Again, in Exodus 20:11 we read, "For in six days the Lord made heaven and earth, the sea, *and all that in them is,* and rested the seventh day. . . ."

Galaxy Formation

From the foregoing discussion it will be appreciated that condensations of "primordial material" are most problematical. On the galactic level, however, the difficulties are persent on a far grander scale. In the case of our own galaxy, at least, one must explain the intricate makeup of the disc—its nucleus and spiral arms containing some 100 billion stars, the hundred or so globular clusters (each containing several tens of thousands of stars) that revolve around the galaxy as satellites, and the galactic corona (see Figure 4).

Many cosmogonists have been unwilling to tackle the question of galactic origins. Alfvén displays a healthy respect for the problem, admitting readily that our "knowledge" of star formation does not appreciably enhance our understanding of galaxy formation:

> But even this approach to an explanation eventually leads us into serious difficulties. To begin with, the analogy with star formation is of little help because our grasp of its later phases is still dim. Further, we should not expect any major resemblances because the end product, a galaxy, differs so much from a star, and not only in size. Even more serious is that the theory of star formation assumes that the condensing mass consists exclusively of koinomatter (regular matter). The theory, of course, readily lends itself to antimatter, but it falls down when confronted with a mixture of koinomatter and antimatter: an ambiplasma. By its very nature, ambiplasma must incur annihilation, which may be of fundamental importance.[25]

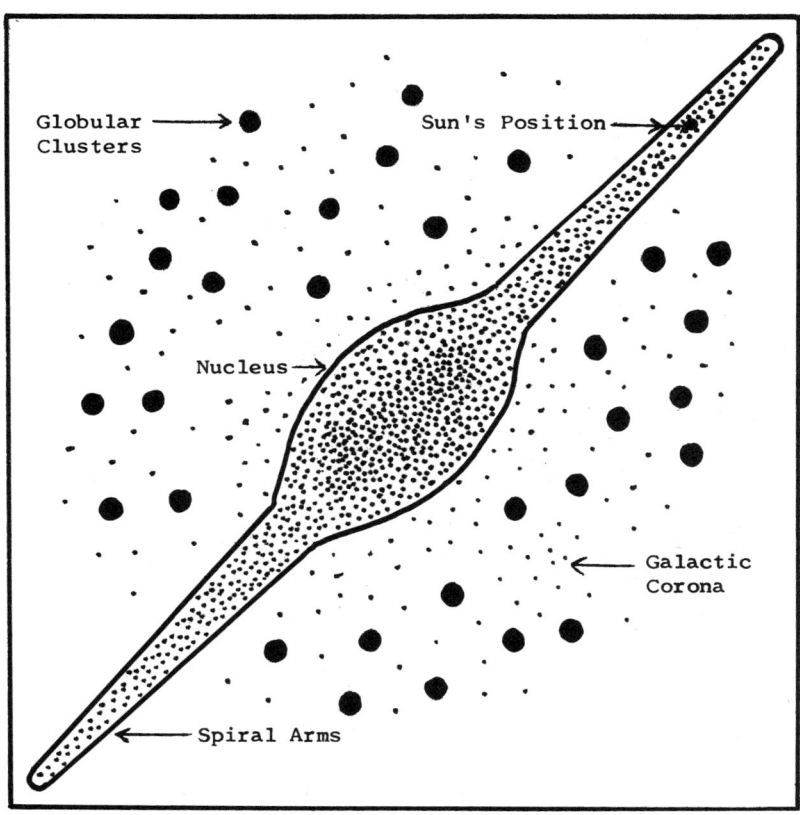

Figure 4. Our galaxy, edge-on view, showing galactic corona and globular clusters (satellites of the galaxy). No evolutionary theory has explained the origin and maintenance of the galaxy or its satellites.

The early stages of galaxy formation are incomprehensible enough, but, he adds, "The further development of galaxies poses a much more formidable problem."[26] The *Encyclopedia Brittanica* concurs with this view, terming this whole area "a challenge to cosmogonical thought."[27]

While the popular literature on the subject speaks blithely of "protogalaxies" as though they were an everyday reality, none has ever been observed, and no satisfactory model of one has ever been put on paper.[28]

Galactic Evolution

Do galaxies gradually evolve from one type to another over millions or billions of years? The current view is that *they do not*. Just how this position has become respectable constitutes an interesting historical study.

We find in the heavens several distinctly different types of galaxies —normal spirals, barred spirals, ellipticals of varying degrees of flatness, and irregulars. Several decades ago Hubble arranged these into his well-known "tuning-fork diagram" shown in Figure 5. It was his belief that galaxies evolved from left to right on the diagram starting with a round elliptical, gradually flattening, and eventually developing into a spiral type via the upper route. Finally,

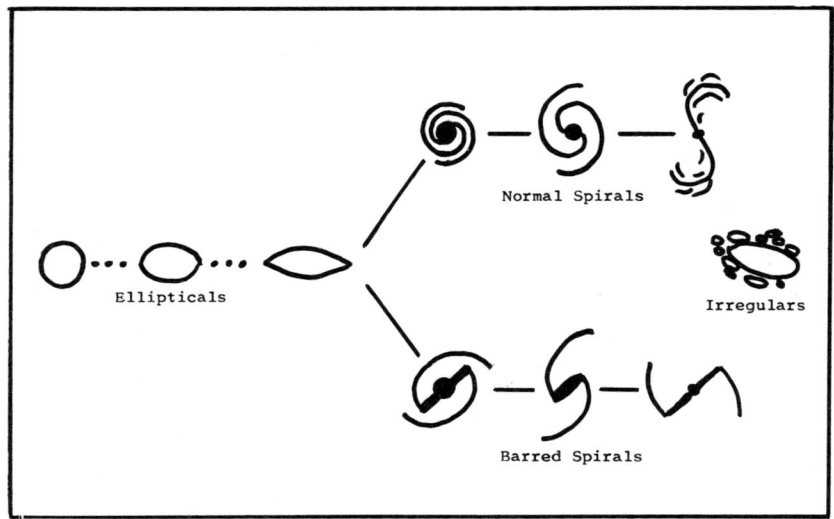

Figure 5. Hubble "tuning-fork" diagram of galactic types. Hubble believed that galaxies evolve from left to right along the upper route; Shapley held that the evolution was from right to left. The consensus today is that galaxies do not evolve from one type to another.

he proposed that they lose all structure from their spiral arms and form an irregular galaxy.[29]

Shapley, on the other hand, felt it more reasonable that they should evolve from right to left. But the important thing seemed to be that, at all cost, they should *evolve*.

In both schemes the upper route of the fork was followed, and no satisfactory explanation was offered for the existence of the barred spirals—those possessing a straight bar-like structure at their center. Even today these constitute a real puzzle. Hodge states:

> Another important dynamical problem that is not solved is the problem of explaining the existence of the bars in the barred spiral galaxies. These masses of stars do not obey any reasonable dynamical model and may be held in place by some non-

Figure 6. Barred Spiral Galaxy in Eridanus (NGC 1300). Astronomers are at a loss to explain how the bar is maintained over long periods of time. The problem is solved very neatly by a recent creation.

gravitational force such as a strong magnetic field. Just how this can work is not yet known[30] [see Figure 6].

The barred spiral galaxies are best explained by a recent creation. On the basis of what we know today, these structures must be extremely young, or the bars would long since have been bent into spirals in keeping with Kepler's Second Law.

Neither the Hubble nor the Shapley theory was based on actual physical evidence. Today it is generally felt that angular momentum considerations rule out such evolution from type to type. Abell summarizes the situation as follows:

> There is much doubt, however, that galaxies evolve from one type to another at all. The fact that different kinds of galaxies are flattened by different amounts almost certainly results from their having different amounts of angular momentum—that is, from their different rotation rates. In other words, galaxies might always have had essentially their present forms (at least since their formation), the form of a particular galaxy depending mostly on its mass and angular momentum per unit mass.[31]

It is gratifying to see that many astronomers are no longer attempting to make a dichotomy between "young" and "old" galaxies. Hodge writes:

> Our conclusions, then, are that the sequence of the classification of galaxies is not an evolutionary sequence. . . . The best evidence available now indicates that they are all of approximately the same age, at least all of those near enough to our galaxy for this to be estimated.[32]

The Problem of Planets

Although there remains an unshakeable confidence among the general pseudo-intellectual public that the earth and other planets condensed from "the same cloud that formed the sun," the real savants in the field are at a loss to explain just what is supposed to make the small particles of material aggregate together into a larger body (if indeed one can even take the smaller particles for granted).

Thomas Gold of Cornell, writing on "Problems Requiring Solution," lists as Problem No. 1: "the method of agglomeration of solid pieces. How do they manage to stick together, especially over a certain range of size?"[33] Iron particles, he submits, might stick together by magnetism up to a certain size but beyond that there is a "difficult gap between objects that are centimeters or a meter in size, and those that are gravitationally active (a kilometer or more in size)."[34] "This gap is the most difficult to bridge, because as yet gravitation is not in the picture."[35] He then mentions the possibility that comets might form nuclei of accretion, but fails to explain where *they* came from.

Hoyle takes a different tack. He has conceived the ingenious idea of freezing the fragments together with water.[36] Unfortunately, however, he fails to disclose where his H_2O was synthesized. Also, he concedes the possibility that heat from the sun could melt the ice and sabotage the whole scheme. It is also well to note here that all space probe analysis of planets in our solar system to this date indicate an absence of extraterrestrial water. It is questionable then whether one should feel free to postulate water elsewhere in space as Hoyle does.

An earlier idea of Hoyle's involved the use of oil or pitch as a binding agent. Virtually everything from "chewing gum" to "baling wire" has been attempted to fasten planets together, but still the problem remains.

The December 23, 1966, issue of *Time* carried a typical sensationalistic article concerning the imagined formation of another solar system in the constellation Monoceros. Based on a paper by Low and Smith in *Nature*,[37] the article described observations on the twelfth magnitude star, R Monocerotis. The object, according to the details given in the original paper, is nothing more or less than a hot star surrounded by a thick blanket of gas and dust. And yet the paper was given the very presumptive title, "Infrared Observations of a Preplanetary System."

There is no experimental evidence presented that the object is indeed contracting as it is supposed to be. It may actually be expanding from the heat of the star. In fact, much of the observed debris may have been spun off from the star; nothing is securely established concerning the rotation of the star *or* the cloud. Thus, what may well be just another degenerative phenomenon, has been interpreted, with a generous measure of wishful thinking, as a "creative" process.

Let us keep firmly in mind the stark fact that our solar system is the only planetary system that has ever been observed. All the other billions of solar systems that are supposedly out there somewhere have been inferred by very questionable statistical rationalizations rather than solid physical evidence.

What *have* been observed are several binary systems in which one member of the system is extremely dim or even dark, and hence invisible with our best telescopes (astrometric binaries). In such a case the existence of the companion is *inferred* by the wavy path of the bright member. The best authorities still disagree on whether such a dark object should be considered an oversized planet or a small star.

Multiplicity of Star Types

One might derive the impression that, compared to the biological world, the stellar world is somewhat monotonous—that there are stars, stars, and more stars. This is hardly the case, however. Their diversity in both structure and function is staggering. Indeed, "one star differeth from another" (I Cor. 15:41) to the extent that no two are exactly alike.

Stars can differ in size, mass, density, color, brightness, temperature, rotation rate, composition, spectral lines or bands, stability, magnetic field strength, nature and extent of atmosphere or envelope, period (for variable stars), radio emission, corpuscular radiation, and many other factors such as whether they are single, binary, or members of a more complex system.

Ideally, there should probably be as many categories of classification as there are stars. But for practical reasons some fairly broad arbitrary groupings have been set up. Even an abridged list of the types of stars and stellar objects that are encountered in the literature would be too lengthy to include in this paper.

"Missing Links"

The burden of proof is upon the evolutionist, who claims that

CRITIQUE OF STELLAR EVOLUTION

every object is serially related to other objects, to demonstrate observationally the *intermediate* stages between the various types. In many cases there has not even been a theoretical treatment of the imagined transition. Some of the specific obstacles that exist will be considered at this point.

(1) *Pulsating Stars* are unstable stars that alternately increase and decrease in brightness. There appears to be an accompanying oscillation in size, like a balloon being alternately inflated and deflated. Many distinctly different types exist; a few of which are (a) the RR Lyrae variables, with short periods of from 0.3 to 0.7 days; (b) the classical Cepheids, with periods of 1 to 50 days; (c) the W Virginis variables, with similar periods but 1 to 2 magnitudes fainter; (d) Mira-type variables, with long periods of from 80 to 1000 days; (e) semi-regular variables; (f) irregular variables; and (g) spectrum variables.

How a "normal" star is supposed to lose its stability and evolve into a pulsating star is indeed a great mystery. And how it is then supposed to regain its stability and evolve into still another type is equally baffling. Inglis concedes, "Why the star began to pulsate in the first place is not understood completely, but we know that some unbalanced forces must have developed that caused an initial expansion or contraction"[38]—which is about as specific as the Delphic Oracle. Obviously the question concerns the internal structure of stars which cannot be observed; hence guesswork and imperfect, oversimplified models are the only tools at our disposal.

(2) *T Tauri Stars* are highly unstable reddish objects that are claimed to be the link between interstellar clouds and Main Sequence stars. Well over a thousand of these stars have been identified in the galaxy.

But the T Tauri stars differ radically from the model predicted by stellar evolution theory. They are surrounded by thick and highly active outer atmospheres. Rather than pulling in matter from the surrounding space as might be expected, they are ejecting vast quantities of material *from* the star! Also they show a great overabundance of lithium, which would have no conceivable means of building up to that level during the star's "short" history, especially considering that thermonuclear reactions have supposedly not yet started.

George Herbig, astronomer at Lick Observatory, after discussing these peculiarities at some length, presents this summary:

> What physical processes or attributes could account for the distinctive features of the T Tauri stars: Their extremely active and luminous chromospheres, their massive ejections of surface material, their variability in brightness, their high lithium abundance? None of these phenomena are predicted by the modern theory of the contraction of young stars. Each is still a complete mystery.[39]

The logical conclusion is that the T Tauri stars are *not* the link between interstellar gas and Main Sequence stars that the theorists are so desperately seeking; the "real link" must still be missing.

(3) *Planetary Nebulae* are slowly expanding shells of gas surrounding certain very hot stars (see Figure 7). Stellar evolutionists have been, for some time, trying to establish planetary nebulae as a link between red giants and white dwarfs. It is generally agreed that they have a catastrophic origin such as an eruption of the central star. But, according to Meadows, ". . . no explosion producing such a nebula has ever been observed."[40]

Perhaps the leading authority on planetary nebulae today is Lawrence H. Aller of U.C.L.A. who states in a recent article, ". . . we may someday find a young object that is evolving into a planetary . . . but none is now known."[41]

Inglis reviews several "possible candidates for the job of supplying the universe with planetary nebulae" such as novae, Wolf-Rayet stars, RR Lyrae stars and red giant irregular variables, and concludes, ". . . none of these seems to fill the bill completely; astronomers are left with another puzzle to solve."[42]

(4) *White Dwarfs* are extremely small stars that are thought to consist mostly of "degenerate matter"—that is, matter that is presumed to have collapsed to a fantastically high density. (The possibility that they were created *as* white dwarfs is not even entertained as a hypothesis.)

Current dogma has it that red giants evolve into white dwarfs.

Figure 7. Planetary Nebula in Aquarius NGG 7293). Such nebulae are alleged to be an evolutionary link between red giants and white dwarfs. However, none has ever been observed in the process of evolving from anything else or to anything else.

We are told that our sun will some day go the way of all stars that have exhausted their supply of hydrogen—dissipating itself to become a red giant, and then somehow collapsing into a white dwarf. However, the "route" that is taken on the Hertzsprung-Russell diagram to reach the white dwarf "stage" is only surmised by compounding hypothesis upon hypothesis. According to Brandt, "Precisely how the future sun reaches this area of the H-R diagram is unknown. The path may be along the sequence of subluminous hot stars . . . since these objects are commonly thought to be very advanced in their evolution."[43] Obviously, guesswork abounds.

Abell concurs: "The evolution . . . from red giant to white dwarf is speculative only. Perhaps the star goes through a stage of variability, or emits material as a planetary nebula."[44]

We become increasingly suspicious when we note that some astronomers claim white dwarfs to be remnants of supernovae, while others maintain that white dwarfs evolve *into* supernovae! Regardless of what the facts may eventually turn out to be, evolution must, for the present, be served.

It should be apparent to the thoughtful Christian that the entire system of stellar evolution has been built upon a premise that is implicitly atheistic. The uniformitarian mind demands that every astronomical object be explained by some "previous stage of development." Never is there a willingness to admit a bona-fide creation at *any* point.

Age Discrepancies

One of the more entertaining aspects of this study is a consideration of some of the inconsistencies that come up with respect to the cosmic time scale. When modern theorists attempt to force an evolutionary framework upon a degenerating universe, such discrepancies are bound to occur, and many of the problems become increasingly worse the more that is done for them.

(1) *Age of Universe:* Let us compare the age of the universe according to various authorities in the field of astronomy. Their lack of agreement should speak volumes to us concerning the reliability of their dating methods:

Estimated Age of Universe	Authority
4.3-5 billion years	Gamow[45]
7 billion years	Peebles and Wilkinson[46]
10-15 billion years	Ashford[47]
70 billion years	Shklovski[48]
trillions of years	Alfvén[49]
infinitely old	Hoyle[50]

One thing is eminently certain. Not all of these men can be right. Yet at least four of them are considered to be first-rate cosmogonists.

What "dating methods" are used? The cosmogonist simply picks a number that he feels is large enough to encompass all the imagined evolutionary processes of ages past. But no two men can quite reach agreement as to what *has* taken place in the past.

Would any of these men be willing to face an honest creation at the time in the past specified? Of course not! They have a most evasive way of dealing with the problem of creation, pushing it farther and farther back in time, but never coming to grips with the real heart of the matter. Typical of the cosmogonists is Alfvén who says, "We beg leave to sidestep the question 'What happened before then?' "[51] Prior to this point in time the "model" ceases to be "relevant for us."[52]

The smaller estimates are based on inferred recessional velocities of distant galaxies as calculated from observed red shifts. Implicit in such a calculation is the assumption that the red shifts (displacement of spectral lines toward longer wavelengths) are in fact due to a Doppler effect. There are today astronomers, such as Gerald Hawkins of Boston University, who do not accept this interpretation.[53] Most frequently the alternative explanation that is offered involves some sort of "tired light" phenomenon.

Recent research on quasars has rendered the Doppler interpretation more than a little questionable. *One quasar displays five different red shifts.* The following is taken from the 1968 news bulletin of the American Institute of Physics:

> Experimental and theoretical work being done at the University of California (San Diego), Kitt Peak Observatory in Arizona, and California Institute of Technology shows that several different red shifts can be fitted to the absorption spectra of a single quasar. In the most extreme case, one quasar displays 5 red shifts that range from 1.36 to 2.20. Obviously only one red shift can be due to the motion of the entire object, so something must be proposed to account for the others.[54]

(2) *Spiral Gaxalies:* A very serious age discrepancy is observed in the spiral arms of galaxies. This writer first became aware of this source of embarrassment to evolutionists when reading *Galaxies and*

Cosmology by Paul W. Hodge several years ago. Hodge presents the problem as follows:

> The rotation times for spiral galaxies are approximately 10^8 years, halfway out from the center, but the ages of the spiral galaxies are approximately 10^{10} years. Therefore, one would expect that a spiral arm formed at the beginning of the galaxy's history would now be wound up 100 times. In actual fact most spiral arms of galaxies show only one or two complete turns.[55]

A typical spiral galaxy is shown in Figure 8. If it were as old as is claimed, it would be coiled up into a tight disc, with no lanes showing between the hundred or so turns in the arms.

Theoreticians had hoped that the difficulty could be resolved

Figure 8. Normal Spiral Galaxy in Virgo. If such galaxies are as old as is claimed, their arms should be wound up 100 times. In actuality they rarely exhibit more than two complete turns. This is possibly the most glaring age discrepancy facing astronomers today.

rather simply by showing that the entire galaxy turns as a unit—that the arms are frozen into a permanent shape by a magnetic field. But Halton Arp of the Mount Wilson and Palomar Observatories rejects this explanation in a recent article: "The magnetic field which runs through the gas in an arm is not strong enough to give appreciable rigidity, and in any case the stars are not coupled to this magnetic field."[56]

Something else was therefore proposed—the density-wave theory. According to this idea, alternate regions of condensation and rarefaction rotate around the galaxy at constant velocity. However, Arp quickly shows that this is no panacea either: ". . . There is a whole class of spirals that contain little or no disc in which the density waves could be transmitted."[57]

Arp then suggests that the spiral arms may simply be the tracks of material ejected from the galactic nucleus. Differential rotation would form such tracks into a spiral pattern. However, Arp fails to give a convincing explanation of why such ejections that occurred near the "beginning" have not yielded highly coiled systems; we are back to our original problem. It would seem more logical to believe that spiral galaxies are considerably younger than has been supposed.

(3) *Globular Clusters:* These are roughly spherical assemblages of stars that orbit around our galaxy as satellites (see Figure 9). It is currently believed that such clusters are "very old" because they appear to be "highly evolved."

Some age estimates of globular clusters (e.g., M3 and M5) run as high as 26 billion years.[58] Obviously, the men who make such claims do not enjoy close fellowship with those who hold to a 7-billion-year-old universe. The more one studies the utterances of present-day astronomers the more one realizes how little concord exists. We are beset today with a hodgepodge of mutually contradictory ideas, brought about by a desire to superimpose an evolutionary framework on a degenerating universe.[59]

In the case of the M3 cluster an embarrassing situation has come to light. The problem, somewhat oversimplified, is this: If the cluster is as old as is claimed, why does it contain a number of

Figure 9. Globular Cluster in Canes Venatici (M3). The age of this cluster has been estimated at 26 billion years, in serious conflict with the generally held view that the universe is only 7-10 billion years old.

"young" stars?[60] These relatively hot blue Main Sequence stars could not have existed for any great span of time, or their fuel would long since have been depleted.

As an explanation for this dilemma we are asked to believe that the blue stars condensed billions of years later than those in the rest of the cluster. But from what? The cosmogonist is woefully lacking in raw materials here, since globular clusters are notorious for their lack of interstellar material.

(4) *Binary Stars:* Pairs of stars that revolve about a mutual center of gravity are called binaries. It is now generally conceded that both members of such a pair were formed at the same time.[61]

CRITIQUE OF STELLAR EVOLUTION

Yet one member of the pair is often a "young" star while the other is a "highly evolved" star.

Sirius, a nearby system, consists of two components: Sirius A, a bright blue Main Sequence star; and Sirius B, a dim white dwarf. Sirius A is supposed to be a "young" star because fuel is being consumed at such a prodigious rate that it could not have been doing so for very long. Sirius B, on the other hand, has supposedly evolved through all the many stages leading to a white dwarf including T Tauri, Main Sequence, and red giant.

How can these things be? How can one star of a binary system appear young while the other appears old, yet both are acknowledged to be the same age? Theorists in the field seem satisfied with the explanation that Sirius B simply "evolved faster." With such a flexible theory one can play this game any way he pleases.

Like biological evolution, it explains too much; any set of data can be rationalized to fit the theory by one means or another. A theory that is this insensitive to the observational data stands little chance of ever being overthrown.

Conclusions

1. There are many weak links in the hypothetical evolutionary life cycle of a star. The weakest of these is the alleged spontaneous birth of stars from interstellar material. Both scientific data and Scripture militate strongly against the doctrine of continuous star formation. This idea has undoubtedly come about as a consequence of the implicitly atheistic assumptions that underlie the majority of present-day astronomical speculations.

Observation and revealed truth both point to the creation of all stars at a definite time in the past *by processes totally dissimilar to present processes*. The present astronomical economy involves degeneration, dissipation, and "running down" in stars, whereas there must clearly have been an initial period of organization and "winding up."

2. The problem of how galaxies are supposed to structure themselves from primordial material is one of the most enigmatic questions in the whole realm of cosmogony. Few cosmogonists have

been willing to undertake study of this problem. Those who have attempted it have failed disastrously.

The question of the inability of galaxies to maintain their structure over long periods of time is one that needs serious study by Christian men of science. This would appear to be a promising avenue of research for establishing a recent creation.[62]

3. There is still no acceptable evolutionary explanation for the existence of planets. According to our present understanding, solid particles would fail to agglomerate to form even small chunks of material, let alone planets. That planets do form spontaneously is held today strictly as an article of evolutionary faith.

4. Astronomical dating methods appear to be entirely devoid of scientific value, since they involve guessing at an evolutionary history for the object being dated. The fact that astronomers disagree widely on such imagined histories accounts for the many serious age discrepancies in the literature today.

Age estimates are continually being inflated to keep step with the philosophical views of the times. Why, if cosmogonists are actually in possession of the truth at any given moment, must they change their theories and age estimates the next moment?

5. The evolutionary approach is utterly bankrupt when it comes to explaining the ultimate origin of anything. To the evolutionist, each stage of development requires a previous stage. Never can there be a true beginning. Yet scientific data and Scripture both demand such a beginning. The most satisfactory explanation for the origin of stars, galaxies, and planets is a rapid and miraculous creation which endowed the heavens initially with all the diversity of structure and function that we observe today.

Acknowledgments

I am greatly indebted to Dr. Emmett Williams, fellow member of the Bob Jones University Science Department, whose thoroughgoing knowledge of thermodynamics was most helpful on numerous occasions. Mr. Gary Guthrie of the Bob Jones University Mathematics Department was kind enough to provide a final check on my calculations, while Dr. Stewart Custer, Dr. Fred Afman, and Mr. Arend tenPas of our Bible faculty assisted in questions of interpretation of the Scripture portions cited; all three of these men concurred with the position set forth in this paper. Comments and suggestions by these five colleagues were greatly appreciated since there is such an appalling dearth of Christian literature on the subject.

REFERENCES

1. G. Abell, 1969. Exploration of the universe, 2nd ed. Holt, Rinehart, and Winston, New York, p. 572.
2. S. J. Inglis, 1967. Planets, stars, and galaxies, 2nd ed. John Wiley and Sons, Inc., New York, p. 325.
3. J. C. Brandt, 1966. The sun and stars. McGraw-Hill Book Co., Inc., New York, p. 111.
4. Quoted in L. H. Aller and D. B. McLaughlin, 1965. Stellar structure. The University of Chicago Press, Chicogo, p. 577. The statement was originally made in a lecture on star formation, *NUFFIC* International Summer Course in Science, 1960.
5. R. Jastrow and A. G. W. Cameron, eds., 1963. Origin of the solar system. Academic Press, New York, pp. 39-53.
6. *Ibid.,* p. 43.
7. *Ibid.,* p. 44. The mass of the cloud divided by its radius squared must be equal to 7.6×10^{-3} gm/cm^2. Using cgs units,

8. *Ibid.,* p. 42.
9. *Ibid.,* p. 42. The sun's radius is 432,000 miles. One hundred times this value is 43,200,000 miles or 6.95×10^{10} meters. The volume of the condensed material V_2 is $4/3\pi r^3$. Using MKS units,

10. The use of C_p rather than C_v is called for in this calculation since the volume is not constant.
11. It can be shown that such a system should radiate away about half

of its energy as it contracts. (See C. M. H. Smith, 1966. A textbook of nuclear physics. Student edition. Pergamon Press, Oxford, p. 757.) If this energy were to remain in the cloud, its temperature would increase to 200,000°K rather than 100,000°K for T_2. Recalculating for this situation we still obtain about -30 eu/mole. Another objection that might be raised is that the initial cloud might be far larger and more massive, condensing into a cluster of stars rather than a single star. However, the same order of volume and temperature ratios would obtain, and our basic argument still stands.

12. T. Page and L. W. Page, eds., 1968. Stars and clouds of the Milky Way. The Macmillan Co., New York, pp. 246-253.
13. Brandt, *op. cit.*, p. 60.
14. For the condensed material at 100,000°K, the force outward is 7.1×10^{28} newtons; the force inward is 8.2×10^{28} newtons. However, the outward force due to rotation has been ignored in this calculation.
15. These equations may be combined to give

This is an expression for the radius at which the outward and inward forces are equal. It is not especially useful for our present purposes, however, because of the temperature uncertainty.

16. Jastrow and Cameron, *op. cit.*, pp. 43, 44.
17. Page and Page, *op. cit.*, p. 210.
18. G. Mulfinger, 1967. Examining the cosmogonies—a historical review, *Creation Research Society Quarterly*, 4:57-69.
19. Brandt, *op. cit.*, p. 112.
20. *Ibid.*
21. Jastrow and Cameron, *op. cit.*, pp. 40, 41.
22. *Ibid.*, p. 41.
23. *Ibid.*, p. 42.
24. G. H. Herbig, 1967. The youngest stars, *Scientific American*, August, pp. 30-36.
25. H. Alfvén, 1966. Worlds-antiworlds. W. H. Freeman and Co., San Francisco, p. 77.
26. *Ibid.*, p. 78.
27. Encyclopedia Britannica, 1964, "Cosmogony," p. 580.
28. The magnitude of the problem may be surmised from an issue of *Sky and Telescope*. On page 302 of the November, 1969 issue a model is described in which three cosmogonists started with 115,000 small gas clouds already arranged in a flat disc and already moving at the proper rotational speed! Is there no limit to how much contriving is considered legitimate?
29. See P. W. Hodge, 1966. Galaxies and cosmology. McGraw-Hill Book Co., Inc., New York, pp. 6-14, 116, 117, for a good discussion of these early theories.
30. *Ibid.*, p. 123.

31. Abell, *op. cit.*, p. 629.
32. Hodge, *op. cit.*, p. 122.
33. Jastrow and Cameron, *op. cit.*, p. 171.
34. *Ibid.*, pp. 171, 172.
35. *Ibid.*, p. 172. This difficulty is discussed in John C. Whitcomb, 1964. The origin of the solar system. Presbyterian and Reformed Publishing Co., Nutley, N. J., p. 12. Also Whitcomb's paper in the September, 1967, *Creation Research Society Quarterly* lists nine obstacles with which the best theories of the solar system are unable to deal successfully.
36. *Ibid.*, p. 68.
37. F. J. Low and B. J. Smith, 1966. Infrared observations of a pre-planetary system, *Nature,* 212:675, 676.
38. Inglis, *op. cit.* (Reference No. 2), pp. 275, 276.
39. Herbig, *op. cit.*, p. 35.
40. A. J. Meadows, 1967. Stellar evolution. Pergamon Press, Oxford, p. 151.
41. L. H. Aller, 1969. The planetary nebulae—part II, *Sky and Telescope,* 37:348.
42. Inglis, *op. cit.*, p. 298.
43. Brandt, *op. cit.* (Reference No. 3), p. 118.
44. G. Abell, 1964. Exploration of the universe. First edition, Holt, Rhinehart, and Winston, New York, p. 532.
45. In Gamow's The creation of the universe, 1952 (p. 32 in the Bantam Books edition), he assured us that a former discrepancy had been rectified, and that the age of the universe had been securely established at 4.3 billion years. (Prior to that it had been 1.7 billion.) Yet in a later book he had increased the estimate to 5 billion. See G. Gamow, 1958. Matter, earth, and sky. Prentice-Hall, Inc., Englewood Cliffs, N. J., p. 518.
46. P. J. E. Peebles and D. T. Wilkinson, 1967. The primeval fireball, *Scientific American,* June, p. 28.
47. T. A. Ashford, 1967. The physical sciences—from atoms to stars. 2nd ed. Holt, Rinehart, and Winston, Inc., New York, p. 677.
48. Article entitled, Universe 70, not 10 billion years old, Shklovski says, in *Scientific Research,* October 1967, p. 23.
49. Alfvén, *op. cit.*, p. 68.
50. F. Hoyle, 1960. The nature of the universe. Signet Science Library, New York, p. 113.
51. Alfvén, *op. cit.*, p. 70.
52. *Ibid.*
53. Hodge, *op. cit.*, p. 161 (see Reference No. 29).
54. Physics in 1968—News from the American Institute of Physics, p. 12.
55. Hodge, *op. cit.*, p. 123.
56. H. Arp, 1969. On the origin of arms in spiral galaxies, *Sky and Telescope,* 38:385.
57. *Ibid.*, p. 385.
58. J. A. Coleman, 1963. Modern theories of the universe. Signet Science Library, The New American Library, New York, p. 121.
59. Evidence for a degenerating universe was discussed in G. Mulfinger,

1968. Degeneration processes in the cosmos, *Bible-Science Newsletter*, September, 1968, p. 1.

60. Inglis, *op. cit.*, p. 363.

61. S. S. Huang, 1967. The origin of binary stars, *Sky and Telescope*, 34:369, 370.

62. Another matter that should carefully be studied by Society members is the inability of comets to remain intact over long periods of time, and the implications of this fact on the date of creation.

XXVI

THERMODYNAMICS: A TOOL FOR CREATIONISTS (REVIEW OF RECENT LITERATURE)

EMMETT L. WILLIAMS*

I. Introduction

Thermodynamics is a course that causes many an undergraduate to shudder mentally. The use of odd cycles and strange systems leads many students to feel that they are exploring an Alice-in-Wonderland world.

To add to these difficulties the approaches to thermodynamics are myriad. One can plunge into the thermodynamics of equilibrium, non-equilibrium, steady state, reversible, irreversible, isolated, closed, or open system processes to name a few.

New books on thermodynamics usually offer fresh approaches to the subject showing the science to be in a state of flux. Also scientists are critically evaluating the science at the present time.[1-3] This may lead to even more novel thermodynamic interpretations.

Regardless of the present turmoil, principles of immense scientific importance have been developed in this discipline. That these principles are of tremendous generality and affect all other sciences is obvious from the forementioned varied approaches to and applications of thermodynamics.

Thermodynamics deals with the "mystical" quantity called energy, particularly its possible transformations. Every natural process uses this quantity since it "appears" to be what enables nature to operate. Energy can be defined as the ability to do work without

---

*Emmett L. Williams, Ph.D., is chairman, Department of Physics, Bob Jones University, Greenville, South Carolina.

resorting to any mathematics. For further study on the energy concept see references 4-8.

Historically, thermodynamics developed from the study of heat engines and the problems involved in converting heat into mechanical work, which is the basis of most of our modern industrial operations.

The first principle or law of thermodynamics is the conservation of energy. Energy can be neither created nor destroyed: it is transferred from one place to another, or changed into various forms. Some other ways to express this idea are as follows: The loss of energy anywhere is always compensated by an equal gain of energy somewhere else.[9] If any system is carried through a cycle (the final state being precisely the same as the initial state), then the summation of the work delivered to the surroundings is proportional to the summation of the heat taken from the surroundings.[10] In Robert Mayer's own words,

> I therefore hope that I may reckon on the readers' assent when I lay down as an axiomatic truth that, just as in the case of matter so also in the case of force [the then current term for energy], only a transformation but never a creation takes place.[11]

Or simply, the energy of an isolated system always remains constant.

The second principle or law of thermodynamics is more subtle. There are several different statements of this idea. Each reveals a new aspect of this concept:

Carnot: Given an engine that is reversible and that operates between two fixed temperatures, then no other engine operating between these same temperatures can exceed this engine in efficiency.[12]

Planck: It is impossible to construct any cyclic device that can extract heat from a reservoir and produce no other thermal effects whatever.[13]

Kelvin: It is impossible to construct any cyclic device that can extract useful work from an isothermal system.[14]

Clausius: Heat cannot pass spontaneously from a body of lower temperature to a body of higher temperature.[15]

Caratheodory: In the neighborhood of any given state of any

closed system there exist states which are inaccessible from it along any reversible, adiabatic paths.[16]

The entropy in an isolated system is a monotonically increasing function of the time.[17]

It is obvious from reading these statements that certain processes are impossible in "nature" and certain natural processes are unidirectional. Thus the second law of thermodynamics, ". . . epitomizes our experiences with respect to direction taken by thermophysical processes."[18]

Actually natural processes tend to go in a direction that leads to degeneration of the system involved.[19] Living and non-living systems tend to wear out, age, break down, or decrease in complexity.

Briefly then, it can be said that conservative and degenerative processes operate in nature.

Looking over the various statements of each principle, one may wonder how these are related to the process of "evolution." First, evolution is taken to be thermophysical process. The sun is supposed to be the driving force for evolution on the earth. It is a process that is active now (i.e., evolution is assumed to be a continual upward process).[20] An evolutionist, Sidney Fox, states, "Evolution, however, has put together the smallest components; it has proceeded from the simple to the complex."[21]

Evolution is presumably a "creative" process, not conservative or degenerative. Proponents consider molecules-to-man evolution as a building, bettering process. Evolutionists would claim that once something is evolved it can evolve into something better supposedly because of environmental "pressures." Although evolved inorganic and organic entities can be conserved and are subject to degeneration, the prevailing "spirit" of nature is one of evolutionary development.

Thus observable conservation and degeneration (science) conflict with necessary evolutionary betterment (philosophy). It is this conflict that creationists have explored to show the fallaciousness of the molecules-to-man concept as a natural occurrence in a *real* world.

II. Creationist Interpretations of First Law

Since conservation processes operate in nature, creation is finished.[22-23] Thus evolution, as a creative process, is impossible. This has been the basic thrust of creationist arguments spearheaded by the writings of H. M. Morris.[23-25] He has provided an excellent scriptural basis for the first law of thermodynamics.[24-25] A philosophical consequence of the first law of thermodynamics, pointed out by writers,[26-28] is that the universe has either always been in existence in its present state, or was brought to this state by processes not operating now or by direct acts of creation. Conservation processes can only preserve what is already present. Such processes cannot be used to explain the origin of anything.[28-29]

The uniformitarian hypothesis that the present is the key to the past can be viewed in light of conservation principles.[29] Since all present geological processes are not creative, then extrapolation of these processes into the past is a self-contradiction according to Morris. Again conservation processes cannot be used to explain origins.

In the realm of astronomy and cosmology the steady state and continuous creation ideas of Hoyle violate the first law.[30-31] The

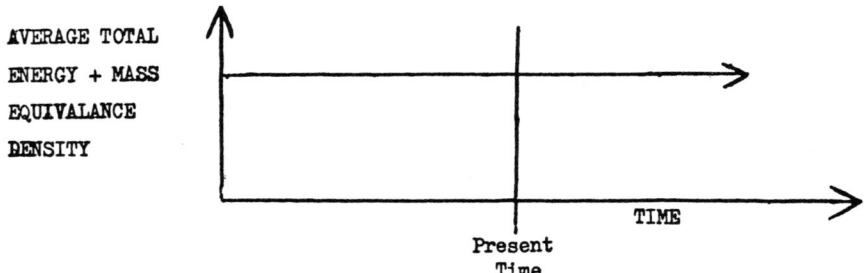

Figure 1. Average energy density versus time. In a finite universe there is the same amount of energy today as there was 1,000 years ago, and there will be 1,000 years from today, according to the first law of thermodynamics.

continuing creation of matter out of nothing by natural processes has never been observed, but thermodynamic concepts for the evolutionist have never stood in the way of evolutionary necessity!

A plot of energy vs. time for a finite universe according to the first law is shown in Figure 1.[31] Barnes[32] suggests that this principle came into operation after the origin of mass and energy.

Some members of the Creation Research Society engaged in a brief and unique discussion of the relationship of conservation principles in the physical sciences and "after its kind" biological conservation. The purpose of the correspondence was to unify the two concepts into a single conservation hypothesis: This reviewer initially asked for comments.[33] Harold Armstrong wrote a brief analysis of the conservation principles from physics.[34] Armstrong and Williams[35] discussed the need to specify what is meant by order. This may be the key to developing concept. Lammerts[36] suggested the following:

> Except for degenerative changes and losses (as extinct species) the total number of species determining DNA units now existing is the same as the number originally created. The law of conservation of energy essentially states that the total energy content of the universe remains constant both inorganically as regards atomic reactions and biologically as regards the inheritance of an original total number of species determining DNA units.

McDowell,[37] using information theory concepts, postulated that

> The total information implicit in all the bodies (including the total information upon the genes which they carry) of all creatures which are alive upon our planet at any given instant cannot exceed the total information coded upon all the genes which they carry.

Or similarly,

> The total information implicit in all of the bodies (including the total information coded upon the genes which they carry) of all creatures which have lived since the original creation, live now, or ever will live upon our planet cannot exceed the total information coded upon all the genes of all of the creatures which came into being at the original creation.

This discussion is still open for comment from others.

Williams approached conservation processes in biology from a qualitative thermodynamics viewpoint.[38] Initial-final state methodology was used to illustrate conservation of kinds of living organisms. Figure 2 shows this idea in a simplified manner. This methodology offers possibilities as a way to analyze living systems thermodynami-

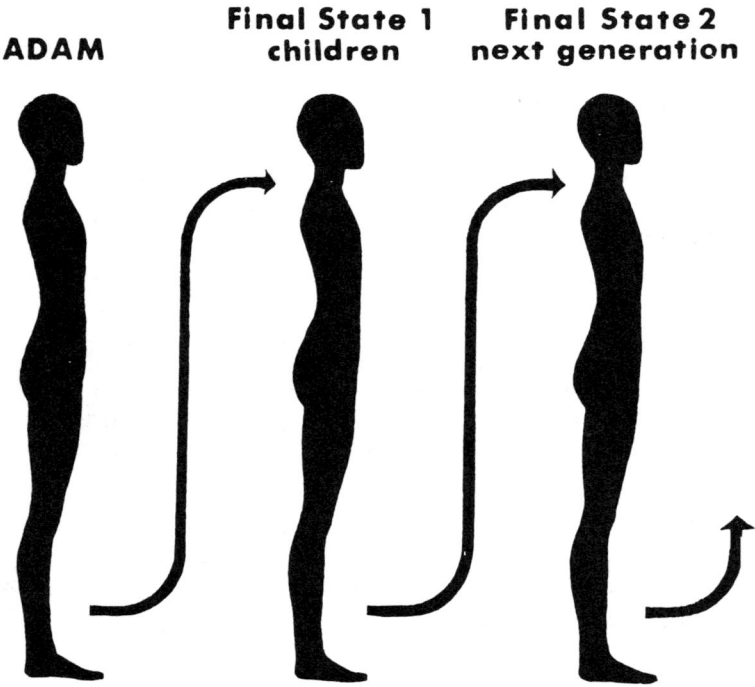

Figure. 2. Schematic diagram of reproduction and growth of succeeding generations from initial created state.

cally. The use of this method eliminates the need of evolutionary contrivances to explain the order of living systems in a world of increasing disorder. The creationist approach shows that order can be conserved, although the original order must have appeared by miraculous means.

III. Creationist Interpretations of the Second Law

A. General

The major creationist effort has been in developing applications of the second law of thermodynamics. Degenerative processes in nature are opposed to imagined molecules-to-man evolution. This contradiction was first explored by Clark.[39] He termed universal natural disordering as the law of morpholysis (to lose form). Morris[40-42] developed the concept further and also provided a scriptural basis for the second law.

B. Degenerating Universe

Since the order of the universe appears to be decreasing, it must have been a state of high order at some past time. The analogy used is the unwinding of a clock as it runs down. Some creationists[43-46] interpret this as evidence of a definite creation in the past, the winding up. Also others[47-48] have used the phenomenon of increasing disorder to state that the universe is not eternal, for if it were, it would have already run down to complete disorder.

Clark[49] has an excellent discussion of the application of the second law to a finite or infinite universe. The argument is essentially that, if the second law applies to all isolated parts of the universe, it will apply also to the whole.

Clark and Williams[50] in separate treatises have noted how cautious evolutionary scientists are when prescribing the dictates of the second law to the universe, yet proceed with "reckless abandon" when developing an evolutionary origin for the same universe! Williams postulated that the universe can be treated as an isolated system based on biblical evidence, and not on scientific information.

Mulfinger[51-52] has applied the second law to existing processes in the universe and to supposed evolutionary processes. He claims,[52]

"Every star is a dynamic system undergoing *degenerative* changes." This is based on observational data and runs counter to the evolutionary "propaganda" about the birth of stars. Mulfinger shows thermodynamically that star formation by condensation is impossible; and notes that all known processes in the universe are degenerative.

C. *Degenerating Man*

Creationists[53-54] claim that man has been degenerating since Adam. One can arrive at this conclusion by consistent application of the second law. It should be remembered, however, that the effects of decay processes have not overridden the stabilizing influence of conservation processes.[54]

Mutations are biological examples of degenerative changes in biological systems. Although mutations are used as a possible mechanism for imagined upward evolution, this claim cannot be substantiated. Reasoning according to the second law necessitates that mutations are harmful, and creationists[55-61] have used this idea effectively. Observational data are on the creationist side in this dispute.

Williams[62] qualitatively viewed living organisms from a thermodynamic standpoint assuming degenerative processes. Such an approach is possible and dispenses with evolutionary reasoning to circumvent the second law where life is concerned. It is interesting to note that scientific facts are fitted easily into a creationist framework.

D. *"Chemical Evolution"*

One of the required steps in "evolutionary history" is that of chemical upgrading. Smaller atoms "evolve" into larger atoms and molecules. Simpler molecules change into more complicated ones, and finally life spontaneously generates on the proper molecules in a suitable place.

These speculative stages of molecules-to-man evolution are on extremely weak ground scientifically. Here is where normal disordering processes unquestionably "rule" the inorganic and organic

THERMODYNAMICS: A TOOL FOR CREATIONISTS

worlds. Clark[63] recognized that evolution is basically a chemical problem. The experiment done by Miller and Urey[64] have offered evolutionists their greatest hopes. Scientists[65-69] including creationists have been quick to point out the defects of this approach from thermodynamic considerations.

Debate at this level involves the question of open and closed systems. Why do evolutionists insist on open systems? Definite advantages are gained by using open systems. Mass and energy can flow through the boundaries of such a system. When a step is necessary in evolutionary change, an open system can be *imagined* so that an excess of reactants can be added to cause the chemical reaction to proceed drastically to the product side by the well-known LeChatelier principle.

Suppose a reversible reaction, $A + B = C$, is possible, but from thermodynamic considerations very little C forms. Assume C is more complex than A or B and is needed in an evolutionary sequence. It can be fabricated in an open system by forcing the reaction to the right by adding an excess of A or B.

But the "evolutionary game" is not finished yet. The product C can be selectively removed from the reaction site, and evolutionists may claim that, in a natural situation, C could diffuse away from the site. More C can form from the reaction than would be expected thermodynamically and huge quantities of the complex compound can be made available.

Thus C is ready for further evolutionary processing thanks to an open system—and *intelligent planning*. Forcing chemical reactions in a preferred direction is one of the latest fads of evolutionists,[70-71] but the possibility of such a process existing naturally is almost nil.

It is essential to note that brute natural processes do not act this way. Rather natural processes follow the second law, which requires that a natural, non-living system drive toward equilibrium, not toward increasing complexity. As Rusch[72] noted, directed experimentation is all good "clean fun" in a chemistry laboratory or in the mind of the evolutionist, but the laboratory is where it ends.

Another way to avoid second law consequences is by imagining a catastrophic event that drives a system far from equilibrium (similar to an explosion). Fluctuations develop that cause the disturbed system to move to a state more ordered than the explosion (metastable state).[73-74] Evolution, then, proceeds supposedly from the new "ordered" state. Again the probability of such happening in a natural situation is slight if not impossible.

Also the order referred to in the new state is questionable. The system must be closely controlled to insure that the proper state rather than total chaos is developed from the transition. Unguided natural processes are not this selective, and as predicted by the second law a disordered state will more likely result.

One stands in awe of the unnatural means evolutionists resort to in order to get their processes to "work in the right way." If something is needed for further evolution, schemes are concocted to provide the necessary material. If evolution needs to follow a particular path, then evolutionists say it does so. Evolution does not thrive on straight science; it needs blessed events.[75] Scientific miracles are necessary. Why? Simply so evolution can be made to avoid observable degeneration. Evolution from molecules-to-man is more miraculous than creation.

E. *Intelligence and Degeneration*

The only way to work around natural disordering is to use intelligence. Creationists[76-78] have pointed this out, but evolutionists will not be deterred by the realization that natural events will not work like a controlled experiment, or that "evolutionary processes" cannot select their properties or paths as intelligent men can.

F. *Evolution and Probability*

Probability can be related[79-80] to the second law by the Boltzmann formulation,

$$S = k \ln w \tag{1}$$

$$\text{or,} \quad dS = k \ln \left(\frac{w_2}{w_1}\right) \tag{2}$$

where S is the entropy of a given state, k is Boltzmann's constant, and w is the possible number of microstates of the given state.

THERMODYNAMICS: A TOOL FOR CREATIONISTS

Consider a natural transformation between state 1 and 2 with total possible microstates of w_1 and w_2 respectively. If $w_1 > w_2$, then state 1 has a greater probability of formation than state 2 by the second law (because of its higher entropy). If the system goes from state 1 to state 2, then $\left(\frac{w_2}{w_1}\right) < 1$ and entropy decreases (the improbable happens).

Thus every time the improbable occurs the second law is violated. The big problem that exists in trying to apply this idea is that it is almost impossible to determine the possible microstates for complicated systems.

Scores of creationists have shown how improbable evolution is. One would expect the probable to happen in nature.[81] If the improbable continually occurs, it would not be considered improbable but probable. To say that evolutionary events are improbable is to say that the chance of their happening is slight. The problem does not end here. Evolution, by its very nature, would have to proceed in a sequence of improbable steps.

For sake of argument, assume the probability of an evolutionary step is 1 in 10^{20} possibilities. The next evolutionary step necessary to continue the ordering operations would have a probability of 1 in $(10^{20}) \cdot (10^{20})$ or 1 in 10^{40} if both steps have equal probabilities. Connected sequential steps would become phenomenally improbable the further the process goes. An ordering step must be followed by another ordering step, etc. Actually the system would proceed towards disorder (probable occurrence).

This unbelievable sequence of improbable steps may lead a person to ask just how probable is the improbable? The word never is appropriate. Evolution is so improbable that it will never occur; the idea is that if you wait long enough for any event with a finite probability, it will occur. "Long enough" may be never.[82] A quote of Boltzmann (1898) will help illustrate this.

> One should not imagine that two gases, in a 0.1 liter container, initially unmixed, will mix, then again after a few days separate, then mix again, and so forth. On the contrary, one finds . . .

that not until a time enormously long compared to $10^{(10^{10})}$ years will there be any noticeable unmixing of the gases. One may recognize that this is practically equivalent to never.[83]

There is a finite probability that gases can unmix; however it is meaningless because it is so low. Kittel,[84] has another excellent example of the meaning of never.

It has been said[85] that "six monkeys, set to strum unintelligently on typewriters for millions of millions of years, would be bound in time to write all the books in the British Museum." This statement is misleading nonsense, for it gives a misleading conclusion about very, very large numbers. Could all the monkeys in the world have typed out a single specified book in the age of the universe?

Suppose that 10^{10} monkeys have been seated at typewriters throughout the age of the universe, 10^{18} sec. This number of monkeys is about three times greater than the present human population of the earth. We suppose that a monkey can hit 10 typewriter keys per second. A typewriter may have 44 keys; we accept lower case letters in place of capital letters. Assuming that Shakespear's *Hamlet* has 10^5 characters, will the monkeys hit upon *Hamlet*?

The probability that any given sequence of 10^5 characters typed at random will come out in the correct sequence (the sequence of *Hamlet*) is

$$\left(\frac{1}{44}\right)^{100,000} = 10^{-164,345}$$

Where we have used $\log 44 = 1.64345...$. The probability that a *monkey-Hamlet* will be typed in the age of the universe is approximately $10^{-164,316}$. The probability of *Hamlet* is therefore zero in any operational sense of an event, so that the original statement at the beginning of the problem is nonsense; one book, much less a library, will never occur in the total literary production of the monkeys.

What happens . . . if we do not specify the title of the book, but agree to accept any known book? There may be about 30×10^6 distinct titles of books: the largest library, the Library of Congress, contains about 15×10^6 books and pamphlets. Note that the total production of the monkeys is equivalent to 10^{24} short volumes of 10^5 characters each, but you will find that none of these duplicate any existing book.

Evolution is statistically as hopeless as the situation just illustrated. When dealing with large numbers nothing but this is to be expected. There is a finite probability that I could stand in Greenville, South Carolina, and throw a baseball to the moon. But, how many evolutionists would wager a month's salary that I would accomplish the feat? Yet the same people will spend a lifetime defending the same degree of probability concerning evolution.

Clark notes[86] anyone invoking such unusual chance undermines the very basis of science. Science is based on probable occurrences and once chance is admitted as a "mechanism," everything becomes indeterminate. A scientist could never rule out chance in any of his studies and scientific work would be impossible to perform.

The high odds against the formation of complex organic compounds such as DNA and proteins by chance have been discussed.[87-92] The chance that "nature" could organize anything is slight.[93-98] Probability is just one of the many mathematical arguments against evolution. Evolutionists themselves have shown little faith in present evolutionary theories from a mathematical standpoint.[100]

G. *Origin of the Second Law*

Barnes states[101] that the second law came into operation after the universe was created completely. Morris suggests[102] that the origin of the second law was connected with the Fall.

IV. *Conclusions*

Creationists have utilized thermodynamics reasoning effectively in their opposition to evolutionary speculation. It is one of the most fertile areas of creationist thought. Not all of the creationist ideas can be explored in such a brief review. Interested students should study the references and all past issues of the *Creation Research Society Quarterly* for a better knowledge of the subject.

REFERENCES

1. P. T. Landsberg, ed., 1970. Proceedings of the international conference on thermodynamics (held in Cardiff, U. K., 1-4 April). Butterworths, London.
2. E. B. Stuart, B. Gal-Or, and A. J. Brainard, eds., 1970. A critical review of thermodynamics. Mono Book Corp., Baltimore, Md.
3. B. Gal-Or, 1972. Entropy, fallacy, and the origin of irreversibility, *Annals of the N. Y. Academy of Sciences*, 196:305.
4. W. Ford, 1972. Classical and modern physics I. Xerox, Lexington, Mass., pp. 392-4—A brief, easily understood discussion of energy transformations.
5. E. L. Williams, 1969. A simplified explanation of the first and second laws of thermodynamics: their relationship to Scripture and the theory of evolution, *Creation Research Society Quarterly*, 5:138—A brief section on the importance of energy transformations.
6. J. Kestin, 1966. A course in thermodynamics. Blaisdell, Waltham, Mass., pp. 157-60—A brief, rigorous discussion of energy.
7. R. A. Millikin, D. Roller, and E. C. Watson, 1965. Mechanics, molecular physics, heat and sound. M.I.T. Press, Cambridge, Mass., pp. 65-79—Work, power, and energy concepts developed historically.
8. L. Tisza, 1966. Generalized thermodynamics. M.I.T. Press, Cabridge, Mass., pp. 3-52—Interesting discussion of the development of thermodynamic concepts.
9. Ford, *op. cit.*, p. 394.
10. J. H. Keenan, 1970. Thermodynamics. M. I. T. Press, Cambridge, Mass., p. 10.
11. A. L. King, 1962. Thermophysics. W. H. Freeman & Co., San Francisco, p. 7.
12. F. H. Crawford, 1963. Heat, thermodynamics and statistical physics. Harcourt, Brace & World, New York, p. 209.
13. *Ibid.*, p. 215.
14. *Ibid.*, p. 214.
15. Kestin, *op. cit.*, p. 410.
16. *Ibid.*, p. 460.
17. Crawford, *op. cit.*, p. 237.
18. King, *op. cit.*, p. 78.
19. E. L. Williams, 1966. Entropy and the solid state, *Creation Research Society Quarterly*, 3(3):18.
20. J. Huxley, 1960. At random: a television interview (in) Issues in evolution (Evolution after Darwin III). Sol Tax, ed. University of Chicago Press, p. 41.
21. S. W. Fox, 1971. *Chemical & Engineering News*, 49(50):46.
22. Williams, *op. cit.* (reference No. 5).
23. H. M. Morris, 1971. Proposals for science framework guidelines, *Creation Research Society Quarterly*, 8:147.

24. H. M. Morris, 1963. The twilight of evolution. Baker Book House, Grand Rapids, Mich.
25. H. M. Morris, 1964. The power of energy, *Creation Research Society Quarterly*, 1(1):18.
26. O. L. Brauer, 1967. God of the universe watching over the earth, *Creation Research Society Quarterly*, 3(4):4.
27. Morris, 1964, *op. cit.*
28. T. G. Barnes, 1970. Origin and development of the universe, *Creation Research Society Quarterly*, 7:51.
29. H. M. Morris, 1965. Science versus scientism in historical geology, *Creation Research Society Quarterly*, 2(2):19.
30. G. Mulfinger, 1967. Examining the cosmogonies—a historical review, *Creation Research Society Quarterly*, 4:57.
31. D. Penny, 1972. The implications of the two laws of thermodynamics in the origin and destiny of the universe, *Creation Research Society Quarterly*, 8:261.
32. T. G. Barnes, 1966. A scientific alternate to evolution, *Creation Research Society Quarterly*, 2(4):5.
33. E. L. Williams, 1969. Letter to the editor, *Creation Research Society Quarterly*, 6:155.
34. H. Armstrong, 1969. Letter to the editor, *Creation Research Society Quarterly*, 6:201.
35. E. L. Williams, 1969. Letter to the editor, *Creation Research Society Quarterly*, 6:201.
36. W. E. Lammerts, 1970. Letter to the editor, *Creation Research Society Quarterly*, 7:50.
37. I. McDowell, 1971. A law of biological conservation, *Creation Research Society Quarterly*, 8:189.
38. E. L. Williams, 1971. Resistance of living organisms to the second law of thermodynamics: irreversible processes, open systems, creation and evolution, *Creation Research Society Quarterly*, 8:117.
39. R. E. D. Clark, 1967. Darwin: before and after. Moody Press, Chicago.
40. Morris, 1963, *op. cit.* (reference No. 24).
41. H. M. Morris, 1970. Biblical cosmology and modern science. Baker Book House, Grand Rapids, Mich., pp. 111-139.
42. Morris, 1964, *op. cit.* (reference No. 25).
43. Penny, *op. cit.*
44. R. E. D. Clark, 1961. The universe plan or accident? Muhlenberg Press, Philadelphia, p. 25.
45. B. Davidheiser, 1969. Evolution and Christian faith. Presbyterian and Reformed Publishing Co., Nutley, N. J., p. 220.
46. G. J. Van Wylen, 1959. Thermodynamics. John Wiley & Sons, New York, p. xi.
47. Brauer, *op. cit.* (reference No. 26).
48. Barnes, 1970, *op. cit.* (reference No. 28).

49. Clark, 1961, *op. cit.*, pp. 29-37.
50. E. L. Williams, 1970. Is the universe a thermodynamic system?, *Creation Research Society Quarterly*, 7:46.
51. Mulfinger, *op. cit.* (reference No. 30).
52. G. Mulfinger, 1970. Critique of stellar evolution, *Creation Research Society Quarterly*, 7:7.
53. R. D. Shaw, 1970. Fossil man: ancestor or descendant of Adam?, *Creation Research Society Quarterly*, 6:172.
54. Williams, 1971, *op. cit.*
55. Morris, 1964, *op. cit.* (reference No. 25).
56. G. C. Lockwood, 1971. The second law of thermodynamics and evolution, *Creation Research Society Quarterly*, 8:8.
57. Morris, 1971, *op. cit.* (reference No. 23).
58. Morris, 1963, *op. cit.* (reference No. 24).
59. Morris, 1970, *op. cit.*, p. 124 (reference No. 41).
60. I. McDowell, 1970. Thermodynamics and original information, *Creation Research Society Quarterly*, 7:183.
61. A. E. Wilder Smith, 1970. The creation of life. Harold Shaw Publishers, Wheaton, Ill.
62. Williams, 1971, *op. cit.* (reference No. 38).
63. Clark, 1967, *op. cit.*, p. 127 (reference No. 39).
64. S. L. Miller and H. C. Urey, 1959. Organic compound synthesis on the primitive earth, *Science*, 130:245.
65. D. E. Hull, 1960. Thermodynamics and kinetics of spontaneous generation, *Nature*, 186:693.
66. E. L. Williams, 1967. The evolution of complex organic compounds from simpler chemical compounds: is it thermodynamically and kinetically possible?, *Creation Research Society Quarterly*, 4(1):30.
67. W. E. Lammerts, 1964. Discoveries since 1859 which invalidate the evolution theory, *Creation Research Society Quarterly*, 1(1):47.
68. P. A. Zimmerman, 1964. The spontaneous generation of life, *Creation Research Society Quarterly*, 1(1):13.
69. D. T. Gish, 1972. Book Review. *Creation Research Society Quarterly*, 8:277.
70. I. Prigogine, G. Nicholis, and A. Babloyantz, 1972. Thermodynamics of evolution, *Physics Today*, 25(11, 12):23, 38.
71. Hull, *op. cit.*
72. W. H. Rusch, Sr., 1966. Analysis of so-called evidence of evolution, *Creation Research Society Quarterly*, 3(1):4.
73. Prigogine, *et al., op. cit.*
74. P. Glansdorff and I. Prigogine, 1971. Thermodynamic theory of structure, stability, and fluctuations. Wiley-Interscience, New York.
75. Williams, 1967, *op. cit.*
76. Lammerts, 1964, *op. cit.*
77. B. Davidheiser, 1971. Science and the Bible. Baker Book House, Grand Rapids, Mich., p. 69.
78. Smith, *op. cit.*, p. 152 (reference No. 61).

79. J. D. Fast, 1962. Entropy. McGraw Hill, New York, pp. 47-61.
80. Williams, 1966, *op. cit.* (reference No. 19).
81. Barnes, 1966, *op. cit.* (reference No. 32).
82. C. Kittel, 1969. Thermal physics. John Wiley and Sons, New York, p. 63.
83. *Ibid.,* p. 45.
84. *Ibid.,* pp. 65-66.
85. J. Jeans, 1930. Mysterious universe. Cambridge University Press, p. 4.
86. Clark, 1961, *op. cit.,* pp. 32-35 (reference No. 44).
87. G. E. Parker, 1970. The origin of life on earth, *Creation Research Society Quarterly,* 7:99.
88. W. L. Henning, 1971. Was the origin of life inevitable?, *Creation Research Society Quarterly,* 8:59.
89. A. J. White, 1972. Uniformitarianism, probability and evolution. *Creation Research Society Quarterly,* 9:32.
90. A. E. Wilder Smith, 1968. Man's origin, man's destiny. Harold Shaw Publishers, Wheaton, Ill., pp. 59-80.
91. J. F. Coppedge, 1971. Probability and left-handed molecules, *Creation Research Society Quarterly,* 8:163.
92. J. J. Grebe, 1967. DNA studies in relation to creation concepts, *Creation Research Society Quarterly,* 4:25.
93. Williams, 1966, *op. cit.* (reference No. 19).
94. Mulfinger, 1967, *op. cit.* (reference No. 30).
95. H. Armstrong, 1970. Comments on scientific news and views, *Creation Research Society Quarterly,* 7:121.
96. F. W. Cousins, 1970. Is there life in other worlds? A critical reassessment of the evidence, *Creation Research Society Quarterly,* 7:32.
97. Penny, 1972, *op. cit.* (reference No. 31).
98. H. B. Holroyd, 1972. Darwinism is physical and mathematical nonsense, *Creation Research Society Quarterly,* 9:5.
99. H. Armstrong, 1970. Comments on scientific news and views, *Creation Research Society Quarterly,* 7:80.
100. P. S. Moorhead and M. M. Kaplan, eds., 1967. Mathematical challenges of the neo-Darwinian interpretation of evolution. The Wistar Institute Press, Philadelphia.
101. Barnes, 1966, *op. cit.* (reference No. 32).
102. Morris, 1963, *op. cit.* (reference No. 24).